TRIALS AND TRIUMPHS
WOMEN OF THE
AMERICAN CIVIL WAR

TRIALS AND TRIUMPHS
WOMEN OF THE
AMERICAN CIVIL WAR

Marilyn Mayer Culpepper

Michigan State University Press
East Lansing
1991

All Michigan State University Press books are produced on paper which meets the requirements of American National Standard of Information Sciences—Permanence of paper for printed materials ANSI Z39.48-1984.

Michigan State University Press
East Lansing, Michigan 48823-5202

Printed in the United States of America

00 99 98 97 96 95 94 93 92   2   3   4   5   6   7   8   9   10

Library of Congress Cataloging-in-Publication Data

Culpepper, Marilyn Mayer.
  Trials and Triumphs: Women of the American Civil War/by Marilyn Mayer Culpepper.
    p.   cm.
  Includes biblographical references (p.   ).
  ISBN 0-87013-296-2 (alk. paper)
  1. United States — History — Civil War, 1861–1865 — Women. 2. Women — United States — History — 19th century. I. Title.
E628.C85 1991
973.7'15042—dc20   91-52579
                                                                        CIP

Contents

Acknowledgments

Grateful acknowledgement is made to the following:

Material appearing on pages 252–56, 270 and 372 originally appeared as "An Iowa Woman in Wartime," by Marjorie Ann Rogers, *Annals of Iowa* 35/36 (1961). Copyright © 1961 Iowa State Historical Department. Used by permission of the publisher.

Material appearing on pages 26, 269–70 and 271 originally appeared as "The Sharp Family Civil War Letters," ed. George Mills, *Annals of Iowa* 34 (1959). Copyright © 1959 Iowa State Historical Department. Used by permission of the publisher.

Material appearing on pages 117–18, 123, 282–83, and 285 originally appeared as "Civil War Wife: The Letters of Harriet Jane Thompson," ed. Glenda Riley, *Annals of Iowa* 44 (1978). Used by permission of the publisher.

Material appearing on pages 116 and 195–96 reprinted from James C. Mohr, ed.: *The Cormany Diaries: A Northern Family in the Civil War*, Copyright © 1982 University of Pittsburgh Press. Used by permission of the publisher.

Material appearing on pages 110, 123, 133, 167, 287–88 and 294 reprinted from the Letters of George and Amanda Chittenden. Used by permission of the Indiana Division, Indiana State Library, Indianapolis.

Material appearing on pages 91–92 and 291–92 reprinted from Mary D. Robertson, ed.: *Lucy Breckinridge of Grove Hill: The Journal of a Virginia Girl, 1862–1864* (Kent, Ohio: The Kent State University Press, 1979). Used by permission of the publisher.

Illustration and Photograph Credits

Cover:
Text from the Burwell Letters. By permission of the McCain Library and Archives, University of Southern Mississippi.

Untitled. By permission of the U.S. Army Military History Institute, Carlisle Barracks, Pennsylvania.

Endsheets:
New Year's Day, 1864. *Harper's Weekly: A Journal of Civilization* (2 January 1864): 8–9. Courtesy of Special Collections, Michigan State University Library.

Page 8:
Shirley House. By permission of the Old Court House Museum Collection, Vicksburg, Mississippi.

Page 54:
Untitled. Reproduced from the Collections of the Cincinnati Historical Society.

Page 88:
The House-tops in Charleston During the Bombardment of Sumter. *Harper's Weekly: A Journal of Civilization* (4 May 1861): front cover. Courtesy of the New York Historical Society.

Page 130:
Untitled. LC-B8171-306. By permission of the Library of Congress.

Page 166:
View of a hospital at Fredericksburg, Virginia, May 1864. Courtesy of the New York Historical Society.

Page 204:
The Shell. *Harper's Monthly Magazine* (December 1908): 45. Courtesy of the Michigan State University Library.

Page 242:
Members of Soldiers Aid Society, Springfield, Illinois, c. 1863. IChi-22103. By permission of the Chicago Historical Society.

Page 274:
Womens Central Relief Association Inside View at Cooper Union, 29 April 1861–7 July 1865. 38.120.3. By permission of the Museum of the City of New York.

Page 314:
Ladies of the U.S. Sanitary Commission, 1863. Courtesy of the New York Historical Society.

Page 354:
Peace—Fourth of July, 1865. *Harper's Weekly: A Journal of Civilization* (8 July 1865): front cover. Courtesy of the New York Historical Society.

Introduction

Every schoolchild has heard about Fort Sumter and Gettysburg and Appomattox, but relatively few Americans, young or old, know much about the activities of women during the Civil War. Most historians gloss over the experiences of women who for four years took over men's work on the homefront. Whether they stayed at home and managed the farms and businesses or whether they went out to the battlefields as nurses and hospital matrons, the women of both sections found their lives profoundly affected by the war.

The diaries, letters, and memoirs of Civil War women present a collage: a composite of women's actions and reactions, of joys and sorrows, of failures and accomplishments. This is their story—told by them in their own words. Continuity, philosophy, military history, and statistics are kept to a minimum in order to give center stage to the women. Unfortunately, it is impossible in so short a work to be all-inclusive. A mere sampling is presented here, the spotlight focusing not on famous women but on the lesser-known "heroines" of the era.

Clearly these women do not necessarily speak for *all* women. There were scores of variants to the views of these women, divergencies that tend to echo the dissension which characterized those tumultuous years.

Writing about two sections so sharply divided in views and attitudes that they took to the battlefield over those differences obviously precludes the use of "all" or "never" or "always." Instead, such blanket terms have been more accurately tempered with a qualified "some" or "many" or "a few." And yet, despite their differences, the similarities of the women of both sections were even greater, and therefore in this work Northerners and Southerners are grouped together for the purposes of discussion. The women of *both* the North and the South were loyal to their section and eager to support the war effort with words and work. They all suffered intense anxieties over the safety, health, and comfort of their loved ones. Many were displaced by the war; many made immense sacrifices and underwent severe deprivation. For countless women the end of the war meant starting anew.

There could be dozens of ways to organize this material and other writers or readers might well choose another arrangement. In fact, relegating these women to any single category presents a challenge in itself. In this thematic development the various women could fit into almost any or every chapter. Women, for example, were patriotic, anxiety-ridden, self-sacrificing, enterprising, and energetic. These chapter divisions reflect major categories and the author's attempt to use an organization other than a formal chronological ordering of material. Molding some six hundred different writing styles into a unified whole offers an additional challenge.

The hundreds of quotations have been relatively untouched. The whimsical punctuation and the peculiar spelling of the era have been left intact. A few changes have been made in paragraphing and capitalization and a few periods have been added to facilitate the reading of letters and diary entries which start with a capital letter and conclude three pages later with a period—or a dash. Often the uniqueness of the expression is part of its charm. I therefore have usually omitted the interruptions caused by the repeated interjection of "[*sic*]"; the reader can be assured the quotations have been checked, rechecked and checked again for accuracy.

Granted, there is far greater space devoted to Southern women; however, the battles were fought at their doorstep, it was they who suffered most from displacement, pillaging, and harassment.

Furthermore, most of the Civil War women diarists were Southerners and, of course, most were among the well-to-do planter class. These were the women who had the time and the education to write.

Unfortunately, little space is devoted to the problems and contributions of black women during the war years. The omission is neither an oversight nor a deliberate exclusion. Obviously, the war brought immense changes to Negroes. It brought freedom and independence and a new beginning. However, as a result of the strict enforcement of the laws prohibiting the teaching of slaves to read or write, there are very few diaries or letters extant written by black women. To be sure, there were many exceptional black women, among them Charlotte Forten, the teacher of freedmen; Susie King Taylor, the nurse; and Harriet Tubman, the worker for the Underground Railroad, for the Union Army, and for the education of blacks. To examine the everyday experiences of black women from the standpoint of their owners, or from the material in the few primary sources available, or from pure conjecture would distort the focus of this research based on women's eyewitness accounts of life during the Civil War. Black women did, indeed, contribute significantly to the war effort. Their real story, however, unfolded during the Reconstruction years.

There are few conclusions drawn here. The material is presented with as little interpretation as possible—the women must speak for themselves and their times.

The bibliography is limited to only those sources most helpful in depicting the role of Civil War women. To add clarity, diaries and collections of letters are alphabetized whenever possible by author rather than editor. A reader consulting a source in a library would also do well to check under the editor's name. When referring to particularly brief sources (some diaries and reminiscences), I have not deemed it necessary to include specific page numbers. Although my original intention was to use only unpublished diaries, letters, and reminiscences, I soon discovered that plan would exclude many of the most interesting personalities whose writing had already come to light and been published. As a result, the final product is a

3

combination of both published and unpublished material. The diaries and letters of a few men have also been included when that material helps illuminate the role of their mothers, wives, sisters, or lovers.

I have been greatly remiss in not consistently referring to the women as Mrs. or Miss or as "Jones" or "Chesnut." I have known many of these women for more than a decade now. I have laughed and anguished and grieved with them. To call them by formal titles or by their last names would belie our friendship, the familiarity I have come to feel for them.

It is with deep regret that I return my Civil War friends to their slumbers. I have found them to be feisty, fanatical, coy, devious, crafty, steely, calculating, predatory, indomitable—and incredible.

Some were warm and gracious, pulling up a chair and welcoming me into the family circle, grasping my arm at times to impart an observation or a word of wisdom. Others bristled at having a horrid Yankee looking over their shoulders. Some, preoccupied with social activities and the companionship of high-ranking army and government officials, had little time for me. A few prided themselves on their abrasiveness and their denunciation of any of my views contrary to their own. Some proved stalwart forerunners of the feminists of the latter years of the twentieth century. There were several I was delighted I was not in competition with—for a husband, for social position, for an administrative post, or as a raconteur. Several I wished were living next door. Many will continue to live in my heart and my memory for the rest of my life.

My heartfelt appreciation for the introduction to these women goes to the librarians and archivists in the more than sixty libraries I visited while conducting my research. The library at Michigan State University warrants special commendation: Fred Honhart and the staff of the University Archives and Historical Collections; the resourceful Interlibrary Loan and the Special Collections staffs; Michael Unsworth of the Social Science Division, and Sue Iversen of Microforms.

Duke University is also truly outstanding. Its incredibly fine staff has been most generous in sharing the library's wealth of material.

At the Indiana Division of the Indiana State Library, Marybelle Burch was an invaluable aid in locating scores of diaries and letters. Special gratitude goes to Gordon A. Cotton, Director of the Old Court House Museum at Vicksburg; Caldwell Delaney, Museum Director of the City of Mobile; Ralph Draughon, Jr., Curator of Manuscripts at the Historic New Orleans Collection; and Peer Edwin Ravnan, Archivist, of the Middle Georgia Archives, Washington Memorial Library, Macon.

I thank Sidney E. Berger at the American Antiquarian Society; Susan K. Barnard at the Atlanta Historical Society; Thomas M. Czekanski at Beauvoir, Home of Jefferson Davis, Biloxi, Mississippi; Eugene Zepp at the Boston Public Library; Herbert Brinks, Calvin College; Archie Motley, Corey Seeman, and Theresa McGill at the Chicago Historical Society; Galen R. Wilson, Constance Gordon and Andrea P. Mark at the Chicago Public Library; Mary Jane Neely at the Cincinnati Historical Society; Alesandra M. Schmidt at the Connecticut Historical Society; Benedict Markowski and Mary Karshner of the Burton Historical Collection, Detroit Public Library; Guy Swanson at The Museum of the Confederacy; Mary Wolfshill at the Library of Congress; Virginia Daley, Linda McCurdy, and Patricia S. Webb at the William R. Perkins Library, Duke University; James J. Holmberg of The Filson Club; Gordon L. Olson at the Grand Rapids Public Library; Sally Childs-Helton, Indiana Historical Society; Dennis P. Kelly and Retha W. Stephens at Kennesaw Mountain National Battlefield Park; Brenda Lawson and Virginia Smith at the Massachusetts Historical Society; Jim Johnson at Memphis/Shelby County Public Library and Information Center; Ruth Ellen Bauer of the Minnesota Historical Society; Elsa Meyers at the New Jersey Historical Society; Jean Wentworth of the Historic Mobile Preservation Society; Alice Gillisse at the New Bern Historical Society; Catherine C. Kahn at the Historic New Orleans Collection; Valerie Wingfield and Rob Scott at the New York Public Library; Margaret Heilbrun and Patricia Paladines at the New York Historical Society; James P. Quigel, Jr. at the Pattee Library, Pennsylvania State University; Gayle Shackelford and Peggy Krohn at the Pensacola Historical Society; Bill Bynum at the Historical Foundation of the Presbyterian and Reformed Churches at Montreat, North Carolina; Abigail Yasgur at the Schlesinger Library, Radcliffe College; Edward Skipworth at Special Collections, Rutgers University; Elfrida M. Raley at the South Carolina Historical Society; Wayne C. Moore, Archives and Manuscripts Section at the Tennessee State Library; Robert W. Clark at the Southwest Collection at Texas Tech University; Elizabeth Alexander at the P. K. Yonge Library of Florida History at the University of Florida; William Cooper, Jr. at the King Library, University of Kentucky; Herbert J. Hartsook at the South Caroliniana Library at the University of South Carolina; Terry Latour, Sandra Boyd, and Alexandra S. Gressitt at The McCain Library and Archives at the University of Southern Mississippi; Kevin Ray at Washington University Library in St. Louis; Christian S. LaRoche at the Historical Society Museum of Valparaiso, Florida; Denise Montgomery at Valdosta State College Library; Kenneth F. Thomas, Joint Collection Western Historical Manuscript Collection—State Historical Society, St. Louis; and Patricia M. Hodges of the Special Collections at Western Kentucky University.

I would particularly like to thank my longtime friend and colleague here at Michigan State University, Pauline Adams, for her valuable help and encouragement. Some of the material in chapter 9 was taken from an article we co-authored for the *American Journal of Nursing* in 1988; some of the examples in chapter 3 came from papers we presented jointly at professional meetings. Another special colleague, Arnella Turner, contributed many helpful suggestions and support. Fellow American Thought and Language professors Jeff Charnley, Perry Gianakos, and David Anderson were most resourceful. My typist Jo Grandstaff has proved extremely knowledgeable and efficient. To Dr. Richard Chapin, recently retired Director of the Michigan State University Libraries and the MSU Press, I am greatly indebted. Fred Bohm, the current director of the Michigan State University Press, has provided both vision and expertise. I was most fortunate to have the competent Julie Loehr overseeing the production of this book and to have had Kristine Blakeslee as my adept copyeditor. Most of all, I thank my husband Tom, for his patience, his understanding, his critical reading, and his vitally important counsel.

—MMC

CHAPTER I

A Nation Torn Asunder

I could not wish you away from the place of danger, for *duty* and *honor* demand that every true man should "take his life in his hand" & stand ready to defend his family & his country, but I pray God may be with you all, and shield your dear heads from harm. If I were only a man, how gladly I would take my place with you. Have no fear or anxiety about *home*—the women will manage at home, while the men are doing their part in war.

—*Julia Fisher*, November 1861

One need not be a student of history to recall that the roots of the Civil War dated back to the early days of our country. The sectional discord manifest in the formation of our government and the location of its capital continued to escalate with time and was only temporarily compromised in 1820 and 1850. Divisions over the extension of slavery into the territories and, of course, over slavery—the South's "Peculiar Institution"—itself, set father against son, brother against brother. Abolitionist rhetoric, the Kansas–Nebraska Act, the formation of the Republican party, the Dred Scott decision, John Brown's raid on Harper's Ferry, and the election of Abraham Lincoln inflamed long-festering animosities which finally erupted in the South's secession and the "irrepressible conflict" that both sides were initially convinced would be of short duration. The firing on Fort Sumter merely served to bring the enmity to a head.

The war's raison d'être, the real issues at stake? Historians have long waged their own civil war over what each side was fighting for—or against. One camp insists that the South, believing they were being squeezed out of land and power by an industrialized North, was ostensibly fighting over protection of their states' rights; another camp maintains that the North was valiantly fighting to save the Union and to eradicate slavery. The more rational of the analysts, however, argue that, as with most wars, the contest probably revolved around the practical concerns of economics and the resultant, radically different lifestyles.

The bitterness and deepfelt hatred endemic to any war are intensified in a civil war where civilians on the homefront, as well as soldiers on the battlefield, meet in repeated homesoil confrontations with the enemy. An enemy thousands of miles away in another country is one thing; however, an enemy maneuvering its cannons into position on the outskirts of town, or brandishing pistols as he pillages one's house and livestock before setting a torch to the ravaged remains, is quite another.

In the late 1850s (and obviously with the onset of the war itself) long-standing sectional differences seemed only to exacerbate. The hotly contested political, social, and economic issues which divided the nation also succeeded in severing close family ties and in creating bitter enmity between lifelong friends as well. In the South, small pockets of Unionists refused to secede with their states and were eventually overtaken—their occupants either subdued or banished. In many areas of the North the Copperheads (Northerners who sympathized with the South) were vilified and ostracized. In the enemy-occupied areas of both sections, physical and verbal harassment overcame both reason and morality. In the border states, animosities seethed.

Some of the most engaging depictions of the myriad conflicting viewpoints espoused in Tennessee and Kentucky and the social ramifications they entailed are to be found in the diary of young Johanna Underwood, daughter of the Warner Underwoods, a pro-Union family living near Bowling Green, Kentucky. (The story of

the eviction of the Underwoods during the Confederate occupation of the town is covered in chapter 4.)

Even prior to the war, "Josie," while visiting her married sister
in Memphis, was incensed by talk of secession.

> Several gentlemen called. It was dreadful to hear how they
> talked. Mr. Western [her brother-in-law] and Mr. Grafton [a
> favorite suitor] did not hesitate to say they would be glad to
> see the country divided—that there was no similarity of interest
> in the two sections North and South—no love between them
> and the sooner separated the better—Worse than useless to
> be trying to live as one country and forever working against
> each other. Dear Pa charged me to avoid political discussions
> but goodness alive! how can I sit quietly and hear such talk
> as this. (Nazro, 7)

A few days later, Josie pointed out that even at a gala New Year's
Eve Ball

> the subject of secession like Banquo's ghost *will not down*
> but will come up—no matter what the place or time,—especially
> if Will Webb and Tom Grafton meet. Last night it was
> Mr. Webb's bad taste—that started the subject—then we
> were all off like horses in a race. I as bad as any of them.
> (Nazro, 10)

Still later, Josie recorded Mr. Grafton's bitterly partisan comments
following a heated conversation with Mississippi's Governor Foote.
Interjected, of course, was her own fervent hope for a peaceable
solution to the Nation's problems.

> "The Governor and other old foggies like him, don't appreci-
> ate what the condition of the South will be if Lincoln is al-
> lowed to carry out his abolition principles—and I for one am
> ready to fight to the death to prevent it."

In her diary Josie retorted:

11

But why not fight for Southern rights *in* the Union—why wish to divide this great country that your forefathers and mine sacrificed so much to establish.

Mr. Grafton continued:

"How could Washington dream a Lincoln—a low born clod hopper would ever be elected president of the United States? And he never was either—only a part of the Country wants him and the sooner we separate forever from that part—the better for the South."

Relieved when the music resumed, Josie noted:

I was glad the dancing stopped his talk. It is plain to see that the older—wiser people are for preserving the Union in spite of their antagonism to Lincoln and his party—but it is dreadful to hear how so many of the younger men talk—Mr. Western advocates secession as a fundamental principle for any free country. . . . (Nazro, 11)

A week later, following a semi-successful Secessionist parade in Memphis, Josie continued her tirade against the Secessionists.

The hardship of the position of the Unionists in Tenn. and Ky., like Pa, Uncle Joe and others is that they are just as much opposed to Lincoln and his policy as the recessionists are and Pa was a Bell and Everett Elector and did all in his power—to prevent Lincoln's election—but he is no less a lover of his country, because a party he regards untrue to the constitution were successful. He thinks for that very reason all true patriots should, stand true to the old flag and to the whole country and he says—he opposes secession *most*—out of his love for the South, for disunion will be her ruin—for if there is war—it will surely be in the South and the whole land desolated and laid in waste and slavery will certainly go if the Union is dissolved. The only way, he thinks, is for the South to remain in the Union if she would maintain *any* of the "Southern rights" she is clamoring for. (Nazro, 15)

Upon her return home to Bowling Green, Josie found the divisiveness increasing.

The feeling is growing more and more bitter between Union people and secessionists try as we will to maintain the same outward show of friendship. There is a lack of sympathy in hopes and fears that is felt when not expressed. (Nazro, 42)

In a subsequent diary entry, Josie attempted to sort out the divergent views of her family on the subject of disunion.

Dear Pa believes in maintaining the Union—for the good of the *whole country* and thinks any division of the country will hurt the South far more than it will the North—in fact will *ruin* the South and he still hopes if Kentucky does not secede she may some way avert a war and bring about reconciliation between the sections. Mr. Girder and Mr. Western from different standpoints, hoot at the idea of any patched up peace— Mr. G., says "*Whip* the South back and give her her rights and kill off the fire eaters north and south and maintain the constitution as it is and uphold the old flag against traitors north and south" and dear Ma agrees with him—both opposed to any neutrality. Mr. McCann does not believe in slavery— though he thinks the Government had no right to meddle with it in the States where it already exists—but thinks the South should not be allowed to secede—for admitting that doctrine is ruin—Mr. Western believes slavery an essential condition of the inferior races—ordained by God and he also believes in States Rights and secession—so the arguments rage in one way or the other all the time. . . . (Nazro, 45)

The controversy, Josie noted, often raged at the dinner table with guests now and then overstepping their bounds and becoming obnoxious in their political harangues. On just such an occasion Josie's mother took command.

But dear Ma couldn't help hitting back—for Pa's sake—and when we rose from the supper table she said "Mr. Norton, (she had always called him E. before) you will excuse me from going into the Parlor with you—and of course you would not wish to be asked ever again to become a guest in the home of Unionists after the sentiments you have expressed." (Nazro, 42)

The resignation of Josie's Uncle Wint (her mother's younger brother) from West Point and his subsequent enlistment in the

Confederate army created a deep family rift and completely devastated Josie's mother.

> We are all distressed and dear Ma is heart broken. Uncle Wint has resigned! He wrote "he had not before understood the true conditions of the conflict and as much as it grieved him to withdraw from the service of the government that had educated him and the profession he loved—and above all to go against the opinion and advice of brother Warner (Pa) whom he honored and loved above any other living man—he could not conscientiously fight any longer against the South—so had sent in his resignation."
>   Pa said "just what I feared" and tried as best he could to comfort Ma—who wept in terrible distress just as though Wint were dead—and indeed said over and over again "Oh! if he had only died or been killed defending the flag and the country for which his fathers fought—before he turned traitor"—"to think of my father's son fighting against this country" and so she grieved in a heartrending way—for all her patriotic family pride had been centered in Wint and his resignation nearly kills her. She begged us all never to mention his name to her again—to let him be as one dead. Too bad! too sad! How can we do that for he has always been like our brother. How bitter, how hard everything is getting. . . . (Nazro, 67)

Later, Josie wrote:

> Ma does not cease to grieve over Uncle Wint's resignation—though she hasn't mentioned his name since and when we heard he had joined the Confederate army, she cried again like her heart would break—saying over and over "O that I should live to see the day that my father's son would fight against this country"! (Nazro, 69)

With the firing on Fort Sumter, the line between "acceptable callers" and "unacceptable callers" was quickly drawn in many Northern as well as Southern homes. As would be expected, Josie's antipathy for "rebels" intensified as the weeks passed. Her rancor was clearly evident in her response to a former friend's request to call upon her.

14

Yesterday I drove in town and whilst sitting in the carriage a man in Captain's uniform, came up to speak to me and I recognized Terah Freeman, whom I had not seen since I was at school in Russellville and he at college there. The soldiers dress, a moustache and two years had changed him quite a little. It was he who had bowed so low the day before, and two other Tennessee boys I had known in Russellville. He asked me if he could call. I told him "Not in that uniform" which surprised him no little, as he said "He supposed of course I was a Rebel" and I answered, "Why should you have supposed that? Did you ever in the old school days hear me express great admiration for Benedict Arnold"? and then I told Uncle Lewis to drive on. . . . (Nazro, 75)

Several days later two Confederate officers, whom Josie had known "as plain Misters" during her Memphis visit, arrived in Bowling Green with their regiment and asked "if they might call."

Ma decided they should not, so we kept the messenger waiting a long time whilst I wrote note after note, tearing up one and writing another, trying to write a refusal, without offense. . . . (Nazro, 75)

Although Josie appeared to have been seriously attracted to the Mr. Grafton of her Memphis visit, she was discouraged from maintaining correspondence with "a Rebel."

The Underwood family represented just one of countless families who suffered the anguish of divided loyalties. At least one mother had three sons fighting for the Confederacy and three for the Union. Ardent Confederate Sarah Morgan, of Baton Rouge, had three brothers serving with the South, two of whom gave their lives for their country. A brother-in-law sided with the North and served in the western theatre of war. Although Sarah's eldest brother, Philip Morgan, was torn between Union and Confederate sympathies, he took the Oath of Allegiance, but refused to fight against his countrymen. Eventually, despite their extreme distaste at having to live amongst the hated Yankees in occupied New Orleans, Sarah and her family were forced to abandon their itinerant refugee life and seek the protection of Philip and his wife in the Crescent City. During the ensuing months, friction was kept to a minimum within the household by her brother's prudent diplomacy, a kindness which happily was not lost on Sarah.

> There are no Southern young men left in town, and those who remain would hardly be received with civility by Miriam [her sister] and myself. Of the Yankees, Brother has so much consideration for us that he has never invited one to his house since we have been here, though he has many friends among them who visited here before our arrival. Such delicacy of feeling we fully appreciate, knowing how very few men of such a hospitable nature would be capable of such a sacrifice. Thinking we need company, Brother frequently invites what he calls "a safe old Secessionist" (an old bachelor of fifty-three who was wounded at Shiloh) to dine with us; thinking it a fair compromise between the stay-at-home youth and Yankees, neither of whom this extremely young man could be confounded with. (Dawson 1960, 389–90)

A few weeks later she again remarked on her brother's thoughtfulness.

> Every time he hears good news on our side, he tells it just as though it was on his side, instead of on ours; while all bad news for us he carefully avoids mentioning, unless we question him. (Dawson 1960, 393)

In later life, writing with the wisdom of hindsight, Eliza Frances Andrews apologized to the memory of her father, a staunch Unionist, for the disrespect she and her family showed him by bringing on "scenes that were not conducive to the peace of the family."

> Youth is impulsive, and prone to run with the crowd. We caught the infection of the war spirit in the air and never stopped to reason or to think. (15)

Although the young people were remorseful after their passionate outbursts, Eliza confessed:

I am afraid, that first and last, we made the old gentleman's life a burden to him. In looking back over the sufferings and disappointments of those dreadful years the most pathetic figure that presents itself to my memory is that of my dear old father, standing unmoved by all the clamor of the times and the way-wardness of his children, in his devotion to the great republic that his father had fought for at Yorktown. I can see now, what I could not realize then, that the Union men in the South—the honest ones, I mean, like my father—sacrificed even more for their cause than we of the other side did for ours. . . . They were gentlemen, and most of them slaveholders, who stood by the Union, not because they were in any sense Northern sympathizers, but because they saw in division death for the South, and believed that in saving her to the Union they were saving her to herself. They suffered not only the material losses of the war, but the odium their opinions excited; and worst of all, the blank disillusionment that must have come to them when they saw their beloved Union restored only to bring about the riot and shame of Reconstruction. (16–17)

Sarah Butler Wister, daughter of Fanny Kemble, the famous English actress, and Pierce Butler, saw her family split by the war: her father and younger sister sympathized with the Confederacy, and she and her mother allied with the North. Sarah suffered great distress when in August 1861 her father was arrested (and later released) on suspicion of treason. Shortly after Fort Sumter, Sarah predicted in her diary her sister's reaction to the commencement of hostilities.

She thinks that the taking of Ft. Sumter will put an end to hostilities as the North will see that the South is in earnest, & is so very unwilling to fight, itself!!! She will open her eyes a little when she arrives here & finds every man of her acquaintance enlisted. (289)

Katharine Hubbell, of Bridgeport, Connecticut and New York City, little dreamed that her October 10, 1860, marriage to Joseph Bryan Cumming, of Augusta, Georgia, would lead to a four-year separation from her beloved Northern family. As a Northern bride living with her Southern in-laws during the war, "Kate" found herself suffering the loneliness and isolation of a stranger in a foreign land. Further complications arose when her brother Henry enlisted in the Union Army and her husband and his four brothers joined the Confederate Army. Residing with a close-knit family, long steeped in Southern tradition and possibly, at times, slightly uncomfortable with an alien in their midst, required grace and limitless tolerance, both of which "Kate" Cumming apparently had in abundance. Letters from her mother were usually condensed "one page letters" subject to be opened for inspection and carried under a flag of truce. At times, the separation seemed almost unbearable (K. H. Cumming 1976).

Although she had been born in Charleston, South Carolina, Septima Collis "became a *Union* woman" when she married a Northern soldier just four months before the war began. Her divided loyalties culminated with the death of her brother, who had fought for the Confederacy, and the serious illness of her husband, an officer with the Union forces.

> . . . although I had many relatives and hosts of friends serving under the Confederate flag all the time, I never fully realized the fratricidal character of the conflict until I lost my idolized brother Dave of the Southern army one day, and was nursing my Northern husband back to life the next. (18–19)

Both Northern and Southern women's diaries recount impassioned verbal sparring with family members and friends. In her May 21, 1861, diary entry, Sarah Bovard, of Alpha, Indiana, lamented her divided family: "I take the children and go to mother's but do not stay long. She abused the Republicans—called them thieves, liars and everything bad . . . my feelings hurt." A few months later she noted: "Mother comes by going to meeting, stops long enough to wish old Lincoln dead."

Sallie Florence McEwen, of Franklin, Tennessee, concluded her May 6, 1862, diary entry with the notation that

> Mrs. L. Bailey was at our house this evening; she is completely changed from a Secesh woman to strong union; she left our house almost in tears; she got a Secession talk rather too strong for her union nerves.

Not only were families divided, but in some areas the war pitted neighbor against neighbor. Sallie Pendleton Van Rensselaer, writing in her diary from Berkeley Springs (admitted to the Union in 1863 as part of West Virginia), mirrored the feelings of great numbers of western Virginia residents.

> . . . I am a Virginian, every drop of blood that flows in my veins is Virginian, but my being Virginian, don't make me a Secessionist—it, on the contrary, makes me a Unionist, for I think Va's good, is in holding to the Union, to the Constitution & to the Laws. (6 January 1862)

Two days later she reaffirmed her convictions.

> My love to and for my State is *great*, but that to my country is *greater, far far greater*. (8 January 1862)

Five days later she wrote of the enmity caused by the war:

> No one can imagine the bitterness that now exists between what were once called friends. (13 January 1862)

Although many Union sympathizers fled northward as war became imminent, some either could not or would not move to safe Union territory. "Miss Abby," a schoolteacher in Atlanta during the Civil War, walked a tightrope for fear of publicly displaying her ardent Unionist sentiments and thereby suffering banishment and/or a loss of her teaching position. As a consequence, she repeatedly choked back heartfelt tears over Northern losses and smothered exuberant cheers over Southern defeats. Speaking for her small coterie of loyal friends, she wrote: "We have learned our lessons well,—

can cry when we would laugh—and laugh when we would cry" (6 May 1864).

Particularly distressing to "Miss Abby" were church services which denigrated the Federal government and offered prayers for its annihilation.

> A solemn Sabbath this has been. Though sick in soul & body—I went to church. Devotion was not the impetus that sent me there—but a restlessness—a feeling that I could not bear this suspense alone. I must mingle with the multitude—and perhaps some friendly hand would clasp mine—some voice whisper—"Courage"! "Faith"! . . .
>
> I wondered too—what would be said in the pulpit today; and if there would be thanksgivings for *victories*. Though our present pastor has never preached war—but the gospel; and has not as many ministers have done—*instructed* God how to deal with the "vile enemies who are fighting against us." Victory was prayed for as usual . . . [and a special meeting convened] for the purpose of praying that our enemies might be defeated, and we gain the victory. All were urged to be present, and with united hearts present this petition to the Court of Heaven. . . .
>
> I bit my lips to keep the color in them, and was afraid my next pew neighbors would hear my thoughts. I actually held my hands firm together, to keep them from flying up imploringly—for I trembled with fear, lest God would hear these prayers which were to be offered, and those who had prayed for the coming of this "enemy" as the saviors of their country—must again sink in despair. (15 May 1864)

Sherman's inauguration of the Atlanta campaign warmed "Miss Abby's" heart and on May 24, 1864, she noted:

> I met a gentleman—a Southern Unionist staunch & true; he was walking with a Confederate officer—and bowed very slightly and sedately. After he passed, something, which often impels us to look back, made me turn my head; at that instant, his head turned too, & his face was covered with smiles. I knew then, his heart was as glad as mine—but our intuition, schooled as it has been these years—tells us where to laugh, & when not to.

"Miss Abby," keenly aware of her isolation as a Unionist in Confederate territory, was often shocked by the bitterness she observed among Southerners.

> Have I been always thus alone? Was there always war & terror & tumult about me? and never any sunshine & brightness and peace? Was there always somebody praying for vengeance?— and ladies saying as one said the other day—"I wish there was a sea of blood between the North & South—so broad and deep, it could never be crossed"! And another who lived not a hundred miles distant, who was making haste to refugee said— "I rather every one of my children (she was the mother of four) should be laid out on the *cooling board*, than to have the Yankees get my niggers." (30 May 1864)

Loyalties also differed markedly within political parties. Everyone, it seemed, had a different idea about the war and how it should be conducted. Abolitionists saw the war as an attempt to free the slaves, other soldiers and civilians sought the reunification of the country. Some Northerners wanted a fight to the finish to reestablish unity, still others hoped for peace and conciliation. The latter group of antiwar Democrats, called Copperheads or Peace Democrats, commanded large followings in some areas and were maligned in others. Anna Mercer LaRoche noted in her diary that the name "Copperhead" was used because "that snake is ready to strike at any moment without cause." As a peace proponent she wrote:

> Peace and conciliation—How we need them—We are of the obnoxious party—against the war & find times hard for us. (Francis 26 February 1863)

Anna LaRoche and her prominent Philadelphia family were such rabid Copperheads that Anna vehemently resisted having "Mott" Francis, a handsome, bright New Yorker, introduced to her "because he is such a Republican." As they continued to meet at social gatherings of family and friends, Anna struggled with her emotions. "I have taken a great dislike to him on account of his politics &

21

will not be won over" (Francis 17 May 1864). In a later undated diary entry, she commented: "I like him ever so much & I do not wish to as he is a 'republican.'" Love finally won out, however, and nine months later, Anna and "Mott" were married.

The fiery patriotism that sparked the previously mentioned Sarah Morgan and Eliza Andrews was widespread among Southern women during the war. In fact, the zealous devotion of the women of the South to their cause has often been credited with having prolonged the Civil War for months after the Confederacy had been virtually defeated. (Northern women, to be sure, exhibited comparable loyalties, however, the proximity of the enemy and the devastation wrought by the army "bummers" fueled Southern hatred of the Yankees to near fanaticism.)

According to many authorities, women were the Confederacy's best recruiters. Perhaps women were blissfully unaware of the death and destruction of the battlefield or perhaps having so long and so faithfully looked up to their fathers, husbands, and brothers as their "male protectors" they continued to cast their soldiers in the role of defenders of defenseless women and children. In any case, Southern women appeared to cling to the romantic image of their men as gallant warriors. One woman expressed the sentiments of many of her contemporaries when, buckling the armor on her patriot husband, she remarked, "I had rather be the widow of a brave man than the wife of a coward."*

Ella Gertrude Clanton Thomas, for example, proudly noted:

> My husband will go—My brother Jimmie will leave in the same co . . . and I am proud to see them exhibit the noble, manly, spirit which prompts them to go. It proves that southern blood has not degenerated in consequence of the life of luxury and ease we have been living.

---

*The same exhortation was chanted by the women of Eucheeanna, Florida, when during the early days of the war they marched about town urging on the men with "Go boys, to your country's call! I'd rather be a brave man's widow than a coward's wife." That day sixty volunteers responded to their dramatic appeal (Reddick, 1).

In the same entry, she explained:

> When Duty and Honor call him it would be strange if I would
> influence him to remain "in the lap of inglorious ease" when
> so much is at stake. (13 July 1861)

Young Southern ladies often refused to be seen in the company
of a man eligible for service who was not in uniform. Some Confederate women sent "stay-at-homes" petticoats and nightcaps to
shame them into enlisting. Kate Cumming expressed the almost
universal Southern conviction that all men—and women—should
be actively engaged in contributing to the war effort.

> I also said a man did not deserve the name of man, if he did
> not fight for his country; nor a woman, the name of woman,
> if she did not do all in her power to aid the men. (K. Cumming
> 1959, 191)

Death on the battlefield, the ultimate sacrifice for the Southern
cause, was considered glorious by many women (usually those with
no family members serving with the armies). Josephine Clay
Habersham, in reflecting on the death of a soldier friend, noted:

> It was a sad, *untimely* death, but oh! how glorious to die for
> one's Country. I can imagine no higher destiny for a noble
> minded man! (92–93)

At times Alice Ready envisioned herself in the hero's role, a soldier
bravely defending his country. Since her gender denied her that
option, she took immense pride in her brother's service, even though
it might eventuate in his death.

> How I glory in being a Southern born, and a *rebel*. I never
> before wished I was a man—now I feel so keenly my weakness
> and dependence. I cannot do or say anything—for "it would
> be unbecoming in a young lady." How I should love to fight
> and even die for my Country—our glorious beautiful South—
> what a privilege I should esteem it, but am denied it because

> I am a woman, however the Feds seem to fear the women as much or more than the men. To us they give the credit for the number of men the South has in the field. I thank God I have a brave Brother to fight his country's battles. He may fall, but it will be in a glorious cause and although an only and a darling Brother—I had far rather this should be, than have him at home remaining idle while there is so much to be done. Mama says I talk wildly. It is what my heart feels and head approves. (83–84)

Not infrequently, as the war progressed, Southern women, incensed by what they deemed cowardice, gathered in the streets to shame the troops for retreating. Mary Loughborough described such a scene following the siege of Vicksburg. As the groups of weary soldiers straggled past, the women demanded to know where they were going.

> "We are running."
> "From whom?" exclaimed one of the young girls of the house.
> "The Feds, to be sure," said another, half laughing and half shamefaced.
> "Oh! shame on you!" cried the ladies; "and you running!"
> "It's all Pem's fault," said an awkward, long-limbed, weary-looking man.
> "It's all your own fault. Why don't you stand your ground?" was the reply.
> "Shame on you all!" cried some of the ladies across the street, becoming excited.
> I could not but feel sorry for the poor worn fellows, who did seem indeed heartily ashamed of themselves; some without arms, having probably lost them in the first break of the companies.
> "We are disappointed in you!" cried some of the ladies. "Who shall we look to now for protection?"
> "Oh!" said one of them, "it's the first time I ever ran. We are Georgians, and we never ran before; but we saw them all breaking and running, and we could not bear up alone." (43–44)

Thousands of women, however, were torn between their patriotism, their inherent pride in their kinfolks' enlistment, and the

24

promise of safety assured by hiring a substitute. Sarah Wadley, for example, was a staunch Southern patriot, who repeatedly railed against any thought of submission.

> . . . submission; submission! Why do I speak that disgraceful word, why do I think it for a moment; victory or death is our only alternative, worse than death would be our conquest by the Yankees, that is now the most hateful word in our language. (2 March 1862)

Yet when it came to her brother Willie's enlistment, she expressed mixed feelings. Sarah's intense Confederate loyalties gave way to some conflicting thoughts about the risks Willie faced, his ultimate contributions to the war, and his attempts to secure a substitute.

> I sometimes think I have false ideas on this subject, and that Willie is perhaps doing his duty better by remaining to assist Father who so much needs him than by going into the camp where he would not assist our country any more, but still I cannot help feeling it as a stain, a cause for blushing, that he should have a substitute. (16 November 1863)

Willie's substitute proved to be expensive and at first Sarah weighed the price against the hazards involved:

> his price is ten thousand dollars in money, a horse, saddle and bridle, and to provide a house and bread stuff for his family during his absence, it is a high price to pay but a little one to receive when one is going to a life of peril and hardship only *for the price*. (16 November 1863)

Unfortunately, the South at that point was rigidly enforcing the conscription of every able-bodied man available and the substitute papers were returned with the notation, "No more substitutes received except in case of the sickness or disability of the party procuring them." In her confusion, Sarah confided to her diary: "I don't know what to wish, I can't bear the thought of Willie's going away, and yet I am anxious for him to serve his country" (16 March 1862).

It was far easier, of course, to know what one's neighbors should do. Kate Foster noted in her diary:

> There are some young men here I think ought to be drummed out of society—the idea of one man staying when his country calls for aid and so anxiously too. (25 June 1863)

Never for a moment should it be inferred that all Southern women exulted in the enlistment of their husbands and/or brothers, Sarah Wadley being a case in point. However, many Confederate women's diaries reflect an enthusiasm not often exhibited in the more realistic diaries and correspondence of Northern women. Lizzie Little, of Illinois, for one, urged her fiancé to put off volunteering for as long as possible.

> But George if I am allowed to say anything, do not go yet, wait. Let some battles be fought, see the power you have to contend with, for I believe it is a fierce one. The South will not be conquered in a day as some here vauntingly boast but in the end we may hope may we not for complete victory. . . .
>   Now George do not go until it is necessary. We need some intellectual thinking men to help make a new government, a new Union and let the loafers of our cities, the scum of society show their valor ere the working efficient men take the field. When it comes to that then I would say *go, go.* (Avery 22 April 1861)

Maria Sharp was particularly bitter about her husband's enlistment in the Second Regiment of the Iowa Volunteer Infantry:

> You wanted me to make the children think you done right by going away but i cant teach them that when i know it is not right so i dont teach them anything (489).

Ann Cotton, of Marietta, Ohio, chided herself for agreeing to her husband's volunteering to join the Union troops as a surgeon. Within three months after his departure she was already regretting his enlistment.

I daily regret having given my consent to your going away. I do not know what possessed me, that I did so. I do not think it will be of the least benefit to you or anyone else, for as to conquering the south, I do not believe it will ever be done. . . . It is dreadful to live as you are doing & all for nothing too . . . don't you wish sometimes that you had not gone? Now tell the truth! (28 December 1862)

A few days later, she confessed:

I am more a wife than a patriot, & although I do care for my country, I care for you much more. I know that this is all very selfish but I can not help it, especially as I am naturally selfish! (1 January 1863)

By June 2, 1864, Ann's patience was wearing even thinner as she denounced the hiring of substitutes.

If the war lasts much longer it cannot be carried on by volunteering alone as almost all good loyal men are gone, but there is a great many butternuts [Southern sympathizers], & they ought to be compelled to go. It would please us here very much if such men as Mr. Follette were obliged to go, but as the law now is, he would not go if he were drafted, as he could get a substitute. I do not believe in such a law & hope it will be abolished, as it is only the rich who can be benefited by it. It is a great pity that all the traitors in the North could not be killed off instead of our best men, don't you think so?

To enlist (and sometimes, in which town to enlist), to take one's chances in the draft, or to hire a substitute presented men and their families with important options. Northern states and towns frequently offered a wide range of bounties (bonuses) to men who would enlist and thus help meet that area's conscript quota. Janette Stoddard, of Fairgrove, Michigan, wrote to her sister Laura Jane, of Kalamazoo County, Michigan, to announce the birth of her three-day-old son and to explain the circumstances of her husband's enlistment.

27

But blame him not for enlisting. He did not do it until driven by the heavy draft that is pending. Other towns in better circumstances are buying up our men at a rapid rate so that the draft is likely to take nearly all that remain. One of about ten men who have recently enlisted only one beside Crosby has been credited to this town while others are getting 200 to 300 dollars for enlisting for other towns. Crosby for the sake of helping his own town was credited here with the promise of only 100 and now they basely refuse even *that* and told him to go where he can do the best. He may be able to get his credit changed but it is uncertain. Money is a very small thing in comparison with the risk of life incurred but to those who leave dependent families behind, it is essential. . . . When the conscripts, the men enlisted for other places, and the skadoodlers, have all left the neighborhood, I presume there will not be ten men in town. I believe the most of the towns are raising their quota but this is one of the meanest of all mean places. We have been so unfortunate as to get into it and must abide by the consequences. (20 August 1864)

Janette thanked her sister for offering to help purchase a substitute for her husband, but added "from [what] we can learn of the prices of substitutes now they are beyond our means" (20 August 1864).

Unpopular conscription laws enacted by both Union and Confederate governments stirred up great unrest in both sections. Particularly resentful were the families who suffered so gravely from the seemingly unfair exemption clauses. The South's immunity for planters owning twenty or more slaves, the Twenty-Negro Law, in particular, infuriated small farmers owning few or no slaves. To many Southerners it became "a rich man's war and a poor man's fight." Loudly and repeatedly, small farmers voiced their anger at having to do all the fighting while their rich counterparts lolled around at home.

Although the conscription bills stimulated volunteerism among men on both sides who wished to avoid the stigma of being drafted, the substitution clauses were hotly contested. In the North, Congress's passage of a law making every man between the ages of twenty and forty-five subject to army service, yet permitting the sending of a substitute upon payment of $300, gave rise to draft riots.

28

The New York City Draft Riots of July 1863 brought murder and mayhem to a location seemingly far removed from the field of battle. As the drawing of names at draft boards in the city began, thousands of disgruntled New Yorkers (many of them foreign-born) resorted to mob violence in protest to the draft system which they believed clearly discriminated against the poor. The draft's provision that allowed men to hire substitutes for $300 (a sizable sum in those days, especially to a day-laborer) seemed grossly unfair and their low wages and the continually escalating prices further fueled the unrest. Furthermore, the city's poor, many of them Irish, were convinced that the increasing numbers of free blacks from the South attempting to enter the New York City job market presented a serious threat to their jobs. Seeking vengeance on the blacks as the source of their troubles, the mob gathered strength in numbers and courage from liquor and commenced indiscriminate attacks on blacks and anyone they judged to be associated with the draft or the Republican party. Troops were called in to supplement the city police force, but before the rioting had ended, more than one hundred people had lost their lives. Shortly after the riots, which struck fear into the hearts of New Yorkers, Maria Daly noted in her diary:

> I saw Susanna Brady, who talked in the most violent manner against the Irish and in favor of the blacks. I feel quite differently, although very sorry and much outraged at the cruelties inflicted. I hope it will give the Negroes a lesson, for since the war commenced, they have been so insolent as to be unbearable. I cannot endure free blacks. They are immoral, with all their piety. (Hammond 1962, 251)

Virginia Fox wrote to her husband of her sleepless nights during the riots and declared, "I would have given any sum for a pistol here for those nights" (20 July 1863).

The draft and the substitution system angered citizens in small towns as well. Benton Lewis's mother wrote to her son describing the resentment exhibited in Cannon and Courtland, Michigan, and noting the towns' solutions to quotas.

> . . . now I will tell you how they got along with the draft in
> Cannon   you must remember Cannon is a very patriotic
> town and had only six men to furnish for the last call so they
> called a meeting and agreed to raise 300 dollars and pay each
> man that would enlist   they did not levy a tax but got every
> one to sign that would and those that were exposed to the draft
> paid 25 dollars each   after that was done Bill Young paid
> one of the men four hundred dollars out of his own pocket
>   so he sent a substitute and is free for three years him-
> self   that is the way to do it. . . . the most of the towns will
> fill their quotas by inlisting but Courtland is doing nothing
> they threaten to resist but I guess they will cave when the time
> comes. (20 September 1864)

The popularity of "Exemption Clubs" was explained by Annie
Cox in a letter to her fiancé, Gideon Winan Allen, a law student
at The University of Michigan.

> The draft came off last Thursday. 117 were drafted in the
> city [Madison, Wisconsin], probably not more than 20 of the
> number will go, for they all belong to some one of the exemp-
> tion clubs of the city. I wish you could join. They pay $50 and
> if drafted the company make up the $300. (15 November 1863)

In Oxford, Wisconsin, Mary Burwell wrote to her husband of an
attempt by some of the townspeople to initiate a tax "to keep some
men here at home that is just as able to go to war as you are."
Although the proposal was voted down, it was scheduled to come
up for a vote again. Mary fervently wished women would be allowed
to vote for she would do all she could "to put it down" (Winter
1864–5). Some men, to Mary's thinking, were *not* more equal than
others!

Life was further complicated for a soldier and his family by the problem of whether or not he should reenlist. In a letter of February 19,
1864, Lois Davis, of Dracut, Massachusetts, counseled her sons

> . . . [I] hope you have not taken a hasty step and are now
> repenting it. I mean reinlisting. Perhaps now the excitement
> has somewhat subsided you almost repent it; but so it is and

we must all make the best of it. I could have wished it otherwise but I must not be selfish for I know our country requires just such noble true patriotic men as you are. Yours was no base hirelings to leave home and friends to share the fortunes and fate of war, not for gold was you bought, but true loyalty which caused you to take up armes in your country, cause I know quite well you could not come home and settle down to any civil pursuits in life untill the rebelion is over, and too that you will have more money, but the maney long months of hardship that must intervene before your time is out is hard to think of but Dear boys dont be discouraged yours is a holy cause a just cause and may the God of battles watch over and protect you is my constant prayer.

Enmity, of course, is inherent in all wars; however, Southerners exhibited an unusually malevolent hatred of Yankees. The violence and looting of Sherman's troops no doubt served to exacerbate their animosity.

General William T. Sherman himself was well aware of the utter loathing of Southern women for the Federals. In a letter to his wife he wrote:

> I doubt if history affords a parallel to the deep and bitter enmity of the women of the South. No one who sees them and hears them but must feel the intensity of their hate. Not a man is seen; nothing but women with houses plundered, fields open to the cattle and horses, pickets lounging on every porch, and desolation sown broadcast, servants all gone and women and children bred in luxury, beautiful and accomplished, begging with one breath for the soldiers' rations and in another praying that the Almighty or Joe Johnston will come and kill us, the despoilers of their homes and all that is sacred. (Sherman 1909, 268–69)

Even from the very earliest days of the war, however, Southern women displayed a daring feistiness that continued to characterize their relationships with the hated Yankees throughout the war. Kate Foster and her friends living near Natchez, Mississippi, for example, deplored the intrusion of the Yankees in their heretofore peaceful community.

> The Yankees come to our church in crowds and are by degrees
> filling the pews up with their hateful blue coats where "our
> grey" last sat and listened with swelling hearts to the word of
> God. I cannot bear to be nearer than three or four pews. They
> are such dirty creatures.

In the same entry, Kate wrote disparagingly of the fraternization
of some of her acquaintances with Northern soldiers:

> Some of the young ladies around Natchez are receiving atten-
> tion from the Yankees. I think it shows *so* little character not
> to resist love of admiration more. (20 September 1863)

On another occasion, Kate told her diary:

> We ought not to speak of a Yankee and one of our soldiers
> in the same breath. The meanest of our men are ten times
> better and more of gentlemen than the best of the Yankees.
> We saw the Provost Marshall and a more conceited, conde-
> scending and would be gracious man I never saw. (25 July 1863)

Kate and her fellow Southerners were positively outraged to hear
of one of their own *marrying* a Yankee. At least one young lady
sought to avoid censure by insisting that her fiancé was "Not a
Yankee. He's a Westerner, from Illinois." In one Southern church
the organist steadfastly refused to play for the wedding of a parish-
ioner who was marrying a Union soldier. Finally, when the bishop
ordered her to play, she complied reluctantly, dressed in mourning
and played in a funereal tempo (L. W. P. Fletcher, passim).

Particularly in occupied territories, enforced submission and the
resultant collision of two opposing loyalties and two different sets
of values produced incessant harassment that was freely engaged
in by both the occupation troops and the local citizenry. Northerners quickly learned that Southern belles could often become bel-
licose when sufficiently provoked by Yankee intruders. Many a
Southern lady proved herself anything but the docile, fluttering,
demure woman of book and legend. As their tormentors
increased in numbers and in offenses, Southern women discovered

they could harass in return—that they could give as good as they got. True, some women reported they "sugared" their Yankee oppressors and thus prevented many atrocities; others, however, took more direct action. One woman, upon being kissed on the street by a Yankee, simply drew a pistol and shot him.

Southern women usually remained cool and undaunted even when Yankee mauraders threatened to "blow their brains out" unless they surrendered their valuables. Lucy Buck told of one woman's being accosted by a Yankee intruder who pulled out his pistol and took deliberate aim at her. When she refused to allow him to wrest her jewelry box from her, he fired his gun (or snapped the cap) "full in her face without producing any impression." In the scuffle that ensued she "dealt the miscreant such a blow as sent him reeling from her" (Buck, 274–75). When a Yankee officer put a pistol to Mary Hort's head and then threatened her with his dagger, Mary stood her ground and announced defiantly: "If you kill me I shall go straight to heaven. I am a Christian" (April 1865).

Soon after its takeover by the Federal troops, New Orleans became famous for the confrontations between "Beast Butler" (the appellation given General Benjamin F. Butler, commander of the occupation forces, by the women of New Orleans) and the "she-adders of New Orleans" (Butler's terminology for the Crescent City's Confederate female population). The women's derogatory comments insolently whispered within hearing distance of the Union soldiers, their haughty gathering up of their skirts to avoid contact when a Federal soldier passed, their vicious spitting on the Yankee invaders, and their slamming shut of window blinds at the sighting of a Federal officer's passing, led Butler to issue his famous proclamation to the women of New Orleans. (A copy of the order is on display at the Historic New Orleans Collection.)

Headquarters Department of the Gulf,
New Orleans, May 15, 1862.

General Order No. 28.

As the officers and soldiers of the United States have been subject to repeated insults from the women (calling themselves

33

ladies) of New Orleans, in return for the most scrupulous non-interference and courtesy on our part, it is ordered that here-after when any female shall, by word, gesture, or movement, insult or show contempt for any officer or soldier of the United States, she shall be regarded and held liable to be treated as a woman of the town plying her avocation.

By command of

Major-General Butler.

Geo. C. Strong, *A. A. G., Chief of Staff.*

One of the most notorious conflicts centered around General Butler and Mrs. Philip Phillips. Although her husband was a promi-nent lawyer in Washington and she a popular Washington socialite, Eugenia Phillips, her two daughters, and her sister became such out-spoken opponents of the Federal government that at length the four-some was arrested and imprisoned with Rose Greenhow in the Greenhow home. Through the help of Edwin Stanton and Judge Advocate Keyes, Mrs. Phillips, her daughters and sister were released and given three days to pack prior to their removal south beyond Union lines. After a brief stop in Richmond, Mrs. Phillips and her family settled in New Orleans where she soon found a comfortable niche among the hotheaded Confederate women of the city. After the surrender of the city, she enthusiastically participated in their spirited resistance to General Butler and his ultimatums. During a particularly tumultuous period in New Orleans, Mrs. Phillips met General Butler in a one-on-one showdown. Charged with laugh-ing as the funeral procession of a Union officer passed her home, Mrs. Phillips refused to apologize to General Butler, saying her laughter was the result of a children's party, whereupon she was exiled to Ship Island and held incommunicado with anyone save General Butler and her maid. Following her release, Mrs. Phillips and her family were ordered out of New Orleans into Confederate territory. For the remainder of the war they made their home in La Grange, Georgia (Phillips-Myers; Kinchen 1972, 116–21).

Now and then contending loyalties had a lighter side. In a letter to Jennie Chamberlain, Cavalryman Gilbert W. Chapman reported an afternoon's merriment at his headquarters in Virginia, a scene best described by Gilbert himself.

> We are quartered on a large plantation near James City, Va and thire [sic] are some fifteen or twenty good buildings in which we are quartered. An old man some sixty years old owns the plantation and he has some five or six daughters Secesh every one of them the worst kind but Kilpatrick is just the one to manage such birds as they are. . . . The other day the General had gone off on official business of some kind or other and there was a crowd of his staff officers got one of them to playing on the piano and singing. She sang the "Bonny Blue Flag" and "Dixie" and several other songs that contained secession sentiments of the strongest kind. *Old Kill* (as we call him) came back just as she was doing her best on "Dixie." The General called out, "Corporal of the Guard arrest that woman and lock her up" and she was arrested and locked up in the Smoke house for twelve hours and when she came out the Genl made her sing "The Star Spangled Banner." Oh but didn't she hate it—but she had to do it or go into the Smoke house. I tell you what Jennie—it was fun for us boys. She pretended for a while that she didn't know it but the Genl said that he knew that she did and must sing it and so she did. (Chamberlain 4 October 1863)

During the occupation of New Orleans, the women proved particularly recalcitrant, their stubbornness exhibited in the Battle of the Handkerchiefs. In 1862, as a large contingent of paroled rebels were dispatched from the city during the occupation, a "group of children, wives, and maids gathered on the levee to wave farewell and to bid them Godspeed." The women's arrogance antagonized the Federal officers until finally at the point of bayonets the women were driven from the rooftops. The soldiers handily defeated "the enemy" and prided themselves on confiscating "300 handkerchiefs, 600 parasols and umbrellas and flags" (Battle of the Handkerchiefs).

Throughout history, flags have served as the tangible, often emotion-wrought symbols of a country's land and its people. Flags during the Civil War were no exception. During the war years, women made, presented, raised, defended, hid from the enemy, wore, and even flaunted flags as expressions of their devotion to their country. Some of their proudest moments were devoted to putting their talents and needles to work creating flags and presenting them to favorite companies. Knowing their handiwork would serve as a rallying point on the battlefield imbued their creators with a special pride.

Even small flags became loyalty badges. In defiance of the Federal occupation troops, anti-Union women in Baltimore strolled about town wearing Confederate flags on their bosoms. Fannie Beers, while visiting her mother in the North, became suspect for her Confederate sympathies. Her loyalties came up for question when it was whispered about town that she was in possession of a Confederate flag given her by her "Rebel" soldier husband. Although the flag was only a small cloth emblem, it was highly prized by Mrs. Beers as a very precious gift. As a safeguard against search and seizure, Mrs. Beers carefully employed library glue and pasted it over her heart for safekeeping (Spring 1861).

Federal orders that "All devices, signs, and flags of the Confederacy shall be suppressed" was a red flag to many women such as Sarah Morgan, who recorded in her diary her intention to devote all of her

> red, white, and blue silk to the manufacture of Confederate flags. . . . Henceforth, I wear one pinned to my bosom—not a duster, but a little flag; the man who says take it off will have to pull it off for himself; the man who dares attempt it—well! a pistol in my pocket fills up the gap. I am capable, too. (Dawson 1960, 24)

There seemed to be no bounds to the hatred many Southerners felt for Yankees. They frankly wished them dead. Following a battle, Southerners frequently exhumed and reinterred decaying Yankee corpses hastily buried too close to their homes, or as an alternative realigned family cemetery fences in order to further distance themselves from the despicable bodies. As the Yankees passed in front of her Nashville home, Rachel Craighead commented in her diary: "I suppose . . . many of them [are] going to their graves but I am wicked enough to say I don't care—wish every one of them may be bagged" (Spring 1862). On a visit to a nearby graveyard, Mrs. Craighead noted: ". . . there were a number of Yankees buried in our graveyard. I think it outrageous to fill up our Cemetery with such trash" (Spring 1862).

Virginia C. Tarrh was so furious that a Yankee soldier had been buried in the family's plot that "when I found it out, I had the fence moved, thereby putting him outside" (T. Taylor 1903, 194).

Even at the war's end, Emma LeConte represented the vast numbers of Southern women who were completely unwilling to capitulate.

> *We* give up to the Yankees! How *can* it be? How can they talk about it? Why does not the President call out the women if there are [not] enough men? We would go and *fight*, too—we would better all die together. Let us suffer still more, give up yet more—anything, anything that will help the cause, anything that will give us freedom and not force us to live with such people—to be ruled by such horrible and contemptible creatures—to submit to them when we hate them so bitterly. (90)

Patriotic fervor (or perhaps exasperation over military strategy) prompted scores of women to deplore their gender and wish themselves men capable of marching into battle or directing mass movements of troops. Within days following Fort Sumter, the South's famous diarist Mary Chesnut was already at work reproaching what seemed to her lackluster performances on the part of certain Confederate officials.

> Oh if I could put some of my reckless spirit into these discreet, cautious, lazy men. (Chesnut 1984, 63)

Later, speaking of her husband, she wrote:

> *Now*, when if ever man was stirred to the highest for his country & for his own future—he seems as utterly absorbed by Negro squabble, hay stealing, cotton saving. . . . If I had been a man in this great revolution—I should have either been killed at once or made a name & done some good for my country.

Lord Nelson's motto would be mine—Victory or Westminster Abbey. (Chesnut 1984, 179–80).

Although Confederate patriot Sarah Morgan regretted the bitterness engendered by the war, she at the same time deplored the role of women as bystanders.

> This is a dreadful war, to make even the hearts of women so bitter! I hardly know myself these last few weeks. I, who have such a horror of bloodshed, consider even killing in self-defense murder, who cannot wish them the slightest evil, whose only prayer is to have them sent back in peace to their own country,—I talk of killing them! For what else do I wear a pistol and carving-knife? I am afraid I *will* try them on the first one who says an insolent word to me. Yes, and repent for it ever after in sack-cloth and ashes. *O!* if I was only a man! Then I could don the breeches, and slay them with a will! If some few Southern women were in the ranks, they could set the men an example they would not blush to follow. Pshaw! there are *no* women here! We are *all* men! (Dawson 1960, 24–25)

Sarah Morgan vehemently denounced the surrender of New Orleans, and once again wished herself an active participant in the war.

> O that from the Atlantic to the Rio Grande their vile footsteps should have been allowed to press our soil! Give up to them? Rather than submit, I would that, all gathered together, we should light our own funeral pyre, and old men, brave soldiers, fair women and tender children should all perish hand in hand in the bright flames we would send up to Heaven as a memorial to our toil, sorrow and suffering. If I was a man! O if I was only a man. (Dawson 1960, xxi)

Caroline Kean (Hill) Davis, of King William County, Virginia, expressed a similar longing to play a more dynamic role in the war effort.

> I have the greatest desire to be active and useful now. I sometimes wish I was a man that I might take my place among the

gallant defenders of our rights instead of being contented to work in the sphere in which Providence has placed me. . . . (13 February 1865)

Bewailing the subordinate role of women, Julia LeGrand imparted observations in her journal that might well endear her to twentieth-century feminists.

> In the meantime we are leading the lives which women have lead since Troy fell; wearing away time with memories, regrets and fears; alternating fits of suppression, with flights, imaginary, to the red fields where great principles are contended for, lost and won; while men, more privileged, are abroad and astir, making name and fortune and helping to make a nation. (52)

A paragraph later she continued:

> I can't tell you what a life of suppression we lead. I feel it more because I know and feel all that is going on outside. I am like a pent-up volcano. I wish I had a field for my energies. I hate common life, a life of visiting, dressing and tattling, which seems to devolve on women, and now that there is better work to do, real tragedy, real romance and history weaving every day, I suffer, suffer, leading the life I do. (52–53)

A number of adventurous women not only wished they were men, but actually donned men's clothes and joined their country's troops as soldiers. Sarah Emma Edmonds, for example, dressed as a man, and apparently served as an orderly, a mailboy, and as a male nurse before she contracted malaria and her identity was suspected. In fact, Sarah appears to be one of over 400 women who posed as men and actually served in the ranks during the war. Even greater numbers retained their female identities, yet assumed men's roles on the battlefield as standard-bearers or even sharpshooters. Madame John Turchin led her husband's regiment into battle when her husband became seriously ill and was unable to leave his sick bed. Kady Brownell, of Rhode Island, fought with her husband's regiment, earning a handsome reputation for herself as a sharpshooter and swordsman.

Commitment to their cause spurred scores of women to undertake dangerous wartime espionage activities. The fashions of the day—hoops, reticules, parasols, corsets, and elaborate hair styles—provided ideal hiding places for smuggling military secrets and coded messages through enemy lines. On several occasions, crucial information provided by women helped determine the outcome of a battle. Mrs. Rose O'Neal Greenhow, one of the most famous of the Confederate spies, sent messages to General Beauregard that helped the Confederacy to their victory at the Battle of Bull Run. Despite being placed under house arrest when her espionage activities were discovered, "Rebel Rose" covertly continued to send important military information out of Washington to top officials in Richmond. Eventually, her work as a spy lead to her incarceration in Old Capital Prison and to banishment to Confederate territory.

Another famous Southern spy, Belle Boyd, following her graduation from Mount Washington Female College and her debut in Washington, conclusively settled a ruckus between her mother and a Union soldier attempting to invade their Martinsburg home by grabbing a pistol and killing the intruder. Although she was immediately charged with murder, a military hearing vindicated Belle as having acted rationally in defense of her mother and her home.

Volunteer work nursing wounded soldiers proved much too tame for Belle, and soon the enterprising young lady began devoting her talents to espionage activity on behalf of the Confederacy. Employing the techniques of a femme fatale, Belle openly flirted with Union officers as she picked their pockets—and their brains. On one occasion she cleverly eavesdropped through a crack in a hotel floor on a secret council of war meeting, and hurriedly conveyed the information to grateful Confederate officers. Stonewall Jackson himself wrote Belle in appreciation of her aid.

> I thank you, for myself and for the army, for the immense service you have rendered your country to-day.
>
> > Hastily, I am your friend
> > T. J. Jackson, C.S.A.

Belle became famous throughout the country for her midnight horseback rides through enemy lines and her fearless spying activity in the midst of enemy shelling. She was twice imprisoned and twice banished to the Confederacy (Boyd).

While a student at Oxford Female College in Ohio, Virginia Moon, later known as "Miss Ginger," became increasingly displeased with the pro-Union sympathies of the college authorities. In a fit of pique, she drew out her pearl-handled revolver, and one by one shot out the stars of the United States flag raised above the college buildings. She was immediately dismissed and sent home to Memphis where she devoted her time to nursing activities and passing along to Confederate military leaders information inveigled from Union soldiers in the then Federally-occupied city. In the spring of 1863, while ostensibly visiting her sister and brother-in-law in Ohio, Virginia was arrested by the Federals on suspicion of attempting to convey to waiting Rebel officers an important dispatch involving the plans of a secret revolutionary faction for a potential Confederate-Northwestern alliance. Also charged with carrying morphine and quinine for Confederate hospitals in her hoopskirt, Virginia was accused of being "an active and dangerous rebel in the employ of the Confederate government. Has contraband goods and rebel mail and is the bearer of dispatches" (O. Smith 1955, 103).

Highly indignant over the prospects of being searched by a man, Virginia quickly pulled out a revolver and warned her captor "If you make a move to touch me, I will kill you, so help me God!" Virginia's audacity and her threats to report him to her friend, General Burnside, somewhat cowed Captain Harrison Rose who left her momentarily to arrange for her removal to the Provost Marshal's office, whereupon Virginia snatched the secret dispatch from her bosom and hurriedly swallowed the incriminating evidence.

Although she was paroled to the South, she continued her espionage activities, but was once again arrested while traveling in Virginia, was imprisoned at Fortress Monroe, and was soon returned to the Confederacy (O. Smith 1955; Kinchen 1972).

Elizabeth Van Lew conducted her espionage work for the U.S. Secret Service from an ideal vantage point—her home in Richmond, the capital of the Confederacy. Dubbed "Crazy Betsy," Elizabeth traded on her nickname as a cover for her intrepid "underground" operations. Although her refusal to make shirts for the South Carolina soldiers and her repeated visits to Federal inmates in Richmond's infamous Libby Prison may have appeared peculiar and somewhat unpatriotic to her neighbors, suspicions as to her possible espionage activity were usually dismissed as aberrations of an unbalanced old spinster. As "Crazy Bet," Elizabeth gathered information from prisoners and hospital patients about the location, strength, and movements of Confederate troops which she quickly passed along to Union officials. Additional top secret information was supplied by a young black woman whom Elizabeth had freed and educated and who, through Elizabeth's scheming, was strategically placed as a spy in Jefferson Davis's home. Military secrets awaiting delivery were frequently written in cipher or in invisible ink and hidden about the mantelpiece in the Van Lew library. Other messages were rolled into little balls later to be fitted together at Union army headquarters. The Van Lew home also became a sanctuary for escapees who were hidden behind spring doors in secret rooms of the once-beautiful mansion. When at last some of her actions came under suspicion, she was sent threatening notes sinisterly marked with a skull and crossbones.

> Old Maid
> Is your house insured?
> Yours truly
> White Caps

Eventually she was ordered not to take food to the Union men in the hospitals and to discontinue supplying meals to prisoners;

however, Elizabeth was never caught in the act of spying and thus continued her "craziness." It was said that much of the information gleaned about Richmond during the war was gathered thanks to the efforts of Miss Van Lew. Following the war, General Grant showed his appreciation by rewarding her with a job as Postmistress of Richmond during his two terms as president (Van Lew).

In her diary, Belle Edmondson candidly admitted transporting contraband between Federally occupied Memphis and her home in Shelby County, Tennessee.

> At one o'clock Mrs. Facklen, Mrs. Kirk and I began to fix my articles for smuggling, we made a balmoral of the Grey cloth for uniform. . . . All my letters, brass buttons, money & in my bosom. . . . (16 March 1864)

Patriotism and survival clashed head on in many Federally occupied areas where local citizens were invited/required to take the Oath of Allegiance to the U.S. Government. The pledge was rigidly enforced in some areas; citizens who refused to comply were banished to the Confederacy—or what was left of it. In other areas the Oath was somewhat haphazardly administered. Failure to take the Oath was often used as grounds for exiling particularly outspoken, hostile Southern patriots. Usually, it was a basic requirement for obtaining food or supplies from the Federal troops, securing a job, or retaining possession of one's home. Thousands of Southerners resigned themselves to taking the Oath as their only means of survival. Families with fathers, brothers, and sons fighting for the Confederacy found the pledge humiliating and degrading—one more forced subjugation to the enemy. In addition to the humiliation, submitting to the Oath further involved a loss of reputation and traitorous feelings of having abandoned their loved ones on the battlefield. To renounce the loyalties and traditions of a lifetime and swear allegiance to the government diametrically opposed to the government of their convictions and interests, to instantaneously forgive and forget their terrible sufferings and losses was incomprehensible to most loyal Southerners.

Many Southerners preferred exile to taking the detested Oath of Allegiance. For others, although their consciences damned them as hypocrites and liars, reality dictated submission. Some compromised their scruples and submitted to the Oath, secretly convinced that an oath agreed to forcibly was in no way binding. Some, like Sarah Morgan, as she attempted to enter Federally occupied New Orleans with her sister and mother to live under the protection of her eldest brother, prayed for Confederate soldiers on the battlefield while the unsuspecting Federal officers attempted to administer the Oath.

Then came a bundle of papers on board carried by another, who standing in front of us, cried in a startling way, "Sarah Morgan!"—"Here" (very quietly).—"Stand up!"—"I cannot" (firmly).—"Why not?"—"Unable" (decisively). After this brief dialogue, he went on with the others until all were standing except myself, when he delivered to each a strip of paper that informed the people that Miss, or Mrs. So-and-So had taken and subscribed the oath as Citizen of the United States. I thought that was all, and rejoiced at our escape. But after another pause he uncovered his head and told us to hold up our right hands. Half-crying, I covered my face with mine and prayed breathlessly for the boys and the Confederacy, so that I heard not a word he was saying until the question, "So help you God?" struck my ear. I shuddered and prayed harder. There came an awful pause in which not a lip was moved. Each felt as though in a nightmare, until, throwing down his blank book, the officer pronounced it "All right!" Strange to say, I experienced no change. I prayed as hard as ever for the boys and our country, and felt no nasty or disagreeable feeling which would have announced the process of turning Yankee.

Then it was that mother commenced. He turned to the mouth of the diminutive cave, and asked if she was ready to take the oath. "I suppose I *have* to, since I belong to you," she replied. "No, madam, you are not obliged; we force no one. Can you state your objections?" "Yes, I have three sons fighting against you, and you have robbed me, beggared me!" she exclaimed, launching into a speech in which Heaven knows *what* she did not say; there was little she left out, from her despoiled house to her sore hand, both of which she attributed to the at first amiable man, who was rapidly losing all

44

patience. Faint with hunger, dizzy with sleeplessness, she had wrought on her own feelings until her nerves were beyond control. She was determined to carry it out, and crying and sobbing went through with it.

I neither spoke nor moved. . . . The officer walked off angrily and sent for a guard to have mother taken before General Bowens. Once through her speech, mother yielded to the entreaties of the ladies and professed herself ready to take the oath, since she was obliged to. "Madam, I did not invite you to come," said the polite officer, who refused to administer the oath; and putting several soldiers on board, ordered them to keep all on board until one could report to General Bowens. Mother retired to the cabin, while we still kept our seats above. (Dawson 1960, 382-84)

Thanks to the intercession of Sarah's brother, the Morgans were permitted to enter New Orleans, but only after Sarah's mother, with Sarah's brother's help, had feebly "managed to hold up her right hand and say 'Yes' to the oath" (Dawson 1960, 387).

A few weeks later, Sarah was still experiencing qualms of conscience about the Oath.

How about that oath of allegiance? is what I frequently ask myself, and always an uneasy qualm of conscience troubles me. Guilty or not guilty of perjury? According to the law of God in the abstract, and of nations, Yes; according to my conscience, Jeff Davis, and the peculiar position I was placed in, No. Which is it? Had I had any idea that such a pledge would be exacted, would I have been willing to come? Never! The thought would have horrified me. The reality was never placed before me until we reached Bonfouca. There I was terrified at the prospect; but seeing how impossible it would be to go back, I placed all my hopes in some miracle that was to intervene to prevent such a crime, and confidently believed my ill health or something else would save me, while all the rest of the party declared they would think it nothing, and take forty oaths a day, if necessary. A forced oath, all men agree, is not binding. The Yankees lay particular stress on this being voluntary, and insist that no one is solicited to take it except of their own free will. Yet look at the scene that followed, when mother showed herself unwilling! Think of being ordered to the Custom-House as a prisoner for saying she supposed she would

have to! *That's* liberty! that is free will! It is entirely optional;
you have only to take it quietly or go to jail. That is freedom
enough, certainly! There was not even that choice left to me.
I told the officer who took down my name that I was unwilling to take the oath, and asked if there was no escaping it.
"None whatever" was his reply. "You have it to do, and there
is no getting out of it." His rude tone frightened me into half-
crying; but for all that, as he said, I had it to do. If perjury
it is, which will God punish: me, who was unwilling to com-
mit the crime, or the man who forced me to it? (Dawson 1960,
392–93)

The journal of Catherine Devereux Edmondston also testified to
the South's revulsion of the Loyalty Oath.

They say to us, "This Oath or see yourselves plundered by
Yankees and negroes alike; This Oath or turned out of your
house and loved home." Swear anything—both possible and
impossible—say light is darkness—heat is cold—Andy Johnson
is a gentleman—Seward is truthful—Yankees are honest—what
you will! I assent to it all, and hate you while I do it.
(Edmondston n.d., 108)

The Oath of Allegiance raised grave questions for Elizabeth Curtis
Wallace and her husband whose Norfolk County, Virginia, plantation had been a "no-man's land" seesawing back and forth between visitations by Confederate as well as Union forces.

What are we to do? Shall we take the oath and remain at home,
with some certainty of protection, or shall we go South? These
are the questions that agitate us now. The Yankee-negro-
soldiers did such havoc among the people on their way that
many have gone to town and taken the oath to keep from starvation. (80)

The knowledge that they would be stripped of all of their property
if they did not take the Oath, coupled with the fear that they might
be considered traitors by the Confederacy if they did submit, further complicated the Wallaces' dilemma.

46

The whole day has been engrossed with the subject of the
Oath. Poor George [her husband] cannot speak of it without
tears. Joe is distressed and Mr. Reed also and seem to feel that
it may be their duty to sacrifice themselves for their families,
not their property; that is nearly all gone already. We are all
poor, and the question now is shall we accept poverty and freedom in the Confederacy or shall we accept slavery and the
remains of our fortunes in the United States. It would be cruel
in our Confederate Government to frown upon the many who
have taken the oath in tears and bitterness. (80)

At the end of the war, Louisa McCord's mother, despondent over
the terrible turn of events, decided to sell her home in Columbia;
however, that transaction required taking the despised Oath of
Allegiance, a step her mother could not bring herself to take.

Finally Dr. Reynolds [a long time family friend] persuaded her
to do it, undertaking to do it himself at the same time. One
of the saddest sights I ever saw was that couple walking arm
in arm to the Provost Marshall's office, my mother in her
shabby black dress and her rusty crape veil. It was like a pitiful, pitiful funeral. (Smythe, 79)

Refusal to take the Oath of Allegiance often became "a private
war" as in the case of Lizzie Hardin, her sister, and her mother who
were arrested in Harrodsburg, Kentucky, ostensibly on the rather
innocuous charge of having waved their handkerchiefs at their hero,
Brigadier General John Hunt Morgan, when he visited Harrodsburg
in 1862, but more probably for being fanatical Southern sympathizers. Although their Unionist friends pleaded with them to take
the Oath and thus obviate almost certain banishment, they steadfastly refused. Even the promise of release from jail failed to sway
the trio. Given a copy of the Oath, they were instructed to examine it and present their answers the following morning.

The oath was as strong as the English language could make
it: to uphold the government of the United States in act and
in words, almost in our very thoughts; to pledge eternal enmity
to the rebellion and all engaged in it; to give them no assistance

47

nor hold any communication with them directly or indirectly. Finally we swore that we took this oath freely and voluntarily and below, where the name was signed was printed, "The penalty for the violation of this oath is death."

And yet this oath was taken by many who argued that it was compulsory and therefore not binding either legally or morally. Some took it from the fear of leaving their wives and children without protection in a land where we seemed to breathe oppression with the air. Others took it only because they did not choose to be imprisoned and many after taking it went without hesitation into the Southern Army. I think it would have been better had no Southerner ever taken the oath but at the same time I saw some cases— *a very few*—where I could not but excuse it. (Hardin 1963, 124)

The next morning at the courthouse:

We were at length called to the table where standing in a row we were asked if we had read the oath.
"Yes, we have."
Mr. Riley then asked me what my answer was.
"I don't feel like taking it," I said, looking, Ma said, as though some nauseous mixture had been offered me, the very sight of which made me sick.
"And you?" to Jimmie.
"I will not take it."
"Will you take it?" to Ma.
"Never." (124–25)

Finally, when neither persuasion nor intimidation proved effective, the Hardins were exiled to Georgia and spent the remainder of the war at Eatonton. The Hardins typified hosts of Southern sympathizers living in Federally occupied territory who were willing to accept imprisonment and/or banishment rather than submit to the Oath of Allegiance. Julia LeGrand no doubt spoke for thousands of her compatriots in writing, "Let me lose what I may by refusing" (63).

Mildred Elizabeth Powell, a defiant young Missouri woman with decidedly Southern sympathies, was so outspoken in her advocacy of the Southern cause that she was arrested September 29, 1862, and imprisoned at Palmyra, ostensibly

> as a punishment for the many offenses that I had committed against the government in discouraging enlistment, persuading my friends to fight against the administration and a great many other things. . . . (151)

Given the opportunity to take the Oath of Allegiance and be paroled, Mildred not only refused, but retorted that she "had rather die in prison than to perjure myself before God and man" (167).

Her curt refusal to accept an introduction to the Provost Marshal and a sarcastic letter to Federal officers, which even she deemed as possibly "injudicious-imprudent," failed to endear her to her Union "persecutors." Finally, after months of imprisonment and following frequent heated interchanges, her captors lost patience with the spirited young lady and banished her to the isolation of the Nevada Territory.

Further amplification of Mildred Powell's story is found in a letter written by George Smith Avery from his headquarters in Palmyra, Missouri, and found in the Chicago Historical Society Collection. The letter, addressed to Avery's future wife, Lizzie Little, refers to the arrogant behavior and imprisonment of a Miss Crath, apparently Miss Creath, who shared the friendship and the rabid Secessionist views of Mildred Elizabeth Powell. Miss Powell appears to have been arrested while visiting at the home of Elder Jacob Creath, Margaret Creath's father. According to George Avery's letter:

> The greatest enemy that we have to contend with here at present is secesh in ladies apparel. Not longer ago than yesterday a person by the name of Miss Crath [Creath] came to Lt. Col. Gault's Office under a fictitious name & obtained a pass of him to visit the prisoners confined in the Military Prison. Soon after he issued the pass he learned that she was not the person that she represented herself to be—whereupon he ordered the document taken from her, which was done. The ladie's [sic] dignity thus being insulted—she returned to his office, & endeavored to obtain redress by forcibly applying her

fist to the Col's face. She dealt several severe blows. The Col.
being too modest to assent. He finally remanded her to the
jail there to await his pleasure. He released her on conditions
that she would make an apology before the Regiment for the
offense. She has not yet fulfilled the conditions, & it is my
impression that she will not. She is the daughter of Secesh Rev.
Crath [Creath]. The ladies are a nuisance about the prison.
(23 February 1862)

Staunch Confederates categorically denounced all friends and
neighbors who took the Oath as cowards and traitors. Amelia
Bourne complained in her diary:

> Henry Jones come home this evening—he is just from Camp
> Douglas—has taken the "Oath." Oh! how terrible to think of.
> So *many* of those, who *pretend* to be of Kentucky's brave boys
> to *disgrace* themselves. Yes they have lost all *self* respect: of
> course they don't expect their relations or friends to respect
> them. I would much rather see my brother brought home a
> corpse than return as *he has*. *Disgraced*. (22 January 1864)

A preference for death for her brother rather than submission
was far more than an impulsive outburst of patriotism for Kate
Carney, of Murfreesboro, Tennessee. When her brother Will finally
agreed to the Oath of Allegiance, Kate did her best to avoid him
when he visited their home and repeatedly lamented to her diary:

> Why didn't he die, before returning to bring eternal disgrace
> on the family. He has ever been a draw back. I could have
> stood his dying much better. . . . I had rather our throats were
> all cut, or turned beggars on the world than that Bro. John
> should disgrace himself by taking that dirty oath. How little
> brother Will thinks of his family. It will ever be a stain on his
> poor little children. (380)

Just as waving handkerchiefs at the enemy in occupied territory
proved a dangerous activity, so was the seemingly traitorous act of
praying for the *wrong* president or of omitting the Prayer for the
President, which was an integral part of Episcopalian church liturgy.
Newspaper accounts told of the famous episode at St. Paul's church

during the occupation of New Orleans where on a September Sunday in 1862 the service was interrupted by a Union officer who lustily informed the congregation that

> As this church is solely devoted to the service of the Lord Jehovah and as Abraham Lincoln is not prayed for I by command of Major General B. F. Butler order this imperious nest of secession heretics to be dispersed and these doors to be closed. (Battle of St. Paul's)

It is difficult, of course, to determine the precise exchange of words, but the courageous parishioners (primarily women and old men) were said to have retorted fearlessly, "We'll go when we feel like it, not before." (It is doubtful whether the Federal officials were as infuriated by the congregation's refusal to *start* praying for the health of President Lincoln as they were incensed by the congregation's refusal to *stop* praying for the health of Jefferson Davis.)

The traditional Episcopalian Prayer for the President continued to be the source of considerable conflict throughout the Federally occupied territories. Many Southerners stubbornly persisted in requesting divine aid and an ultimate victory for President Davis and the Confederacy. Some churches attempted to omit the prayer entirely. Judith McGuire described a Richmond church service following the Federal takeover of the city the preceding week:

> Another gloomy Sabbath-day and harrowing night. We went to St. Paul's in the morning. . . . I could not listen; I felt so strangely, as if in a vivid, horrible dream. Neither President was prayed for; in compliance with some arrangement with the Federal authorities, the prayer was used as for all in authority! How fervently did we all pray for our own President! Thank God, our silent prayers are free from Federal authority. (351)

Worshipers in other areas of the occupied South were pressured into a token mumbling of at least some kind of vague, superficial (and certainly hypocritical) entreaties for Lincoln and the Union. Emilie McKinley expressed great sympathy for a Vicksburg church

51

whose minister was denied permission to omit the prayer for President Lincoln and his officers during the church service on Christmas Day, 1863. (Vicksburg was occupied by this time and Union officials, of course, insisted that the prayer be offered for Lincoln and not Jefferson Davis.) So angered were several of the worshipers that as the congregation bowed in prayer, "five ladies present could not with their own consent offer prayers for their welfare, so rose and left the church" (Christmas 1863).

Forty-eight hours later, the ladies, refusing to stoop to an apology, were banished from Vicksburg for showing disrespect to the President. Notices of their exile were posted on the street corners (Christmas 1863).

Southern diaries and reminiscences are replete with tales of confrontations over the Prayer for the President. Louisa McCord Smythe described the problems encountered by the minister of her church in Columbia, South Carolina.

> About this time, maybe a little sooner, Mr. Shand was in great trouble about the church. He was ordered to read the prayer for the President of the United States. It may sound very childish to you who have never known the bitterness of a conquered people, but we simply would not consent to such a thing, and the church was closed. Then Mr. Shand was notified that should the church remain closed another Sunday it would be given to the negroes. The dear old man went the rounds of his flock explaining to them his position, telling them that he would read the prayer the next Sunday, to save the church and begging them to stand by him. Of course we all went. We couldn't do otherwise. (77)

As they entered the church, Mrs. Smythe, her family and friends, made their way through the smirking, arrogant Union soldiers who, she reported, had come to lord it over the congregation.

> The service went on all right. The congregation was quite large, but of course very few men. In those days everybody knelt down in the bottom of the pews with their backs to the minister. As the prayers began everybody took this position—

52

the officers generally, as I remember did not, but stood—we were all kneeling until Mr. Shand began the prayer for the President and then by a common impulse, for there had been no consultation as far as I now know, there was a great rustle over the church, and every individual stood upright. As soon as that prayer was finished down went the congregation again with the greatest devotion. I wish you could have seen those officers—What could they do? Their eyes flashed fire and they evidently breathed out wrath—swelled with wrath—nearly burst with wrath, but we were all so decorous, so devout, so dignified and the prayer went on so steadily from the pulpit that there was simply nothing to do. The church was saved, and from that time till I left Columbia the congregation always stood through that prayer. The officers generally were conspicuously absent. (77–78)

To be sure, all war is cruel; however, diarists, journalists, politicians, letter writers, and speakers repeatedly referred to the American Civil War as "this cruel war." A new nation, as Lincoln so eloquently put it, was testing whether it could long endure. In less than one hundred years after its founding, America's land, people, political parties, and churches were rent asunder. A patriotic fanaticism divided families and aligned neighbors and friends and sections against each other in undying enmity. It was perhaps not surprising that a country could be so divided as to economics, politics, religion, morality, and lifestyles; the miracle is that it could ever be put back together again.

CHAPTER II

Slaves, Soldiers, Free People

> If the negro should be set free by this war, which I believe he will be, whether we gain or not, it will be the Lord's doing. The time has come when his mission has ended as a slave, and while he has been benefited by slavery the white race has suffered from its influence.
>
> —*Kate Cumming* 6 October 1863

To attempt to discuss all of the ramifications of slavery would be an exercise in futility. To ignore the question of slavery, however, would be to overlook one of the most important concerns of the Civil War period. The repeated references to blacks, the intimate impartings of private thinking that permeate the diaries and letters of women during the Civil War period, bear testimony to the racism prevalent in both the North and the South. At the same time, these personal outpourings provide remarkable insights into some of the most hotly contested issues of the times: attitudes toward slavery, toward the possible deportation of slaves, toward the employment/impressment of blacks in the armies, toward emancipation, and toward the efforts of Northern women to assist and educate the freedman.

Slavery, for many Southerners, had long been a way of life, (although in 1861, only a minority owned slaves*) and slave owners were accustomed to their positions of authority and privilege.

*The South's four million slaves (about one third of the South's 12,000,000 people) were owned by 384,000 whites with only about 1,800 owning 100 or more slaves (Boatner, 764).

Many poor white *non*-slave holders cherished their enviable position of being at least one step removed from slavery, and yearned for the day when they too would come into their own, purchase a few slaves, and partake of a life of leisure. Laws prohibiting teaching slaves to read and write, preventing the congregation of slaves, and forbidding their possession of firearms confined blacks to servitude.

Owners who might now and then have experienced a twinge of conscience over the holding of men and women in bondage were somewhat inhibited by law, economics, and tradition from extricating themselves from the "Peculiar Institution." There were legal intricacies governing manumission, and even the most compassionate owners, knowing their "hands" had no skills with which to support themselves, were deterred from setting their slaves free. Disposing of their slaves by selling them off was frowned upon as the process frequently involved the separation of family members and the possibility of their purchase by cruel, insensitive owners. Thus, planters who had inherited slaves were, to a certain extent, bound to "the system."

Martha Jane Crossley, of Perote, Alabama, expressed concern over her Negroes.

> I am troubled to know what do with my negroes for another year. I do not wish to hire them out of the family, for fear they may form bad habits and be badly treated, and it seems that it will not be to the interest of any of my brothers and sisters to take them. I shall let them go among my people for nothing however and earn my own support some way before they shall be hired where they are not cared for. (615)

Reminiscing about her childhood years in Vicksburg, Annie Laurie Broidrick pointed out:

> My father never bought negroes or "flesh" as it has been called, unless requested to do so by his own servants who sometimes fell in love with, and wished to marry other planters' slaves. Then "marster" was begged to buy the desired one so that they should not be separated. Almost all our slaves were inherited property, having been in the family for years. (4)

In response to the attacks by Northern abolitionists, Southerners countered with the rationalization that slavery was "a positive good." Convinced that blacks were childish, uneducable, improvident, and unable to look after themselves, slave owners believed themselves magnanimous in providing food, clothing, and shelter for otherwise destitute heathens. Furthermore, were they not saving these poor wretches from eternal damnation by providing religious instruction for them?

Mary Sharpe Jones, widow of the Rev. Dr. Charles Colcock Jones, famous for his work as a missionary evangelist among the Negroes of the South, apparently subscribed to the popular "paternalistic" attitude toward slavery, although at the same time urging radical reforms.

> The workings of Providence in reference to the African race are truly wonderful. The Scourge falls with peculiar weights upon them. With their emancipation must come their extermination. All history from their existence proves them incapable of self government. They perish when brought in conflict with the intellectual superiority of the Caucassian race. Northern Philanthropy & cant may rave as much as they please, but facts prove that (only) in a state of Slavery such as exists in the Southern States, have the negro race increased & thriven most. We would point to the History of the Brittish West India Islands and to New England, with her starved & perished Blacks, not that we have done our duty to them here. Far from it.
>
> I feel if ever we gain our Independence, there will be radical reforms in the system of slavery as it now exists. When once delivered from the interference of Northern abolitionism, we shall be free to make & enforce such rules & reformations as are just & right. In all my life I never heard such expression of hatred & contempt as the Yankees heap upon our poor servants. One of them told me he "did not know what God Almighty made negroes for; all he wished was the power to blow their brains out." (M. S. Jones 1959, 76–77)

In her recollections of 1860 and 1861, Cornelia McDonald, of Virginia, despite her Southern sympathies, deplored the South's attempts to justify slavery. She was adamantly opposed to Southerners who urged the revival of the African slave trade, and to those who advocated secession with an idea of legitimizing the infamous trade once again.

I never in my heart thought slavery was right, and having in my childhood seen some of the worst instances of its abuse, and in my youth, when surrounded by them and daily witnessing what I considered great injustice to them, I could not think how the men I most honored and admired, my husband among the rest, could constantly justify it, and not only that, but say that it was a blessing to the slave, his master, and the country; and, (even now I say it with a feeling of shame), that the renewal of the slave trade would be a blessing and benefit to all, if only the consent of the world could be obtained to its being made lawful.

They agreed that it was owing to the restrictions put upon the trade that the slaves suffered in the passage; and but for the laws against the traffic, and if it was legitimate they would be far happier if brought away from their own country even as slaves, than they could be if they remained in freedom and barbarism. They insisted also that it was to the interest of the Cotton States and the dignity of the South to revive it. Such men as Mr. James M. Mason, Mr. Ran. Tucker, and many others did not hesitate to avow their intention in case the South did secede and achieve her independence to use their best endeavors to establish the iniquitous practice again. Many there were, however, who did not go so far and though they were no advocates of slavery or the slave trade, were unwilling to be dictated to by a hostile section, and were in favor of secession for the sake of independence. (11–12)

As the war lengthened from months into years, the blockade and tremendously inflated currency continued to eat away at Southern finances. Some Southerners, had they not done so before, gradually began to question the economics—even the morality—of the whole slave system. Although she and her husband owned slaves, Ella Gertrude Clanton Thomas at one time confided to her diary:

> . . . to you my new journal, my new friend, I will confess that what troubles me more than any thing else is that I am not certain that *Slavery* is *right*. The doctrine of self government I suppose of course to be right. . . . But as to the doctrine of slavery altho I have read very few abolition books (Uncle Tom's Cabin making most impression) nor have I read many pro slavery books, yet the idea has gradually become more and more fixed in my mind that the institution of slavery is not right. . . .

58

Owning a large number of slaves as we do I might be asked why
do I not free them? This if I could, I would not do, but if Mr.
Thomas [her husband] would sell them to a man who would
look after their temporal and *spiritual* interest I would gladly
do so. Those house servants we have, if Mr. Thomas would
agree to it, I would pay regular wages but this is a subject upon
which I do not like to think and taking my stand upon the
moral view of the subject, I can but think that to hold men
and women in *perpetual* bondage is wrong. (23 September 1864)

Another Civil War diarist, Kate Stone, whose family owned some
one hundred and fifty slaves, wrote in retrospect:

. . . my first recollection is of pity for the Negroes and desire
to help them. Even under the best owners, it was a hard, hard
life: to toil six days out of seven, week after week, month after
month, year after year, as long as life lasted; to be absolutely
under the control of someone until the last breath was drawn;
to win but the bare necessities of life, no hope of more, no matter how hard the work, how long the toil; and to know that
nothing could change your lot. Obedience, revolt, submission,
prayers—all were in vain. Waking sometimes in the night as
I grew older and thinking it all over, I would grow sick with
the misery of it all.
 As far as Mamma could, the Negroes on our place were pro-
tected from cruelty and were well cared for; they were generally
given Saturday evening and had plenty to eat and comfortable
clothes. Still there were abuses impossible to prevent. And constantly there were tales circulated of cruelties on neighboring
plantations, tales that would make one's blood run cold. And
yet we were powerless to help. Always I felt the moral guilt of
it, felt how impossible it must be for an owner of slaves to win
his way into Heaven. Born and raised as we were, what would
be our measure of responsibility?
 Although the war swept from us everything and life since
'65 has been a long struggle for the necessaries of life, I have
never regretted the freeing of the Negroes. The great load of
accountability was lifted, and we could save our souls. . . . (7–8)

Not a few Southerners (as well as Northerners) believed the only
real solution to the race problem lay in Negro deportation. Keziah
Goodwyn Hopkins Brevard, alone and sounding somewhat frustrated

in her attempts to cope with the planting and harvesting responsibilities of a bustling plantation, apparently found her diary a sympathetic listening ear for her vexations during the several months prior to the firing on Fort Sumter. Keziah's frustration with her insolent slaves and with the system itself no doubt reflected her own problems as well as the concerns of many of her contemporaries. Her hatred of the abolitionists, her belief in emancipation accompanied by deportation of blacks, her fear of slave insurrections or poisonings typified views held by great numbers of Southerners.

> How can a Southerner love those whose highest glory would be to know we were exterminated to give place to a people far inferior. I wish every vessel that would go to Africa to bring slaves here could sink before they reached her soil. I would give up every ct. I own on earth if it could stop the slave trade. My reason is this—we have a hard time with them & I feel for those who are to come after us. (20)

Following Lincoln's election, she bemoaned:

> Oh my God! This morning heard that Lincoln was elected—I had prayed that God would thwart his election in some way & I have prayed for my country. Lord we know not what is to be the result of this—but I do pray, if there is to be a crisis, that we all lay down our lives sooner than free our slaves in our midst—no soul on this earth is more willing for justice than I am—but the idea of being mixed up with free blacks is horrid! . . .
>
> I would give my life to save my country. I have never been opposed to giving up slavery if we could send them out of our country . . . if the North had let us alone. The Master & the servant were happy with our advantages—but we had had vile wretches ever making the restless worse than they would have been & from my experience my own negroes are as happy as I am—happier—I never am cross to my servants without cause & they give me impudence, if I find the least fault, this is of the women, the men are not half as impudent as the women are. . . . God be with us is my prayer & let us all be willing to die rather than free our slaves in their present uncivilized state. (27–28)

Keziah also lamented her humane treatment of her slaves and their impudence in return.

> I wish Lincoln & Hamlin could have died before this & saved our country's disolution—The south ought to go out of the U as it is—Northern Abolitionists hate us so they ought to be glad we are not part of them—they groaned to know we could live—poor wretches now pray for your own sins & let us answer for ours. Oh that such wretches as N. Abolitionists could be blotted from the records. I hate their principles. I go as much for patriarchal feelings for my or our blacks as anyone does— but I do not go for mixing the two races—I ever have lamented their being brought to America. God gave them a country to themselves & there they ought to have remained. I should not say this, for if God had designed it—he would have had it so— we must believe his ways are right. Lord help us. . . .
> Gods ways must be right—he has put them here for some wise purpose & I know should leave all in his hands & not murmur as I do. But it is hard for a poor lonely female to take impudence. I have taken gross impudence hundreds of times & let it pass unpunished. This would not hurt me as it does if I was indifferent to them—but I am constantly administer- ing to their comforts & do it literally—let anyone look over my annual accounts & I feel proud to know it. I have never looked on them as beasts of burden—working for my pleasure. I think I am responsible for all I do for them and to them. . . . (30)
> I hope and trust in God as soon as Secession is carried out. We of the south begin to find a way to get all the negroes sent back to Africa & let the generations to come after us live in more peace than we do. I can't see how we are ever to be safe with them in our midst. I wish every soul of them were in Africa contented in their own homes. . . . As long as they are here & number so many more than the whites there is no safety any way. . . . (37)
> We know not what moment we may be hacked to death in the most cruel manner by our slaves. Oh God devise a way for us to get rid of them quietly & let us all be better Christians. (86)

Many Northerners, even many of the most zealous abolitionists who spoke, wrote, and fought for the eradication of slavery, were openly hostile to the acceptance of blacks as voters, co-workers, neighbors, or holders of public office. Southerners certainly had no monopoly on racism.

Both sections were greatly divided in their attitudes toward one of the most controversial concerns of the war—whether or not to enlist blacks in the armed services. Their employment in the Union Army marked one of the first steps down the slow, tortuous road toward greater social acceptance of blacks.

In the North, Lincoln's call for volunteers attracted large numbers of free blacks, and as the fighting continued, the question of arming blacks as soldiers presented innumerable problems for both sections. The sentiments of many Northerners were no doubt epitomized in the diary entry of Maria Lydig Daly, of New York City:

> It was a very interesting and a very touching sight to see the first colored regiment from this city march down the street for the front. They were a fine body of men and had a look of satisfaction in their faces, as though they felt they had gained a right to be more respected. Many old, respectable darkies stood at the street corners, men and women with tears in their eyes as if they saw the redemption of their race afar off but still the beginning of a better state of affairs for them. Though I am very little Negrophilish and would always prefer the commonest white that lives to a Negro, still I could not but feel moved. (278)

The correspondence between Sophia Buchanan and her husband, John, on duty in the South with the Union forces, frequently included diatribes against slavery and all of its attendant evils. The letters from Sophia's husband served to document her conviction that slavery was essentially the cause of the war.

> . . . this accursed sin slavery, which is at the root of all our trouble . . . . the South fighting to maintain slavery forever, & if possible to extend it over the whole land & re-establish . . . one of the barbarities of the dark ages, the abominable slave trade. . . . [Why would] part of our own loved America . . . ever become so perverted, & degraded as to try to ruin so wise &

good a government, as our's has ever been. God grant [that] his righteous retribution, may fall upon the heads of those, who have attempted this, sown the seed of secession, & brought on this most cruel and senseless of wars. (Blackburn 1965, 55)

As for enlisting Negroes for combat service, John Buchanan wrote Sophia that in his judgment, based on his experiences in South Carolina, blacks were too servile to make good soldiers.

> I have seen none of these *Colored Gemmen* as yet who would be capable of fighting & will venture the assertion, such is their servility, that fifty of their Masters would put to flight a Reg. of them. Poor helpless Creatures, raised as a farmer Raises Stock, allowed a Peck of Corn a week for subsistence, a gill of salt, to season this . . . & with an abject servility which is painful, it would be equal folly to employ them on either side. (Blackburn 1963, 81)

A staunch Baptist, John Buchanan was appalled by the conditions of the Negro in the South.

> The slave Mother presses her child to her Bosom with all the seeming love & tenderness of the enlightened Christian mother but it is beyond her power to develop the Mind of her offspring & thus they live and thus they die. Oh what an accursed Institution this is, how full of wickedness & cruelty. If there had not existed another sin on this continent, this is sufficient of itself, to call down the Judgments of a Just God & I think this unholy Rebellion may be traced to this Peculiar, *very Peculiar* Institution. (Blackburn 1963, 82–83)

After further observation of the Negroes, their abilities, and their stamina, John changed his mind and reasoned that blacks would be welcome additions to the Union army.

> . . . I have seen Regs of Colored men & must confess that where the necessity exists, I would as soon they would shoot *Mr. Reb* as to do it myself. It is a joke upon their masters to lose their property & then have *it* turn round and fight them. (Blackburn 1963, 84)

Some Northerners believed that it was the responsibility of blacks just as much as whites to share in the defense of their country. One Northern woman, discouraged by the war news she was reading, asked her husband, a physician with the Union forces:

> Do you see many contrabands? It is reported that they are all driven by their owners south, as they are the cause of this war—although innocently. I do not like to see their black ugly faces—I wish they might all be kept away from our free states.

She concluded her remarks with:

> I think it is time to take the Negroes & let them die & be killed off instead of our best men. They could work if not fight. (Cotton 3 March 1863)

George Farmer, serving with the Union Army, wrote to his family in New York City, indicating that the use of Negro troops was depleting not the black, but rather the Rebel ranks. White soldiers, he pointed out, hovered around the rear of their black troops:

> . . . they hustled their men into some sort of a line ordered them forward and then left them.
> No prisoners was taken by the black troops but every wounded Rebel in front of their line was bayonetted to death. A wounded rebel Officer yielded himself a prisoner to a black Sergeant—The reply was Dont see dat an you fix me off if you had me now I fixes you. He was stabbed to death.
> This is no doubt the feeling of the Nigger troops and when the Rebels discover that Wounded and prisoner or prisoner means certain death they will not be so anxious to fight the niggers. (1864)

Obviously, most Southerners were vigorously opposed to this proposed innovation on numerous economic as well as social grounds. The conscription of slaves, of course, meant a great financial loss to a slaveholder. Relinquishing his human property involved not only the sacrifice of considerable material wealth, but also a serious reduction in farm output resulting from his depleted (or nonexistent) workforce.

For most Southern white supremacists, their ingrained racism made the prospects of living/fighting with blacks as their equals absolutely unthinkable. As yet another deterrent, introducing army troops of free blacks would seriously complicate the practice adhered to by many well-to-do slave owners of sending along a black "servant" to tend to the care and feeding of his "master."

The possibility of reprisal was unquestionably a serious consideration, particularly in areas where blacks constituted over 80 percent of the population. For decades, plantation owners, in a determined effort to ensure subservience and prevent the potential for insurrection, had carefully and systematically searched their slave quarters for weapons, and they were firmly convinced that arming blacks ostensibly for the defense of their country was, instead, arming them for violence and mayhem.

Prodded in many instances by Yankees, contrabands at times became a serious menace to farms located in remote areas. Kate Stone described the chaotic conditions around their plantation, Brokenburn, in northeastern Louisiana.

> This country is in a deplorable state. The outrages of the Yankees and Negroes are enough to frighten one to death. The sword of Damocles in a hundred forms is suspended over us, and there is no escape. The water hems us in. The Negroes on Mrs. Stevens', Mr. Conley's, Mr. Catlin's, and Mr. Evans' places ran off to camp and returned with squads of soldiers and wagons and moved off every portable thing—furniture, provisions, etc., etc. A great many of the Negroes camped at Lake Providence have been armed by the officers, and they are a dreadful menace to the few remaining citizens. The country seems possessed by demons, black and white. (184)

As the threat of a possible insurrection increased daily, Kate was sure the government in Washington

> has done all in its power to incite a general insurrection throughout the South, in the hopes of thus getting rid of the women and children in one grand holocaust. We would be practically helpless should the Negroes rise, since there are so few

65

men left at home. It is only because the Negroes do not want to kill us that we are still alive. The Negroes have behaved well, far better than anyone anticipated. They have not shown themselves revengeful, have been most biddable, and in many cases have been the only mainstay of their owners. (298)

Slave owners in the border states, ever hopeful of a Congressional act compensating them for their "servants," were often reluctant to see blacks become Federal soldiers. Although an ardent Union supporter, Frances Dallam Peter, of Lexington, Kentucky, reflected her racial biases as she noted in her diary:

> ... the negro regiments that have been raised at Port Royal and elsewhere have proved a failure, the negroes refusing to work and deserting on every occasion and of the celebrated Kansas regiment only 148 are left and Gen. Saxton has petitioned to be removed to some other command as he is tired of [the] negro and every thing about him. So say some of the papers, and others make out that every thing is going well and the black soldiers are so patriotic and etc. I doubt it. The first account is by far the most probable. From all I have observed of the negro he is much too averse to work, too timid to make a good soldier, and has got it into his head that liberty means doing nothing. I think it is acting against the Constitution to make soldiers of the blacks, and however much the abolitionists may say to the contrary, they will find in the end that this arming & equiping of negro regiments is a mere waste of time and money. . . . (14–15)

A few weeks later, she expanded on the subject of enlisting blacks.

> ... Adjutant Gen. L. Thomas made a speech to the soldiers at Cairo [Illinois] yesterday, in which he spoke of the matter of receiving colored men into the lines and reprobated in the way in which some of them had been treated, instancing some cases in which they had been returned to Slavery (some of the soldiers when they get hold of a negro have been in the habit of selling them). The camp of rendezvous for blacks which is now at Cairo will soon by order of Gen. Hurlbut be removed to Island No. 10 where they will be employed in tilling deserted farms. I expect when the negroes hear of this they won't feel

so anxious to run off to the soldiers. Sambo doesn't like hard work especially if it has to be done regularly. And I have noticed that since Mr. Lincolns January proclamation, and since they have found out that the soldiers make them work just as hard if not harder than their masters they don't take half as much interest in them and are not near as willing to do things for them, as when the army first came here. (24)

By the spring of 1864, although basically opposed to "making soldiers out of blacks," Frances was resigned to the enrollment of Negroes for military service and advocated Kentucky Governor Bramlette's support.

> We don't know yet what side Gov. Bramlette will take but if he is wise he will support the Government and not attempt to resist the enrolling of negroes. Mr. Lincoln did not make that enrollment law. It was Congress and as Congress decided that all persons from 20 to 45 without regard to color should be enrolled we cannot resist the carrying that law into effect, without beng as much in a state of rebellion as any of the Confederates, and having a Civil War in our midst.
>   Such a course would be fraught with evil to us in every way. We would have our slaves set free, as was the case with the Confederate States, and would have no hopes of compensation. Our Kentucky troops would be sent out of the State; the whole State overrun with armies and devastaed by war. (50)

As the employment of blacks in the Confederate forces gained more proponents later in the war, Ella Gertrude Clanton Thomas (known as Gertrude Thomas) questioned President Davis's proposals.

> President Davis in his message says that we are better off than we were this time last year but when President Davis advocates the training of Negroes to aid us in fighting—promising them as an inducement to do so *their freedom*, and in the same message intimates that rather than yield we would place every Negro in the Army—he so clearly betrays the weakness of our force that I candidly confess I am disheartened. I take a woman's view of the subject but it does seem strangely inconsistent the idea of our offering to a Negro the rich boon—the priceless reward of freedom to aid us in keeping in bondage a large portion of

his brethren when by joining the Yankees he will *instantly* gain the very reward which Mr. Davis offers to him after a certain amount of labor rendered and danger incurred. Mr. Davis to the contrary, the Negro has had a great deal to do with this war. . . . (17 November 1864)

Catherine Edmondston also pointed to the general antipathy of Southerners toward the arming of blacks in her January 9, 1865, diary entry.

This negro question, this vexed negro question, will if much longer discussed do us more injury than the loss of a battle. Gen Lee advises the Conscription & ultimate Emancipation of 200,000 Slaves to be used as soldiers. One or two rabid partizan papers, Democratic, I might almost say Agrarian to the core, seize on the proposal, hold it up to the people, to the army, in the most attractive lights. They promise the white soldier that if the negro is put in the army, for every negro soldier fifteen white ones will be allowed to return home. They use it as an engine to inflame the passions of one class against another, tell the poor man that the War is but for his rich neighbor's slaves, that his blood is poured out to secure additional riches to the rich, etc., etc., nay one paper, to its shame be it said, the Richmond Enquirer, openly advocates a general Emancipation! as the price for fancied benefits to be obtained by an alliance with England & France. Actually it offers to sell the birthright of the South, not for a mess of pottage, but only for the hope of obtaining one.

But so it is. Coming as it does on the evacuation of Savannah when we are almost ready to sink under the accumulation of Yankee lies & Yankee bragg, over their boasted Victory over Hood, our money depreciated & depreciating daily more & more, deafened on one side by loud mouthed politicians who advocate "Reconstruction to save Annihilation," "Reconstruction as a choice of Evils," & on the other by the opponents of the Government who expatiate with alas too much truth upon the mismanagement, the waste, the oppression which, cast our eyes which way we will we see around us, threatened again with a new suspension of Habeas Corpus, the Constitution daily trampled under foot by Impressment Laws & Government Schedules, what wonder that many unthinking people catch at this straw as at hope of salvation & delivery from present misery without pausing to ask themselves what will be their condition when they have accepted it. But sounder & better councils will prevail. This beaten and crushed Aboli-tionist, the Enquirer, will find that the body of the people are against him, that the foxes who have lost their tails are too few in number to govern those who still retain theirs. Slaveholders on principle, & those who hope one day to become slaveholders in their time, will not tacitly yield their property & their hopes & allow a degraded race to be placed at one stroke on a level with them. (Edmondston 1979, 652–53)

In time, some of the most ardent Southern racists began advocat-ing the conscription of blacks as a practical means of reducing the black population. Mary Akin, wife of Warren Akin, a Confederate congressman, was extremely candid in expressing her attitude about employing black troops.

Every one I talk to is in favor of putting negros in the army and that *immediately*. Major Jones speaks very strongly in favor of it. I think slavery is now gone and what little there is left of it should be rendered as serviceable as possible and for that reason the negro men ought to be put to fighting and where some of them will be killed, if it is not done there will soon be more negroes than whites in the country and they will be the free race. I want to see them *got rid of soon*. (117)

Mrs. Akin somewhat agreed with her brother that by "putting our negros in the army to fight, they will turn against us as soon as they can." She wrote to her husband:

. . . I think there is much truth in that but we are like the man with the elephant, and I am wanting to see them put where they will stand some chance of being killed as well as white folks. (122)

Finally, but only as a "last ditch effort" in March 1865, the Con-federate government authorized the enlistment of blacks as soldiers. Prior to that time, however, they had requested slave owners in cer-tain areas to "volunteer" some of their "hands" (or had outright im-pressed them) to help build fortifications and work on the railroads or to serve as cooks or hospital attendants. Not infrequently, owners were required to provide the workers as well as their tools and food.

In January 1862, Kate Stone, from her northeastern Louisiana home, noted:

> Gen. Polk has called on the planters from Memphis to the lower part of Carroll Parish for hands to complete the fortifications at Fort Pillow, forty miles above Memphis. A great many Negroes have been sent from Arkansas, Tennessee, and North Mississippi, and now it comes Louisiana's time to shoulder her part of the common burden. A man was here today with Gen. Polk's appeal. He had been riding constantly since Monday from one plantation to another, and nearly everyone had promised to send, some half of their force of men, some more, some less. (83)

With the Federal takeover of Southern territory, blacks were actively recruited by or impressed into the Union army. Mary Jane Reynolds, of Loudon, Tennessee, wrote to her husband in January 1864:

> They have issued an order to take all the negroes that belong to rebels and put them in regiments and Henry [one of their slaves] has been very much troubled for fear they would take him. He came in the other day to know the precise meaning of loyal citizen. The circular said to take all that did not belong to loyal citizens and he did not understand exactly the meaning of loyal. I have not heard of them taking any about here yet. (28 January 1864)

A month later, however, she reported the recruiting officers at work attempting to enlist their slaves.

> There are men going around now making up colored regiments. There was a negro recruiting officer here the other day and last night there was a white one stayed all night. . . . He did not tell his business till this morning. He tried to get Hen and Ab [two of their slaves] to enlist. I understand that John West has turned some of his over to the government and got three hundred dollars a piece for them. Don't you think father had better do his so. (Early February 1864)

On another occasion she wrote:

> There has been several enrolling officers here trying to get Henry and Ab to volunteer but I don't think they have much notion of it. Henry said he did not want to leave here. That he told you he would stay here and take care of father while he lived and father told him as long as he stayed he would protect him and try to keep him out of the army. (16 February 1864)

Several weeks later, she informed her husband:

> I understand that they conscripted Ed Kline and Dick Blair and all the other negroes that were working on the railroad and took them off. (7 April 1864)

When attempts failed to lure Southern blacks into the Union army or to work on the building of bridges and fortifications, more drastic methods were employed. In June 1862, Kate Stone wrote:

> The excitement is very great. The Yankees have taken the Negroes off all the places below Omega, the Negroes generally going most willingly, being promised their freedom by the vandals. The officers cooly go on the places, take the plantation books, and call off the names of all the men they want, carrying them off from their masters without a word of apology. They laugh at the idea of payment and say of course they will never send them back. A good many planters are leaving the river and many are sending their Negroes to the back country. We hope to have ours in a place of greater safety by tomorrow. (126–27)

In defense of her workforce, Kate Stone's mother probably did what most Southerners did to keep their slaves out of the hands of the Yankees.

> Mamma had all the men on the place called up, and she told them if the Yankees came on the place each Negro must take care of himself and run away and hide. We think they will. (125)

71

Even in Kentucky the Federal impressment of blacks was not always admirably conducted. In a December 1863 diary entry, Frances Peter deplored the heartless conscription of blacks from Sunday evening church services in Lexington.

> . . . The darkies met with a great mishap this evening. Just as their churches were being dismissed a number of soldiers who had been stationed outside rushed upon the unsuspecting negroes capturing all the men they could lay hands on. The darkies in great terror ran in all directions, some jumping out of the church windows and all doing their best to elude pursuit, sometimes in a most laughable manner, stout, hale men pretending to be crippled & hobbling along with their canes. The soldiers however caught a good many whom they sent off to Camp Nelson [a training camp for Black soldiers] to work on the wagon road they are going to make to Cumberland Gap until they can get hands enough to finish the railroad. It was right mean of them to be 'pressing' the darkies on Sunday and all dressed in their 'go to meetin' clothes, and not even give them time to take off the latter. . . . (43)

During the Federal occupation of Huntsville, Alabama, Mary Jane Cook Chadick observed an appalling scene similar to the one Frances Peter described.

> Such a scene! While the negroes were all assembled at church, the Yankees surrounded the building and, as the men came out, seized them. Some got away and succeeded in hiding from their pursuers. Others were run down by those on horseback. The black women were running in every direction, hunting their husbands and children. It is really heart-rending to a looker on. These are their friends—the Abolitionists! (22)

Abolition preachers further contributed to the turmoil occasioned by the Union troops. In numerous November entries in her 1863 diary, Mrs. Chadick pictured a chaotic Huntsville as hundreds of blacks, induced by the army or by preachers, took their first steps toward independence by walking out on their owners.

Yankees came into town in considerable force, took up all the able-bodied black men to fight for them, telling them that they wanted them to go and hold Nashville, while they (the Yanks) went out to fight our army. Several negroes, who had previously gone to them, came in today and removed their families. (28)

Later she wrote:

Today an abolition preacher from Ohio made a speech to the darkies, which has caused a good deal of excitement among them. Many of them have left today. Many families are without servants. (28)

On November 22 and 24, Mrs. Chadick's racist and secessionist biases intermingled.

The dead body of a Yankee lieutenant was brought to town and buried. Killed in a skirmish near Mooresville. The "African fair sex" crowded around the body, putting roses upon it and muttering, "Poor fellow! Killed by old Secesh." They have all just been listening to an Abolition sermon from one Jones of Ohio, who is doing all in his power to stir them up to rebelling by telling them that they are free now and here, that Lincoln made them so last Jan. 1.

He told them that they must stay here, and send out their husbands, children and sweethearts to help crush out this rebellion, that their masters are bound to support them and take care of them, and pay them for all the work they have ever done, that the hand of God is in this thing, and that He has opened up the way for them to come here and set them free, and when we are subjected, they (the blacks) are to occupy this country.

Another Abolition speech today. Two flags, bouquets and a haversack were presented to the eloquent speaker by the fair darkies, whose names, he assured them, should be sent up to Lincoln. These speeches are having a telling effect. All the servants about town flock to hear them. My own asked permission to go, but most of them are too free for this. (28)

Sherman's sweep through middle Georgia en route to Savannah in the fall of 1864 left Mary Jones Mallard (who was pregnant and expecting her baby in December) and her widowed mother, Mary Sharpe Jones, helpless victims of the army's foragers. Their plantation at Montevideo in Liberty County, Georgia, was repeatedly searched and pillaged, their livestock carried off or ruthlessly destroyed, the ladies insulted, and their slaves impressed by the army or encouraged to leave. Mrs. Mallard wrote in the journal she and her mother kept:

> They [slaves] took off today: Jane, Morton, George, Ebenzer, Little Pulaski, our house servant Jack, & Carpenter Pulaski. Seeing the two last men going away, Mother called to the soldier who had been in charge, "Why are you taking my young men away?" He said, "They need not go if they do not want to." She then asked, "Boys do you wish to go or stay?" They immediately replied, "We wish to stay." She then said, "Do you hear that? Now by what right do you force them away?" They had Pulaski laden down with our Turkeys & wanted Jack to drive one of the carts. So they were all carried of[f]: carriages, wagons, carts, horses, & mules, servants, with food & provisions of every kind & as far as they were concerned, leaving us to starvation. (M. S. Jones 1959, 48)

The next month, following the birth of a baby granddaughter amid the tumult created by the Federals, Mrs. Jones continued describing in their journal the enrollment of blacks for work in the Union army.

> They are now enlisting the negroes here in their service. As one of the officers said to me, "We do not want your women but we mean to take the able bodied men to dredge out the river & harbour at Sav[annah], to hew timber, make roads, build bridges & throw up batteries."
> They offer $12 p[e]r month. Many [Negroes] are going off with them. Some few sensible ones calculate the value of $12 p[e]r month in furnishing food, clothing, fuel, lodging, &c, &c. Up to this time, none from this place has joined them. I have told some of those indisposed to help in any way & to wander off at [their] pleasure that as they were perfectly useless here it would be best for me & for the good of their fellow servants, if they would leave & go at once with the Yankees. They had

seen what their conduct was to the black people: stealing from them, searching their houses, cursing & abusing & insulting their wives & daughters, & if they choose such for their masters to obey & follow them. The sooner they went with them the better, & I had quite a mind to send on a request that they be carried off. (74–75)

Lincoln's Emancipation Proclamation freed the slaves, of course, but only in those states still in rebellion. In reality, the Proclamation as issued on January 1, 1863, freed relatively few slaves at first. The border states were exempted from the decree and the Southern states simply disregarded it. In many areas as yet untouched by Federal rule, the slave system and the buying and selling of human beings went on as usual. That Southerners would want to sell their slaves in order to obtain at least partial recompense for what could possibly become a total loss made economic sense, but the compulsion of some Southerners to *buy* slaves right until the end of the war defies comprehension. Hindsight is always better than foresight, however, and apparently the system was so ingrained and their confidence in a Confederate victory so unshakeable that an ultimate defeat was inconceivable. Extravagant dreams of eventual compensation for their slaves must have distorted the thinking of border state slave owners as well.

In Alabama, Parthenia Hague told of "Mr. G.," who, some six months before Lee's surrender, purchased two Negro slaves for a total of $13,000. His wife scolded him "for his indiscretion in buying negroes at that time, as we believed that they would soon have an opportunity of leaving, if they chose to do so." However, "Mr. G." laughed, saying, "Wait till you get to the bridge before you cross the river." It was indeed a foolish expenditure, for six months later, following the collapse of the Confederacy, the two slaves returned to Columbus as free men (160–61).

And yet, "Mr. G." was certainly not the only Southerner buying slaves during the final months of the war. As late as January 1865, Mrs. Akin wrote her husband: "Mr. Land has sold Oscar his wife & children, four of them, for twenty thousand dollars" (121).

Other Southerners were discovering that hiring "servants" was wiser than buying "servants."

> ... News from Southern papers goes to show that the value of negroes is greatly depreciated. The hire of a servant for one year, being nearly, or quite equal to his fee simple value. This is pretty much the case here. The negro is not a very marketable article at present. People do not care to risk buying a species of property which if it does not 'take wings and fly away,' like riches, at least of late years, often makes good use of its legs and runs off. And that is generally the last his master sees of him unless he should take it into his head to return of his own accord. So most persons prefer hiring to buying. Only yesterday a likely negro man was sold for $250. . . . (Peter 1976, 48)

Elizabeth Curtis Wallace and her husband, whose plantation in Norfolk County, Virginia, was alternately visited by Confederate forces and camped on by the Union forces, experienced numerous problems with their black labor.

> Mr. Wallace suffers a great deal from the carelessness and thoughtlessness of the negroes. So do I. We have come to the conclusion that it would be much better for us if all the negroes would leave us for then we could hire white people who, now that the negroes are all crazy with freedom, would be more faithful and more interested in their labours. (15 April 1863)

A few months later, she wrote:

> These free negroes give us a deal of trouble by working as they please. Our crops when harvested will cost more than it would sell for. It is the last crop Mr. Wallace will plant under the present circumstances. (6 October 1863)

At least one slave was convinced of his net worth. Catherine Edmondston told of overhearing a conversation between Frank, a family member, and Sharper, a young slave.

> Had an amusing illustration of the value in which Cuffy holds himself today. Sharper and Frank were playing in the lot when

Little George came up with the sheep. Sharper began to banter him about his size, and among other things wound up by telling him he "warn't wuth a hundred dollars." "How much are you worth?" said Frank. "Me! I wurth 500 dollars." Frank, not wishing to be outdone said, "And how much am I worth?" Said Sharper with an air of disdain, "Youse white. You ain't wuth nothin.'" (24)

As they gradually became aware of their freedom, most slaves left their plantation homes to follow the army or to attempt to make a life for themselves. The loss of their "hands," the sometimes gradual, other times abrupt departure of their former slaves, forced many wealthy plantation families to struggle with work that had heretofore been done by a staff of a dozen or more house servants and scores of black fieldhands. The descent from their former lofty status as virtual dictators to legally proposed social equality with their former slaves was a displacement difficult for many a Southerner to accept. Even in un-liberated areas, as rumors of their freedom circulated, blacks became increasingly more independent and whites increasingly more incensed.

In May 1864, Lucy Fletcher complained:

I cannot help wishing the Yankees would take the whole race—they are so insufferably lazy & puffed up with their own importance. We only keep one servant this year, and she will probably cost us at least $1,500. We have to pay $300 for hire, her board is worth at the lowest calculation $1,200 for she is the most enormous eater, unfortunately, that I have ever seen, & her clothes at least $200 more. To crown all, she is the most inveterate whiner & complainer, and has been keeping her room now, for several days, and I fear, will be of little account, as she has a chronic disease of the womb, which is very prevalent among them. While I cannot help thinking she is much better able to go about & help at least with the work, than I am. . . . I cannot of course insist on her coming down, if she says she is not able,—& so I have been drudging heavily until I feel sometimes, perfectly worn out. I am finding out, by experience, how utterly inefficient & worthless, most of our servants are—I finished the whole week's ironing with the exception of four pieces, before dinner on Saturday—for which Viney generally takes two days.

Some Southern women looked upon their departing slaves as un-grateful wretches. Kate Foster wrote in her diary on July 16, 1863:

> The negroes are flocking to the enemy in town. . . . They are an ungrateful set and we are all tired of them.
> I think negroes are a lot of ingrates and God punishes us for ingratitude as much as for any other sin. Let the foe take all the negroes—they are welcome to them and the sooner we are rid of them the quicker we will whip our enemy. (28 July 1863)

Four months later, she was forced to admit:

> John, Sarah & Rose have left and I did the washing for six weeks, came near ruining myself for life as I was too delicately raised for such hard work. (15 November 1863)

Other slave owners viewed the loss of their workforce with con-siderably less venom. Although Grace Brown Elmore predicted a bleak future for the blacks, she took the time to personally discuss the alternatives with several of her slaves.

> I tried to present as plainly as possible all the hardships we would have to undergo, that it would not be a life of ease to any. On the other hand, I told her how false and wicked the Yankees had been in their conduct to the negro, how women and children had been abused just so soon as they had ceased to be an amusement and excitement to them. (30)

Later, she wrote:

> We talk very fully to them about the probability of freedom . . . and we tell them they will find freedom harder than slavery. . . . Phyllis [one of the slaves] says she expects to work, and when I suggested she might not get work, she replied, "No fear of her not getting on, with such a smart husband, who could turn his hand to anything." Each one thinks himself or herself specially adapted to succeed and will find out too late there is a vast dif-ference between having a few thousand free colored people living in the South, and 4,000,000 let loose to support themselves. (86)

Phyllis reported that the slaves did not really know what lay ahead but that "the commonest idea was that each man would have his farm house, stock and plenty to eat and drink, the plantations were to be divided among the negroes who lived there" (87).

As the situation worsened, Grace admitted: "If we lost everything, I believe I'd prefer the servants leaving us. Being without money, we would find it impossible to provide for so many and they would be a trouble and a care" (29). During the final days of the Confederacy, Grace informed the servants that "they could go when they liked, for we had no money to pay for their services, or food to sustain them" (87).

Although a great many owners attempted to conceal the knowledge of freedom from their slaves for as long as possible, others gathered them together and attempted to explain the situation and the problems involved for everyone. Sarah Wadley wrote of her father's discussion with his slaves.

> Father gave all the negroes choice yesterday evening, told them they might go with Willie to a place of safety or they might bundle up their things and go to the Yankees, to take a *free* choice, they might have done so in reality, Father would not have hindered them, but they every one chose to go with Willie. Some were not sincere, for Mr. McCormick says that Mr. Duvall is sure he saw one of them, he thinks several, with the Yankees this morning when they left. I was passing through the hall yesterday morning and overheard one of the railroad negroes talking to Father, something was said about going to the Yankees, "No, Mars William," Abe said, "I come from Georgia and you did too and I calculate to die by you." (49)

When their caravan en route to Georgia was stopped at the Mississippi River (see chapter 4) and the Wadleys were about to return home, Sarah's father once again spoke to his slaves:

> . . . and Father called up the negroes to tell them the decision; they were all attentive while he told them, and while he added that he had seen in those few days all kinds of suffering that

he ever expected to see, he had seen the graves of negroes as thick as the heads before him, he had seen acres of the most miserable little huts opposite Natchez where the negroes were staying, and negro women up to their knees in water paddling out clothes, for want of tubs, he had passed one plantation where there were a hundred negroes with no overseer and they had not a morsel of salt and but little meat; all the able bodied negro men were put in the army, the others were left to shift for themselves. Father told them that he thought he should be able to feed and clothe them for another year here, but that if he were to be discovered in the attempt to cross the river he should be "as powerless as Nancy's baby there." The negroes assented, Mark said he was willing to go back and save what little was left, and so they all said. (93)

Gertrude Thomas noted in her diary:

This morning Mr. Thomas [her husband] assembled the servants together—told them that numerous reports were about town, that it was extremely probably [sic] that the Yankees would free them, that they would then be obliged to work—that he would have to hire some one and had as soon pay them wages as any one else and advised them to wait quietly and see what would be done. (8 May 1865)

Following news of the collapse of the Confederacy, Susan Bradford Eppes's father walked the floor all night, unable to comprehend the defeat. Sadly, he summoned his slaves to come up in the yard, at which time he announced:

My people, I have sent for you to tell you that you are my people no longer; the fortunes of war have taken you out of my hands—you are free men now. It is no longer your duty to work for me and it is no longer my duty to feed and clothe you but I shall continue to do this until suitable arrangements can be made. I hope each of you will stay on at his accustomed work and I can assure you that my feelings toward you have known no change and will not unless you give me cause. We are no longer master and slave but we can still be friends. (271)

Regarding emancipation there were about as many views and attitudes as individuals. Frances Dallam Peter wrote on Monday, October 19, 1863:

> ... I for one would not be at all disgusted at having Ky [Kentucky] slaves emancipated. ...
>
> It is an undoubted fact that we are much nearer emancipation now, than even last year. People are getting more accustomed to the idea, and do not think it near so terrible as they used to. It is rather significant that at the present writing it is considered nearly if not quite as cheap to buy negroes as to hire them. Clothing and food being so much higher than in former times. Every thing is tending to decrease the value of the negro as a servant, and to make a great many people look forward to the time when this state will be a free one. The time is not yet come for such a change; but unless the 'signs of the times' are very deceptive, it will be affected in due course of time. (39)

Anna Cabot Lowell, a Northerner, became incensed over a discussion of slavery and made clear in no uncertain terms her convictions

> that it was most wicked & unchristian—yet that I should not dare to abolish it at once, now, if I had it in my power— & that as for the Republican party, they did not cause this war, nor enter into it with any plans of abolishing slavery, but simply in self-defence, to save our Republic wh[ich] the South has been, for years plotting to ruin. They certainly wished to prevent the *extension* of Slavery, & the establishment of a Slave empire. They hoped, too, & I, for one, did most earnestly, that this war might be a step towards the future abolition of Slavery. If man will not abolish it, I believed & was sure God would, & that not many years hence. (7 August 1861)

Even love letters between two Northerners erupted into controversy when the subject was emancipation. George Smith Avery, who favored emancipation only if accompanied by deportation, wrote to Lizzie Little (later to become his wife):

We will let no differences of opinion, however great they may be, lessen our affection: But you must not presume for a moment that I can ever endorse your doctrine—it is tinctured to much with John Brownism. I cannot believe that you have so much sympathy for the *African* as is indicated in your language. I cannot believe that you wish to associate in any way with that race. If your doctrine were carried out how long would it be before you would have to extend to them the hand of fellowship.

I do not wish to argue with any person concerning the Negro—I am sick of the very name; but let me say just here, that this war has been brought on mainly by persons advocating the same doctrine which *you*, (My Lizzie) endorse. And I will say further that those who have been the most effectual in bringing about this Bloody Contest are the last to rally in defence of their sacred rights. I will venture to say that you may go along the whole line of the northern Army, & you will not find more than one out of ten who will step out & say that he is an abolitionist. I can speak at least for one Company in the exended catalogue, & that is Co. "P" 3rd Mo Cav. It has not a man who will endorse abolitionism. Now what think you of the unmerited name that is applied to us? "*Nigger Thieves*"—think of it. Dearest, you well know my opinions concerning this agrivated question. (23 February 1862)

Lizzie had decidedly different views from those of George. Their discussion grew more vehement in their exchange of letters.

If our Administration does not declare the Slaves Emancipated ere four weeks pass by I fear we are lost. Philips says it will be too late when the Federal flag waves over New Orleans & Charleston. I pray heaven Lincoln be not too late. He surely ought to see where alone any good to us has its source. If he does not I hope Jeff Davis will so that the poor black man may be free. If they are not the "Glorious Republic" will be a thing that has been. (12 January 1862)

George Avery responded on January 26, 1862, informing Lizzie that he was definitely not risking his life to free the slaves.

Lizzie you must not make an Abolitionist out of me. I fear you do not comprehend my real motives for engaging in my country's service. I will assure you of one thing that it is not for the emancipation of the African race I fight. I want nothing to do with the negro. I want them as far from me as is possible to conceive. Already we have more colored population in the northern states than is agreeable or profitable. Then why fight for more. Slavery is acknowledged to be a local institution hence it is governed by local law. This being the case we the people of the free states have no right even if we were so disposed to interfere with that "peculiar institution." Each state is vested with power to regulate her own domestic affairs, & I am in favor of that right being enjoyed to its fullest extent. I would not sleep one night in the "Tented-Field" to free every slave in America if they were to remain on our soil. You may have a more favorable opinion of the African than I have—it is your right. No Lizzie, I am simply fighting for the Union as it was given to us. I want nothing more. I will have nothing less. When President Lincoln declares the slaves emancipated I will declare myself no longer an American citizen.

In concluding his letter, George wrote:

> It is the attraction that my Dearest possesses that has in a measure actuated me to take up arms. Where can I better protect you or defend your rights than in the battlefield in these times of peril. I trust no political differences will make our affection less strong.

During their courtship, a time when two individuals would most likely be putting forth their greatest efforts to be agreeable, another Northern couple, Annie Cox and Gideon Allen, were at odds regarding politics and emancipation. Both Annie (a Wisconsin teacher) and Gideon (a law student at The University of Michigan during most of the war years) were against slavery; however, Gideon was apparently a Copperhead—a Northern Democrat who opposed the war. Annie, a Republican, believed in the abolition of slavery and wrote Gideon that on the subject of their political differences

> . . . you and I shall have to agree to disagree. I think slavery incompatible with union, freedom or advancement—therefore should be removed. If "God foreordains everything that comes

to pass" then this war was created for a good purpose. Man with all his buried hatchets and peace pipes could not have prevented it—therefore we have only to await the revealing of His will. . . . Slavery will not exist longer. (15 February 1863)

Whether their freedom came during or at the conclusion of the war, many blacks found themselves in a precarious position. Those who remained with their former masters often suffered along with the plantation owners from lack of food and clothing. Many who left of their own accord or who were lured from the plantations by the Yankees became homeless wanderers, drifting from one area to another seeking work, land, food, and shelter. Some of the more fortunate found jobs in the fields working shares with the planters. Some looked to the Federal government to supply them with sustenance and shelter. However, as long as the war continued, the Federal government's first concerns were obviously with the war effort—blacks and their problems took a back seat. By following the army and hovering around the Union encampments, the former slaves could often obtain handouts. (In time the numbers of Negroes who attached themselves to the armies became so great as to inhibit military operations.) Without food from the Federals many were hard put to secure provisions for themselves and their families.

Although the Freedmen's Bureau was established by the Federal government in the last weeks of fighting, there were few provisions made for the vast numbers of blacks freed at the end of the war. To be sure, blacks found their freedom glorious, but survival on their own in a cold, often hostile world was something of a challenge. The history of the Negroes' struggles, the development of the bureaus and aid societies organized to assist them, and the work of the Federal government on their behalf would require volumes of explication rather than brief paragraphs. It would constitute a grave oversight, however, to omit mention of the thousands of Northern women who went south to help succor and educate the freed blacks. Perhaps the experiences of even a few teachers will illustrate some of the problems and the successes of the forerunners of the flood of women who went to the aid of Southern blacks after the war. The laws prohibiting the teaching of slaves to read or write left them illiterate and ill-prepared for life in the world beyond their plantation. It should have come as no surprise that one of the freedman's greatest needs was education.

During the course of the war, various efforts were made to help the freed blacks in their transition from servitude to freedom. Numerous Northern organizations such as the New England Freedmen's Society, the American Missionary Association, and the Western Freedman's Aid Commission sponsored workers, most of them women, to go to the occupied territories to help the newly liberated Negroes. In connection with these organizations or with the Federal government, scores of women found their niche putting their teaching and nursing skills to work to aid the Southern blacks. Dr. Esther Hill Hawks, a graduate of the New England Female Medical College, volunteered her services to the Federal government as a physician and as a nurse. Despite her medical degree, the U.S. government refused to hire her in the medical service, and Dorthea Dix rejected her as a nurse. Apparently Dr. Hawks was too young and too pretty to meet Miss Dix's requirements for older, plain-looking women. Dr. Hawks's compulsion to make some vital contribution to the war effort, or at least to society in general, prompted her to join her husband in seeking to remedy some of the physical and literacy problems of the freedmen in Florida and the Sea Islands. It was in Jacksonville, Florida, that she jubilantly recorded in her diary:

> Monday morning! Just three months ago to-day I commenced the first free school in Florida! Three months! They have been short, but I look with pride and pleasure on the work done! I have a large, orderly and intelligent school; The scholars love me and I love them, most of them have made excellent improvement. . . . I feel that I can look upon my labors here as successful. (79)

Dr. Hawks's school was indeed remarkable in its early attempts at racial integration (and age integration—numerous black soldiers sat in on the sessions in whatever free time they could manage). However, as more and more blacks were enrolled, more and more white children were withdrawn and forbidden by their racist parents to attend classes. Unfortunately, the work of the Northern teachers often went unappreciated by the citizens of either section.

Lucy and Sarah Chase, Quaker ladies from New England, decided that their role lay not with nursing but with teaching and set to work in January 1863, by appointment from the Boston Educational Commission and at a salary of $25 per month, to help care for and teach the 2,000 homeless blacks on Craney Island. In May 1863 the freedmen were moved to the mainland (Virginia) and there the Chase sisters continued their schools and helped the former slaves to establish themselves on the "government farms." The sisters' letters home reflected some of the contempt held by the Southerners for "the nigger teachers."

> Dear Ones at home:
> Sarah and I are domiciled with the man who wrote the following, to Dr. Brown [Superintendent of Negro Affairs]; "Dr Brown, Sir I wish you would be kind enough to let me know if those ladys that were at my house to day are coming up here to teach school   if they are I shall be obliged to move my family for we have never been used to Negro equality nor to White Ladys going in the kitchens and kissing the Negroes. Sir, I am a union man and ever shall be but I am not an abolitionist nor never can be as fer you I believe you are a perfect Gentleman you have always treated me as such and I am willing to do all I can for you and the Government but if you allow those Ladys to live on the farm you will get very little work done by the Negroes and it will end my peace fer this year as fer Mr. Giny [?] he need not give himself any trouble about their teaching my children I am able to school my children as yet without sending them to a Negro school.
>
> > Yours Respectfully,
> > Wm Wakefield, Overseer"
> > (Swint 1966, 78)

Esther Otis, while a student at Oberlin College, joined three of her classmates in 1863 in accepting commissions from the U.S. War Department to go south as teachers of the contrabands. In some of her schools, the numbers of enrollees eager for an education exceeded the capacity of the schoolrooms—in one case "one hundred and fifty . . . contrabands in one small room." As was true of many of the black schools, students of all ages begged for the opportunity to learn to read and write. Esther Otis was particularly moved by a Negro preacher who came with his Bible and promised to give her five dollars if she would teach him to read anywhere in it.

At various times during her sojourn in the South, Esther worked as a matron at the hospital, organized schools as well as taught in them, visited the camps, distributed clothing, and taught Sunday school classes. Often her bed in her makeshift quarters was a pile of overcoats. Her classrooms were also something less than ideal.

> Had a poor dirty room to teach in. Shall have some work to do to get it in shape. Never mind I have been doing that more or less ever since I came South. I am glad of the experience I have been getting. (6 September 1863)

The work of Northern women in helping to educate newly emancipated blacks was a start but was in no way a total solution to the problems at hand. Freedom for four million former slaves created a multitude of obstacles and hardships. Freedmen's camps floundered for lack of funding. As a result of overcrowding, disease, and malnutrition in the camps, hundreds of Negroes suffered and died. Efforts to employ blacks in newly occupied territory as field workers often resulted in conditions that closely resembled their prewar enslavement. Their "promised land" turned out to be exactly that— land promised but never delivered. Had their "forty acres and a mule" materialized; had more provisions been made for their eventual emancipation; had the South itself been less impoverished at the end of the war; had not greedy Carpetbaggers and Scalawags taken advantage of them; had Sourtherners been willing to receive their former slaves on a more humanitarian basis; had Northerners not felt threatened by their competition in the workforce—the freedman's and freedwoman's situation might indeed have been far different.

CHAPTER III

Anxiety—The Irrepressible Companion

Never until my visit to Alabama had I fully realized the horrors of suspense,—the lives of utter self-abnegation heroically lived by women in country homes all over the South during the dreary years of the war.

Every day—every hour—was fraught with anxiety and dread. Rumor was always busy, but they could not hear *definitely:* they could not *know* how their loved ones were faring.

Can imagination conceive a situation more pitiable?

Ghastly visions made night hideous. During the day, the quick galloping of a horse, the unexpected appearance of a visitor, would agitate a whole household, sending women in haste to some secret place where they might pray for strength to bear patiently whatever tidings the messenger should bring.

—*Fannie Beers* 1888, 53–54

In the preceding excerpt from her book, *Memories*, Fannie Beers, a nurse and the wife of a Confederate soldier, movingly depicted the incessant anxiety which plagued the waking hours and murdered the sleep of untold numbers of both Northern and Southern Civil War women. Were their loved ones at the battlefront safe, comfortable, healthy? Would the hated enemy invade and occupy their homes and property? Should they remain and attempt to protect their homes or should they search for refuge in safer areas? Were their husbands or sons getting in with the wrong company in the army, acquiring bad habits—drinking, smoking, gambling? Where would the money for food, clothing, shelter come from? How could they survive the growing labor shortages and escalating taxation? How could they manage a home, a family, and a farm without the help and mainstay of a husband? How could they maintain their own health amidst the strain from worry and overwork? What would happen following the war? After the thrill and excitement of soldiering would their husbands be willing to return home to the cares and routine of family life? Thus ran but a brief sampling of the problems confronting women on the homefront.

The ever-present threat of the death "of one's own house and blood," of course, eclipsed all other anxieties. As the slaughter continued and the numbers of casualties mounted (sometimes as many as 25,000 to 44,000 dead, wounded or missing in a single battle), families everywhere suffered, if not from their own grievous losses, then from their heartfelt compassion for the losses which ravaged their friends and neighbors. Gnawing fear became an irrepressible companion.

For some women there was a daily agonizing wait for news brought in by the evening train.

> Ill news came heralded by signals well understood. Loud prolonged and piercing screams . . . from the 'iron horse,' which broke the stillness of the night as it came rushing in. . . . Each quivering head stood still—waiting for the aged father, with slow, dragging steps, to return from where the news was read, with messages which gave relief to some, and confirmed the bitterest and most dreaded fears of others. (T. Taylor 1903, 34)

Somehow, no amount of forearming oneself, no amount of "steeling oneself" against adversity could minimize the actual shock of reality. Knowing her two sons were involved in the fighting around Winchester, Virginia, in the fall of 1864, Lois Wright Richardson Davis, living near Lowell, Massachusetts, was tortured by fear that the fighting would leave her bereft of one or both of her sons. Her worst fears came true in the dreaded letter from her one remaining son, Charles, reporting the tragic news of his brother's death in combat. Adding to her own deep grief was her son's request that she combat. Adding to her own deep grief was her son's request that she carry the news to a fellow townswoman (a Mrs. Foster) of the death of Mrs. Foster's husband. Mrs. Davis reported the painful visit in her next letter to her son.

> I went to Mrs. Foster with your letter. Poor thing it was heart rending to hear shrieks and moans. She was hear yesterday, she was quite calm. It seems she to was expecting sad news, she had watched the papers. She was standing in the door when I went up asked if Mrs. Foster lived there. She said "This is Mrs. Foster, what is it? What is it! 'Tis Charleys mother I know I see his eyes. Tell me, tell me quick." She had not heard a word untill I went there. (2 October 1864)

It would be difficult to imagine the torment suffered by Catherine Cooper, of Maury County, Tennessee, who sent ten sons and five grandsons to the war. Of the sons, five lost their lives, four returned home wounded, only one escaped unhurt. In a letter to her sons on April 6, 1863, she wrote:

> I heard Thomas is in the hospital, which almost derainged me. I think sometimes my trials are greater than I can bear.
>
> My dear children I long to see you, but try to be patient, and prepare for all events. James, Thomas be assured I will be mother to your wives and children in your absence.

Death eventually hit home in the Cary Breckinridge family of Botetourt County, Virginia, when in May 1864 news arrived of the death of Lucy's brother, Gilmer, at Fort Kennon. Informing Gilmer's wife, "Sister Julia," proved a traumatic experience for heartsick Lucy and her sister Eliza. Apparently no words were needed for

> . . . Sister Julia just looked at her [Eliza's] face and with an agonizing shriek fell down. She told them not to tell her, that she knew what we had heard. I pray God I shall never witness such a heart-rending scene again. Today she looks as if she had

had a long illness, so pale and wasted, and just lies still moan-
ing, and takes no notice of a thing except little Johnny. Poor
Mamma! She has to think so much of Sister Julia that she has
but little time to think of her own loss. He was a greater comfort to her than any of her children. He was always so loving
and confiding. . . . (182)

Three days later Lucy wrote:

Dear Sister Julia, there is little left to make life desirable to her.
If God should take my love! Oh, it is too terrible a thought.
I have thought so constantly and so hopefully about him today. It makes me tremble to find how entirely my happiness
in this life depends upon him. (183)

Instantaneous death on the battlefield was perhaps a greater blessing to a soldier and his family than the gradual ebbing away of life
resulting from ultimately fatal wounds that insidiously sapped their
victim's energy, his will to live, and finally drained away the last
vestiges of life itself. The slow, agonizing death of her brother, a loss
recorded by Rachel Craighead in a lengthy succession of diary entries,
was a tragedy reenacted in thousands of families in both sections.

Rachel Craighead, a zealous Confederate patriot, was sure her
"heart would burst" when her father, a prominent Nashville banker,
was arrested after the Rebel abandonment of Nashville in February
1862 and sent to the penitentiary for refusing to take the Oath of
Allegiance to the U.S. government. His subsequent release, however,
was merely a lull in the anguish that awaited the family. In October
1862 the family became increasingly apprehensive over the safety
of Rachel's brother, Bud, fighting with the Southern forces around
Perryville, Kentucky. Rachel despaired to her diary:

My heart is most broken. Is my brother kill[ed]. Oh! Lord—is
it thy will to crush us so. I am real sick with crying. I feel *almost*
like there is not a drop remaining in [the] vial of wrath which
has been poured upon our heads. If I am sinning—I beg for-
giveness. (19 October 1862)

On October 20, 1862, Rachel's husband brought home the dreadful news that Bud had indeed been killed. It then befell Rachel to tell her parents.

> I went in to tell Ma & Pa. How I did hate to do it. Poor Pa & Ma. Pa got up. He has been walking the floor all day. He says his peace is broken forever on this earth. His only boy, his pride, the idol of Ma's heart. Oh! if I could write as I feel. . . . (20 October 1862)

For a time the family's grief was miraculously, although temporarily assuaged, by the news that Bud was not dead but instead had been seriously, although perhaps mortally, wounded. Immediately, Rachel's anxious parents rushed to Bud's bedside, there to keep a constant vigil over his three months of agony. At Christmastime Rachel joined them in attending Bud in his final days. Now and then Bud rallied, evidencing vague signs of improvement; more often, however, his condition worsened as Bud himself slowly abandoned all hope of recovery.

December 25 passed with Rachel's scarcely knowing it was a holiday. On December 26 Bud became "very low spirited." In her diary Rachel painfully detailed her brother's suffering.

> "You will all go home but me. Tell Tom [Rachel's husband] I wanted to see him so bad. Tell Uncle Wile . . . too. Ma I wish I could fight once for home. Oh! but Ma I did fight so hard for you all—but I want to fight once for home. It is so bad to be left to dwindle away. That's what I am doing—dwindling. I wish Jesus would come and take me away now—not leave me to dwindle away."

On January 4, Bud appeared to be dying and Rachel mourned:

> I never, never can forget this day when the destroying angel seemed winnowing around with his terrible wings, when it seemed as if Bud's life was blowing away as chaff before a strong wind. (4 January 1863)

93

Ten days later, Bud was still clinging to life and Rachel wrote:

> He was very comfortable all day until 4 o'clock when he was taken suddenly sick. We thought he was dying. He said "God Bless you all!" Called us each said he was dying. He said "Then Ma won't have her son . . . I'll be in heaven. I'll watch over you all when I go there. God bless. God bless you." Our poor hearts are wringing with anguish but he said *"don't cry for me!"* He is perfectly resigned to his fate . . . but what will I do without my brother. His coming home is all we have had to look forward to since he left. What a desolate home ours will be without Bud. (14 January 1863)

The family's torture as they helplessly witnessed Bud's rapidly deteriorating condition intensified as Bud repeatedly pleaded with them:

> "Sis for heaven's sake give me something. . . . Pa please throw me out the window or break my poor leg off—anything to ease me." (January 1863)

While there was yet life the family found reason to hope; however, the long suspenseful months of special diets and gentle, loving care unfortunately were to no avail. Bud's death left Rachel and her family absolutely devastated. In the weeks that followed, Rachel became increasingly depressed.

> I wish I could sleep forever. Whenever I wake the first thing [is] something *dreadful* has happened. I remember my dear brother has gone from us—then my heart aches . . . that dreadful thought that he'll never come home. All's a blank. Nothing to look forward to. . . . Oh! Bud if we only had you with us. As Pa says the sacrifice is too great for anything. If it could have been otherwise and our soldier had been left to us—but all is over.
>
> I thought it dreadful when I was here waiting to hear from Bud from day to day. I thought I could [not] suffer more but I find the certainty of desolation is worse than the agonies of suspense but there is no alternative but to endure. (1 February 1863)

Time, the great healer, failed to ease Rachel's grief. Each week for years thereafter, Rachel noted in her diary: "three weeks . . . ," "thirty-four weeks . . . ," "fifty-five weeks . . . ," or "three hundred and seventeen weeks since my dear brother died." Her moroseness continued and nine months after her brother's death Rachel explained in her diary: "Ina says I think it a sin to laugh. I tell her she is mistaken. I don't want to laugh—that's all" (3 October 1863).

Morbidity preyed on Rachel's physical and mental health for almost a year after Bud's death. Even eighteen months later, in August of 1864 when the family took a vacation trip to Newport and New York (a strange holiday for Confederates!), Rachel, still in mourning, was a reluctant participant in most of the vacation activities, refusing to dance and attending the theater begrudgingly.

As is true of any war, tales of death and horror abound in Civil War diaries and letters: of mothers rushing to the bedside of wounded sons only to be confronted with the heart-rending news that they had arrived too late; of parents waiting in the depot for a train to carry them to a loved one recovering in a field hospital, only to discover that dear soldier's coffin being unloaded from an incoming train; of a distraught wife-mother searching a battlefield and finding her husband and two sons lying dead among the carnage, her wails of grief audible a mile away.

Tragedy usually struck without warning. Angie, the future Mrs. George Hurlbut, was apparently helping to earn her living by working as a dressmaker. During the course of what had been a gay afternoon's fitting, Angie was stunned by the tragedy that unfolded before her eyes.

> Oh, George, such a scene as I witnessed here last Tuesday eve. I hope I shall never see such grief again. I was here fitting a dress for cousin Amelia Marlow, Dora's sister. Her husband was in the Army. Amelia was so happy. She talked of her husband all day, and several times exclaimed, "Oh, Angie, you don't begin to know how I love my husband." Just before supper Mr. Webb, her brother-in-law, brought the word that her husband had been killed. I thought of those I love and have

drawn them still closer to my heart lest one cord should be severed. (8 October 1864)

One of the most chilling experiences was that described by Mrs. P. G. Robert, a nurse serving in Richmond's Clopton Hospital, who recalled the shock suffered by a young bride living just a block away from the hospital.

> A bride of six weeks, going to the door on her way out, returned to tell her mother that the next door neighbor's son had been killed and was being carried into the mother's house. Her mother hastened with her to the door, only to find that the soldiers had mistaken the house, retraced their steps, and were coming up their own steps, bearing the groom who but six weeks before, in the pride and strength of manhood, went to join his regiment; although he held in his pocket a furlough for several days, he could not let his regiment go into active service without him. The mother, taking in the incident, caught her daughter in her arms and bore her into the parlor and laid her on the floor on the identical spot where six weeks before she had stood as a bride. (Missouri Division 1920, 88–89)

Separating truth from rumor posed one of the most difficult tasks of the times. Partisan newspapers, both North and South, boasted of victories to camouflage defeats, minimized their own casualties, and maximized those of the enemy. Confederates as well as Federals heard only what they wished to believe and promptly rejected as untrue news contrary to their hopes and desires. There were widely circulated reports (long before April 15, 1865) that Lincoln was dead, that Jeff Davis had been killed, that the English were siding with the South, that the French were sending ships and troops to aid the Confederacy, that Gettysburg was a great Southern victory, that Washington had been taken, that the Confederacy had "gone up," that a counter revolution had divided the North.

The incessant spread of rumor bred additional tension in women's already stress-filled lives. Telegraph and railroad lines were frequently disrupted and scores of newspapers in the South had closed down. At times, communication, other than word of mouth, came to a complete standstill, and as a result near-panic often set in. Emily Harris's diary entry could have applied to almost any community.

> People are in an awful state of excitement. They may, almost, be said to be flying about with streaming hair. They are just ready to believe anything they hear provided it is horrible. I never have heard so many false rumors before. Some things are, however, distressingly true. (Racine 1990, 365)

Sarah Butler Wister noted that people were "perfectly tormented by rumours" and "the exhausting rises & falls of expectation" (284–85). Refusing to give credence to the flurry of unsettling rumors that kept infiltrating the area, Henrietta Barr, of Ravenswood, Virginia, told her diary:

> Nothing more to add to yesterday's rumours. Mr. R. Park called, contradicted some of the reports. So we live; one day we hear an exciting tale which is pronounced unfounded on the next. I am getting so skeptical I am afraid I shall not believe the truth if I ever should be fortunate enough to hear it again. (30 July 1862)

Henrietta's general distrust of all rumor must have accounted for her denial of the news of the Union victories at Gettysburg and Vicksburg in July 1863.

> A rumor reaches us of a great battle at Gettysburg. Of course Gen'l Lee is victorious although the Yankee papers are not willing to give him full credit for it. . . . A report that "Vicksburg has fallen" I do not credit. I must have better proof than mere hearsay.

Anna Cabot Lowell, who lived near Boston, described the news of the First Battle of Bull Run and the Union rout. At first citizens rejoiced over reports that the Union forces had won a great victory—then came rumors of a possible defeat instead.

> We were dreadfully shocked. We drove to the telegraph office to try to get the last paper—It would not come till ¼ before

7—we drove for half an hour & returned. "All the papers
bought"—On the way, we could see groups of eager, anxious
faces gathered round some man who was reading the news to
them. Sometimes on fences, sometimes on door steps, or at
shop windows, these groups were collected. (22 July 1861)

Despite women's frantic attempts to obtain information, the
newspapers they so eagerly sought and the flurry of extras that augmented regular publication often tended to stir up more turmoil than
they resolved. Catherine Devereux Edmondston reported in her diary
her husband's proposal, "were he an Autocrat," to put a stop to the
war and restore peace to the land by *"one single order."*

"Certainly," said I, "you would order everybody, everywhere
to lay down their arms and go home." "No," he said, "I would
stop *all* Newspapers. This war is now fed and fanned by
newspapers. They have lighted the fire, but they cannot control the conflagration." (32)

Poor communication and the consequent spreading of misinfor-
mation compounded the suffering of hundreds of wives and mothers.
All too few death reports proved false—a confused hospital attendant's
giving out wrong information, and a loved one turning out to be
alive after all. However, Johanna Underwood, of Bowling Green,
Kentucky, recorded one such miracle following the Battle of Shiloh.

Josie and her mother had watched with pride as Josie's fifteen-
year-old brother Warner marched off with the Union troops—"so
handsome in his Lieutenant's uniform."

Dear Ma is so proud of him though it nearly broke our hearts
when with the regiment—he marched through town on the way
South—perhaps to battle and death, though I hope to glory
and victory. (Nazro, 134)

Unfortunately, Josie's morbid fears proved prophetic, when days later
Josie's mother was summoned to Pittsburg Landing to care for young
Warner, wounded during the fighting at Shiloh. The sounds and
sights around the Landing must have struck terror into the heart

of Mrs. Underwood as she observed the surgeons "amputating arms and legs in a little cabin and throwing them in a pile out the window." As she began her desperate search for Warner, her growing fear that she might be too late to see her son alive was at first confirmed:

> Asking one of the attendants if he knew anything of Lieut. Underwood, he said—"Yes madam, he had that cot there by you—he died this morning and has just been taken out." "In God's name—where have they taken him" exclaimed Ma as she sank upon the cot. Just then, Pa came up with the news that Col Hawkins of the 11th Kentucky had taken Warner home with him on a boat that had already gone. The poor dead Lieut. was another Underwood and dear Ma's grief for his mother's sorrow was measured by what her own was for the moment. (Nazro, 140)

The Underwood situation was reversed in the case of Julia Wheelock (Freeman), who was teaching school in Ionia County, Michigan, when a neighbor girl interrupted classes with the news that Julia's brother had been seriously wounded in the Battle of Chantilly. The following morning Julia set off with her sister-in-law on an arduous train and boat trip to Alexandria and a frenzied search through fifteen hospitals which culminated in the wondrous news that her brother was "doing well." Later, the information was retracted and wife and sister learned that death had already claimed its victim (Journal).

Mary Chesnut told of a woman offering up ecstatic prayers of thanksgiving that the report of her son's death had been in error. Her elation quickly changed to anguish as "the hearse drove up with the poor boy in his metallic coffin." Mrs. Chesnut then queried:

> Does anybody wonder so many women die? Grief and constant anxiety kill nearly as many women as men die on the battlefield. Miriam's friend [the bereaved mother] is at the point of death with brain fever; the sudden changes from joy to grief were more than she could bear. (Chesnut 1981, 371)

Contrary to popular wisdom, "no news" did not necessarily signify "good news." Mail was slow and irregular. Rumor was speedy and unreliable. It was sometimes months or even a year before a wife could learn of the fate of her husband or a mother her son. "Not knowing," that interminable waiting for news, must have been excruciating. Sarah Chapin, of Courtland, Michigan, was understandably distraught in writing to her husband:

> It is now four weeks since I have heard from you, except an account I have read in the *Eagle* stating that you were wounded at the Battle of Murfreesboro, but not stating how severely. I need not tell you that my anxiety is very great to know where you are and what your circumstances are. And it seems to me sometimes as though I cannot possibly wait much longer without knowing though I am well aware that I may be obliged to wait a great while. . . . (28 January 1863)

A few days later, Sarah Chapin at long last received a letter from her husband written from his hospital bed in Nashville, Tennessee. She responded at once.

> And what would I not give to know what is your present situation. I tell you my Dearest one, it is a heart rending thought to me to know that my dear husband (one who in sickness has ever been on hand to attend to the slightest want) has had so great an amount of suffering to endure in a strange land and with no friendly hand except that of strangers to administer ought to his comfort. I can hardly contain myself at the thought. And it seems to me that I could almost fly until I had reached your couch that I might be with you and take care of you myself.

In another paragraph:

> I have tried to keep up as good courage as possible and shall continue to do so. Oh Theodore, if you can only get well enough and they will only let you come home, what a consolation that would be to us all. (6 February 1863)

For almost six months Theodore Chapin wavered at death's door. Upon occasion he was encouraged about his recovery; more often he was convinced his condition was terminal. Letters to his wife,

Sarah, in what he believed were his final moments, served to exacerbate Sarah's anxieties. On January 22, 1863, Theodore sent home explicit directions for the financial transactions to be completed upon his death.

> My Dearest, Dearest wife, my sweet, sweet babes, I am going to write a few lines to you ere my spirit takes its final leave. Last night the vital just flickered in its socket. Today I have a little added and will improve it in this way. It is hard for one to give it up for the sake of wife and babes and I have thought that I should not. I NEVER, NEVER should have been here. . . .
>
> In regards to paying the debts Sarah, I think it best to not pay the mortgage until the other debts are paid. If the Doctor should take advantage of it. . . .

Theodore concluded his letter:

> Now Sarah, my gentle patient wife, your Father, your Mother, your Edward, your Jacky, and my Sweet Babes, goodbye, goodbye. I have no doubt that [when this] letter shall reach you, and in all probability in less than 36 hours, my body will be in the ground and my spirit shall be with you if possible when you read this letter. They have removed me to another hos'l that makes no difference as I need not tell you where to direct any more [letters]. I have looked at your and Gene's likeness 26 times today and wished that I could be with them when I died.

A letter from General Hospital No. 8, Nashville, written on June 22, 1863, brought to a close the Chapin papers.

> Mrs. Chapin
> > Madam
> Your letter of June 17th came to hand this morning requesting that your husbands things might be sent to you. We wrote to you shortly after his death telling you how they might be obtained but probably you did not receive it. In order to have them sent you will have to get a Power of Attorney and an Identification before some Justice of the Peace and send a receipt for the effects and $3 in money to defray Express Charges when they will be immediately sent to you.

His Effects are
   Cash $1.03   1 Knapsack   2 Dress Coats   1 Pr pants
1 shirt   1 Pair Drawers   1 testament   some envelopes
1 Cap Cover   1 pair mitts and a few other little things.

I have carefully enquired of the nurses and Ward Masters who tended him while here and none of them knew of his having a Gold pen or pencil case and think that he brought none here.

If you should ever want to find his grave you can do so by examining the Books of the Medical Director of this place. The graves are all numbered and registered on his books. Our Hospital No. of dead is 413 but I do not know the No. of the Grave. You can easily find out if necessary.

Yours Very Respectfully
I Remain
J. S. Baldwin
Clark—No. 8 Hosp.
(Chapin 22 June 1863)

Hospital nurses and matrons were commonly barraged with letters from wives and mothers eagerly seeking information concerning their husbands and sons. One mother, desperate in her hope that the "intelligence" of her son's death would prove untrue, implored Mary Martha Reid, a matron-nurse in the Florida hospital in Richmond, for word about her son.

> Oh for some certainty regarding my boy's fate. This state of suspense will soon put me in my grave. I have sat by the window & watched for my boy's coming, week after week, week after week, from day light 'till dark, & through the long sleepless nights have been startled by every sound, until I have felt that I should lose my reason.
>
> Since I first heard that my darling had been killed I have through every discouragement from friends & circumstances, entertained the hope that he was living, that I shall yet welcome him to his home. . . . (26 February 1863)

In the case of Mrs. P. G. Robert it was the nurse herself who sought news of her husband. While her husband was serving as a chaplain with the Louisiana forces, Mrs. Robert volunteered her services as a nurse at a Richmond hospital. After weeks of not hearing from her husband, her anxiety apparently mounted to the breaking point. No messages could be sent through the lines to the city.

> It was only through occasionally meeting the wounded men that we heard anything that was going on at the front. On the morning of the sixth day, on reaching the hospital, one of the ladies rushed up to me with the statement that a man had been brought in the night before from my husband's regiment and was in the third story of the building, and that if I would go up and see him I could probably hear some tidings of my husband. When I reached his side I found he had just fallen into the first sleep since being wounded. (Missouri Division 1920, 87)

Despite her friend's insistence that she waken the wounded man, Mrs. Robert could not find it in her heart to disturb his desperately needed sleep. The soldier's nurse, however, offered to trade places, and for what seemed an eternity, Mrs. Robert conducted her vigil.

> For two long hours I sat and fanned him, hardly knowing whether I wished that he would wake or not. My anxieties and fears were so great that I felt perhaps ignorance in my case might be the last happiness I should ever know. (Missouri Division 1920, 87)

Even when, after two hours, her patient awoke, Mrs. Robert, fearing his answer, could still not bring herself to question him. First she responded to his request for coffee.

> When he told me how anxiously he wished the cup I rose and went downstairs immediately to get it, still without asking him the question I so much longed yet dreaded to have answered. On my return he took the cup eagerly and drained it to the last drop. Then I felt that I must know something, and trying to steady myself as much as possible I said, in a tone as calm as I could command, "You are from the Second Louisiana?" "Yes, madam," he said with pride, "I am from the Second Louisiana." "Do you know the chaplain?" I then asked with quivering lips. "Oh, yes," he said, "he helped to put me in the ambulance last night."

Is it any wonder that I broke down completely, and to the man's astonishment, burst into tears. It was the first tidings I had had since five terrible engagements had taken place, and I had heard not one word from my husband; and to learn that the night before he had been well and able to help a wounded man into the ambulance was a relief beyond the power of language to express. (Missouri Division 1920, 88)

Reliable information was always difficult to obtain. Waiting for news among the throngs gathered around the telegraph office or while sitting alone in the bleak solitude of one's home, must have seemed endless. Worse yet must have been the tortured suspense suffered by women living close to a battlefield and compelled to stand shuddering on a nearby hillside as the thundering cannons signaled yet another murderous conflict in which a beloved son or brother or father was engaged. From distant Lynchburg, Susan Blackford heard the cannons at the First Battle of Bull Run (First Manassas) and wrote:

The sound of the cannon were distinctly heard on the hills of Lynchburg, and we well knew that a great battle was being fought from early morn until sunset, and that not only the fate of our country and our homes was at stake, but that each boom which stirred the air might be fraught with the dying sigh of those we loved best. Mrs. Robert C. Saunders, whose husband was in the battle, stood all day on one of the hills near her home in Campbell and listened in agony to every gun. . . . I remained at Father's with Betty Colston and the children waiting and trembling, at one time on my knees praying for my husband's safety and at another trying to prepare myself for the worse news should it come. (36)

Worries over the health of their fighting men came close to topping the list of anxieties tormenting women on the homefront. Their fears were well founded, for even more to be feared than death or a mortal wound on the battlefield should have been the pervasive epidemics of contagious childhood diseases and camp illnesses that ran rampant through the troops. Tens of thousands of soldiers, particularly those from rural areas who were heretofore unexposed to measles and mumps, quickly contracted the diseases, often as early as in the assembly areas. Camp diseases, such as diarrhea and dysentery, malaria, and typhoid fever, were responsible for almost ninety thousand deaths among the Federal troops alone (Steiner 10). Almost a million and a half cases of malaria resulted in the deaths of over ten thousand Northern soldiers. Lack of isolation of contagious cases, lack of knowledge in preventing and/or treating the diseases, and lack of sanitary conditions and procedures greatly contributed to what amounted to "natural biological warfare." Disease was quickly spread, for as Dr. Paul E. Steiner noted in *Disease in the Civil War*:

> Often, water supplies were shared by drinkers, bathers, launderers, cooks, horses, mules, the commissary's cattle, flies, mosquitoes, and other fauna as well as, unwittingly, some protozoa and bacteria coming from skins, nearby latrines, and other obvious sources. Pediculosis was said to have been universal whenever conditions prevented bathing or the boiling of clothes. (7)

The following excerpts from letters from their "soldier boys" must have completely unnerved those families waiting apprehensively back home.

> . . . I take my pen in hand to wri[te] a few lines to you for P[er]ry to inform you that he is sick. . . . He has got the intermittent fever, he has vomi[t]ed every 20 minutes since yesterday morning. (Mayo 1967, 189)
>
> I was sorry to hear that any of you were sick but hope to hear of your recovery soon as the measles are not as fatal at home as they are in camp. (Mayo 1967, 201)
>
> I have been quite sick since our arrival here and have been in the hospital all the time. The march here [Camp Crab Orchard, Kentucky] used me up, for I was not strong enough to stand it. . . . My disease has been general debility, and he is the worst *General* I have ever served under. (Mayo 1967, 239)

Despite a soldier's survival through illness and disease, he was frequently discharged with debilities which handicapped him for a lifetime. Exhaustion, bitterly cold weather, sleeping on the hard ground, malnutrition—the hardships of war—all added to Sophia Buchanan's concerns about her soldier husband's future health.

. . . if you ever live to return, I almost fear you will be a broken down man, in the prime of life. How many have lost that greatest of blessings, health, since entering the service. . . . (Blackburn 1965, 61)

In Oxford, Wisconsin, Mary Burwell was witness to homecomings that brought greater sadness than joy.

William Peirson has got home but he is crazy as he can be, it takes three men to guard him all the time now and they say they don't think he will get well again. Dear husband I hope you will come home all right and as good as you went away. (3 January 1865)

Life was never worry-free for women on the homefront. Accidents (the result of carelessness and inexperience), exhaustion, malnutrition, "high-spirited" exuberance, or "low-spirited" depression were constant threats to soldiers on the march and during encampments, and a nagging concern for the women at home. Members of Garrett Smith Ainsworth's family, of McHenry County, Illinois, were doubtlessly beside themselves with foreboding as Garrett's letters chronicled the death of three of his comrades during the first weeks of his enlistment with the Fifteenth Illinois Volunteers. At their first encampment, Garrett and his new-found friends merrily headed for a nearby river and a refreshing swim, only to return to headquarters an hour later with the company's first casualty: one of the men had drowned. Later that same evening during an electrical storm, another man asleep in a nearby tent died when lightning struck the camp. Days later yet another man was drowned, lost overboard as their company was being transported by steamer down the Mississippi to its new headquarters. On Garrett's brief furlough home, a freak gun accident claimed the life of a trainman and sent Garrett and his friend to court as material witnesses.

Civil War diaries, letters, and reminiscences reverberate with tales of accidents, gunfights, foolish daredevil pranks, and show-off antics that helped decimate the ranks and caused great consternation on the homefront. On September 8, 1861, Perry Mayo wrote:

106

A couple of Company G's men were going through with the manual of arms. One was giving orders and the other going through with the exercise (not thinking the gun was loaded), when the orders were given, ready—aim—fire. The gun was aimed at the breast of the person giving orders and the whole charge went throug[h] him killing him instantly, but such things are so common that I hardly ever make note of them.

Later that month, Perry commented:

. . . we have lost two men, One died and the other had his arm shot off while in a row caused by gambling for money. (21 September 1861)

Letters from husbands and brothers detailing the incompetence, drunkenness, and immorality of some of their commanding officers gave rise to grave doubts on the part of the women at home as to the quality of leadership in both armies. John Tallman, for example, took a dim view of his commanding officer who was "known among the boys as the Whiskey Commander from his keeping himself well soaked in the article . . . " (25 May 1864). Virgil Andruss accused his commanding officer of being "a drunkard and a thief." Virgil was delighted, however, that justice was being served for the colonel was soon to be brought before a court of inquiry for his conduct (11–14 September 1864).

Even while in training, Jacob Lauman, a soldier with the 7th Iowa Volunteer Infantry, quickly became disillusioned with his superior officers and wrote to his wife:

We have been brigaded and I am now under command of a Genl. who knows precisely as much about Military matters as a Horse does about a holiday, and no more, and we turn out every day at two o'clock for drill in this Camp of Instruction, what a farce, and are paraded around for two hours by a man who has to be told what command to give and how to do it *every time*. . . . (8 January 1862)

Susan Blackford's husband could scarcely have dispelled her "gloomy outlook" on the war when he informed her:

> The army is very badly generalled and the result is there is
> much demoralization and want of confidence. Bragg ought to
> be relieved or disaster is sure to result. The men have no faith.
> (224)

Few anxieties were assuaged by Perry Mayo's letter home with one
of the worst indictments of officers.

> The Capt is dead drunk more than half his time. He doesn't
> get out of his tent to take command of the company more than
> two days in the week. This is a pretty rough charge, but I am
> prepared to substantiate the truth of the statement. (195–96)

Families were invariably concerned about the quantity and quality
of food their loved ones were being allotted in the army. Perry Mayo's
mother no doubt winced when she read her son's letter of December 1, 1862, telling of his Thanksgiving dinner.

> I suppose you would like to know how I spent Thanksgiving
> so I will tell you what myself and a partner . . . had for dinner—
> one cup of coffee each (which is the staff of life for a soldier),
> two pieces of fried pork (the last we had) and four crackers a
> piece and each cracker contained from ten to thirty worms vary-
> ing in length from ⅛ to ½ an inch. . . . We broke them into
> our coffee to scald them and dipped them out with a spoon
> as they came squirming to the top.

Frightening tales of food poisonings around army camps further
added to homefront worries. Mary Burwell warned her husband:

> Mother says that the Southerners poison the oyster beds and
> then they are put up and sold to the Soldiers, and a great many
> has lost their life in this way, and now dear Andrew for the
> sake of your dear wife and baby, and all that is dear, be on
> your guard for such things as these, don't eat any more oysters
> for fear they are poisoned. (13 November 1864)

The likelihood that their menfolk might succumb to lapses of religious or moral convictions, or take up with bad company, or become addicted to tobacco, or alcohol, or gambling, made many

women apprehensive. Through her tears, Charley Ingersoll's mother wrote from Owego, New York:

> . . . I will only write what I wished to say before you left but could not command my feelings. I wish to impress upon your mind the importance of trusting in God and striving to obey his commands, for by so doing you will be prepared for the right discharge of every duty. Take the word of God for the men of your counsel and adhere strictly to its truths and principles in all your ways. As your lot is to be among strangers, O may the Lord be your friend; may he guide you in all your ways. . . . I suppose you will smile at this scribbling, but the tears come so fast I can hardly see to write. (Rundell 1964, 332)

Charley's mother also warned her son about the evils of theatergoing in her letter of December 8, 1863:

> You seem to be very much taken up with the Theatre. I hope you will not get in bad company by going. I never had a very good opinion of Theatres and exhibitions or anything of a fictitious character. It seems to me as though the performers who make that the business of life, will not have a very solid foundation for happiness in time to come. Life is a stern reality, and it is the duty of everyone to improve the golden moments as they pass in some way that will honour God, for this will be most conducive to our own happiness. (Rundell 1964, 357)

In still another letter, Mrs. Ingersoll wrote:

> Your father says you must be a good boy and try to take care of your health. We was very glad to hear that swearing was prohibited in your company and hope that card playing and all such vices are also. We do hope you will never attempt to play cards or practice whatever is wicked. . . . If you have any leisure moments, I hope you will try to spend them in some useful way. . . . (Rundell 1964, 334)

It was somewhat surprising that swearing, card playing, and theatergoing were frowned upon by Charley's family, and yet alcohol (we assume in moderation) was condoned. On at least one occasion, Charley's father took a bottle of brandy and "Troutmouth" to

Charley's brother as his company passed through town and even his mother expressed concern over the safe arrival of a bottle of whiskey which they had sent him.

Mary Burwell extracted a promise from her husband before he left for the army to "stop swearing," a promise she was not hesitant to remind him about.

> I hope you are striving to do as you promised me when you went away. You know you said you would stop swearing. I think a great deal of that promise. Read the little book you took away with you and pray to God every night that you have the chance to and then we will both be doing the same thing at the same time. (25 September 1864)

During his first weeks in service, Mary's husband found himself surrounded by fellow soldiers who either had made no such promise or who had long since forsaken their resolve.

> Mary I knew that I am wicked before I came here but I am sick and ashamed of wickedness. There are some here that take delight in cursing and swearing. It is just one continual string of swearing and card playing, but dear wife I have made a strong resolve to keep from all evils and vice of all kinds and I want your prayers to help me in my undertaking. (11 September 1864)

The absence of a chaplain in her son's regiment alarmed George Chittenden's mother:

> I am sorry you have no chaplain in your Regiment. I think it would be a great satisfaction to have regular service on Sabbath and the assistance of a faithful Minister in sickness and death to give solace and council in the last hours of those who fall away from home and friends. (11 August 1861)

John James Hervey Love, serving as a surgeon with the New Jersey Volunteers, explained to a friend the impossibility of carrying a "church tent" with them from camp to camp and the consequent decline of religious fervor.

> It is hard, very hard for one to retain his religious sentiments
> and feelings in this Soldier life. Every thing seems to tend in
> a different direction. There seems to be no thought of God of
> their souls etc. among the soldiers. (18 October 1862)

Ann Cotton, of Marietta, Ohio, repeatedly implored her husband
to live a good, Christian life.

> I hope & expect to have you meet me with a clear conscience,
> you know that the *greatest* objection I had to your entering
> the army was the fear that you would not lead a truly christian
> life while there, & I know you will find it hard to do so. I love
> you very much dear husband but I would a thousand times
> rather hear of your death than have you live dishonored &
> disgraced. You promised to lead such a life while gone, as to
> gain the respect of your associates & to bring home a name
> of which your children can well be proud. Oh! what would
> not a loving father do for the best interest & *happiness* of his
> children. (19 October 1862)

Fear of that "old devil alcohol" and its potential for careless, possibly fatal accidents or licentious behavior preyed upon the minds
of vast numbers of wives and mothers. Harriet Jane Thompson
gingerly reminded her husband of the dangers of the habitual use
of alcohol.

> Will you let me give you a little advice. I am younger than you
> and whenever we were at home if I said anything to you about
> drinking you did not like it and thought you knew when to
> drink and when not but please do not get in the habit of it.
> You are just as apt to get in that habit as anyone. Now do not
> be angry at what I have said for it is all in kindness. (222)

Apparently her advice was ill-received, for she later wrote:

> In one of your letters that I got last week I thought you spoke
> as though you were angry. You said for me not to be fretting
> that you would try and take care of yourself. I suppose it was
> in answer to what I said about your drinking. But I cannot
> help but feel uneasy for there are quite a number in the

111

> Regiment even from our place that does like liquor and I pre-
> sume will have it and I know when you are at home you can
> most always take a drink along and I hope you are not angry
> at me at what I said. . . . (297)

Drugs, of course, were not a twentieth-century invention. Ned
Homans, of New York City, wrote his "Dear Little Duckie," Fannie
Eells, of Cleveland, Ohio, of his experiments with "the Divine Weed"
and "hasheesh." And it seems, out of curiosity, Fannie, too, tried
"the weed." Ned scolded her for her "curiosity" and promised to
give up billiard playing and cigar smoking in order to save money
for their forthcoming marriage. He did not promise to give up "the
weed," however.

> I've remembered your injunctions Darling about smoking and
> am remarkably temperate in my use of the "Divine Weed." (8
> February 1864)

In another letter, Ned commented facetiously:

> Talking about Hasheesh I mean to get you to let me make some
> long wished for experiments with that Drug—For the benefit
> of Science you know. (9 January 1864)

Benton Lewis's mother wrote from her home near Grand Rapids,
Michigan, admonishing her son not "to be tempted to do wrong
such as drinking swearing gambling or any of the vices so prevalent
in the army" (26 May 1863). She concluded her letter in true motherly
fashion: "Let me know what you get for wages and bounty and what
you done with your clothes."

At times Mrs. Lewis's uneasiness over her son was superseded by
worries over the desertion of her son-in-law, Maynard, from the
Thirteenth Michigan Infantry in October 1862.

> I tell you what Hett [Benton's sister and Maynard's wife] is full
> of trouble. She is so poor you would not know her. I never
> saw her look so bad as she does now. She never knew what
> trouble was before. She has come and her face is all cried up. . . .

She has done and said everything in her power to have him [her husband Maynard] go back to his regt but I guess she wont make it out. I am afraid he will keep on untill he is taken and then death will be his portion but I hope that may not be for her sake. (14 February 1864)

Much as women longed for the speedy return of their dear ones, the potential for desertion loomed ominously in the backs of their minds. Dissatisfaction with army life, lack of confidence in one's superior officers, poor or scanty army rations, failure to gain promotion, and concern over one's family at home often made for disgruntled soldiers and frequently led to desertions. Punishment usually resulted in imprisonment, a court martial, and possible death before a firing squad. The army's dispatch of deserters was particularly gruesome, and as a consequence, women on the homefront constantly cautioned their loved ones against taking "French leave" or deserting.

The following account depicted the grisly execution of several hapless army deserters.

Arrived at Beverly Ford, Virginia, on the Rappahannoak August 2nd 1863 remaining here until September 16. During our stay at this place five deserters were caught. They had their court martial trial and was found guilty and was sentenced to be shot. They were kept in a farmhouse about ½ mile east of camp. When the day and hour came for their execution the whole 6 corps was ordered out to witness the execution. When we got about half way to where the execution was to take place [we] came to a halt. After waiting here some time we were ordered to about face and we went back to camp. Come to find out there was 3 of those deserters were Catholics and they did not want to die untill they had their sins pardoned so their sentence was postponed 3 days. A catholic Priest was soon produced, and pardoned their sins. When the 3 days had expired we were all ordered out to witness their execution.

When we arrived to the place we were formed in two lines. The Deserters were taken from a farm house that was near by and marched down in front of us. The Catholic Priest marches with them muttering words of consolation. The martial band followed up playing the Death March and their drums were

113

muffled, making the occasion more sollem. The Deserters were marched around where their graves were dug. Their coffins which was mearly rough board boxes were plased over their graves and each one was seated on their own coffins. There each one could see his final resting place. . . . Then to that were cousins were seated on the out side. One of them got up and went and kissed the other one and bade him goodby. Then went back to his seat. Each one was then asked if they had anny thing to say. They all shook their heads no. They was then blindfolded. A squad of 60 men was marched up in front of them with loaded guns. Half of them were loaded with blank cartiges. The order was soon given to reay, ame, fire and they were all except one swept back on to their coffins in an instant. One of them would fell off one side had he not been caught by a man standing near by. The Surgeons was there to examine the remains and they were all pronounced dead. There was nothing more for us to see so we were marched back to camp.

Before leaving this plase there were to more Deserters caught. One of them was drumed out of camp. The other one was sentenced to be shot. When the day and hour came for his execution the army was moving to Culpepper. The fifth corps came to a halt to witness the execution. About the same saremony was went through.

The preceding description was corroborated by scores of other accounts of the punishment dealt out to deserters, many of whom had gone A.W.O.L. in attempts to provide for their destitute wives and children. Although the latter cases garnered sympathy from their compatriots, strict military discipline was enforced and the executions were enacted before great assemblages of soldiers in an effort to discourage future desertions.

The immorality which was thought to pervade the army camps troubled families at home. (The term "hooker," of course, derived from the hordes of women who trailed the troops of that famous general.) Husbands frequently commented on the baseness of camp life, as did Lizzie Avery's husband, George, in a letter written in June 1864:

Every day I become more & more disgusted with this moral desolation which seems everywhere to pervade the Army &

especially here [Headquarters of the First Division, Seventh Army Corps, Little Rock, Arkansas].

Men and women—married & unmarried—black & white seek only to gratify their sensual desires, & it matters little whether or not there is a comingling of the races—time and place is of little or no consideration. I do not believe there is more than one woman in a thousand in the whole southern Confederacy who is virtuous, & the men are universally libertines.

Our Army says: Well, we have only one short life to live, & we cannot afford to loose these three years. We will make the most of the opportunities presented to us; but at the same time, we will expect our wives at home to maintain a character which is beyond suspicion. Enough of this.

You will wonder what has put me in this strain. Of late I have been so situated that I could watch the progress of human depravity.

I thank God that I am free. I have no fear for the future—the one thought that I have such an one as My Lizzie for a wife is sufficient to arrest any temptation. (22 June 1864)

The droll comment by William Wilcox from Taunton, Massachusetts, in a letter to his wife, Lizzie, concerning a camp follower may not have seemed quite so humorous to Lizzie. He noted that "a girl" had stayed all night in camp in the 55th regiment and the next morning "looked as if she was played out. I should not wonder if she was" (7 November 1862).

A friend of William Hertzog's wrote *not* to his family, but to Will, describing a splendid new recruit his company had picked up. However, the new volunteer turned out to be a woman and much to the men's disappointment had to be discharged. Hertzog's friend continued his letter with details of "houses of ill repute" around his encampment in Pulaski, Tennessee.

. . . there is four hore houses here where a man can get a single Trump for 3 Dollars five Dollars all night in Tennessee money. . . . (21 November 1863)

For Harriet McLellan, anxieties about her husband that were to plague her entire married life took on new dimensions during their otherwise happy reunion in July of 1864:

> How happy to meet Lee once more. I have been true to him, has he been the same to me. Alas, I feel instinctively that he has not. Lee I fear has dissipated much. While I was praying God's mercy upon him, & living a pure & holy life, he was indulging in scenes of revelry. (30)

No doubt few husbands admitted to their infidelities; however, Rachel Cormany's husband was the exception and his confession was a crushing blow to Rachel.

> This has been indeed the saddest week of my life. My heart is almost broken. It is with the greatest effort that I keep up—I have prayed God for grace to overcome. . . . It takes all the powers of my mind and soul to bear up under this my greatest of sorrows so as to hide the anguish of my heart. I have forgiven with all my heart & have resolved to try to forget it & put forth my greatest efforts to make him happy. He seems almost heartbroken over his missteps & I feel that it needs an effort to save him from despair. He has vowed to me that henceforth no such missteps shall befall him. God will help him & we shall be happy again. (Mohr 1982, 582)

At least one irate wife accused her husband, recently returned to his company following a furlough, of having brought home "the snake bite." Mary Caroline Belcher, of Henry County, Virginia, sent her husband a scathing letter accusing him of having infected her with "the snake bite." Her husband, Granville, was shocked by her accusations and had no easy time extricating himself from the charges.

> I suppose you are very uneasy about yourself as well as myself. I was thunderstruck yesterday evening when I herd that it was whispered about in the neighbourhood that I had got snake bitten in richmond and gone home and left the bite at home. You need not suffer kow oneasiness about that. if I was under the gallows to be hanged I would say that I never tutched a woman since I left home. (16 March 1862)

Lurking in the backs of the minds of numerous women was the frightening possibility that following an action-packed, adventurous army life, their soldier husbands and sons might find home life dull and commonplace. Letters from the warfront about dreams of seeking fortunes in the West or in Mexico frightened many women who looked forward to a calm, peaceful postwar existence surrounded by family and friends. Kate Starks, hoping her husband would be discharged in two months, wrote to him on April 11, 1864:

> . . . They will be two of the longest months that ever I experienced for they will be passed in anxiety and suspense. . . . Oh how I do hope that you will get home and then we can be so happy if you will only be content to stay at home and I will try to make home as pleasant as possible. . . .

Ann Cotton, as did legions of other women, openly expressed her fears over her husband's ennui following the war.

> I am so afraid you will not be happy at home after having led such a wandering life but I will try & hope for the best. (16 February 1863)

On another occasion, she reflected on their first Thanksgiving day separation in their ten years of married life:

> I wonder if we will all be alive & together in a year from now, & if so will we be as contented & happy as we have been. I am afraid that *we* will never be so happy together again, as we were, for we will learn to do without each other, & it may be, that our love will die out altogether. You see I say *we*, but *I* do not think *I* could live at all if such were the case. I imagine all sorts of things & make myself very unhappy, but I try not to. . . . (27 November 1862)

In a letter addressed to "my own dear William," Harriet Jane Thompson coyly (or uneasily!) wrote:

> I received your kind letters . . . and I was very glad to hear that you had got to a stopping place. . . . You are liking the place so well and seem to enjoy a soldier's life so much I do not know but there is some danger of your liking it so well you will not care anything about living with me any more. Do you think

117

there is? But to be in earnest about it I think you are too true a husband for that but I am glad you are enjoying yourself but hope it is not in forming bad habits. . . . (296)

Sometime later, "Jennie" was again perturbed by her husband's continued enthusiasm for military life. Her loneliness seemed to aggravate her insecurity.

> It seems that you are enjoying a soldier's life. Perhaps you enjoy yourself better than you do at home, but if you can be cheerful it is better for you and I have wished a great many times since you left that I could be but I cannot for it seems as though I was left all alone. No one cares for my feelings nearer than a Father and Mother. But I cannot help myself and I must put up with it. I never was worthy of such a kind husband and do not know as I ever will be enough to make home pleasant to you. I do not know as I ever will have the trial of making home cheerful and pleasant to you. I do not expect it. (302)

Hundreds of letters to their lovers (a term devoid of the twentieth-century sexual implications) reflected the concerns of many young women over the psychological changes that a savage fratricidal war might induce. Might their lives of challenge and danger lure their lovers westward following the war, rather than homeward? Might their fiancés suffer a change of heart having fallen prey to the charms of some pretty new face? Might the horrors of war take their toll and send them home insensitive and inhumane?

Evidence of a rapidly developing emotional callousness offended Mary Chesnut as she observed groups of men apparently waiting on a train platform.

> I saw men sitting on a row of coffins, smoking, talking, and laughing, with their feet drawn up tailor fashion, to keep them out of the rain. War hardens people's hearts. (Chesnut 1981, 456)

Alarm bells no doubt sounded in Lizzie Little's consciousness as she read her fiancé's report from the battlefront describing his unit's reluctance to take prisoners. Lizzie responded quickly, although cautiously.

> Dearest you told me you take few prisoners. May I say a little-word, may I say, be merciful. Not that I do not think you so. But dearest as you say it is terrible to shoot a man begging for life on bended knees. I cannot think of it. It chills this Life Blood. I always told you this was a barbarous warfare, pardon dearest & understand me. I know that you probably act under orders, to an extent, but, perhaps I had better not have spoken of it but you will pardon me for saying just that one word. It seemed so terrible. (Avery 7 September 1862)

Sometime later, Lizzie wrote:

> Dearest if I could only tell how you are, if all the carnage & destruction through which you have passed had (or has) left you unharmed, I would be more content, but my loved one this suspense is terrible. (4 September 1863)

George's confession that he was "not the George of three months ago" and that he thought he would "never be a civilian again" further entrenched Lizzie's anxieties.

Martha Derby Perry's worries about her husband, John Perry, a surgeon with the Union army, must have soared when she read his letter of May 24, 1864, written from near Hanover Junction. He explained that he could "scratch only a few lines, being up to my elbows in blood."

> It seems to me that I am quite callous to death now, and that I could see my dearest friend die without much feeling. This condition tells a long story which, under other circumstances, could scarcely be imagined. During the last three weeks I have seen probably no less than two thousand deaths, and among them those of many dear friends. I have witnessed hundreds of men shot dead, have walked and slept among them, and surely I feel it possible to die myself as calmly as any,—but enough of this. The fight is now fearful, and ambulances are coming in with great rapidity, each bearing its suffering load. (184–86)

As the carnage continued, a feeling of apathy appeared to permeate all the ranks. Writing from Marietta, Georgia, on June 30, 1864, as he approached Atlanta, General Sherman also confessed to having become hardened to death and suffering.

> It is enough to make the whole world start at the awful amount of death and destruction that now stalks abroad. . . . I begin to regard the death and mangling of a couple thousand men as a small affair, a kind of morning dash. . . . (Sherman 1909, 299)

In time, women also began to question their own sensitivities. As the war dragged on and the lists of the dead and wounded lengthened, some women were shocked to find themselves becoming inured to the horror tales of the battlefield and the depredations on the homefront. Mrs. Henry Dulaney was "struck with the great change these times have effected in my own character and feelings."

> Familiarity with hardships and annoyances and difficulties of every kind have accustomed me to thinking with less distress of the deprivations of the same kind endured by our soldiers, and a constant repetition of descriptions of death and suffering has hardened me, and I hear now of acres of dead and cities full of wounded with less sensibility than was at first occasioned by hearing of the loss of half a dozen men in a skirmish. As blow after blow falls, and our hearts are in a measure seared by the constant touch of the fire, we grow graver and older, and take a great shock more quietly than we would have taken a triffling annoyance a year ago. (M. M. Andrews 1929, 53)

In recounting the details of a family with five sons fighting for the Confederacy, the father (a widower) and sisters suddenly left homeless and destitute as a result of the war, Judith McGuire's sympathy was tempered by the fact that "Sad as this story is, it is the history of so many families that it has ceased to call forth remark" (110).

For many a young lady there was always the latent fear that her handsome fiancé might find some new beauty more to his liking. Nettie Watkins bided her time and waited for young Edwin Weller to settle down and realize his true happiness lay in a permanent alliance with her. Throughout much of their correspondence, Ed was prone to tease her with letters about "the good looking ladies" he met and "the gay old times" he was enjoying in the service.

On December 24, 1863, from Wartrace, Tennessee, Ed wrote:

> There is to be a Christmas Party about two miles from here at a place called Bell Buckle tomorrow night. I have an invitation to attend but hardly know whether I shall go or not. There is a few very good looking ladies up there, and will be at the party I am told. I shall have a gay old time if I do go you can bet. (63)

In March 1864 Ed commented:

> The next day [after a dance] I called . . . on some young ladies in the aristocratic part of the town. They were Secesh but very fine looking ladies, the best I have seen in my travels in the south. We had a very fine time, got pretty well acquainted with three or four of (what they call here), the aristocracy of the south. (70)

Again from Wartrace, from Ed to Nettie:

> I am going to call on two young ladies tomorrow who live about three miles above here. They have a piano and are said to be good players and singers beside being good looking. I anticipate a gay time. (65)

Fortunately, none of the beauties could match Nettie and on November 15, 1865, Ed and Nettie were married.

Nor were wives removed from the possible estrangement of their husbands. General William Pender made the mistake of flippantly writing his wife about a very innocent flirtation carried on at a dance for soldiers in Suffolk, Virginia.

> I was at a little gathering two nights ago, and had a very nice time dancing and flirting with a very nice girl. I am trying to get her to knit you a sac for the hair, but she said that she is not going to work for my wife, but will do anything for me. . . .

Mrs. Pender was furious.

> Now, I ask you candidly, in your sober senses, why you wrote me such a thing as that? Was it to gratify your vanity by making me jealous, or to make me appreciate your love still more? You are very much mistaken. I feel indignant that any women should have dared to make such loose speeches to my husband and that he should have encouraged it by his attentions, for you must have gone pretty far for a woman to attempt such a liberty . . . nothing you have ever said—nothing you have ever done, nothing you have ever written in this whole of our married life—ever pained me so acutely or grieved me so deeply.

Needless to say, General Pender was extremely contrite and the rift in what appeared to be a very happy marriage was soon smoothed over (40–46).

In addition to their concerns over the welfare of their boys at the front, there were countless worries at home for women to contend with. Death, of course, took no holiday on the homefront. There were few families untouched by infant mortality or the death of a favorite young niece or nephew.

Ill children always evoke anxiety. During the war years the practice of medicine was still in "the dark ages" and many areas, having sent their ablest physicians to the warfront, were experiencing severe shortages of doctors. As a consequence, youngsters with high fevers, convulsions, and persistent digestive and bowel irregularities often suffered dire consequences. One can scarcely envision Susan Blackford's personal grief and the torment she must have undergone in writing her husband of the sudden death of two of their children, both within a fortnight of each other. Her trauma worsened with the loss of yet another child who died within an hour of his birth.

Measles, smallpox, and diphtheria epidemics ravaged entire towns and communities. Amanda Chittenden wrote from Franklin, Indiana, to her husband, a physician serving with the Union forces.

> For one week, including the first of last week and the latter part of the week before, there were eight deaths in town, and I think there is an average of two or three each week. (24 January 1864)

Harriet Jane Thompson detailed the illness and sorrow that surrounded her on the homefront.

> There is a great deal of sickness round here. You know William Christy. He buried his wife one week ago last Sunday and one of his girls that was grown up was buried the Tuesday following and There are six of them sick now. His wife had Typhoid fever and all the rest have the Dyptheria. Indeed I feel almost afraid to stay here sometimes. . . . (301)

From the first days of the conflict, Louisa Brown Pearl's heart was torn between her husband, a devout Unionist who fled to Detroit with their daughters to escape Confederate persecution/imprisonment, her son John who enlisted with the Confederate army, and her conviction that she must remain in Nashville to protect the family home.

> My husband is exiled on account of his northern birth & for adhering to the old government. My daughters preceded their father about four weeks. I have remained here hoping to save something from the wreck of our property & thinking I may do something for my son who is in the army fighting for the South. I am daily expecting to hear of a battle in which he must take part. (309)

Although Louisa's chief concerns naturally centered on the well-being of her son on the battlefield, her anxieties mounted with her inability to obtain any word through the lines for months at a time from her husband and daughters in Detroit. Family worries were soon multiplied by the problems of obtaining food for her twelve boarders and nine "servants" and the fears attendant on the impending takeover of Nashville by the Federal troops. The latter, the retreating Confederate troops and the Federal occupation of Nashville, constituted some of Louisa's less pressing worries according to her February 7, 1862, diary entry:

> I cannot be greatly alarmed at the thought of their coming. Fighting & the consequent suffering & bereavement, terrifies me more than any thing. (312)

Despite her bravado, Louisa's determination to remain in Nashville left her quite alone and fearful of being ordered out or burned out of the city. With the approach of the Federal troops, Nashville citizens embarked on a general mass exodus.

> . . . everybody is on the move, hacks, carriages & drays are in requisition & by twelve nothing of the kind can be had for love or money—thousands have left town & are still going, leaving their houses empty. (313)

Several sentences later, she continued:

> I will stay where I am, if the army makes no resistance. . . . I have picked up my clothing & some valuables where I can easily pack them & sit trembling by awaiting the next news. (313-14)

Although the Confederate government storehouses had been opened and provisions distributed to the citizens to prevent their falling into the hands of the Federals, the food situation gradually worsened.

> We are in anything but a pleasant situation—we have no market, no paper currency—no bread carts, no milk carts, no coal carts nor anything else. (317)

Louisa confided to her diary that her war experiences were engendering a new, somewhat frightening sense of independence that she coupled with a reaffirmation in the "will of God."

> Yesterday was my birthday. I am fifty one years old. . . . Before
> this, I should have learned the one great lesson, which is, that
> in all circumstances, even under chastisement, we should ever
> be patient & humbly submissive to the will of God. This I trust
> I do feel in some degree. All my life I have shunned responsi-
> bility & have been so dependent on the love of my friends for
> happiness—now I am compelled to think & act for myself &
> every one whom I called friends have been taken from me &
> I have only John that I can even hear from—but "There is a
> Friend that sticketh closer than a brother" & to him I can
> always go. Blessed be his name. (311)

Fears revolving around their economic woes, concerns about
ministering to the needs of their children at home, problems of operating farms or plantations with a dwindling labor supply (in both
the North and the South) led many women to question their own
mental and physical health from time to time. Emily Harris assessed
her own sanity and in an entry in October 1864 confessed to her
journal:

> It is seldom I stop to think of how I feel, much less write about
> it, but tonight I feel so unusually depressed that I cannot [help]
> casting about in my mind to see what is the matter. I left
> home . . . with Mary and Quin . . . to celebrate the anniver-
> sary of their marriage. I forgot all I wanted to carry with me.
> I lost some money. I felt unwell. I came home and found my
> sick ones not so well. I heard that the troops [with David—her
> husband] . . . were ordered *to sleep with their shoes and cartridge
> boxes on.* After supper the topic of conversation was Death. Our
> faithful dog—Boney, has howled ever since dark. What ails me,
> I do wonder? (Racine 1990, 345)

Octavia Stephens, of east Florida, became increasingly depressed
over the prolonged absence of her husband and their consequent
financial problems. On August 5, 1863, she wrote her husband:

> I think if we fight much longer we will come down as low
> as slaves, and I think we had better give up, and have our hus-
> bands with us. Slavery if such it will be, will be much harder
> when we are subdued after our husbands are killed. Oh how
> I wish the war never had started.

Fate proved to be particularly cruel to Octavia. The commencement of hostilities and her husband's taking up arms to fight with
the Confederacy marked a sudden disruption to Octavia's happy,
affluent antebellum plantation life. It was left to Octavia to over-
see the black workforce and the operations of their plantation.
Somehow tragedy seemed to stalk Octavia's every move. The first
blow fell with the death of her baby; next a Federal invasion
threatened their St. Johns River home and Octavia was forced to
leave their plantation for a refugee life with her aunt in Thomasville,
Georgia.

Throughout their separation, Octavia's letters reiterated her anxieties, her loneliness, her hope for a speedy conclusion to the war
and the safe return of her husband. The latter was not to be, however,
for in March 1864 came word that Octavia's husband, Winston, had
been killed in a skirmish near Jacksonville. One week later, tragedy
struck again with the death of Octavia's mother. That same week,
however, the sun shone when Octavia gave birth to a son.

Grief over the death of her husband and her mother a week apart
proved almost too much for Octavia to cope with.

> All looks so gloomy now. I feel as though I had but little to
> live for. I try to do my duty to my children & live for their
> sake, but have not the heart to do anything, all the pleasure
> of my life was wrapt up in Winston, he was almost my life, it
> seems as though I could not do without him much longer, I
> can not realize the whole truth, it seems dark & mysterious.
> (Spring 1864)

Anxieties also took their toll on Martha Jones, of Versailles,
Kentucky. The chronicle of worries, hardships and responsibilities
recorded in her tiny handwritten diaries was typical of the experiences
of thousands of women who were struggling to maintain at least
some degree of normal family life at home while their husbands were
serving with the armies. Whether because of disposition, delicate
health, family situation—or a deep-seated premonition of the trials
yet awaiting them, Martha Jones, and others like her, were exceedingly

anxiety-ridden. One surmises that, at least in Martha's case, their families often contributed to their anguish.

> Father came up and among other things said he heard I made Willis [her husband] go in the army. I cried nearly all day. (29 July 1863)

Each of Martha's diary entries recorded the weather, a record of her sewing for the day—"a chemise for Lizzie," "a vest for Willie"— and a summary of her daily routine. Almost invariably there was a plaintive yearning for "my dear husband," which each day grew more desperate. Martha Jones's troubles continued to mount with the loss of a daughter to scarlet fever and her consistently thwarted plans to join her husband for at least a brief visit at his warfront encampment. Her nights, according to her diaries, were sleepless and only now and then punctuated with the elation (and consequent sleeplessness) of intermittent letters from her husband. Martha's death at age thirty-seven, two years after her husband's death at Fort Harrison in October 1864, is not surprising.

The debilitating sleeplessness that haunted the nights of Martha Jones was repeated in diary after diary. Many women who could submerge their anxieties in frantically busy days met their bête noire at night. The nights became interminable for the countless women who tossed and turned and worried the hours away. All too often their sleep was shattered by hideous nightmares or portentous dreams. Harriet Jane Thompson lamented to her husband:

> Oh, how I wish this war was over. Everyone is in continual excitement and fear all the time. My fear is that you will get sick. . . . I dreamed last night you were sick and I started to come to you but I could not get started. I got to the cars and they were so full I could hardly get in but I did get a seat and then they were so heavily-loaded they could not run and it seemed as though I could hear you calling me to come to you quick and I woke up crying. You cannot imagine how glad and thankful I was to find it only a dream still I have felt worried all day for fear something is going to happen but I hope not. (224)

What little peace of mind Southern women could summon was often disrupted by the increasingly insolent, rebellious attitude of their slaves and the ever-present possibility of slave uprisings. Maurading bands of guerillas, bummers, deserters, and "pyromaniacs" kept the women of both sections on tenter hooks. These troubles, along with the rumor or reality of enemy troop movements in nearby areas, produced a constant state of agitation for many Southern women. Emily Harris succinctly expressed the latter anxiety when she reported in terror that she and her neighbors were

> in a dreadful state of excitement, almost wild. The Yankee army are advancing upon Spartanburg we fear. They are now destroying Alston and Columbia. . . . It has been impossible for me to sit or be still or do any quiet thing today. I am nearly crazy. (Racine 1990, 364)

To be sure, there were exceptions to the frenzied days and sleepless nights that kept many Civil War women teetering on the edge of physical and mental collapse. Some few Civil War diarists made no mention whatsoever of the war or perhaps alluded to it only fleetingly or tangentially. Social life, parties, visiting, fashions, family activities, and gossip occupied the greater part of their waking hours.

Most Civil War diarists and letter writers, however, described a tortured existence, clouded with constant worries about their soldiers on the battlefield and about their own personal and family concerns on the homefront. George Hurlbut's friend Angie (later to become his wife) poignantly depicted the truly courageous role of the women at home and reminded her fiancé:

> You wrote that the horrors of the battlefield would be too much for the minds of the fair sex. Am I to infer from that, George, that you think our minds are too shallow? I believe there are women who possess as brave and noble hearts as was ever called to beat in the bosoms of men. I think the hearts of women suffer more real sorrow than those that are called to still their beating upon the battlefield. They are at rest and know no more pain; we are left [to] mourn their loss, and hide our anguish deep in our own hearts. (9 June 1864)

It was these legions of women, no doubt, who gave credence to Robert Selph Henry's conviction (K. Jones 1955, v): "The harder part of war is the woman's part."

CHAPTER IV

The Refugee Experience

Such an excitement! A perfect *caravan* of *"refugees"* passed
up the road before dinner. Carriages, wagons & horses—about
50 servants in the crowd, singing "Dixie," at the top of their
voices—families from Farquier—Oh! it was a sad, sad sight—
And to think we too may be fleeing ere long—And where to?—
for danger seems all around.

Fannie Page Hume 14 March 1862

The terms "refugee," "displaced," and "homeless," familiar desig-
nations in the annals of late twentieth-century history, were also
terms applied over a century ago to some tens of thousands of itinerant Southerners during the Civil War. Although wars invariably
involve mass movements of men and supplies, the Civil War was
notorious for its upheaval of families, principally those comprised
of lone women and children.

The early months of the war saw only a trickle of "displaced persons": Confederate sympathizers caught in Federal territories moving southward and counterbalanced more or less by a similar
movement of Union sympathizers heading northward. As the war
progressed, however, and as Federal troops began gobbling up one
area after another, occupants of enemy-threatened territories hurriedly sought refuge in what was hoped would be "safe" areas. Soon
a stream of planters and small farmers were scurrying out of harm's
way—a migration quickly followed by a virtual flood of homeless

Southerners, residents of whole towns and cities who were either driven out or frightened out by the enemy. The immensity of the refugee population becomes more impressive when one remembers that battles, encounters, or skirmishes took place in every state in the Confederacy and that one after another, the South's most densely populated cities were taken over by the Union armies. In February 1862 the Rebels abandoned Nashville, Tennessee. Two months later, New Orleans was occupied by Federal troops, Vicksburg was taken over in July 1863, Atlanta in 1864, followed by Savannah, Columbia, and finally, Richmond.

For some Southerners there was a choice: to remain and attempt to protect their homes and valuables or to frantically gather up what possessions they could and strike out for the security of less embattled areas. For many, however, there was no choice. Families, forced to watch helplessly as their homes were confiscated for officers' quarters and hospitals or maliciously torched in retaliation for real or imagined offenses, were left with no option but to leave. Unfortunately, for most refugees there was not just one displacement but many. Moves were often executed in the dark of night and were almost always fraught with uncertainties of where to go, what to do, and how to secure even the barest essentials of life—food and shelter.

Although some relocations involved a traumatic wrench from family, neighbors, and familiar surroundings, other moves proved convenient, even at times pleasurable. The least chaotic moves, of course, were those familiar disruptions to both Northern and Southern family life as daughters packed up and headed back to their girlhood homes seeking the support and protection of their parents when their husbands left for the armies. Soldier husbands, deeply concerned over the welfare of their wives, often urged them to return to their family homes. It was with just such a move in mind that Granville W. Belcher wrote his wife, Mary Caroline, in Henry County, Virginia, in November 1862:

> I am very sorry that you are so mutch dissatisfied you must
> move to your Father's and stay there til I come home. if your

Father and mother are willing for you to come back and make that your home. . . .

Those were the days, one recalls, of close family ties, when many households included elderly parents, uncles, aunts, in-laws, orphaned nephews, nieces, or cousins all residing under the same roof. For the most part, the augmented living arrangements seemed to prove congenial. A married daughter accompanied by her two or three small children was usually given an enthusiastic welcome back into the bosom of the family. On occasion, however, the return home evolved into a "private civil war"—a clash of generations or personalities. Amanda Chittenden who, accompanied by her young daughter, made her wartime home with her parents in Indiana, confided in a letter to her husband:

> Mother gets so near crazy sometimes and keeps up such a continual worrying that I am almost persuaded to run away sometimes. Home is the hardest place to find comfort. . . . (13 April 1862)

For a few fortunate Southerners, their displacement involved relatively little turmoil. Kate Robson, for example, was living "the good life" in Atlanta with her husband and two children in an expensive, newly built home. Each afternoon, according to her husband's directions, their coachman, resplendent in livery, appeared with their phaeton and horses ready for an afternoon of "making calls" or shopping. A "good cook" her husband "had bought" in Madison prepared the family's meals; Kate's clothes were cared for by a black maid who had attended her since childhood and had been presented to her as a wedding gift by her father. A nurse girl cared for the children; yet another "servant" was responsible for the washing and ironing; the household chores were given over to an Irish housekeeper. Kate's good fortune miraculously continued, however, and as the Federal troops advanced into Tennessee and northern Georgia in November 1863, her husband, in an effort to protect his family and his finances, sold his prosperous grocery business in Atlanta and "invested his entire capital in a plantation and negroes" in Albany, Georgia. Kate later recalled:

> My third baby Paul was born in Atlanta in November 1863, and when my husband told me he had sold our home, I had a nervous chill that put me in a bad way.

Even so, Kate's "chill" was minor compared to the problems of her fellow Atlantans.

Although the move necessitated a change of residence, Kate was apparently one of the few Southerners who remained relatively untouched by the war. She later noted, "We lived in peace and plenty in Albany." With the help of ten or more servants, the Robsons (Kate's husband, perhaps by virtue of age or substitute, did not serve with the Confederacy on the battlefield) continued to give parties and engage in an active social life. In her reminiscences she admitted that she suffered only in spirit: "If I had a relative as near as a cousin killed in war I do not know it." Kate Robson was the exception rather than the rule, however.

Many of the earliest displacements involved loyal Northerners who were caught in the wrong place at the wrong time. With the commencement of hostilities, scores of Union citizens engaged in businesses or working as teachers in the South yet unsympathetic to the Southern cause were forced to return to their northern origins. Miranda Spalding's sister, a Northerner living with her husband in Texas, wrote of her harrowing experiences of being driven off their plantation as the Federals approached. Despite her husband's having taken the Oath of Allegiance, they were stripped of their cattle and farm animals. In a desperate effort to return to the North, Mary and her little children took refuge for four weeks in a soldier's tent in New Orleans before boarding a steamer on the Mississippi. En route to Union territory the ship underwent fierce shelling from the Confederates. Mary described the horrors of the trip in a letter to her sister.

> Oh Miranda could you have been an eye witness to the scene
> when myself and children were huddled down behind the coal

and the cannon and shell of the Confederates was tearing into our boat from Arkansas shore. Two returning soldiers who had been in the War three years and escaped were killed dead on our board. (2 December 1866)

Unfortunately, these were merely some of the preliminary episodes in this poor woman's catalogue of wartime tragedies. During the course of the war her daughter died, her son-in-law was killed in service, she adopted the orphaned grandchild, her husband apparently failed in business, her brother was incarcerated as a prisoner of war, and as a final blow, her son succumbed to a protracted illness. Such tragedies were not isolated cases.

For many families there was little or no choice about moving. Transfers, banishments, evictions, and mass evacuation orders by either Federal or Confederate officers offered no alternatives. Innumerable displacements, for example, resulted from orders issued by the Confederate government for the protection of government offices and workers.

Early in 1865, as Sherman approached Columbia, young Malvina Black Gist (later Waring), a young war widow employed by the Confederate Note Department then located in the South Carolina capital, registered considerable reluctance to being moved with her department to the "safety" of Richmond.

> Must I go with the department to Richmond? . . . it is high time I was having some experiences out of the ordinary, and if anything remarkable is going to happen, I want to know something about it; it might be worth relating to my grandchildren! Anyhow, it is frightfully monotonous, just because you are a woman, to be always tucked away in the safe places. I want to stay. I want to have a taste of danger. *Midnight*—But I am overruled; I must go. My father says so; my mother says so. (T. Taylor 1903, 274)

Knowing that Columbia was in imminent danger of a Union army takeover, Malvina left the city "strangely laden."

> . . . I feel weighted down. Six gold watches are secreted about my person, and more miscellaneous articles of jewelry than

would fill a small jewelry shop—pins, rings, bracelets, etc. One
of my trunks is packed with valuables and another with provisions. (T. Taylor 1903, 275)

In many respects, Malvina's experiences were typical of those of
thousands of other refugees throughout the South. There were
delays en route; caring people befriended the stranded girls and hos-
pitably provided them with food and shelter; they suffered loneliness and severe food shortages once they arrived at their destination.
When Malvina's group was detained on the way to Richmond, "utter
strangers" met them in carriages and took them into their homes
for the duration of their stay in Charlotte.

Homesickness and worry about her family were a natural concomi-
tant of Malvina's move. Anxious over the fate of her family during
the subsequent sacking and burning of Columbia, Malvina despaired:

> Shall I ever look into their dear faces again. . . . People who
> have never been through a war don't know anything about war.
> May I never pass through another. Why will men fight? Espe-
> cially brothers? Why cannot they adjust their differences and
> redress their wrongs without the shedding of woman's tears and
> the spilling of each other's blood. (T. Taylor 1903, 275)

Later, upon learning that Columbia was "in ashes," she wrote:

> It [war] is a crushing machine, whose mainspring is anxiety,
> whose turnscrew is apprehension. Are my brothers all dead? Are
> my father and mother still living? These questions put me to
> the rack when I allow myself to ask them. (T. Taylor 1903, 277)

As refugees from throughout the South crowded into Richmond,
food scarcities became acute, prices escalated to unheard of heights,
and Malvina became just one of the thousands suffering from the
shortages. On March 8 she confided to her journal:

> Wish I had been taught to cook instead of how to play on
> the piano. A practical knowledge of the preparation of food
> products would stand me in better stead at this juncture than

any amount of information regarding the scientific principles of music. I adore music, but I can't live without eating—and I'm hungry! I want some chicken salad, and some charlotte russe, and some oxplate, and corn muffins! These are the things I want; but I'll eat anything I can get. Honestly, our cuisine has become a burning question. (T. Taylor 1903, 279)

A few days later her hunger pangs had intensified.

There are so many interesting things I could and ought to write about, but I just can't, because I am so hungry! And having nothing to eat, I am going to bed to fill up on sleep. (T. Taylor 1903, 281)

On March 29, Malvina was anticipating yet another move.

Mr. Duncan brings us the weightiest news. The Confederacy is going to the dogs—or did he say the devil? . . . We may have to fly from Richmond as we did from Columbia. It is a profound secret as yet; but he warns us to be ready to leave on quick notice. Are we to be driven to the wall? I can't believe it! But somehow—somehow—my heart is as barren of hope tonight as the great Sahara of water. (T. Taylor 1903, 283)

For many other women as well, it was mandatory that they leave their native or adopted homes. Not a few women were banished as punishment for "crimes" against the Federal government. Elizabeth Eggleston, of Vicksburg, incurred the wrath of the Federals and was greeted at her door on November 22, 1864, by an officer bearing the following order:

Madam:
I am directed by the Maj. Genl. Comding to inform you that transportation will be provided for you tomorrow—the 23inst—and you will hold yourself in readiness to move to Black River—Also that if you are not ready at the time mentioned that you will be simply taken outside the picket line and be obliged to furnish your own transportation.

Very Respectfully
J.S. Curtiss Capt. & Pro. M.

> You will have your baggage ready to be ex-d by an officer this
> evening who will seal up your trunks.

Despite the fifty-nine year old Mrs. Eggleston's reputation for aiding
anyone in need, Rebel *or* Union, she was charged by General Napoleon
Dana with being a "general busybody, with Rebel interests, Rebel
philanthropist, mail receiver, carrier of smuggled funds to prisoners in jail, etc., etc." and was banished from the city (G. Cotton
Collection).

For having waved their handkerchiefs at John Hunt Morgan, the
Confederate raider and hero, when he appeared near their home
in Harrodsburg, Kentucky, Lizzie Hardin, her mother, and sister were
expelled from Federal territory. Sue Ramsey, the teenage daughter
of the James G. M. Ramseys, was forced to leave Knoxville for singing "Dixie" and associating with known Secessionists. Accused of
laughing at the funeral procession of a Union soldier, Eugenia Phillips
was banished from New Orleans by General Butler (see page 34).
Rose O'Neal Greenhow enthusiastically engaged in espionage for
the Confederacy and was arrested, imprisoned, and sent south. "The
Quinine Lady," Louisa Buckner, was jailed for buying up and attempting to distribute quinine to the Rebels. Scores of other women
were expatriated or imprisoned as spies or traitors.

Thousands of families, including vast numbers of women who were
desperately struggling to keep their families sheltered and fed while
their husbands were with the Confederate forces, were overnight
turned into refugees when the Union army ordered mass evacua-
tions of particular areas. Although Sherman's orders calling for the
evacuation of Atlanta following his conquest and subsequent occupation of the city in the late summer of 1864 were condemned as
cruel and inhumane (even by many Northerners), the general, about
to embark on his historic "March to the Sea," was too shrewd a cam-
paigner to allow a belligerent populace to jeopardize the rear of his
armies. Furthermore, Union military strategists were already well
aware of the advantages to be gained by forcing still more refugees
into already congested Confederate territory. Food supplies, Sherman

reasoned, should be directed to his troops rather than diverted to feed hungry Atlantans, and he adamantly refused to rescind his orders.

Sherman announced flatly in his September 4, 1864, letter to General Halleck:

> If the people raise a howl against my barbarity and cruelty, I will answer that war is war, and not popularity-seeking. If they [Atlantans] want peace, they and their relatives must stop the war. (Sherman 1957, 111)

Shortly after the arrival of the troops, commodious family homes and stately old churches were quickly confiscated and converted into hospitals, barracks, and officer's quarters. Mary Rawson, who was living with her parents in Atlanta during the war years, described the plight of defenseless Atlantans, evacuated at first house by house and shortly thereafter en masse.

> When we were at breakfast this morning Grand-father came and told us that Aunty had been ordered to leave her beautiful home to give place to a *Yankee colonel* who had given her only half a day to move all her property. O cruel soldier! could you not be a little more lenient? Could you not allow her one day for this work?

As Mary helped her aunt pack

> . . . officers were there dictating as to what should be carried away and what should remain and continually repeating the injunction of haste, haste, forgetting that haste makes waste. Tongue cannot express her trouble in leaving she has no home to go to elsewhere. (3)

The problems encountered by Mary's aunt were simply a dress rehearsal for the agonies the Rawsons were about to undergo. For days the family had vacillated over whether to move farther south with relatives—but where her father would be subject to the draft—or whether to head north without money or means of support.

Money to travel was of the essence, however, and Federal orders prohibiting the sale of cotton or tobacco, all of which was to be impressed by the government, seriously threatened any serious plans
for a northerly move. Only properly signed papers would allow Mr.
Rawson to sell his provisions, and day after day Mary's father wear-
ily made the rounds of army offices. Just as the situation appeared
hopeless, army officials suddenly relented, the necessary papers were
secured, and the frenzied packing of trunks was intensified. At last,
the family decided that braving the ice and snow of Iowa winters
was the wiser alternative to risking the conscription of Mary's father
in the South.

Days already too short to accomplish the herculean task of moving were further complicated for Mary and her family by women

> who came to see if we wished to sell anything and on answer-
> ing in the negative they said "well we dont care you have got
> to leave and when you are gone we will come and take what
> we want." And on going out one of them snatched a spur which
> was hanging in the passage saying "we will take this anyhow."
> Oh I was so angry!
> The evening set in and this was to prove our last night in
> our dear sweet home. As I lay in bed long after all quiet the
> house and cheerful paper on the wall seemed to find utterance
> and sorrowed audibly for their departing occupants. . . . So one
> by one the room and pieces of furniture gave vent to their feel-
> ings in words. Then all together they asked us Oh how can
> you leave us. . . . (6)

Finally, the last trunk was made ready and

> On dressing preparatory to the journey I found I had still a
> short time which would be unoccupied. This I determined to
> pass among the flowers. So wandering among the familiar walks
> and beds I gathered some favorite roses. But it was not long
> ere a call from the house recalled me from my reflections. . . .
> The wagons had arrived and the baggage was being rapidly
> stowed away for transportation. The[n] came the parting from
> loved home servants and kindly associations. There was
> mammy who had been living with us ever since I can remem-
> ber. . . . There was Charlotte with her little ones around her

tearfully shook my hand. . . . Taking a sad farewell from servants
and friends we seated ourselves in the ambulance which slowly
moved out of the yard.

In a few moments we found ourselves on the hill on which
stood our school house and from which a fine view of our place
could be obtained. Never, never did this hill look so pleasant
in the setting sun as it now did, and now as I look upon the
groups of oaks and hedges of arbortia I for the first time could
appreciate the words of the song which after [offer] such a beautiful sentiment "the dearest spot of earth to me is home sweet
home." (6)

Thanks to patience and diligence, Mary's father was successful in
obtaining the wherewithal to hire a boxcar and move his family and
many of their possessions out of the city; however, other Atlantans
had neither Mr. Rawson's clout nor capital. Mrs. W. C. J. Garrison
dramatically described the siege of Atlanta and the subsequent eviction of her family. The shelling usually took place at night and during one bombardment, Mrs. Garrison was horrified at seeing a baby
killed in its mother's arms in the streets.

. . . the women and children would have to get of[f] and go
to a mile or two out on the woods on the Side the Southern
army was Located. There would be hundreds going along
together Old men and old woman to[o] feeble to walk would
be carried. About this time my Father had to go to the front.
He was a Captain and after he left us we never Saw him agan
as he was killed. The men and women and children Suffered
with hunger moore than words can express and those in
Sherman's track Sufered for clothes and everything that humanity needs.

On September 2, 1864, Sherman Marched into Atlanta and
took possession of everything, and every boddy. He Sent his
officers to every house to tell the peeple that they ware his prisners. So of course we had nothing els to do bur submit. . . .
Sherman soon got tired of his big Family of women and Children So on the Fourth of September he issued an order exiling
the citizens. we were all Sent out and met at Lovejoy Station
by the Confedert Army. we were turned out in the woods like
cattle. I don't know the exact number but that [there] were
Several Thousand of us. . . .

You speak of tears and weeping but we knew what tears were then. I often wondered if my mother ever slept any. no matter when we woke up at night she was awake. We never undressed for we never knew When we would haft to go. After leaving Atlanta the exiles managed to get to Macon Where we War agan taken prisners by Sherman. He captured Macon with one Battle. He sent us from their Just as he did from Atlanta. This time there was an exile camp prepar[e]d for us a way down at Dawson, Ga where we were provided for.

Union generals, of course, held no monopoly on despotically preempting private property and ejecting the owners. Confederate officers as well helped to swell the refugee ranks with their confiscation and eviction orders. The trials of the Warner L. Underwood family of Bowling Green, Kentucky, for example, dramatically depict the fate of hundreds of border-state families.

During the Confederate occupation of Bowling Green, the Underwood family became prime targets for suspicion and violence as a result of their staunch Union sentiments. Warner Underwood, who knew both Lincoln and Davis well, was shrewdly foresighted in predicting the devastation that would engulf the South as well as the North were there to be a protracted war. As a popular public speaker and writer, his views (frequently reiterated in his twenty-one-year-old daughter Josie's patriotic outbursts) were well publicized, a fact which greatly contributed to the family's precarious situation in a hotly divided Kentucky. As the Confederate forces invaded the area in the fall of 1861, Josie Underwood watched helplessly as the troops took over their yard and barn, plundered the orchards, and milked their cows.

It was only a matter of time before acquisitive Confederate officers began eyeing the Underwood's attractive Mount Air home as potential living quarters. During the ensuing weeks the Underwoods stoically sought to disregard the flurry of rumors about their possible eviction until one cold winter evening their worst fears became reality. In her diary, Josie recreated the terrifying scene awaiting her as she entered the library.

Three soldiers standing in the glare of a bright fire—my dear
father seated on the opposite side of the hearth with a paper
in his hand, evidently a military paper, leaning toward the fire
so that the light of the blazing logs would fall on the paper
that he might read it. Little Johnny by his side with his hand
on Pa's chair and in the background, Jake with some plates and
a tea [cup] in his hand—for he was setting the table and had
come in the library naturally curious. Just as we entered, my
dear father looked up from the paper, to the soldiers saying
"Immediately is a quick word, gentlemen, to a man who has
lived at a place 40 years." "What is it," we asked—going to Pa's
side. Taking Ma's hand in a strong loving and supporting clasp,
he quietly held the paper so we could see it and this is what
we read: "Warner L. Underwood and all persons occupying the
buildings on Underwood's hill, commonly known as "Mount
Air," are required to vacate the premises *immediately* by order
of the General commanding, etc. etc."

It was like a blow that stunned us. Ma sank in a chair, white
and speechless. The orderly I think he was, said "I am sorry
sir to deliver such an order—but had no choice." Pa ordered
his horse—saying I will ride with you to headquarters—we cannot leave tonight. The soldiers went out and waited around
the porch till Pa's horse came. Pa comforted Ma as best he could
and we waited anxiously for his return. When he came we knew
before he spoke that the order remained, only the time was
extended to the 3rd, tomorrow, when we must go, God knows
where or for how long—perhaps forever. (Nazro, 110)

Unable to secure a pass to take them through the lines of Louisville,
Josie's father made arrangements to house his family in an old cabin
about fifteen miles distant, and the Underwoods immediately set
about relocating their slaves with neighboring planters and sending
off their books, piano, and some of their best furniture for safekeeping with friends.

All day we have been trying to pack our things—dismantling
the dear old home—not knowing where we are going, how long
we will stay—or to what we are leaving Mount Air. It is hard,
hard work and these vile Missouri soldiers and even their
officers—are just taking possession of the house—tramping all
over it—handling things and twice today I took things out of

the hands of men who were evidently going to pocket them. A Captain came up the steps to my room, when I was trying to pack things, marched in without knocking and when I arose indignantly and said "Well, sir" he stood looking around and said "Oh! I was just looking over the house—I think I'll have this room for myself." (Nazro, 111)

The Underwoods saw not only the house but much of the remaining furniture appropriated as well. Josie continued:

Col Rich, of the Missouri Regiment asked Ma to leave her room furnished as he wanted to bring his wife there and he would pay for the furniture. Hurried as we were—no time to pack and properly store anything as much as Ma hated to part with her furniture, it seemed the best thing to do, so Ma fixed the room as nicely as possible even leaving the bed made and changes of sheets etc., in the closet and towels on the rack—being glad we would have the extra money for these things—in our uncertain banishment. (Nazro, 112)

Leaving some valuables stored in a "press" in the library they begged Colonel Rich to "let it remain locked—which he said he would do. . . ." The next day, when the Underwoods sent for the money for the bedroom furniture, the request was met with derision. Colonel Rich merely laughed, saying "Did your mother think I was going to pay Union people for anything. That's a good joke. This is only a *small confiscation* we call it" (Nazro, 113).

The confiscation of Mount Air apparently still did not satisfy the enemy, and within a matter of weeks the Underwood household was further disrupted when a longtime friend, jeopardizing his important Secessionist position in the town, arrived in the stealth of night to warn Josie's father of his pending arrest the following day. John Burnam had ridden hard following the Council meeting

to warn Pa for, he said—they might call his action what they chose—if they found it out—but he could not see a friend, to whom he owed as much, further persecuted and stand idly by. He said he must get back to town before day, that no one would know of his absence and he did not want to know what Pa would do—but the only chance was for him to leave. (Nazro, 119)

With no alternative other than being arrested and sent south, Josie's father made his middle-of-the-night escape, leaving his family to struggle along in their tiny cabin (Nazro, 119).

Life had barely settled down for Josie and her mother when three weeks later they were heartened to learn that the Rebels were leaving Bowling Green and they could once again return to Mount Air. Their return, however, left them in a state of shock. Mount Air had been burned to the ground.

> We had not gone very far through the fields before we saw that the trees around the house were all charred and burned and that only the gable end of the house was standing, a smouldering smoke rising about it and as we drove up through the garden—all trodden down like an old common—the last standing wall fell in with a crash and we arrived only in time to witness this final catastrophe and standing there helplessly watched the smouldering ruins of our once beautiful and happy home. Both orchards were cut down—the avenue of big trees leading toward town were all gone—not a fence left on the entire 1000 acres and only the barn and two cabins left of all the buildings. Ruin devastation and desolation everywhere! (Nazro, 125)

In the chaos that prevailed as the Federals bombed the town and the Rebels beat a hasty retreat from Bowling Green, Josie and her family remained with friends, hiding out in a basement while the shells burst round about them. Josie herself narrowly escaped decapitation as shell fragments flew through the yard, even into Aunt Sallie's biscuit dough!

> The biscuit making needless to say was abandoned. Pandemonium reigned supreme. Soldiers were rushing wildly through the streets—cavalry and infantry—horses were being taken anywhere and everywhere found citizens, men, women, and children, white and black were fleeing over the hills to get out of reach of danger—whilst the steady Boom-swish—shriek and *bang*—of cannon shot and shell went on. . . . (Nazro, 127)

Later, Josie wrote:

> The dusk and the darkness came on illuminated in a fearful
> way of burning buildings all over the town—which the Rebels
> had fired before leaving. The biggest fire being half the stores
> on the square one of which belongs to Pa. (Nazro, 130)

Following the Federal takeover, Josie was forced to admit:

> We find that Union soldiers are not much more regardful for
> personal property than were the Rebels—only now Pa has some
> chance of getting his rights redressed and that too, without
> insult. (Nazro, 138)

When the Confederacy approached Harriette Keatinge's husband
(an engraver and still a British citizen) to organize and manage the
Confederate Bank-note Department, the Keatinges decided to move
south and cast their lot with the Rebels. According to Mrs. Keatinge,
their years in Columbia, South Carolina, were halcyon days—until
the onslaught of Sherman's troops in February 1865. The brutal
arrest of her husband and the seizure of their home as officers' headquarters quickly convinced Mrs. Keatinge that the best course for
her three children and an eventual reuniting with her husband lay
in applying for permission to leave with the army as refugees. Permission granted, Mrs. Keatinge, according to instructions, hurriedly
packed two trunks to be forwarded to her at a later date (baggage
valued at $23,000 which she never saw again) and "left the house
to the mercy of the mob."

All along the way on the exhausting trek from Columbia to
Fayetteville, North Carolina, swarms of impoverished women and
children, left completely devoid of food or shelter, joined in the motley
procession trailing the troops and their endless entourage of wagons
and ambulances.

> As no house, barn, store-house or mill was left standing on
> their march but, was burned to the ground by the soldiers, there

was nothing else these people could do. It was either starvation or follow the army for the bacon or hard-tack it gave them. (11)

Of the march, she wrote:

> Every village was laid in ashes, every store, house and fence was burned, every mill was first used to grind their stolen wheat and corn, and when there was sufficient flour and meal for their nee[d]s, the soldiers burned the mill, wheat and corn leaving nothing for the defenceless women and children to eat, or homes to cover their heads. . . .
> As the troops marched through the country, seldom along roads, but over fields, gardens etc. they destroyed everything. Men were detailed to precede these troops and search the woods and country for cattle or horses, when they accumulated a large number they were driven in herds and corralled in some large field. . . . The stolen sheep, cows, pigs, chicken etc. were corralled and the commissary Officers selected those they wanted, then the rest with the horses were shot and left to rot in the sun. This was sometimes a forty-eight hour work. Poor pillaged desolate South! (12)

At night as Harriette Keatinge sought the cool refreshing night air outside the small tent that she and her three children were allotted, she surveyed the encampment of sleeping soldiers mounded grave-like as far as the eye could see.

> Having the appearance in the moonlight of an immense closely filled cemetery, with about three feet between the graves. Above, the stars like so many eyes of those soldiers who had passed over, looking down on the sufferings caused by the cruelty of men.
> Try to imagine a delicate frail woman sitting in front of a camp fire, dependent for food and in constant danger of her life, the only being awake, keeping watch over her children, at the mercy of man and beast. (14)

She queried her reader:

> Can you imagine what it is like to ride all day in a wagon, no rest, no comfort, day after day, no chance to take a bath

or even a wash, to beg for a tin basin of water to wash your childrens faces and your own before going to sleep at night, no towel, no toilet articles of any kind but a comb. To see your clothing growing more ragged and dirty day after day and none to change with, your face and back blistered by the sun and dust and no place to rest your weary, oh so weary! back or head until you get into camp at night? With a baby in your arms, with scarcely nothing to feed her—breast milk dried up from want of nourishment—crying herself to sleep, hungry and sick, if it had rained all day no place to lay your blanket but in the wet and mud—to hush your little ones to sleep and roll them away from the cold and wind. It is impossible for me to describe all this. . . . Oh my God! what days and nights those were. (13–14)

Responsibility for much of the havoc wrought upon unprotected women and their property resided not with unruly, drunken soldiers, but rather with the roving bands of foragers and bummers accompanying the troops. Frightened women chose to abandon their homes and take up the refugee life rather than suffer harassment from merciless stragglers.

As the struggle for Vicksburg began to take shape, the war, heretofore conducted in seemingly remote areas, was suddenly brought home to twenty-year-old Kate Stone and her family. Early in 1863, days and weeks of anxiety eventually culminated in the Yankee forces spreading over the area around Milliken's Bend, Louisiana, a short distance from the family's beloved Brokenburn plantation. As the Stones and their neighbors stood by helplessly, army foragers greedily plundered the countryside appropriating provisions, horses, and slaves for their own special purpose. Ultimately, the questions of whether or when to abandon Brokenburn and move westward were decisively answered one March afternoon. While Kate and "Little Sister" were visiting their neighbors, the Hardisons, a band of armed blacks who had been terrorizing the area suddenly reappeared, stormed into the house and held the girls and their friends at gunpoint while they robbed and pillaged the rooms.

After carrying on this way about two hours they lit matches, stuck them about the hall, and then leisurely took themselves off, loaded down with booty. (197)

Kate and "Little Sister" hastily put out the fires, gathered up their neighbors and what few possessions they could, and raced home, panicked by the men's threat that "they were coming back in a little while and burn every house on the place. . . ." Kate continued:

The next evening, the Negroes from all the inhabited places around commenced flocking to Mr. Hardison's, and they completely sacked the place in broad daylight, passing our gate loaded down with plunder until twelve at night. That more than anything else frightened Mamma and determined her to leave, though at the sacrifice of everything we owned. (197)

The Stones' middle-of-the-night flight on horseback proved an equally terrifying experience. Their path led them through dark, boggy terrain and across bayous created and deepened by the water released when the Federals cut the levees. Their horses became mired in the swampland; their clothes were soaked to the waist; they lost their way; and once Kate heroically swam a bayou carrying her young cousin to safety on the opposite shore. Knowing the Yankees would be in hot pursuit, the little group of seven, badly frightened, family members at one point barely succeeded in evading the enemy by pushing off across a bayou in a leaky dugout, just as the Federals caught up with them at the shoreline. For the next six hours they continued in the boats "in the beating rain and the sickening sun, sitting with our feet in the water," escaping with their lives but with little else. They lost most of their clothing, "all of our likenesses and all the little family treasures that we treasured so greatly."

At Delhi, Kate pictured a scene reenacted in hundreds of towns across the South by refugees caught up in the mad scramble to obtain passage on already overcrowded trains.

The scene there beggars description: such crowds of Negroes of all ages and sizes, wagons, mules, horses, dogs, baggage, and furniture of every description, very little of it packed. It was just thrown in promiscuous heaps—pianos, tables, chairs, rose-wood sofas, wardrobes, parlor sets, with pots, kettles, stoves, beds and bedding, bowls and pitchers, and everything of the kind just thrown pell-mell here and there, with soldiers, drunk and sober, combing over it all, shouting and laughing. While thronging everywhere were refugees—men, women, and chil-dren—everybody and everything trying to get on the cars, all fleeing from the Yankees or worse still, the Negroes.

All have lost heavily some with princely estates and hundreds of Negroes, escaping with ten or twenty of their hands and only the clothes they have on. Others brought out clothes and household effects but no Negroes, and still others sacrificed everything to run their Negroes to a place of safety.

Everybody was animated and excited. All had their own tales to tell of the Yankee insolence and oppression and their hare-breath escapes. All were eager to tell their own stories of hard-ship and contrivance, and everybody sympathized with everybody else. All were willing to lend a helping hand and to give advice to anybody on any subject. Nearly everybody took his trials cheerfully, making a joke of them, and nearly all are bound for Texas. Nobody "crying over spilled milk." Not a tear all day, though one knows there were heavy hearts bravely borne. (191)

Eventually, after several stops along the way, the Stones secured lodgings with the hospitable Wadleys, compatriots living near Monroe, Louisiana. There they stayed for seven weeks of rest and recuperation before continuing their way to Texas for two-and-a-half years of refugee life. Fortunately, their stay at the Wadleys' turned into a most enjoyable experience, thanks to the friendship Kate de-veloped with Sarah Wadley, a young lady about Kate's age, who shared Kate's fondness for diary keeping.

As a border state, Missouri was another of the areas torn apart by internal strife throughout the war. Martha Lamison's refugee ex-periences in many respects mirrored the trials of families who be-came victims of that conflict.

The Lamisons had set out from Ohio eagerly anticipating a promising future in southwestern Missouri. There on 1,300 acres of land they had built a home and

fenced in a garden and yard. We were just getting fixed to live when the rebellion broke out. There was a company formed calling themselves the Homeprotecting guard but in fact they were the home destroying pestilence. They sent us word that if we did not leave in twenty-four hours they would hang the men up like dogs, there was but a few Union men in there. They were nearly all *Copperheads* so we had to leave I had a baby only 2 weeks old that was the first day I had been out doors and we were obliged to pack up and leave. The last night we spent in our own house we expected the Rebels would be on us before morning. Every noise or stir I expected to hear their wild yells. Issac laid with his Revolvers and rifle on either side. The long night wore away. The next day we bid adieu to our homes driven away by *Southern* rule and Southern soldiers. The next day after we left they came on to wreak their vengeance on us. We were gone so they burnt our houses destroyed our fences but we got safe into Kansas. We stoped at Fort Scott. There were several regiments of Soldiers quartered there. There was no hour of the day or night that I would not hear the beat[?] of the drums. I could rock my children to sleep under the shadow of the flag.

We stayed there until Price's Army came in. They had a Skirmish before our door . . . ordered all citizens to leave town if the Rebels gained the day he was going to burn the town. Such another time I hope never to see agin. There was soldiers marching and hauling their heavy guns over the ruf stones, women and children crying. We could not hear ourselves speak. Issac was sick with Billious fever. The children and Myself all had the chills. We only got about a mile out of town when there came on a thunder storm and it was so dark we could not see anything except by the flashes of lightening. We drove out at one side of the road and hitched our horse to a tree and set there all night in our waggon. I expected it would kill Issac but we got on as far as Ossawotomie where Father Isaac and the children got so sick we were obliged to stop and rent a house.

Those were dark days, dark in more ways than one. We were all sick driven away from our home and property our money gone and to add to the rest of our troubles I was nearly blind I could not read the coarsest print could not tell a man from a woman as far off as acrost the room. I could not sew or scarcely cook a meal of victuals but as I got my health my eyesight returned but I shall never be as I was before my hair is sprinkled with grey and at thirty-two I am as old as I ought to be at fifty. We stayed at Ossawotomie about 2 months then we went up to Topeka. We stayed there about one year then come on into Nebraska. Stoped in Plattsmouth and stayed until the Indian trouble broke out when we left and came back again to Palmyra. . . . we live in town in a rented House. We do not own any property, have nothing but a span of horses and wagon and one cow. . . . (Lamison 29 November 1863)

For women who were neither evicted nor evacuated, staying or leaving necessitated a momentous decision. Some deemed it wiser to leave their homes, move their slaves, and live out the war as refugees. Others hoped "protection papers," a guard, or ultimately innate good conscience would help save their property from depredation. Abandoned property was naturally more tempting to the enemy and its wake of ruffians and predators. However, even occupied homes were subject to relentless, repeated searches and ransacking, horrors which were documented by the testimony of thousands of both Northern and Southern victims. "Protection papers" often proved worthless and "guards" could be oblivious bystanders as their cohorts plundered and ravaged. Some "guards" spent their time on verandas sleeping off the previous night's drunken orgy; others gleefully joined in the pandemonium.

Decisions were further complicated by the fear that accepting or securing a guard could oftentimes be misconstrued as a traitorous act. Federal General Williams's offer of a sentinel to protect Sarah Morgan's Baton Rouge home presented numerous problems.

We were so distressed by the false position in which we would be placed by a Federal sentinel, that we did not know what course to pursue. As all our friends shook their heads and said it was dangerous, we knew full well what our enemies would say. If we win Baton Rouge, as I pray we will, they will say we asked protection from Yankees against our own men, are consequently traitors, and our property will be confiscated by our own Government. To decline General Williams's kind offer exposes the house to being plundered. In our dilemma, we made up our minds to stay, so we could say the sentinel was unnecessary. (Dawson 1960, 66)

As her family agonized over whether to seek the protection of her brother, a Union sympathizer, and move to Federally occupied New Orleans, or whether to set out for northern Louisiana, Sarah Morgan attempted to paraphrase Shakespeare.

"To be, or not to be: that's the question." Whether 'tis nobler in the Confederacy to suffer the pangs of unappeasable hunger and never-ending troubles, or to take passage to a Yankee port, and there remaining, end them. Which is best? I am so near daft that I cannot pretend to say; I only know that I shudder at the thought of going to New Orleans, and that my heart fails me when I think of the probable consequence. . . . (Dawson 1960, 342)

Even when circumstances allowed time to pack, there was always the problem of *what* to pack. Sarah Morgan found it difficult to decide between "the dispensable" and "the indispensable."

I wandered around this morning selecting books alone. We can only take what is necessary, the rest being left to the care of the Northern militia in general. I never knew before how many articles were perfectly "indispensable" to me. This or that little token or keepsake, piles of letters I hate to burn, many dresses, etc., I cannot take conveniently, lie around me, and I hardly know which to choose among them, yet half *must* be sacrificed; I can only take one trunk. (Dawson 1960, 38–39)

A few days later the cannonading of Baton Rouge made up the Morgans' minds for them, and Sarah, her nearly hysterical mother, her two sisters, and five nieces and nephews grabbed a few personal items and fled to temporary safety outside the city. A block from home, however, Sarah, with the shells bursting all around her, made a mad, dare-devil dash back home, not once but twice, to retrieve more comfortable shoes, toothbrushes, combs, starch ("to cool our faces"), a lace collar, hair pins, and sundry "little things" (Dawson 1960, 41–42).

Some moves, even ones made with great deliberation, often turned out to be impractical moves. Sarah Wadley's family looked forward to a happier, more secure life in Georgia. However, the Union army aborted their trip at the Mississippi.

As the enemy appeared to be nearing their Monroe, Louisiana home, the William Wadley family, after months of belabored indecision, attempted to gather up their household belongings and their Negroes and head eastward. Days and weeks were devoted to elaborate preparations and the packing and repacking of enormous wagon loads of clothing and provisions. From the start, however, their trip was beset with troubles. First, just before they were to leave, Sarah's sister came down with diphtheria and the family seriously considered giving up their journey. That setback and their difficulties in obtaining their "passes" to travel should have served as warnings of the litany of misfortunes soon to follow.

Before their caravan even got underway, the Negroes became drunk and rowdy while waiting for the wagons to start. Next the Wadleys rode into a hornet's nest. Their wagons broke down regularly and repairs entailed countless delays. Mr. Wadley became seriously ill en route; they struggled through swamps, mud holes, ruts; cantankerous mules caused untold problems as they strained under the burden of excess baggage. The travelers suffered from too much rain, too much sun, and too much mud.

At Natchez, the Wadleys were finally thwarted in their attempted move by the refusal of the officers to promise them safe conduct across the Mississippi River. As they retraced their steps, the Wadleys' frustration over the failure of their long anticipated venture proved to be the least of their worries. Once again their travel was plagued by wagon rollovers, by breakdowns, by wrong roads, by illness, and by fatiguing, frightening overnight encampments. Their ill-fated three-weeks' journey finally ended, the Wadleys set about the backbreaking work of unpacking and resettling.

Decisions about when and where to move created tremendous problems for even the most experienced planter or businessman. For a wife alone, with several small children to care for, the uncertainties were almost overwhelming at times. Although Mary Elizabeth Howes's husband was apparently exempt from the draft because of ill health, she was left alone for fifteen months to manage their six children, their home and their servants, while her husband endeavored to start a new business in the South. For almost nine months, from May 1862 until January 1863, Mrs. Howes did not hear a single word from her husband. At long last his letter instructing her to join him solved her dilemma of when to leave, but decisions about what to take and what to sell and how best to get through the lines left her on the verge of a nervous breakdown. In desperation she confessed to her diary:

> Some say I can go & some say I cannot. . . . I do not know what route to take. No way seems safe enough to venture. . . . I am so perplexed what to do about going & how to sell my things & whether I can get through the lines. O I am so troubled & from want of means. (14)

A few days later:

> I have sold all my beds, & . . . my blankets today & some other things. I do trust I have done right in selling these articles. I am sorely tried. Oh God am I doing right. (16)

Women who before the war had been solely dependent on a husband's plans—or whims—now took on the responsibilities of directing their own futures. Consultation with one's soldier husband was usually an impossibility. Margaret Eliza Lewis McCalla, for example, became worried when Federal troops threatened Knoxville in August 1863. In a letter to her husband then serving as a captain with the Confederate army, she sought his advice.

> I feel a great deal of anxiety just now about our situation here and if I could leave without too great a sacrifice would

155

feel tempted to do it but do not know how I could move with but two horses. Do you think my best plan would be to go through Virginia by railroad? If so I would have to use the money you deposited with me. I would then sell every thing I could here hire out the negroes in S.C. rent a little house somewhere and keep Martha at home. But I ought not perhaps to be troubling you with such things just now as you doubtless are busy enough without any such trouble and I will endeavor to do the best I can. (Partin 1965, 42)

Her husband's response urging her to

remain at home, move nothing, be ready to run Dennis and the boys and horse and buggy in case of a raid and try and see if you cannot gather and dispose of the crop. I do not think East Tennessee will be given up. . . . (Partin 1965, 42)

became lost in the irregular mail service of the times and Margaret failed to receive his "shortsighted" instructions until eight months later. The delay proved fortunate, however, for Knoxville was occupied within days after her original letter and Margaret's move became imperative.

One of the last to leave Morristown, Mrs. McCalla hurriedly packed up her mother, her three small children, "the negroes," and all the possessions she could manage and left for Chester District, South Carolina. She carried with her "all her trunks and bedding, crockery ware and a good deal of kitchen furniture . . . all my wool . . . your clothes . . . all my meat and lard," but she brought "no cows except the white cow and the french broad with their little white calves." She sold his "new hat" and her wheat, but was forced to leave behind "the bedsteads and bureaus, his books, and her piano" (Partin 1965, 43).

Mrs. McCalla's friends and neighbors proved remarkably resourceful in providing her with money and a mare for the move. A Union man, however, a Mr. Staples, was anything but helpful. In a letter to her husband she added: ". . . and it would please me very much to hear of Old Staples getting his reward at the hand of the Southerners when we get possession of East Tenn" (Partin 1965, 44).

In time she wound her way to her sister Effie, in Chester District, and moved into a house owned by her sister which, with the help of neighbors, she made habitable. From the very start, Mrs. McCalla was determined to make her new home into a farm which she could "run for a livelihood and profit"—an endeavor which she successfully carried through in the following months. Although both she and her husband regretted the loss of their valuable collection of books, she later wrote: "I am too thankful for my escape to grieve for what I left behind" (Partin 1965, 44).

After months of being subjected to Federal rule, Margaret Crozier Ramsey left her Knoxville home in July 1864 under a flag of truce. Mrs. Ramsey's troubles then, and in the months to come, must surely have seemed insurmountable. Prior to her departure, she despaired:

> We were robbed of everything—houses burned, ladies insulted. I asked one man how he would like for his mother and sisters to be so treated, he said if they were rebels he would think it all right. The poor ignorant fellow did not know anything about the causes of the war or what he was fighting for. (4)

Like many of her compatriots, Mrs. Ramsey, whose husband's personal and Confederate business kept him out of the state much of the time, had long belabored the wisdom of whether "to refugee or not to refugee." Finally, the banishment of her strong-willed daughter, Sue, for displaying overt Confederate sympathies, convinced Mrs. Ramsey that the time to move had come. Despair and uncertainty about the trip, however, continued to plague her as she explained in her journal:

> We were leaving our native home knowing that we should never return or where we were going or what sorrowful news we should hear after arriving in the Confederacy. (1)

The trials of Mrs. Ramsey's move south via boxcar and "a rough open waggon and broken down horses that had to stop every half hour to rest" soon became inconsequential compared with the tragic news that awaited her as she neared Bristol. There she received word that her dear son Arthur, who had been wounded in battle and was reportedly doing so well, had died of complications following the amputation of his foot.

> I returned to the room threw myself on the bed and cried out in agony—O that is too hard—too much—more than I can bear. (3)

Mrs. Ramsey was inconsolable. Earlier she had suffered the loss of two daughters and now was beside herself with anxiety over the fate of a second son serving with the Confederacy.

> When dear C. [her daughter] died it was a very sore trial and I did nothing but weep for months after. And then dear Ethie but I did not feel like "replying against God." But this was such a shock I wish for death. (3)

Another time she wept:

> I was greatly shocked—cannot express my feelings—had no desire to live. I was so anxious to come on his account, now I had lost my interest in anything. (9)

During the war years while her husband was away on duty with the Confederate army, Martha B. Jones, of Versailles, Kentucky, was consumed by anxiety about whether or not to leave her home and friends and take temporary refuge with her children in Canada. Her diary and letters were tortured debates over whether she and her children could continue to remain much longer in their home. Her son was unable to attend school and conditions, she wrote in a letter to her husband, were such that they could not stay on their farm unprotected.

> If we were in town, I should feel less apprehensive—land is selling very high now. Ma could easily sell her farm and we could remove to Canada or elsewhere & await the termination of the war. I have always been most confident of seeing a cessation of hostilities this fall, but *now* I confess I have abandoned that hope. (11 September 1864)

One month and two days later, Martha Jones's husband was killed by a sharpshooter near Fort Harrison.

Arriving safely at one's destination was clearly no small accomplishment for vast numbers of refugees. Next came the difficult problem of securing lodgings and food. Union victories had set off a chain reaction of escalating numbers of refugees, increased shortages, and soaring prices, and as a result, hotels and boarding houses became prohibitively expensive. Many displaced families turned in desperation to tents, boxcars, and even caves. As an expedient, hundreds of women who could somehow afford to rent a room or two began cooking their meals in a corner of their cramped quarters ("room keeping"), a practice which must have created havoc for the fire departments and fertile fields for insect proliferation. Even those who succeeded in locating rooms or homes with cooking facilities were still hard pressed to buy, rent—or improvise—dishes, silverware, or cooking utensils. It severely tested the fortitude and determination of even the strongest willed women to keep a family together and provide some rudiments of home life during their refugee wanderings. One such courageous woman was Elizabeth Baker Crozier.

In a desperate middle-of-the-night hegira southward, Elizabeth Baker Crozier's physician husband and two daughters fled their home near Knoxville as the Federals approached in August 1863. Hoping to protect their house and at least some of their possessions from the inevitable burning and looting that accompanied occupation, Mrs. Crozier and her two youngest children remained at home. Her attempts to save the house, the piano, the furniture, and clothing went for nought, however, and she and her youngsters soon embarked on an incredible saga of displacement and deprivation. For over eight months, during which time she refugeed for a few weeks or sometimes a month at a time with family and friends, she had no permanent address and no knowledge of the whereabouts of her husband and their two daughters. Many weeks and many miles later, there was a joyful reunion with her daughters and her husband, who was "busily engaged" in a hospital in Covington, Georgia.

Although at last they were together as a family and at least had a roof over their heads, they of course had no household equipment and were reduced to borrowing everything.

> Our cooking vessels consisted of one broken skillet which we did our frying and baking in for sometime. Sometimes it was burnt and others not done. We had a stone bowl which was used for a great variety of things. When we arose in the morning, we all washed in it, then it was thoroughly scoured with soap and scalded with water, then the bread was made up. After meals the dishes were washed in it and then it was nicely cleansed and was kept to hold our drinking water between meals. Often we used it upon the table with soup. It was the chief article in housekeeping.
> I had a beautiful shell that I used as a butter bowl. We often had trouble in getting the fire torch to stand up whilst we were eating. The Doctor made a few things of clay, some plates, a candlestick and some other things, but nothing tasted good from them. We often entertained our company in the summer evenings with the light of a fire torch in the fire place.

Following the war, thousands of refugees returned to find their former homes in ashes, only blackened brick chimneys ("Sherman's sentinels") still standing to remind them of happier days. Now and then returnees discovered their homes ransacked and mutilated but still livable. Even the trip home, however, was often a tortuous, desperate journey. Many never returned to their former homesites, but sought to begin life anew in a totally different location.

With the return of peace and the completion of the doctor's work at the hospital at Cuthbert, the Croziers were further subjected to innumerable frustrations in reaching Tennessee. A railroad ticket, supplied by the United States Medical Director, would supposedly take them to Clarksville. However, two-and-a-half miles out of Chattanooga a surly conductor announced that they would be unable to travel further on their ticket and summarily ordered them off the train and onto the siding. With no money and a great disinclination to borrow any, they eventually secured a room for the night. The next day one of their daughters pawned "her much prized watch for money to take us to Clarksville." Arriving at Clarksville, Mrs. Crozier lamented, "We had just five dollars, no home, no acquaintances, that we knew of, and it was raining." Fortunately, a former pastor's sister took them in for a week until they could find a house, where once again they were confronted with the problem of setting up housekeeping anew.

A remarkable compassion and willingness to share with those who had been dispossessed characterized the women of both sections during the war years and the decade following. Fellow Clarksville residents quickly came to the Croziers' rescue with

> furniture, beds, covering, chairs, tableware, knives, flour, sugar, coffee, hams . . . sometimes money. The young ladies got up a subscription for a horse for the Doctor—all and much more for which we were very grateful. We have not words to express the gratitude of our hearts for these great comforts and blessings.

Securing adequate clothing presented yet another hurdle for refugees. There were innumerable cases similar to that of the two ladies described by Mrs. Crozier who were "out in the yard when they were spied by the enemy, only had on their sunbonnets and calico dresses" and were ordered to leave, their home put to the torch moments later. Mrs. Crozier was just one of the grateful recipients of kindnesses from friends—and from complete strangers.

> At one time we were very scarce of clothing for our family, when my daughters each received a nice dress . . . from friends, and one time, my daughter being in a millinary one day remarked that was a beautiful hat and so becoming to her ($15.00). The next morning, it was sent to her as a present and as she knew no one at the time of the remark that was present, she never knew whom it came from. And at another time, a large box was sent to us and opening it, we found many valuable and useful articles, such as were greatly in need. There were sixteen dress patterns, a bolt of sheeting, several suits of clothing for the Dr. and son, a bolt of domestic, 2 boxes of stockings, socks and everything by the wholesale—linnen . . . gloves, needles, pins, thimbles, 2 bolts of calico with many other little things all being a great relief to us.

Successful adaptation to the refugee life often hinged on an individual's ability to cope with new surroundings and reduced circumstances. Here, once again, refugees had a choice to make: they could engage in bitterness and complaint, making life miserable for themselves and their associates, or they could accept their displacement stoically and attempt to make the best of it.

In her boredom with her relocation, Sarah Morgan bemoaned:

> I would stand another four months of Yankee rule, rather than live that long in Clinton. Yes! and would undergo a weekly shelling besides! (Dawson 1960, xxii)

When Meta Morris Grimball and her family were forced to evacuate their plantation, they took up residence in a wing of a building at St. John's College in Spartanburg. Mrs. Grimball was less than delighted with their accommodations which in comparison with their earlier, far more luxurious homes were very cramped and uncomfortable indeed. In the absence of congenial friends and the socializing that had previously been such an integral part of their lives, Mrs. Grimball found refugee life considerably unappealing. However, in time she came to accept her situation somewhat resignedly and probably spoke for hundreds of her fellow refugees when she admitted in her diary:

> Now I have no home for our Plantation is broken up, our house in Town is only a hire one & upon the whole I may consider myself at home any where my family & trunks . . . are. (76)

The reception accorded the itinerants along the way as well as at their destination was an all-important factor in the refugee experience. In some areas they were accepted with anything but enthusiasm. In particularly congested communities, newcomers were labeled "renegades"; newspaper editorials urged the refugees to "move on." Not a few residents resented the growing numbers of strangers and the competition they presented for the rapidly disappearing food supplies. Kate Stone, so kindly treated by the Wadleys en route, later encountered hostility and discrimination in Texas. Margaret Ramsey despaired to her diary:

> There is but little generosity here—the people have no sympathy for refugees and those who have lost all, because they lost their negroes they feel that loss is greater than anyone, and have no time to think of those who have lost houses, lands, etc. (11)

On another occasion she complained:

> On many accounts it is an unpleasant place to live . . . no sociality—no friendship—no attention to strangers—We have been sick here—Mc Sue and I—no one seems to care or came to enquire if we needed anything. . . . (12)

Most of the diarists, however, marveled over the warm reception they were given in their host communities. As noted, one of the most astounding features of the entire refugee situation was the incredible generosity of great numbers of Southerners, as well as Northerners, who graciously opened their doors to the homeless for days and weeks at a time. Relatives and friends might be expected to share their homes with family members, but during the war years refugees found themselves welcomed into the homes of perfect strangers, many of whom undoubtedly felt fortunate not to be wearing refugee shoes themselves. Sarah Wadley's diary (and those of most Southern women) was filled with notations of her family's gratuitous hospitality to their homeless countrymen as well as to ill and wounded soldiers and the wives or brothers who had come to care for them.

> We have a poor woman staying here tonight for whom my heart bleeds, she went down to the camps on horseback with her baby, only seven months old; to nurse her husband. When she arrived there this morning she found him dead and buried. She is now on her way back to her sad home. She is a very young woman, apparently quite poor, and has no parents living. As I hear her deep and frequent sighs from the adjoining room I can only pity her and be grateful for all the blessings

that surround me. Oh! how many, many such widows this war
will make, nay, has already made; scarcely a family but has lost
one member. (15 October 1862)

When Kate Stone and her family emerged from their wild flight
from Brockenburn, it was the Wadleys who made room in their home
for the five dejected travelers. There two young diarists, Kate Stone
and Sarah Wadley, met and became friends, each recording in her
own diary her impressions of the visit. In catching up on her diary
writing on May 16, 1863, Sarah Wadley noted:

> About the 20th of last month, Mrs. Stone (a lady from the
> swamp) came to Mother to get board for herself and family
> for a week; they had escaped from the swamp in haste and at
> night, lost all their clothing, except what was contained in one
> small trunk, and abandoned their house and furniture entirely
> to the Yankees and *negroes*. Mother . . . could not refuse
> persons in their situation, so they came, Mrs. Stone, Miss
> Kate, Rebecca and Jimmy and Johnny, they are a very pleasant
> family. . . . Miss Kate is a very sweet young lady, so unaffected
> and agreeable.

The proposed one-week stay soon lengthened into an apparently
pleasant seven-weeks' visit. As the Stones were packing to leave, Kate
wrote in her diary:

> Our delightful sojourn at this place is nearly over, and it will
> be many a weary day before we are so comfortable again. They
> are the very kindest people we ever met, and Mr. Wadley, who
> returned a few days ago, is just as generous and kind as all the
> others. To crown all her good deeds Mrs. Wadley this morning
> refused to take a cent for our board all these seven weeks.
> Mamma insisted on it, but both Mr. and Mrs. Wadley declared
> they could not think of such a thing, saying Mamma would
> need every cent she had before she got settled again. Our own
> relations could not have been kinder, and we were total
> strangers to them when they took us in out of the goodness
> of their hearts. May God reward them, we never can. (Stone
> 1955, 220)

To a few women the refugee life was kind, introducing them to new friends, providing them with extended support groups, encouraging them to develop outlets for their talents and pent-up energies. For most women, however, the refugee life was a mean, miserable, loathsome existence, a desperate search for safety, for shelter, for sustenance.

Lee's surrender April 9, 1865, came as a shock to many Southerners, especially the war hawks and visionary die-hards who advocated continuing the struggle in the trans-Mississippi. In the months that followed most of the refugees emerged from their transient quarters and slowly threaded their way back to what had once been home. Somehow, however, things had changed. Their refugee experience, the war, had marked them for life. Home would never be the same again.

CHAPTER V

The Ravages of War

> Destruction stalks every where, and actual starvation is staring the remaining inhabitants in the face. For forty miles there is not an ear of corn and scarcely a cow or a hog. Little children cry for bread, and gaunt famine with a visage of misery and want flies like a destroying angel over the land.
> —*George Chittenden to his wife Amanda 25 July 1863*

War, of course, plays few favorites and death and adversity continuously preyed on their helpless victims in both the North and the South. However, their greater proximity to much of the fighting coupled with the complete upheaval of their economic system rendered Southern women even more vulnerable to the ravages of war. True, some lucky Southerners, by virtue of their fortuitous geographical situation or their cunning in relocating in "safe territory" out of harm's way, escaped the war's being literally brought to their very doorsteps. Thousands of others, however, were forced to watch in horror as their homes and fields were torched, their farms and provisions ransacked, their valuables, everything they held dear, confiscated or wantonly destroyed. Untold numbers of women suddenly found themselves homeless and penniless, reduced in a matter of hours from affluence to penury, scavenging for food, often dependent on handouts from the enemy for the basic necessities of life. The savage pillage, theft, and unconscionable demolition of private property by the soldiers of both armies as they invaded and occupied new territories proved to be among the era's greatest challenges to women's patience, fortitude, ingenuity, and courage.

Although Northern soldiers were credited with much of the villainy, they certainly were not the only culprits. Bushwackers and "bummers" following or tentacling out from Northern as well as Southern armies accounted for millions of dollars worth of damage. Liberated slaves sought retaliation upon former owners and neighbors; deserters embittered by their war experiences looked for recompense from the civilian population; even Southerners themselves vented their anger on displaced Union sympathizers—and occasionally on one another.

In the years following the war, the culpability of officers for the looting and burning of private homes and property has been angrily debated. Even the most conscientious of commanders, however, probably could have had little control over the elements of mass hysteria that pervaded the times. Personal morality and values were frequently superseded by mob rule. Conscience often gave way to most soldiers' convictions that if they did not appropriate food and household goods, the next fellow certainly would.

With the disruption of supply lines, always a top military priority, foraging raids became essential to the survival of the armies. And since most soldiers cooked their own food in camp, "official" foraging parties were enthusiastically augmented by individual and company forays into the countryside for meat and produce to supplement paltry or monotonous army rations.

Perry Mayo, of Calhoun County, Michigan, wrote home proudly describing his company's excursions into the fields around Warrenton Junction, Virginia.

> Since leaving the James River we have had some hard marches, but we get along very well as we could get plenty of fruit and green corn. It would have done you good to see the army go into the cornfields and orchards on the route. They carried every ear of corn out of one fifty acre lot in half an hour, and it was good corn, too. (215)

Edgar W. Clark, of Lansing, Michigan, recalled being bivouacked in northern Virginia, and after hearing chickens clucking in a nearby barnyard, several of his fellow soldiers disappeared, returning moments later with several nice, plump chickens. Edgar noted that he

> took some pains to pull the feathers off in one piece thinking that perhaps I could have some feathers to sleep on that night for the first time since leaving home . . . there was so few that we did not feel them very much but still enough to say that we slept on feathers that night. . . .

Sometime later he wrote of camping near a field in which two or three hundred sheep were grazing.

> But in the course of the next twenty-four hours I do not think there was one left, but lots of pelts scattered over the ground.

On January 31, 1863, Joseph B. Fuson reported in his diary:

> The boys went out jahawking last night and came in with 35 chickens and turkeys and one Rack Koon—we live now tip top.

The armies' confiscation of food, horses, and rail fences (for firewood), popularly referred to as "pressing," no doubt helped the common soldier to rationalize his own wholesale looting of private homes and barnyards. "To the victors belong the spoils" became a byword during the war.

As the months lengthened into years, the utter devastation of the South became a Northern war tactic designed to force the enemy into submission. Criticism still clouds Sherman's infamous march across Georgia and through the Carolinas. However, in reviewing the maniacal fervor of Southern patriots, even after their cause had long since been doomed, one perhaps can better understand the Union army's recourse to drastic measures. The South, most Northerners agreed, must be "brought to its knees."

The word "bummer" became famous during the war as the term contemptuously applied to soldiers or civilian outlaws accompanying the armies (particularly Sherman's) whose vicious plundering and vandalism terrorized the countryside. A correspondent for the *New York Herald* penned the following description of "bummers."

> Any man who has seen the object that the name [bummer] applied to will acknowledge that it was admirably selected. Fancy a ragged man, blackened by the smoke of many a pine-knot fire, mounted on a scraggy mule, without a saddle, with a gun, a knapsack, a butcherknife and a plug hat, stealing his way through the pine forests far out on the flanks of a column—keen on the scent of rebels, or bacon, or silver spoons, or corn, or anything valuable, and you have him in mind. Think how you would admire him if you were a lone woman, with a family of small children, far from help, when he blandly inquired where you kept your valuables. Think how you would smile when he pried open your chests with his bayonet, or knocked to pieces your tables, pianos, and chairs, tore your bed-clothing in three-inch strips, and scattered them about the yard. The "bummers" say it takes too much time to use keys. Colour is no protection from these roughriders. They go through a Negro cabin, in search of diamonds and gold watches, with just as much freedom and vivacity as they "loot" the dwelling of a wealthy planter. . . . There are hundreds of these mounted men with the column, and they go everywhere. Some of them are loaded down with silverware, gold coin, and other valuables. I hazard nothing in saying three-fifths (in value) of the personal property of the counties we have passed through were taken by Sherman's army. (Poe 1961, 74–75)

Despite later protestations by their officers to the contrary, vast numbers of soldiers on both sides were under the impression that their superiors acquiesced in their confiscation of any and all Southern property. In a letter home, Gilbert W. Chapman boasted

> The boys live high. We have the liberty to take anything that we want and so we do—prayers and tears are of no avail. Since the Pennsylvania Campaign when the rebels took everything from the union people of Pennsylvania even to the clothes that they wore. (Chamberlain 4 October 1863)

Other soldiers operated on what seemed to them at least a moral distinction between plundering for food and plundering out of purely malicious intent. Lucius Embree explained in a letter from his encampment near Springfield, Missouri, to his sister:

> We have plenty to eat now. The Boys Jayhawk a great many things. Last night they went from our mess into the Town of Springfield broke open a Cellar—and took all the preserves and canned fruit Nine or Ten Men could cary Together with a couple bushels of the finest Apples I ever saw. There are two or three gallons of as nice chery preserves among them as I ever ate. We have them buried in the Tent with straw and blankets on them. So that if search is made there will be nothing seen but our beds. At first I thought it was stealing to take things in that way, but a "change has come over the spirit of my dreams" and I consider Jayhawking a legitimate trade particularly when the articles taken are food for Soldiers. (29 November 1862)

Most soldiers, however, appeared to blur the distinction, giving little thought one way or another to the ethics of pillaging and looting. Both were blithely accepted as facts of war. In fact, D. G. Crotty, of the Third Michigan Volunteer Infantry, thought it was doing the Rebels a favor to "gobble up" their turkeys.

> Now the good people will remember us, for we spared them the trouble, in a good many instances, of feeding the corn to their turkeys and chickens, which they may need before this cruel war is over. (69)

Anne Frobel and her sister Lizzie, of Fairfax County, Virginia, were just two of the countless women subjected to repeated invasions of soldiers and their subsequent encampment in the fields and yards surrounding their homes. Home owners who were not summarily evicted were incessantly hounded to provide food and accommodations for officers and their wives or lady friends who were accompanying them. Daring not to resist, the beleaguered women prepared hundreds of meals and were rewarded for their efforts by seeing the enlisted men brazenly carry off their poultry and produce. During their encampments the soldiers leveled the woods, depleted the orchards and gardens, and even made off with the Frobels' bees and beehives. Late in the summer of 1861, Anne lamented in her diary:

> This year we had a fine field of rye, as beautiful as I ever saw, as tall or taller than the ceder hedge, with very large finely filled heads although it had been considerably injured by the soldiers continually tramping through it. We succeeded in getting it harvested, and the shocks covered the ground. One evening a very black looking thunder storm was seen approaching, we were looking out noticing the movement of the clouds when all of a sudden the whole field of shocks just lifted up simultaneously and walked off. The pickets had pulled down the fence at every station and stacked the rails so as to form little huts and thatched them thoroughly with the rye. We never saved a single grain. In a few months it all came up along the road side as thick as thick could be. (30)

Despite Anne and Lizzie's being two lone, unprotected women, their attempts to secure guards usually proved futile.

> Lizzie is constantly sending and writing, and sometimes going herself from camp to camp begging and entreating the officers for a guard. They all know how we are here alone, and how shamefully we are treated for they have all ranged round the country as far as they dare go, and acquainting themselves thoroughly with every bodys business. Some times they will allow me and her a guard, and sometimes, "no *Madam* it is Rebel property and we can not make use of our men to protect rebel property," and no protestations to the contrary, or no pictures of our distress will move their, adamantive, obstinate hearts. When they do send us a guard it is four or five men, and we have them all to feed, and at times we are in the greatest straits, send and withdraw them all. Some times when the Soldiers are in the greatest furore, taunting and tearing, cursing yelling, they will trifle and dally until they think all the mischief is done and then send the guard for us to feed. (10)

A year later, on September 30, 1862, Anne reflected on the ruthless destruction of their property.

It is just one year this day since the officers of the Sedgwick brigade came to let us know they were just about moving to occupy this place, and O what a day of consternation and terror it was to us, I shall never never forget! Then we had every thing in abundance. The farm in beautiful order, luxuriant crops growing—everything that heart could wish. And now what a contrast, our beautiful home laid-waste and destroyed, every thing swept off and gone, all the out houses, barns, cattle sheds, fences, hedges, all our beautiful, valuable timber, every tree gone, all our orchards, every thing—only desolation remains—and we almost in a state of starvation and beggary. Nothing remains to us but the old house we live in, and that they constantly threaten to burn over our heads—and to knock down with the cannon at Ft Lyon. (74)

Unfortunately, there was more harassment to come, for Annie and Lizzie were soon overrun by yet another onslaught of Yankees entrenching themselves on the Frobel property and appropriating whatever remaining produce met their fancy.

The front field is literally filled with wagons and horses, all standing thickly together in rows, with streets between. There seems to be more wagons and horses than soldiers, and more officers than men, and as many run away negroes as both, and women innumerable. In one regiment alone, the 6th New Jersey of 150 men, there are twenty seven women. The tents are spread all over the fields and around the house, and although there is such a display of tents, the whole brigade has not as many men in it as Col- Wards regiment had in it last winter, when it was camped on the same grounds. . . . They all seem to think they are fixed down here for the winter, and say they chose this situation because it is less exposed to the wind. No one who has had no experience in these matters can comprehend, or have the slightest conception of the feeling of utter hopelessness, and sinking of heart that comes over one at the thought of being surrounded, and imprisoned and exposed to all the insults and annoyances for months of these detestable abominable people. (77)

Once again, their guard, particularly when he was most needed, proved worthless:

> Our guard drew his pay on Saturday and has been drunk ever
> since and useless to us. He went off this morning under the
> pretence of mailing a letter and staid away all day, and we have
> been tormented with soldiers. (72)

By the spring of 1863 Anne had almost given up caring what would
happen to her and Lizzie.

> Threats are made and I expect it will not be long before the
> same scenes will be enacted here, and it will be our fate to be
> driven forth homeless, to seek a shelter whenever [sic] we can
> find one, but we have been so persecuted and tormented for
> the past two years that I almost cease to care whether they do
> so or not, but rather think it would be a relief, destitute though
> we may be, we could not be much more so than we are now,
> they have taken every thing from us, and to find enough to
> feed us all, is as much as we can do. (126)

Rumors of an impending enemy invasion sent area residents into
a frenetic attempt to outsmart the vandals by ingeniously secreting
their possessions. Now and then advance notice allowed for elaborate packing of books, linens, china, and kitchen utensils for removal to friends' or relatives' homes. Usually, however, there was
little time for the systematic removal of valuables. In haste, women
buried their silver under rose bushes; some hid their jewelry in bird
nests, in trees, or in outhouses. One woman, having carefully secured
her valuables in her ball of yarn, continued knitting industriously
as the greedy soldiers searched her house. The same woman cleverly
concealed bags of flour slipped into the pillowcases on the beds—
and they too went unnoticed. (That ploy was a particularly clever
one, for at the time flour was selling for as much as $500 a bag.)
One old gentleman "banked" his friends' gold watches in his peg
leg. Annie Laurie Broidrick owed her inheritance of the family silver to a "servant" who buried it in boxes under an old storeroom
where it was walked over by unsuspecting soldiers for three years.
Unfortunately the family's cache of money, hidden behind an old
picture, was detected during the first raid on the house. "Layering"
clothes often proved a shrewd maneuver until ultimately their bulk

completely inhibited movement. Sarah Jane Sams wrote her husband that she

> emptied the cotton out of one of our mattresses and filled it very nicely with all of our cloth, blankets, sheets and gentlemen's clothing, sewed it up like a mattress and put [it] under the rest, whether they discover it will be proved by tomorrow I fear. (4 February 1865)

The next day she dressed her children in

> two suits of underclothing and their dresses and wore the same quantity myself, besides three small bags containing needles, cotton and flax thread, tape and buttons. I am a burthen to myself but must try to save a few articles. (5 February 1865)

One Southerner cleverly concealed gold coins by covering them and sewing them on her clothes as buttons. Others stuffed their treasures in their muffs or in the puff in the backs of their skirts. Unfortunately, attempts to hide their costly gold and silver jewelry around their waists or in their hoops were often foiled when callous (or curious!) officers ordered body searches.

Cora Owens detailed in her diary the search of a Mr. Hicks's Louisville home on suspicion of his being president of a "private society of treason."

> They searched Mrs. Hicks & Mrs. Furgerson her sister. Col Mundy, said that the searcher was a woman dressed in Fed. uniform, but Mrs. Hicks believes it was a man. They told her if she did not quietly submit to an examination that it would go hard with her husband & child under arrest & also with the other children. They took off of her everything but her chemise & felt her skin & pinched her & told Mrs. Furgerson that she was very *plump*. They read Mrs. Hicks' letters, tore up her carpets & bedclothes in search for flags [rebel]. (Spring 1863)

Apparently Mrs. Hicks succeeded in outwitting her searchers for the diary continued:

After Mrs. Hicks was searched she went upstairs to dress &
wrapped the flags which she had in the house about her person & dressed before the Feds could find it out. (Owens, Spring
1863)

Voicing her outrage at the insensitive searches of person, Mary
Chesnut complained:

> Our women are now in a nice condition—traveling, your false
> hair is developed & taken off to see if papers are rolled in it—&
> you are turned up instantly to see if you have pistols con-
> cealed—not to speak of their having women to examine if you
> are a *man*—in disguise. I think *these* times make all women feel
> their humiliation in the affairs of the world. With *men* it is on
> to the field—"glory, honour, praise, &c, power." Women can
> only stay at home—& every paper reminds us that women are
> to be *violated*—ravished & all manner of humiliation. How are
> the daughters of Eve punished. (Chesnut 1984, 145)

Among the most threatening invasions of privacy for scores of
women was the fear of their personal letters being read by guffaw-
ing, derisive soldiers. Dozens of diarists described the emotional
trauma of burning personal letters before they could be read and
scattered by the enemy. Catherine Devereux Edmondston despaired:

> . . . I am utterly paperless! Every letter I possessed, mementoes
> of those I loved and lost long years ago, literary memoranda,
> receipts, abstracts, records of my own self-examinings, poetry—
> all, all destroyed. As I look at my empty cabinets and desks
> I feel the void their emptiness causes within my heart. A hatred
> more bitter than ever rises within me. I never thought to shed
> such tears as the burning of Mr. Edmondston's letters to me
> wrung from my eyes. (Edmondston n.d., 103)

Hiding corn and slabs of meat called for great resourcefulness.
General John W. Geary, of the Union forces, wrote to his wife from
his camp near Acworth, Georgia:

> The provisions of the people is also taken without compunc-
> tion, and they are left in utter want. Sometimes they resort

to every subterfuge to hide from the prying eyes of our men
their bacon and other dried meats, one which was found out
yesterday caused no little merriment; several families had
clubbed together to "save their bacon," which they buried in
several handsome *graves* near their houses. Somehow or other
the soldiers smelt the matter, and resurrected about half a ton
of most excellent hams, from the aforesaid "graves." The fame
of the resurrectionists soon spread far and wide, and every grave
was in danger of being opened, but the fourth attempt brought
the business to a close, for the only thing exhumed from it was
the body of a dead rebel, whom our skirmishers had just killed
and buried. (8 June 1864)

There was almost no end to the suffering and deprivation endured
by many Southern women. A brief catalogue of Mrs. Fraser's trials
tends to trivialize her anguish, yet at the same time it presents a
realistic picture of life on the homefront. During the early months
of the war, Mrs. Fraser's house in Marietta, Georgia, which she shared
with her five unmarried daughters, also became home for her eldest
daughter and her nine children when their Florida residence was
destroyed by Union and guerilla forces. Camp fever suddenly swept
through the family, and in a brief period of three months, Mrs. Fraser,
a widow, lost four grandchildren—two to the fever, one to a freak
gun accident, and one on the battlefield.

There was more heartache still to come. Within the year Mrs. Fraser
received news of the death of her only son at Gettysburg. Some
months later when the Yankees occupied Marietta, her fields and
gardens, ripe for the harvest which would provide food for the year,
were decimated by the troops. Fence palings, outhouses, livestock,
pots and pans, linens and silver disappeared almost overnight. Daily
the din of 1,200 soldiers camped around her house was pierced
by the pitiful screams and moans of men undergoing amputations
on the surgeon's table set up under her window. There were further
complications when Mrs. Fraser herself underwent serious abdomi-
nal surgery that saved her life but left her a cripple. Twice attempts
were made to set fire to her house; insults and threats were everyday occurrences. By the end of the war Mrs. Fraser concluded:

> Trouble is now broadcast over our land, and it is dreadful to
> think of the thousands . . . who are now without bread and
> many without homes. To sum up, the whole of our beautiful
> sunny South has been mostly devastated and how they are to
> stand the insults and degradation they have to go through daily
> at the hand of a ruthless foe . . . is a problem that is hard to
> solve. The true Southern people begin now to think it better
> to have fought on until all men, women, and children had been
> laid in their graves.

Although most of Minerva McClatchey's neighbors fled in haste
as the Union forces approached Marietta, Georgia, in preparation
for the 1864 siege of Atlanta, Mrs. McClatchey, with one son and
a niece, determined to remain with the plantation, hoping to save
it from the Yankees. Her husband, ineligible for service with the Confederacy because of the loss of three fingers in a mill accident, had
moved with most of the slaves and the family treasures to the safety
of middle Georgia. In July the Union soldiers took over Marietta
and "in five minutes it seemed as if all creation was here and all
dressed in 'blue'" (201).

The yard and garden were soon overrun with Federal soldiers;
nevertheless, an undaunted Minerva McClatchey fearlessly ran off
the rabble who forced their way into the house and began playing
the piano and dancing in her parlor. She was unable, however, to
prevent the soldiers from making off with her fowls, corn, flour, meal,
honey, molasses, meat, cooking vessels, and pictures. She confided
in her diary: "My feelings of loneliness, helplessness and dread cannot be described" (203).

The Union army's orders prohibiting the sale of anything outside
the picket lines rendered the McClatchey food situation critical. Most
of their provisions had been appropriated by the Yankees and Mrs.
McClatchey was desperate.

> Our provisions, the little we saved, are getting low—we have
> no money and what we are to do, I cannot see. O, dark, dark
> days. My only comfort is that God's promises never fail. I do
> put my trust in him, and believe he will care for us. (204)

Their destitution continued, and on September 1, 1864, Mrs. McClatchey wrote: "But can we get subsistence? It is a poor chance. They will sell us nothing. But we live from day to day, somehow" (207). By trading milk for crackers and other provisions from the occupation troops, Mrs. McClatchey finally managed to secure enough food for survival. Fortunately, she had managed to keep her cow, but she still faced the problem of forage. "We have nothing to feed her on. God help us" (205).

It was indeed a great stroke of luck when a Union officer who was encamped in her yard offered her some "injured hams" which Mrs. McClatchey accepted with deep gratitude. With typical Southern feistiness, Minerva refused to give up to two belligerent Yankees the few chickens she had been guarding to feed her seriously ill son. An argument ensued, and when Minerva admitted that she was a "Reb" the soldiers let out a yell,

> fired their gun off near the house, and meeting some of their comrades at the gate, held a long consultation—I expected they would return and take dire vengeance, but they went off. (204)

Still more trying times awaited Mrs. McClatchey when in October she received word that her son, John, had been wounded in June while fighting with the Confederate forces and had died a month later.

> My God, my God must I believe it—I did not know what it was to have a child cruelly wounded, and to die away from me—I did not know all this time that I have been suffering so much that this last most severe drop was to be added to my already full, and bitter cup. The Lord has been good to me, I must not question his doings. (208)

In December she wrote resignedly, almost prayerfully:

> It seems that I miss my dear John more and more, but I try to repress my feelings. . . . I think of him constantly. It seems wrong to think of anything else—but perhaps I am wrong—

179

the stern necessities of life press upon me, and I must try to
be thankful for the blessings I still have. . . . But my comfort
is that God reigns. He will do right—I will trust Him forever.
I resign my all into Thy hands. Give us poverty, peril, privation or whatever Thou seest fit for us. But oh my God grant
that we may make a family in Heaven, Oh if we may only get
to Heaven—there are no wars—separations no troubles there.
(211)

At one time, as much of the town went up in flames, their home
was almost consumed by the fire. In January 1865, Mrs. McClatchey
was astonished as the townspeople themselves sacked the area's
homes.

Many citizens are almost as bad as the Yankees, one waggon
after another goes by, loaded with plunder of various kinds,
gathered from camps or empty houses. Some people who gathered a great deal of furniture from deserted homes—and lived
high during Yankee occupation of the country, are afraid to
stay now, and have gone north, deserting their ill gotten gains,
which is again siezed [sic], and carried into the country. (213)

In an attempt to save their home near Knoxville, Tennessee, from
being seized by the Federals, Elizabeth Baker Crozier remained with
the house rather than joining her husband and two daughters in
their flight southward. As the enemy's minié balls began pelting the
back porch, Mrs. Crozier and the two youngsters still with her sought
refuge with a sister-in-law living nearby. Within hours, the Yankees
had broken open her temporarily unoccupied home and were busily
engaged divvying up the contents. Granted a few minutes to attempt
to salvage even a few of her valuables, Mrs. Crozier was conducted
by a Federal officer through the rows of sharpshooters occupying
the rifle pits between the two homes. As she opened the door of
her residence

I beheld a scene that I never th'ot of witnessing in my life.
Every lock in the house was broken open, the contents of every
wardrobe, bureau, closet and side board, the front of which
had been broken out, were scattered over every room. I was

overwhelmed with amazement not knowing what to do. My
wine all drunk, my hams, bacon, butter and sugar all gone,
and my faithful old dog stretched upon the garments groaning
most pitifully.

Sometime later, Mrs. Crozier continued:

We have slept in our clothes for more than a week. Oh the
anxiety of a people in the midst of a battle. The cannon roars
day and night. They are constantly belching forth their Breath
of fire from the breastworks of perdition. Friends meet together
to talk and cheer each other, hoping and praying that the Rebels
will soon burst in and remove the iron heel of despotism from
the necks of an innocent people.

For a few days Mrs. Crozier's home was spared the torch. There was
still hope as she wrote:

Our home is still standing, Can it be that it will not meet
the fate of others? We still cast a lingering look toward it, not
yet without hope—not like some I have heard to say their anxiety was so great about their homes that it would be a relief
if all was over. All night the cannon pours forth his mighty,
thundering voice, shakes not only the very earth, but it seems
that the house in which we are will be brought to the ground.

Later that day she watched the flames engulf her home.

Now that great battle begins. . . . At the same time the in-
cendiary was doing his work in our home and as the darkness
of night came on, the light of many of our dear homes illumi-
nated the city with one grand light.

During the course of the war, town after town, as well as broad
areas of the countryside, suffered near annihilation as a result of
the violent invasions of enemy troops. As Sherman cut his swath
through South Carolina, its capital, Columbia, swollen to overflowing
with refugees, primarily women and children from throughout the
South, fell victim in February 1865 to one of the most malicious
assaults of the war. The terror preceding the attack and the horror

of the burning and vandalism that accompanied the takeover of Columbia fueled the diaries of scores of Columbia's outraged citizens. The rape of the city with its attendant pandemonium, however, was merely a repetition, more or less, of the devastation wrought in other areas.

As unregenerate rebels in the first state to secede from the Union, South Carolinians were labeled the "firebrands" of the Confederacy, and were painfully aware of possible massive retaliation for their role in "having started the War." The approach of Sherman's troops drove terrified citizens into a wild packing and secreting of valuables. On December 31, 1864, Grace Elmore noted in her diary:

> Still packing and sending off. All day has the house been turned upside down and everybody engaged in hauling beds, blankets and carpets and crockery about the house, putting up bales and boxes for our destined refuge. . . . (31)

Atlanta and Savannah had been conquered and occupied; bad news was crowding in from all quarters. The future appeared ominous for the Confederacy. Grace continued:

> Today is the last of '64, a gloomy, dark day, the end of a gloomy year. Each year has found us bereft of a portion of our inheritance and further from our independence. This year, God help us, we are almost at the end of the log. Our present situation is darkly, terribly strange, and yet we must not, will not, give up hope. Four years ago if we had been compelled to fly from home we could not have been so downcast, for then we expected to give up home and everything and there were other parts of the Confederacy safe and ready to take us in. But now where shall we find safety, where can we lay our weary heads and rest our sickened hearts? God has been good in deferring our trial so long, but now it has come 'tis a trial of fire. There is not a spot to which we can flee with an assurance of safety. And oh the terrible wrath that is to be expended on us. We are Carolinians, that is our crime, what will be our doom? Sherman said of Charleston, it shall be destroyed "and sowed with salt", can it be supposed he will let Columbia the "hotbed of Secession" stand. God only knows, but this I know, whatever he does, he will find no white faced women to do

his bidding or ask his mercy, our choice would be death rather than dishonor. (31–32)

During the ensuing weeks the Elmores worked feverishly hiding

jars of jelly and preserves in cracks and crevices that will give the rascals some trouble to find before they get them. The spoons, forks and some bottles of whiskey Mother and I have put where they [the Yankees] won't get them, unless the Devil shows them the way. . . . In the short time between darkness and daylight, Billy and I secreted over thirty pieces of meat, I carrying two or three hams at every turn, from the cellar to the third story. Beside this we carried up three sacks of flour, salt and corn. It all had to be done in the perfect silence and no light for fear of watchers outside, for we do not know who to trust beside Billy and Horace [servants]. The day has truly been so full of prosaic drudgery that there is no time for heroics. I had a good lot of poultry killed, and every friend who came in I begged to fill their knapsack, so we were cooking and filling all day. . . . Ah me, the fighting approached nearer and nearer, showing our men were falling back and falling back. About nine o'clock this morning Aunt Sarah left the "Hill" which being the highest point in Columbia was from the first the target for Yankee shells, and sought refuge with us. I am too glad she has come with Mrs. Gen. Hagood and the two little boys, for Mother and I will not be alone. (46)

Just hours before Sherman's invasion of Columbia, Frank and Albert Elmore, Grace's soldier brothers, paid a most welcome, though unexpected, visit to the family home. At the sound of the enemy guns, however, laden with well-filled knapsacks they made a hasty exit.

We could hear the musketry, as we filled their canteens and knapsacks. Mother took charge of Albert's and I of Frank's, and in doing for them had no time for thought. Frank, as I hurriedly folded his clothes, explained to me the rat-tat like so many pop-guns. "They are fighting in the streets, Hurry Grace, hurry." Quickly I crammed in whatever was near at hand, fastened it for him and turned to my other brother. Mother in her excitement could not fasten his pistol belt and this was my last service to him; we followed our boys down the steps, into the yard, to their horses, and bade them God speed. Oh my brave, beautiful, noble Mother, she who has walked so firm, so true, so calm, with never a thought of self, watched her boys till they disappeared, and then for the first time gave way. She wrung her hands, as with their backs turned, she followed them through the garden. I went toward her, but her cry was, "leave me or I'll go distracted," and I left her alone with her God. For myself, I scarce know how I got into the house. I leaned for support against the pantry door, that opened on the piazza, my knees shook and my face must have been white and drawn, as I gazed into the garden watching for my Mother. (48)

My poor Mother bore up bravely, 'Twas well she did, for that day [February 17] was horrible and the night was more so. As our troops passed I stood at the gate. I had *one* bottle of wine and a wine glass which I gave as long as it lasted. We gave all the blankets we could possibly spare, for many of the men had no coats, but ragged jackets, the day was bitter, no sunshine, and they looked cold, but uttered no complaint, nor did they seem dispirited. Even Col Ruttledge needed and asked for a blanket. Some of the men had breadths of carpet wrapped around their shoulders, which roused the fun of those who had more. "Where'd you get your blanket?" they asked, "You'll get out of that before long." "Too much baggage" etc. All greeted us pleasantly as they passed. "We'll come back before long, ladies." "We aren't gone up, ladies," until we actually felt in heart again. They weren't whipped but overpowered. (50)

As the rebels departed, into Columbia swarmed the Union forces. Although the Elmore home was a short distance from town, the riotous soldiers had little difficulty finding it—at first a few bummers and then hordes of fiendish Yankees.

They soon came in crowds, threatened all sorts of things if the doors were not opened. We had no guard, the house was out of town, and we were utterly at their mercy. The servants too got frightened by the numbers that filled the yard and garden, and opened the doors, and in they streamed . . . the wretches walked up and down where they pleased, talking loudly and looking in as they passed the door of the room in which we sat. Some of them went in to Mother's room, broke open the wardrobe, and pulled all the clothes out from the drawers and presses, searching for treasure, laughing and saying coarse things, or talking in loud, rough tones, to intimidate us. Mrs.

Bostick followed them as they went into her room, and searched there, just in time to see one pulling her letters from her desk. She forgot everything in her provocation and I heard her say "How dare you take my letters." His reply I did not hear, but she brought her desk back with her. They went into the parlor, played on the piano, danced, yelled, wrote on the billiard table and were as rowdy as possible, but thank God we suffered no insult. They behaved worse in the yard, stole the servants clothes, ripped open their trunks and boxes, especially ones which they declared contained clothes too fine for any negro, and which they divided among themselves. They went into our store room, took all the flour, meat, and everything they could move away, so that we had nothing left us but what Billy and I had hidden. (51)

Later she wrote:

The lane in front of the house was . . . strewn with all manner of women's wear, handsome dresses, etc. These wretches carried them from the houses into the streets, or gave them to any negro who would be robbed of them a moment after by the next Yankees that came along. No spite seemed too small for them to indulge in. They stole for the mere pleasure of stealing, for they made no use, nor could they of much they stole and destroyed. Every knife, tho' old and almost bladeless, they took from us, and our clothing would have gone too if it had not been sent away. 'Twas well we had a guard; that night was horrible. About dusk I heard a loud voice talking in the yard. Going to the balcony I saw the same bummer who had asked for the shirt; he was asking if we had a guard, for, says he, "if you have not, I'll guard you. Tonight is to be awful work." Just then some one said "There's Gen. Hampton's house burning," to which the demon replied, "Yes it is, for I set it on fire. I meant to save it when I went there this morning, but a dam rebel shot at me while there and I swore it should burn." (55)

Another impassioned diarist described the vengeful firing of Columbia from the vantage point of her family's home on the campus of South Carolina College (later to become the University of South Carolina). Young Emma LeConte and her family were hurriedly packing, ready to move at a moment's notice to safer territory.

185

... I so dread leaving home, for I feel I would never see it again except in ashes. How one grows accustomed to things—a year ago all this would have made me half crazy with anxiety and excitement—now it seems natural. We are prepared for the worst and dare not look even into the immediate future. I cannot even attempt to picture to myself what may happen in the next six weeks, or what may be the fate of our dear, beautiful, old Columbia. (25–26)

In preparation for leaving, Emma had been "hastily making large pockets to wear under my hoopskirt, for they will hardly search our persons." Earlier she had also undertaken to destroy most of her letters and had hidden others knowing they would be "read and scattered along the roads" by the Federals. On February 15, 1865, she wrote:

All is confusion and turmoil. The Government is rapidly moving off stores—all day the trains have been running, whistles blowing and wagons rattling through the streets. All day we have been listening to the booming of cannon—receiving conflicting rumors of the fighting. All day wagons and ambulances have been bringing in the wounded over the muddy streets and through the drizzling rain, with the dark, gloomy clouds overhead.

All day in our own household has confusion reigned, too. The back parlor strewed with clothing, etc., open trunks standing about, while a general feeling of misery and tension pervaded the atmosphere. Everything is to go that can be sent—house linen, blankets, clothing, silver, jewelry—even the wine—everything movable of any value. Hospital flags have been erected at the different gates of the Campus—we hope the fact of our living within the walls may be some protection to us, but I fear not. I feel sure these buildings will be destroyed. (30–31)

The waves of rumors that swept Columbia in the days preceding the Federal occupation were merely a frightening prelude to the horrors that ensued. Enemy shells whistled overhead, mobs of drunken soldiers caroused the streets, pillaging and shouting as they overran the neighborhoods, transforming the city into a veritable inferno as home after home was devoured by the flames.

On February 18, Emma wrote:

> By the red glare we could watch the wretches walking—generally staggering—back and forth from the camp to the town—shouting—hurrahing—cursing South Carolina—swearing—blaspheming—singing ribald songs and using such obscene language that we were forced to go indoors.
>
> The fire on Main Street was now raging, and we anxiously watched its progress from the upper front windows. In a little while, however, the flames broke forth in every direction. The drunken devils roamed about, setting fire to every house the flames seemed likely to spare. They were fully equipped for the noble work they had in hand. Each soldier was furnished with combustibles compactly put up. They would enter houses and in the presence of helpless women and children, pour turpentine on the beds and set them on fire. Guards were rarely of any assistance—most generally they assisted in the pillaging and firing.
>
> The wretched people rushing from their burning homes were not allowed to keep even the few necessaries they gathered up in their flight—even the blankets and food were taken from them and destroyed. The firemen attempted to use their engines but the hose was cut to pieces and their lives threatened. The wind blew a fearful gale, wafting the flames from house to house with frightful rapidity. By midnight the whole town (except the outskirts) was wrapped in one huge blaze. (44–45)

A paragraph later, Emma continued:

> Imagine night turned into noonday, only with a blazing, scorching glare that was horrible—a copper colored sky across which swept columns of black, rolling smoke glittering with sparks and flying embers, while all around us were falling thickly showers of burning flakes. Everywhere the palpitating blaze walling the streets with solid masses of flames as far as the eye could reach, filling the air with its horrible roar. On every side the crackling and devouring fire, while every instant came the crashing of timbers and the thunder of falling buildings. (45–46)

As the destruction intensified, so did Emma's bitterness.

> The Common opposite the gate was crowded with homeless women and children, a few wrapped in blankets and many

shivering in the night air. Such a scene as this with the drunken, fiendish soldiery in their dark uniforms, infuriated, cursing, screaming, exulting in their work, came nearer realizing the material ideal of hell than anything I ever expect to see again. They call themselves 'Sherman's Hellhounds.' (46)

Finally in desperation, having attempted to protect what food and clothing they could from the intermittent showers of sparks carried by the wind, Emma and her family* wrapped themselves in their shawls and blankets, and "went to the front door and waited for the house to catch" (47).

Fortunately, the LeConte and the Elmore homes were miraculously spared. Other Columbia residents were not that lucky. One woman hoped the fact that her husband was northern-born would save her home. Her neighbors apparently clung to the same delusion and confidently stored their belongings in her house until it was packed "from basement to attic." That home, however, suffered the same fiery fate as the heart of Columbia. At 2:00 A.M. the owner bid a sad farewell to her home.

> I took a little bird in its cage, which I could not bear to leave to the flames, in one hand, and my little child's hand in the other, and walked out from under our burning roof into the cold and pitiless street. Hundreds, nay thousands, were there before me; some not so well off as I, for they were invalids. None of us had any pillow but the frozen ground, nor any covering but the burning heavens. (T. Taylor 1903, 331)

The night seemed endless. An exhausted Emma LeConte told her diary:

> Oh, that long twelve hours! Never surely again will I live through such a night of horrors. The memory of it will haunt me as long as I shall live—it seemed as if the day would never come. The sun arose at last, dim and red through the thick, murky atmosphere. It set last night on a beautiful town full

---

*Emma's father, Joseph LeConte, facing certain death or imprisonment by the Federals for his work as Consulting Chemist of the Confederate States Nitre and Mining Bureau, was secreted out of town just prior to the takeover.

of women and children—it shone dully down this morning on smoking ruins and abject misery. (48)

Daylight brought the survivors their ultimate challenge: to bring order out of chaos, to procure provisions and fuel for themselves as well as housing for their less fortunate relatives and neighbors. Heat and food became formidable problems, as farmers refused to venture into town for fear their horses should be impressed. It was often thanks to the generosity of their servants who begged food from the Union soldiers or gathered up provisions from the shops ransacked by troops in the preceding days' melee, that the townspeople kept from starving. On February 17, Emma noted that the servants

> have brought back a considerable quantity of provisions—the negroes are very kind and faithful. They have supplied us with meat and Jane brought Mother some rice and crushed sugar for Carrie, knowing that she had none. How times change! Those whom we have so long fed and cared for now help us. We are intensely eager for every item of news, but of course can only hear through the negroes. (41)

Louisa McCord [Smythe], living in Columbia with her mother and sister while her fiancé was serving with Johnston's army, graphically recounted similar scenes of rampant burning and looting in her reminiscences of the Columbia holocaust. Louisa's aunt and cousin Minna, of Savannah, who were refugeeing with Louisa and her family, joined forces in preparation against the dreaded onslaught.

> As days went on warning came thick and fast, even from the Yankees themselves. A letter was dropped into our yard. . . . I cannot remember the signature but it was, or pretended to be, from an officer in Sherman's army and gave his name, rank, company, etc. It was a most earnest entreaty to all women and children to leave Columbia and gave a very plain warning as to the policy to be pursued by the commanding officers of the army. We were warned to expect the most terrible treatment. By this time everyone was obliged to believe that Sherman was coming and the only thing was to make up one's mind whether

to wait and take what might come, or to try our luck somewhere else. There was little or no accommodation for trav-
ellers—many drove out of town in wagons carrying only a few
clothes and a little food, but many more preferred to stay quietly
and wait for the worst. Our household and Dr. Reynolds were
among the latter. . . . (60)

Although Louisa's household numbered only five women, their
neighbors' household included twelve, as Louisa explained:

> It was altogether a typical "refugee" household, unendurable
> to any but the good manager, and the gentle tempered woman
> that Mrs. Reynolds was. These were specimens of the many
> hundreds of helpless families that quietly awaited their fate at
> the hands of Gen. Sherman. (60)

Despite knowing they would be directly in the line of the shelling
of the "State House," they failed to comprehend the full magnitude
of their plight until:

> Suddenly we heard the first gun, and for the first time heard
> the shriek of a shell pass overhead. It is hard to describe the
> stunned, giddy confused realization that *we* were really being
> shelled—we helpless women and children! (61)

In a relatively short time the firing subsided, but with the cessation
of firing came the Yankees.

> . . . we soon began to hear a distant roar, a far off confusion
> which seemed to come nearer as we listened with our hearts
> in our mouths. Without any warning our back gate was burst
> violently open and in rushed pell mell, crowding, pushing,
> almost falling over each other, such a crowd of men as I never
> saw before or since. They seemed scarcely human in their fierce
> excitement—the excitement of greed and rapine. In one instant
> the large yard was full of them. Like all Southern establishments,
> ours had two or three enclosures within the big outside fence.
> The yard proper, the stable yard, and a yard beyond where the
> servants houses were—then the garden. There were many out-
> buildings, store-rooms, corn houses, etc. Before we could look,
> every door was burst open and every room gutted of its

190

contents. They robbed even the negroes. What they couldn't take they spoiled. I didn't actually see it done but in many places they ripped up feather beds, poured mollasses over the feathers and threw the whole into the wells! I did see men stuffing their pockets with lard and preserves! In a few minutes the ground was honey combed with stabs from bayonets as these wild creatures rushed around prodding the earth in search of buried treasures—we stood petrified and fascinated at the window watching. (61–62)

Once inside the house the men "smashed, tore and pocketed everything they could get at." Luckily, just as several men (one of them brandishing the family's knives) attempted to push past Louisa's mother, the ringing of the doorbell heralded the appearance of General Howard asking permission to use their home as his headquarters. Although unenthusiastic about sharing their home with the officers, they soon realized the accommodation would save their house. General Howard, they knew, would be too ashamed to allow his headquarters to be burned.

As the fires spread throughout the city, Louisa watched the flames lick ever closer.

> I ran to the window and can never forget what I saw—fire in every direction sweeping the whole earth as it seemed, and the wind blowing it right towards us at the most furious speed. Fire is awful enough when you are surrounded by friends and help and comfort, but fire set intentionally, helped on by every device and accompanied by the shrieks and yells, curses, screams and awful antics of thousands of bitter enemies apparently gone mad with hate, is enough to shake the very soul of anything that has the power of or capacity for fright left in its composition. I believe we were no longer capable of fright, for I recollect nothing like terror. I remember sitting down on the floor in my room and burning up all my letters, as I didn't want them to fall into other hands. (63)
>
> The house was twice set on fire and would of course have been burned had it not been for Gen. Howard's regard for his own reputation. He couldn't afford to have his headquarters burned. But it was most evident the determination of the soldiers to burn it. They said over and over (to the servants) that it should burn. Burning cotton was found in the most

extraordinary places, and Gen. Howard would say in his suave manner that it was remarkable how the cotton was blowing about. On one occasion when a ball of it was found burning in the back entry, my Mother answered him "Yes General, very remarkable, through closed doors" and he said no more. He tried to excuse the shelling—when my mother asked him how they as soldiers brought themselves to shell defenceless women and children in their beds—by some platitudes about the sad necessities of war and how he thought of his own children in their little beds, etc. etc., but how *this* had to be in retaliation for the other methods of warfare pursued by us, and then told how some promising young man had been blown up and terribly injured by a submarine torpedo near Savannah. Mamma listened quietly and expressed her sorrow at any one's suffering, but said incidentally as it were, that it was a new idea to make women and children atone for the wounds and death of soldiers. Again the general had no answer. (63–64)

Having succeeded in "punishing" Columbia, Sherman's troops soon moved on. In a final gesture of appreciation to Louisa's family, General Howard detailed two guards to protect the home until the last of the stragglers had left the area.

But no sooner had the general left the house than a small pandemonium broke loose. One of the guards promptly got drunk. The other one, a sergeant, seemed to be a respectable man but desperate and hopeless of doing anything. The tipsy gentleman's hospitality let in anything and everybody that chose to come and the lower floor of the house was for the second time pillaged. What the soldiers left, the "bummers" took or destroyed. Black and white they tore through the house. I suppose knowing the house to have been a general's head-quarters, they thought it had escaped robbery and hoped for much booty. Thank heavens they were disappointed, there wasn't much for them. The sergeant begged my mother to let us girls be taken to some place of safety and he felt sure the house would be completely pillaged and he did not know what worse might happen. Mamma consented to send us, but her blood was up, and she entirely refused to leave the house. Aunt Rache and Minna also went to Dr. Reynolds' but escorted or alone I cannot say—I have forgotten. So we two poor things Hannah and I went out into that "Devils whirlpool", I can't call it anything else, trusting ourselves entirely to our sergeant.

It was a strange feeling that came over us, as following him, we elbowed our way through the rabble passing plenty of men in uniform who seemed in no way to concern themselves to stop what was going on. The morning after the fire when we didn't know what else might be in store for us, or how much our possessions might be taken from us, we had burned every private paper or letter we possessed, except a few trifling notes. I burned all your father's letters except a few that were packed away and couldn't be got out in that moment of hurry. As we went out of the house with our sergeant the impression on my eye was that there had been a snowstorm. The street was white with paper—letters, legal documents—every kind of thing, valuable and worthless strewed the ground. . . .

The next morning we went home greatly relieved to find the house still standing, but what a scene of desolation it all was. Every out-building had its door burst open—fences were thrown down—the garden trampled, furniture broken, books torn up and thrown about, pictures smashed and cut out of their frames and everything small carried away. As we reduced chaos to order we found of course that many things were still left—the oil paintings for instance that were afterwards burned in Henry Cheves house and my mother's bust—but the first look was of utter sweeping destruction. We hadn't a knife or a drinking vessel—the well rope was cut and the well filled with trash and dirt. (68–70)

And yet there was still more suffering to follow: in the wake of the destruction came hunger—and an unearthly, frightening isolation.

Finally fatigue got the better of fears and we at last stayed at home and went regularly to bed. This was a great comfort, and dear knows we had but few. Food was frightfully scarce and what there was was of the coarsest description. Bacon, cornbread made with just salt and water, and biscuits made of the wheat ground up whole, very coarse and always with only salt and water to mix them, were the staple in fact the only supplies of the table. Wagons were sent from Georgia with provisions which the town distributed to those who came for them. For hours there would be a crowd of the best sort of people, standing in line waiting for their chance for a little bit of something to eat. With the reaction I began to fail and had to go back to my sofa and my poor mother of course began to worry, so old Maum Rache was sent to fall in line and try to get me a little fresh meat and white flour. After hours of waiting she got it but the flour was musty and the meat tainted, so we didn't try any more but went back to the old diet. I never like to give a beggar dry bread—I remember too well how those meals tasted—bacon and dry hard cornbread without butter, sugar, milk, or even a mouthful of sweet potato coffee is choky food for a "peaky" convalescent, and I would leave the table sick with hunger. (70)

Communication with the outside world was impossible.

Railroads were torn up, telegraph wires cut, we were isolated from the world, alone in our misery and a prey to the most terrible anxieties and the most awful reports of impending catastrophes. (70)

The silence of the town was so awful. There were no white men (but the old men and little boys), no horses, no wheeled vehicles, no traffic of any kind,—just a dreary waste full of sad women and terrified children and equally terrified negroes. Eighty-five squares of the best portion of our little town lay bare and desolate, a horrible looking waste with the tall chimneys standing guard over cellars full of evil smelling black water. The burned trees and gardens looked so pitiful— Main St., the business street of the town was gone from end to end—only one little lone house left right in the middle of the desert. (71)

Grace Beard was ready for Sherman's troops following the burning of Columbia in February 1865—or so she thought. Realizing that her plantation, thirty miles above Columbia, was in a direct line of Sherman's march, Mrs. Beard, as overseer-owner of their large plantation in the absence of her soldier husband, made a supreme effort to save her provisions and farm animals from Yankee confiscation by establishing a "camp" some distance from her home and thus making her house look deserted. She carefully hid her Negroes away from the house and buried five gallon jars of butter and lard in the woods across the road. For three days and nights she carefully moved and buried. Then, just as she was comfortable and secure in her "camp" came word from an advance guard attempting to alert the citizens of the approach of the Federal troops:

You have fixed yourselves to be literally burned-up. Sherman's orders are to burn all vacant houses and all provisions, besides you can't hide from them, their name is Legion and they march with unbroken ranks across the country. (3)

In desperation she dragged what goods she could back to the house, dressed in as many clothes as mobility would permit, and sat quietly as the Yankees approached "like the locusts of Egypt" to pillage her dressers and trunks. Soon band after band of soldiers swept through the yard and house threatening her and her servants with torture and death unless they divulged the whereabouts of Mrs. Beard's provisions and valuables. Displaying remarkable courage and loyalty, the servants refused to be intimidated despite admonitions that they were free and no longer needed to obey orders from their former masters. Mrs. Beard also held her ground even when the spoilers intimated that women who refused to give up all of their private possessions would be stripped and searched. With great foreboding, she watched the soldiers "shoot all of my hogs, guineas, turkeys" and set fire to the gin house, barn, crib, and stables. Her bravado almost failed her, however, as a soldier in the guise of a protector of helpless Southern ladies continued to harass her. Finally, in a showdown, the suspicious Mrs. Beard ordered him to leave, whereupon he announced menacingly, "I guarded a lady's house near Atlanta and when I asked her for pay she spit in my face so I burned her house up."

Although the war was fought primarily in the South, Northern armies were by no means the only troops guilty of vandalism and pyromania.* In the week preceding Gettysburg, Rebel soldiers wrought havoc on Chambersburg, the Pennsylvania town used as a staging area in the June 1863 deployment of Confederate troops northward and to the east, toward Gettysburg. In a succession of diary entries, Rachel Cormany noted:

---

*See, for example, the Underwood family in chapter 4 (pages 142–46).

This P.M. the Rebs are plundering the stores. some of our merchants will be almost if not entirely ruined. . . . (Mohr 1982, 334)

At 8½ A.M. the rebels commenced coming again. Ga. troops. I was told this morning of some of their mean tricks of yesterday & before. They took the hats & boots off the men—Took that off Preacher Farney. Took $50. off Dr. Sneck & his gold watch valued very highly—took the coats off some, tetotally stripped one young fellow not far from town—Mr. Skinner. We have to be afraid to go out of our houses. (Mohr 1982, 337)

The Rebs are still about doing all the mischief they can. They have everything ready to set fire to the warehouses & machine shops—Tore up the railroad track & burned the crossties—They have cleared out nearly every store so they cannot rob much more. . . . (Mohr 1982, 338)

Thirteen months later Rachel described the return of the Confederates and the burning of Chambersburg. In that town alone, Rebel soldiers destroyed over 500 buildings and caused almost a million dollars worth of destruction to private property.

Just a week this morning the rebels turned up in our devoted town again. before they entered they roused us out of our slumbers by throwing to shells in. this was between 3 & 4 A.M. by 5—the grey back hordes came pouring in. They demanded 500,000 in default of which the town would be burned—They were told that it was imposible to raise that amount—The reb's then came down to 100,000 in gold which was just as imposible. when they were informed of the imposibility they deliberately went from house to house & fired it. The whole heart of the town is burned. they gave no time for people to get any thing out. each had to escape for life & took only what they could first grab. some saved considerable. others only the clothes on their backs—& even some of those were taken off as they escaped from their burning dwellings. O! the 30th July 1864 was a sad day to the people of Chambersburg. In most cases where the buildings were left money was paid. They were here too but we talked them out of it. We told them we were widdows & that saved us here. About 3000 were made homeless in less than three hours. This whole week has been one of great excitement. We live in constant dread. I never spent such days as these few last I never spent—I feel as if I could not stay in this country longer. I feel quite sick of the dread & excitement. (Mohr 1982, 446)

196

"Miss Abby," a displaced Northerner, was incensed by the Rebel depredations going on about her home near Atlanta. In the spring of 1864 she told her diary:

> There is a Battery erected near by, manned by soldiers who are any thing but "protectors". They are engaged in extensive robberies every night; nothing is considered safe which can be carried away. Being no respecters of persons, they call upon all alike;—one night taking four thousand dollars worth of provisions from my neighbor's store room—the next entering a poor woman's house and robbing her of every article of clothing of which she had disrobed herself upon going to bed—and all of her children's garments also. Last night they called at "our house";—broke into the kitchen—carried off two tubs of linen—took every implement lying about the yard—and more than all, they stole my beautiful George—my Turkey gentleman the last of his tribe, I had permitted to live. . . . O, George McClellan—to think your life should be given at last to robber-rebels! It is to be hoped that the man whose name you bear, will never follow your "illustrious example." (16)

"Miss Abby's" distress over the thievery of the Southern soldiers was soon echoed by her Rebel neighbors who bitterly complained:

> "I believe our own soldiers do as bad as the Yankees, and I had as lief one would be here as the other, as far as stealing & badness goes; but of course we don't want the Yankees to come."

Unionist "Miss Abby" was unable to resist adding a sly "Not at all maam!" (48–49).

Sometimes it was the Confederates themselves who destroyed their own property. To prevent their cotton from falling into the hands of the Yankees, the Confederates burned an estimated two and one-half million bales of their own cotton. Following the seizure of New Orleans, it was all too clear that Baton Rouge would be the Federals' next objective. In anticipation, planters immediately touched off a conflagration colorfully described by Sarah Morgan in her diary.

We went this morning to see the cotton burning—a sight never before witnessed, and probably never again to be seen. Wagons, drays,—everything that can be driven or rolled,—were loaded with the bales and taken a few squares back to burn on the commons. Negroes were running around, cutting them open, piling them up, and setting them afire. All were as busy as though their salvation depended on disappointing the Yankees. Later, Charlie sent for us to come to the river and see him fire a flat-boat loaded with the precious material for which the Yankees are risking their bodies and souls. Up and down the levee, as far as we could see, negroes were rolling it down to the brink of the river where they would set them afire and push the bales in to float burning down the tide. Each sent up its wreath of smoke and looked like a tiny steamer puffing away. Only I doubt that from the source to the mouth of the river there are as many boats afloat on the Mississippi. The flatboat was piled with as many bales as it could hold without sinking. Most of them were cut open, while negroes staved in the heads of barrels of alcohol, whiskey, etc., and dashed bucketsful over the cotton. Others built up little chimneys of pine every few feet, lined with pine knots and loose cotton, to burn more quickly. There, piled the length of the whole levee, or burning in the river, lay the work of thousands of negroes for more than a year past. It had come from every side. Men stood by who owned the cotton that was burning or waiting to burn. They either helped, or looked on cheerfully. Charlie owned but sixteen bales—a matter of some fifteen hundred dollars; but he was the head man of the whole affair, and burned his own, as well as the property of others. A single barrel of whiskey that was thrown on the cotton, cost the man who gave it one hundred and twenty-five dollars. (It shows what a nation in earnest is capable of doing.) Only two men got on the flatboat with Charlie when it was ready. It was towed to the middle of the river, set afire in every place, and then they jumped into a little skiff fastened in front, and rowed to land. The cotton floated down the Mississippi one sheet of living flame, even in the sunlight. It would have been grand at night. But then we will have fun watching it this evening anyway; for they cannot get through to-day, though no time is to be lost. Hundreds of bales remained untouched. An incredible amount of property has been destroyed to-day; but no one begrudges it. Every grog-shop has been emptied, and gutters and pavements are floating with liquors of all kinds. So that if the Yankees are fond of strong drink, they will fare ill. (Dawson 1960, 16–18)

The ravages of war left countless women (particularly Southerners) absolutely destitute. Those who had somehow managed to save their homes at least had a place to rest their weary heads at night, a luxury denied thousands of poor, unfortunate victims who had been defenseless bystanders as their homes went up in flames. Some of the homeless found refuge with friends or relatives, who with true Southern hospitality made room for them despite their own already overcrowded quarters and severely straitened circumstances. Other families sought protection from the elements in tents, abandoned cabins or sheds, or in empty boxcars along the railroad tracks. The latter were indeed *temporary* lodgings in the truest sense of the word, for an appalling number of deaths resulted from those dark, damp, unheated, unsanitary quarters.

Finding food for their families sometimes proved even more difficult for women than finding shelter. Mary Gay, of Decatur, Georgia, and many like her, ferreted out kernels of corn in the clutter of their family's bureau drawers which had been seized and scattered about their yards for use as feeding troughs for horses during the encampments of Union soldiers. Mary struck a true bonanza, however, when she discovered the Confederate authorities would exchange bread for the bucketsful of minié balls she and her neighbors collected on the battlefield following the siege of Atlanta.

> I could not be oblivious to the fact that I was hungry, very hungry. And there was another [her mother], whose footsteps were becoming more and more feeble day by day and whose voice, when heard at all, was full of the pathos of despair, who needed nourishment that could not be obtained, and consolation, which it seemed a mockery to offer.
>
> In vain did I look round for relief. There was nothing left in the country to eat. Yea, a crow flying over it would have failed to discover a morsel with which to appease its hunger; for a Sheridan by another name had been there with his minions of destruction, and had ruthlessly destroyed every vestige of food and every means of support. Every larder was empty, and those with thousands and tens of thousands of dollars were as poor as the poorest, and as hungry too. Packing trunks, in every house to which refugees had returned, contained large

amounts of Confederate money. We had invested all we possessed except our home and land and negroes, in Confederate bonds, and these were now inefficient for purchasing purposes. Gold and silver had we none. A more favored few had a little of those desirable mediums of purchase, and sent a great distance for supplies; but they offered no relief to those who had stayed at home and borne the brunt of battle, and saved their property from the destroyers' torch.

What was I to do? Sit down and wait for the inevitable starvation? No; I was not made of such stuff. I had heard that there had been a provision store opened in Atlanta for the purpose of bartering provisions for munitions of war—anything that could be utilized in warfare. Minie balls were particularly desirable. . . .

With a basket in either hand, and accompanied by Telitha [her slave], who carried one that would hold about a peck, and two old dull case-knives, I started to the battle-fields around Atlanta to pick up the former missiles of death to exchange for food to keep us from starving. (255–56)

Soon, Mary and Telitha discovered a veritable treasure-trove.

In a marshy place, encrusted with ice, innumerable bullets, minie balls, and pieces of lead seemed to have been left by the irony of fate to supply sustenance to hungry ones, and employment to the poor. . . . It was so cold! our feet were almost frozen, and our hands had commenced to bleed, and handling cold, rough lead cramped them so badly that I feared we would have to desist from our work before filling the baskets.

Lead! Blood! Tears! Oh how suggestive! Lead, blood and tears, mingled and commingled. In vain did I try to dash the tears away. They would assert themselves and fall upon lead stained with blood. . . . (257)

Jubilantly, Mary and Telitha walked into Atlanta where the minié balls were gratefully accepted and exchanged for baskets brimming over with sugar, coffee, flour, meal, lard, and meat. Mary was ecstatic. "I can never describe the satisfaction I experienced as I lifted two of those baskets, and saw Telitha grasp the other one, and turned my face homeward" (259).

Numerous enterprising women tried with varying success to earn money by baking pies and cakes to sell to the occupation troops.

One soldier wrote from his encampment near Bull's Gap, Tennessee:

> The women around here come into camp with pies biscuit, corn
> bread, etc., which they sell for money when they can get it,
> or trade for coffee sugar salt old shirts, & in fact anything almost
> [that] can be made useful in a family. They are very hard up
> for all necessary articles of clothing and every thing else almost.
> (Potter 18 April 1865)

Unwilling to take the despised Loyalty Oath in order to secure
provisions, Mary Jane Reynolds's family attempted to make ends meet
by baking biscuits for the Yankee soldiers.

> We succeeded in getting fifty bushels of corn last week from
> Jim Viar at one dollar and a half per bushel. We made biscuits
> and rice pies and sold them to the pickets and got green-
> backs enough to pay for it and have 150 dollars left. (16
> February 1864)

At the end of the war, desperate for money for food, Mrs. N. B.
De Saussure got up at 4 A.M. to start "making bread, and any
number of green-apple pies" to sell to the soldiers quartered on the
charred remains of the family's plantation (102). Harriet Simons, a
refugee living in Columbia with her three children, youngest brother,
and stepsons, recalled that though they tried to bake pies to secure
money to purchase food, their messenger returned "with a few scattered remnants and no money." Army stragglers had appropriated
the baked goods.

Many families survived because of the loyalty of their remaining
slaves who shared the food they obtained from the Union army with
their former owners. Towns sometimes were able to provide limited
supplies of food. Emma LeConte explained in her diary after the
firing of Columbia:

> The Mayor issues rations to 7,000 people—all that is left of
> a population of about 30,000. The original population of 12,000
> was enormously increased since the war by refugees and other
> sources. (74)

201

As food stocks dwindled, hungry people waited anxiously for new supplies, among them Emma LeConte and her family, who, fortunately, were in considerably less dire circumstances than most of their fellow townspeople.

> I hope relief will come before famine actually threatens. We have to cut our rations as short as possible to try to make the food hold out till succor comes. Father left us with some moldy, spoiled flour that was turned over to him by the Bureau. . . . We draw rations from the town every day—a tiny bit of rancid pork and a pint of meal. . . . We fare better than some because we have the cows. Mother had peas to feed them, and sometimes we take a few of these from them to vary our diet. Today as a *great treat* Mother gave us boiled *rice* for dinner—some the negroes had brought us in the pillage of the stores. (66–67)

Even if it meant going hungry, Emma's utter loathing of the Yankees was unwavering. "The Yankees are issuing rations but they are only drawn by people in actual need or who have no self-respect" (112).

Emma was not alone in her reluctance to accept food from the Yankees. Following the fall of Richmond, one woman recalled:

> In all this time of horror I don't think anything was much harder than making up our minds to "draw rations from the Yankees." We said we *would* not do it—we *could* not do it! (Avary 1903, 369)

Now and then reciprocal arrangements could be worked out with the enemy troops. Fanny Tinsley, whose husband was serving in the Treasury Department of the Confederacy, felt she must remain at home with her elderly parents. Although fearful at first of the treatment they might receive at the hands of the Yankees, they soon developed a reciprocity whereby her family was given a guard of thirty men for their house and protection for their cows with the understanding that Fanny's mother would "let them have milk for their sick and let the soldiers buy all she had to spare" (Mrs. S. G. Tinsley, 2).

Mary Jane Reynolds, living with her parents in Loudon, Tennessee, wrote to her husband, then in Pennsylvania, explaining the difficulties of obtaining food during the Federal occupation of the area. Providing accommodations for several Yankee officers during their regiment's encampment across the creek turned out to be a wise move.

> One of them gave me half of his tea when he went to leave. The Lieut. that is here now bought two hams, some beef, a little sugar, coffee, a few dried apples and white beans at the commissary yesterday and turned them over to us. They get plenty of rations now and have a much greater variety than the citizens do. I hope we will be able to live if things keep quiet and we have no more changes. (26 February 1864)

To keep from starving hundreds of women were reduced to begging. Although in difficult financial circumstances herself, Mrs. John B. (Meta) Grimball, who was refugeeing in Spartanburg, felt guilty for her inability to share with mendicants.

> Two poor women recently came here to beg, I was not able to give them meal, for I find it hard to get it for my own family, and had no change; but this morning when I was in the Village I passed one of them, & gave her 25¢ having felt badly at refusing her all aid, when she applyed to me at the door. (81)

And yet the foregoing litany of afflictions paled by comparison with the grievous trials suffered by thousands of unfortunate women, both white and black—women who could summon neither the time, nor the strength, nor the will to write. Others, such as General John W. Geary, told their story for them.

> This is the fourth day of the siege [Atlanta], and throughout the live-long day the bursting of bombshells, the booming of cannon, the rattling of small arms. . . . the dead and dying are the features of the day and the night. But there are still worse features than these. *War* and pestilence I have witnessed, but my eyes have been spared until now from witnessing the emaciated and languid form of their skinny twin sister, *famine*. To-day I saw a young mother with a starving child, so poor as scarcely to live, seeking bread at our home. . . . Her husband was a conscript in the rebel ranks, and this is but a specimen of Davis' work. If there is one spot in hell hotter than another, why should it not be reserved for him who has brought such evils on his fellow-man. (29 July 1864)

CHAPTER VI

The Battle Against Privation

> Well, the struggles of the war continued to rage till the South was famine stricken. The material for making clothing was all gone, the wolf was at the door of all those who had been independently wealthy and were reduced to the utmost poverty. There had been no crops raised for four years in the large part of the country. The fences had been burned, the houses had been destroyed and mules taken from the farms and many of the beautiful houses left in ashes. It was a discouraged, nearly broken people and many thousands felt that life was not worth living and gave up in despair.
>
> —*Virginia Norfleet*

Although there is no attempt being made here to present an in-depth discussion of the economics of the war, certain financial aspects warrant consideration in terms of their impact on the lives of both Union and Confederate women. Both sections were plagued by problems of inflation, shortages, soaring prices, speculation, depreciated currency, and higher taxes—problems which had grave repercussions for the battlefront as well as the homefront.

To be sure there were some fortunate women who "never felt the war" and the suffering and deprivation it entailed. Several Northern diarists, who apparently had no immediate family members in uniform and who were economically and geographically well distanced from the strife, appeared completely oblivious to the war.

Life went on as usual in some sectors of the country. Europe and the fashionable resorts of the Northeast continued to attract visitors. New York City, with its art galleries and theaters, still drew crowds of sightseers. Summer homes beckoned their warm weather tenants. (For some Southerners, however, such as Maria Beard Stewart's family, vacation homes soon became year-round refugee sanctuaries.) In many of the large cities, wealthy matrons hostessed sumptuous dinner parties and extravagant galas—festivities which as the war continued underwent only slight modifications in their frequency and lavishness. Maria Lydig Daly was dismayed at the extravagance displayed by many of the women of New York City and in February of 1863 noted in her diary:

> The women dress as extravagantly as ever, and the supper and dinner parties are far more numerous than they have been for several winters. (Hammond 1962, 219)

In Mobile, Ellen Buchanan Screven found the social life much to her liking. There were dances and parties and a private box at the theater, which had been given to her father, a Confederate naval officer, and which she and her husband often shared with friends.

> Such a gay life did we lead there. (Screven)

In January 1865 Kate Cumming confirmed Mobile's lively social scene.

> Mobile is gayer than ever; it seems as if the people have become reckless. I am told that there was as much visiting on New Year's day as there usually is in peace times. The city is filled with military, which is one cause of the gayety. (248)

A few weeks later she wrote:

> Mobile never was as gay as it is at present; not a night passes but some ball or party is given. Same old excuse: that they are for the benefit of the soldiers; and indeed the soldiers seem to enjoy them. (257)

Even in Richmond, even during the last days of the Confederacy, the fashionable set was engaged in what appeared to be, at least in retrospect, a "last chance" social whirl. For some party givers the festivities constituted a determined effort to bring at least a modicum of gaiety into the otherwise rigidly disciplined lives of their "soldier boys." For others, partying was simply a way of life. Judith McGuire, for one, looked askance at the frivolity.

> Some persons in this beleaguered city seem crazed on the subject of gayety. In the midst of the wounded and dying, the low state of the commissariat, the anxiety of the whole country, the troubles of every kind by which we are surrounded, I am mortified to say that there are gay parties given in the city. There are those denominated "starvation parties," where young persons meet for innocent enjoyment, and retire at a reasonable hour; but there are others where the most elegant suppers are served—cakes, jellies, ices in profusion, and meats of the finest kinds in abundance, such as might furnish a meal for a regiment of General Lee's army. . . . (328)

Phoebe Pember, matron at Richmond's Chimborazo Hospital, seemed to be of two minds regarding the gaiety that characterized the city's final days preceding its collapse in April of 1865.

> All this winter of '64, the city had been unusually gay. Besides parties, private theatricals and tableaux were constantly exhibited. Wise and thoughtful men disapproved openly of this mad gayety. There was certainly a painful discrepancy between the excitement of dancing and the rumble of ambulances that could be heard in the momentary lull of the music, carrying the wounded to the different hospitals. Young men advocated this state of affairs, arguing that after the fatigues and dangers of a campaign in the field, some relaxation was necessary on their visits to the capital. (127)

In marked contrast to the unaffected, affluent women revelling in levity and luxury, most women were engaged in a four-year struggle with privation—with inflation and shortages that for some were merely annoyances but which for others assumed life-threatening dimensions.

The economic woes of both sections stemmed from a combination of factors including (1) economies devoted to the production of materiel and the consequent decrease in the production of consumer goods; (2) labor shortages caused by the diversion to the armies of much of the workforce from the factories and farms; (3) the siphoning off of thousands of acres of corn, wheat, and other farm produce by the governments for the subsistence of the armies. In addition the South suffered from the total devastation of large areas of farmland due to military action and foraging and the decrease in the availability of imported goods brought about by the blockade. As a consequence of their preoccupation with "King Cotton," most of the South's manufactured goods—personal items, household goods, farm implements—had been imported. Lincoln's immediate formation of the blockade of Southern ports, therefore, produced serious economic repercussions for the Confederacy.

As a result of their proximity to the battlelines, the rapid deterioration of their currency, and the Union's effective blockade of their ports, the South, without question, suffered the greater economic hardships. By the end of the war, almost all Southerners were in the same straits. As Annie Laurie Broidrick pointed out:

> To be rich during the War was considered a disgrace. Almost every person of note was suffering from poverty, and people were proud of it. Every one gave freely to the cause. (15)

In the South the term "Confederate" quickly gained usage as a word popularly applied to clothing, food, parties, to almost anything shoddy, shabby, or ersatz. Sarah Morgan, upon being invited to attend a military dress parade in a "Confederate carriage," gratefully accepted and later explained in her diary:

> Now, in present phraseology, "Confederate" means anything that is rough, unfinished, unfashionable, or poor. You hear of Confederate dresses, which means last year's. Confederate bridle

means a rope halter, Confederate silver, a tin cup or spoon. Confederate flour is corn meal, etc. In this case the Confederate carriage is a Jersey wagon with four seats, a top of hickory slats covered with leather, and the whole drawn by mules. (Dawson 1960, 233)

Inflation soon surfaced as one of the South's most pressing concerns. As the Confederate government continued to issue more and more Confederate bills, their value plunged disastrously. John B. Jones, of Richmond, watched Confederate currency plummet to a ratio of sixty Confederate dollars to one of gold, then to eighty to one, soon to one hundred to one, and finally, at the end of the war, to absolute worthlessness. Kate Robson remembered distinctly the currency's incredible devaluation:

My husband threw a bundle in my lap and said "Kate I never did hear you say you had enough money. There is three thousand dollars, my half of the profit on a barrell of sugar."

Rampant inflation and growing shortages were promptly reflected in exorbitant prices which sometimes rose to well over ten times their prewar level. In Richmond, for example, toward the end of the war, flour was selling for $1500 per barrel, bacon for $20 per pound, beef $15 per pound, butter $15-$20 per pound, corn $10 per dozen ears. A chicken cost about $50, a watermelon $20, a head of cabbage $10 (J. Jones 1935).

As the value of Confederate currency continued to decline, food shortages in the towns and cities became acute. Farmers, wary of having their horses impressed by the government and unwilling to accept depreciated Confederate bills in exchange for their provisions, refused to come in to the markets. The cutting of the railroad lines made transportation difficult if not impossible for even those farmers willing to send their produce to town. All too often the beef or poultry was odoriferous and spoiled by the time it reached its destination. In addition, food was so scarce that theft by the enemy or by roving bands of guerillas was an ever-present threat.

Shopkeepers and vendors were also reluctant to take Confederate money, insisting on payment in gold or silver instead. Since both of the latter were in extremely short supply, bartering became a common practice. Martha B. Washington recalled:

> By May, 1862, almost all Charleston were refugees. The up-country towns were overcrowded, food was scarce, prices exorbitant; in many instances Confederate money was refused at any price, the farmers preferring to hoard their provisions rather than sell for money they deemed worthless. . . . They refused to sell us provisions, except in the way of barter, and in that light, almost everything, particularly clothing, had a market, but with no means of replenishing, it was not often we could spare our clothing. Going out into the country on one occasion to see what we could get to eat, we had stopped at a farm-house where the woman refused all overtures we had made her. On this day I wore a white waist, known as a "Garibaldi," and then considered most stylish, somewhat on the order of the shirtwaist of today. The woman suddenly turned to me, and said: "I will give you a turkey for your jacket." I replied: "It is not for sale." She kept on urging the exchange; at last she said: "I will give you two turkeys." After hesitating some time, as to whether my wardrobe would allow of the exchange, I consented. Our household consisted of thirteen women and children, and turkeys were a rarity with us! (T. Taylor 1903, 174–75)

A search for food frequently sent Ellen Elmore on ten- to twelve-mile excursions into the York County, South Carolina countryside. Surprisingly, an extremely lucrative source turned up right at home in the trunks containing the family's fancy dress clothes of yesteryear. Once the neighbors learned of the cache, the Elmore women set up a lively business in trading finery for food.

> After a while, it became known that we had valuable stores of household goods and wearing apparel, and from day to day, one or another young woman would come with a chicken, or a pound of butter, or something to trade. The first day a girl came in, she caught sight of an artificial rose, which, among other ball finery, had been rammed into a chest to keep things steady; and upon that she set her heart and offered her chicken in exchange. Imagine the joy of my sister Cornelia, a quick,

impulsive nature, at the discovery of the direction in which the
girl's desires tended. Out of the room she rushed, and hauled
out a lot of flowers, ball dresses, and hats; and from that time
we did quite an extensive millinery business, and had chickens
and butter quite often on the table. Some came for crockery and
clothing. One day a woman took a fancy to some heavy delft-
ware, the remains of an old dinner set, that had been sent to
the plantation years before; and as I emptied the plates on the
cloth (for we were at breakfast when she came), my little niece
said softly, "Lolla" (as she called me) "is going to sell all the plates;
I spec' we will have to eat off the leaves." (T. Taylor 1903, 208)

Since Elizabeth Avery Meriwether's husband did not use tobacco,
the resourceful Mrs. Meriwether cleverly traded his army ration to
the local farmers for eggs, butter, and milk for herself and her children. Hard pressed for $50 to refurbish her Rockaway, she also
finagled an agreement with a wheelwright's daughter whereby she
would trade her "sky blue silk gown" in exchange for the father's
work on the carriage. The trade of a pair of white satin slippers for
fifteen pounds of brown sugar proved considerably more difficult.
When the "tradee" sought to renege on the agreement, the slippers
were shuttled back and forth between the two parties for days until
at long last Mrs. Meriwether succeeded in claiming the fifteen pounds
of precious sugar.

The exchange of two gallons of whiskey for a barrel of flour was
a deal that Susan Blackford was not entirely sure her husband would
approve of; however, the family's hunger necessitated the trade.

> I had a note from Major Jack Langhorne this morning propos-
> ing to exchange a barrel of flour for two gallons of the whiskey
> you have at home. I do not know whether you will like it or
> not but I made the exchange, for I regard a barrel of flour which
> we eat much more valuable to us than the whiskey which we
> do not drink. (151–52)

Gertrude Thomas almost met her match in a shrewd salesman
who refused to sell her two quarts of strawberries for thirty dollars
of Confederate money or ten cents in silver and instead demanded
meat as payment.

A black man came by during the morning with strawberrys to sell at 30 dollars Confederate money or 10 cts in silver, then when I proposed buying them preferred meat and would not take the money. I bought two qts of the finest I ever saw from him giving meat in exchange. In market this morning the money was refused, nothing sold except for silver or gold. (1 May 1865)

In addition to inflation and high prices, increased tax assessments took big bites out of both Blue and Gray incomes.* Emily Liles Harris of Spartanburg, South Carolina, manager of their one-hundred-acre farm while her husband served with the Confederacy, complained to her diary of the financial pinch caused by their mounting taxes.

> I have just returned from a visit to the village. I went up yesterday morning. While there I made a return of our property and the assessor tells me our tax (Confederate tax) will be $581.45. I have the means to pay it, but if we continue to be taxed during the next year as we have last I am afraid our means will utterly fail. I must comfort myself with "Sufficient unto to day is the evil thereof." I gave $5.00 for a pound of soda, $1.00 for a paper of needles, $4.00 for a spool of white cotton thread, $4.00 for a quire of paper. (Racine 1990, 332)

Southerners living on plantations or farms generally fared better by way of food supplies than their compatriots living in cities. However, government mandates that required farmers to turn over 10 percent of their crops to the government were especially hard on the small farmer. Parthenia Hague recalled:

> The first great pressing needs were food and clothing. Our government issued orders for all those engaged in agriculture to put only one tenth of their land in cotton, there being then no market for cotton. All agriculturalists, large or small, were also required by our government to give for the support of our soldiers one tenth of all the provisions they could raise,—a requirement with which we were only too willing to comply. (16)

*See chapter 7 for more detail regarding the problems of Northern farmers (pages 267–71).

Emily Harris recorded her trip into Spartanburg to comply with the government's "tithing orders." She was particularly despondent, however, over the requisitioning of one fourth of her slave labor.

> Friday. Today I went to the village and drove old Press. I paid to the government the tenth of our bacon which amounted to 138 lbs. Dr. Dean has bought some corn at $12.00 per bushel, he is going to try to buy me some but is not certain he can get it. I received warning to send a fourth of our slave labor to the coast immediately. I shall try to pay for a substitute and if I cannot get one I suppose I will be compelled to send one of our negroes, but they shall not budge till they are literally compelled to go. I've sent my husband and that is enough for me to do. A negro was hung today and two more are waiting to be hung in June. I feel bad, there is nothing to be glad about. *All is darkness.* (Racine 1990, 329)

Left to care for the family's plantation six miles north of Jackson, Mississippi, Lizzie Atkinson was repeatedly instructed by her husband not to comply with the impressment of slaves for it would leave her severely impoverished. On January 10, 1863, Thomas Atkinson advised Lizzie:

> I write you this short note to inform you fourteen men left here for Jackson this morning to press in negroes to work here at Vicksburg. As I think we have done our share of the work here wish you not to send any if you can possibly help it. They are going to take about three fourths of the men we have. . . . If these excuses with others you can make will not do any good tell the boy or boys you send that I say they kneed not come if they dont want to they can run away before they get to the depot and go back home and keep shy for a few days until they get away.

Arbitrary requisitions of horses, crops, and Negroes, along with frequent pleas for additional voluntary subscriptions entailed self-denial for many Southerners—or a wrestle with their consciences.

Kate Rowland was annoyed over the Confederate government's appropriation of all the salt in town. To Kate it was a "perfect species of swindling for they only pay 2/3 of the price given for it." This injustice led Kate to rationalize:

> I think a person perfectly justifiable in hiding it from the government. (10 November 1864)

In a diary entry dated March 11, 1865, Judith McGuire commended the altruism of both the farmers of the area and the women of Richmond.

> Fighting is still going on; so near the city, that the sound of cannon is ever in our ears. Farmers are sending in produce which they cannot spare, but which they give with a spirit of self-denial rarely equalled. Ladies are offering their jewelry, their plate, any thing which can be converted into money, for the country. I have heard some of them declare, that, if necessary, they will cut off their long suits of hair, and send them to Paris to be sold for bread for the soldiers; and there is not a woman, worthy of the name of Southerner, who would not do it, if we could get it out of the country, and bread or meat in return. . . . (340–41)

After making generous contributions to the Confederacy, Catherine Edmondston and her husband, Patrick, of Halifax County, North Carolina, looked to their garden, as did many Southerners, for their sustenance.

> This morning came an agent from a committee of citizens organized at Governor Vance's suggestion to collect voluntary subscriptions of meat, meal and flour for the Army. These supplies over and above every man's "surplus" that the Government already has. It must be from his own stock of provisions—what he denies himself for the sake of the Army. On consultation last week we had determined to deprive ourselves of meat at one meal per diem and to give what we save to the Army; but the need is so pressing that we go beyond that and give 500 pounds of meat and 1500 lbs. of meal which we had intended for our own table, and we live on bread and

vegetables. I must bestir myself and make every inch of my garden do its full duty. (99)

The armies' haphazard systems of paying their men and the unreliable mail systems employed to convey that money to their anxiously waiting families resulted in dire financial problems for the women at home. Both Union and Confederate governments were remiss in paying their troops on time. And even when payment was made, the money was usually insufficient, in the face of ridiculously high prices, to keep up a large family at home. General John W. Geary voiced the frustrations of thousands of his comrades of far lesser rank when he repeatedly complained to his wife:

> No paymaster here and I cannot send you a draft. (22 May 1864)
> I have received no pay for three months. You must draw on Mr. Wier to help you out of the scrape. (3 June 1864)

Too few families had a "Mr. Wier" to appeal to for help. Cornelia McDonald grieved for her husband, Angus, who, ill and aged by his war experiences, had become hopelessly despondent over their financial situation. Back pay that Angus had counted on for just such an emergency as the fall and winter of 1863 was not forthcoming.

> "I can get no money for you," he said. "They have refused my pay because I am unable to go on duty. What will you do?" he sobbed out in deepest grief. I wept, too, for him and me and the poor children, for I did not know what I could do. We were homeless as well as penniless. (184)

As indicated in the preceding chapter, enemy invasion and occupation were major contributors to the South's shortages. Louisa Fletcher and husband, of Marietta, Georgia, were utterly demoralized when their hotel, The Fletcher House, and store were burned by Sherman's troops in the fall of 1864. In a December 1, 1864, diary entry she wrote:

Poor Marietta is a complete wreck! It looks sad & deserted! I have no desire to live here any longer than till such time as we can dispose of what property we possess without too great a sacrifice & obtain conveyance to some place where we can enjoy the advantages of civilized society. Here we have no church, no commerce, no business of any kind & nothing to do with. The country people come in with loads of provision but will not sell for money. They want salt, old iron, hides, or something of the kind. Many families have little or nothing to eat. Robbers are coming in from the country & stealing from people's houses wherever they dare in broad daylight. (155)

Dolly Burge, a widow looking after the family's Georgia plantation following her husband's death, was also a victim of Sherman's troops. Her story and her deprivations were similar to those of thousands of Georgians and Carolinians. Mrs. Burge and her young daughter, Sadai, were powerless to prevent the Union soldiers' appropriation of her slaves, her farm animals, and all of her provisions.

But like demons they rush in! My yards are full. To my smoke-house, my dairy, pantry, kitchen, and cellar, like famished wolves they come, breaking locks and whatever is in their way. The thousand pounds of meat in my smoke-house is gone in a twinkling, my flour, my meat, my lard, butter, eggs, pickles . . . are all gone. My eighteen fat turkeys, my hens, chickens, and fowls, my young pigs, are shot down in my yard and hunted as if they were rebels themselves. Utterly powerless I ran out and appealed to the guard.
"I cannot help you, Madam: it is orders." (22–23)

After hours spent watching the ravaging of her house and yard, Mrs. Burge wrote in her journal:

Then, presently, more soldiers came by, and this ended the passing of Sherman's army by my place, leaving me poorer by thirty thousand dollars than I was yesterday morning. And a much stronger Rebel! (34)

Wartime economies in much of the South had long since curtailed the elaborate Christmas gift giving and bountiful holiday dinners of antebellum years; however, the Christmas following Sherman's march through Georgia was particularly austere. Dolly Burge pictured that Christmas in her diary.

> This has usually been a very busy day with me, preparing for Christmas not only for my own tables, but for gifts for my servants. Now how changed! No confectionery, cakes, or pies can I have. We are all sad; no loud jovial laugh from our boys [the slaves] is heard. Christmas Eve, which has ever been gaily celebrated here, which has witnessed the popping of fire-crackers and the hanging up of stockings, is an occasion now of sadness and gloom. I have nothing even to put in Sadai's stocking, which hangs so invitingly for Santa Claus. How disappointed she will be in the morning, though I have explained to her why he cannot come. Poor children! Why must the innocent suffer from the guilty? (43–44)

The next day she wrote:

> Sadai jumped out of bed very early this morning to feel in her stocking. She could not believe but that there would be something in it. Finding nothing, she crept back into bed, pulled the cover over her face, and I soon heard her sobbing. The little negroes all came in: "Christmas gift, mist'ess! Christmas gift, mist'ess!"
> I pulled the cover over my face and was soon mingling my tears with Sadai's. (44–45)

Overcrowding, especially in the large cities, helped generate severe shortages in the South. Even during the early days of the war Richmond began to feel the squeeze as more and more Southerners crowded into the city. Louise Wigfall Wright (Mrs. D. Giraud) explained the influx.

> Many of the private houses received boarders, as the reduction in the purchasing power of their incomes, through the depreciation of the currency, was already severely felt by the people. Yet this was not done for the sake of profit alone. The enormous influx of strangers from other states had to be accommodated. These were brought here by the presence of the

Government, and the proximity of the Army of Northern Virginia, which drew to Richmond hosts of anxious relatives, who waited through the weary weeks and months for occasional tidings, and possible glimpses of their loved ones. (76)

As time passed, it became almost impossible to find living accommodations in Richmond. A dispirited Judith McGuire described her own exhausting search for rooms and the miserable quarters of many of her less fortunate friends: a family of considerable wealth before the war confined to a damp Richmond basement; a mother and her four daughters crowded into one room.

> I cannot mention the numbers who are similarly situated; the country is filled with them. Country houses, as usual, show a marvellous degree of elasticity. A small house accommodating any number who may apply; pallets spread on the floor; every sofa and couch *sheeted* for visitors of whom they never heard before. If the city people would do more in that way, there would be less suffering. Every cottage in this village [just outside Richmond] is full; and now families are looking with wistful eyes at the ball-room belonging to the hotel, which, it seems to me, might be partitioned off to accommodate several families. The billiard-rooms are taken, it is said, though not yet occupied. But how everybody is to be supported is a difficult question to decide. (173)

The food shortages that accompanied the overcrowding drove the prices of eggs, milk, meat, vegetables, pots and pans, sheets and towels, firewood, and personal items to astronomical heights. Judith McGuire told of skillets renting for one dollar per month, of having had milk only twice in eighteen months, of eating one or two meals per day instead of three.

Even family pets were luxuries. In Richmond the daughter of writer John Beauchamp Jones grieved over the death of her aged cat, which had been "stumbling about from debility." Her father overtly sympathized with her, but at the same time secretly breathed a sigh of relief over the consequent reduction in household expenses. The family's parrot, he was convinced, would "*never* die" (J. Jones 1935, 2:258).

218

There were refugees in Richmond toward the end of the war who kept a ton of coal in their rooms, stowed the wood for cooking over the grate under their beds, and tried to fatten up a chicken, tied to the foot of the bed, with boiled peas (Avary 1903, 352–54). Additional problems were the robbers, constantly on the prowl to relieve residents of precious food and heating supplies (Putnam 1867, 341).

Hunger had been such a hardship for one little girl that she clapped her hands in glee over the fall of Richmond.

> "The Yankees have come! the Yankees have come!" she shouted, "and now we'll get something to eat. I'm going to have pickles and molasses and oranges and cheese and nuts and candy until I have a fit and die." (Avary 1903, 369)

Annie Laurie Broidrick recalled the scarcity of food and her emaciated condition during the war years, when she was a child.

> As the enemy came nearer and nearer, we were like rats shut in a hole. Food became scarcer and harder to procure. I remember once, for a childish offence, my mother caught my arm to administer corporal punishment. As she felt its thinness she burst into tears, and cried out, "O! I cannot, my poor little half-starved children, it is not naughtiness, it is hunger." (14)

Although food and housing shortages permeated much of the South, residents of towns under siege, such as Vicksburg and Petersburg, endured extraordinary hardships. Mrs. W. W. Lord and Mrs. James M. Loughborough (Mary Webster) drew bleak pictures of their life in the caves carved in the hillsides of Vicksburg.

> Sunday, June 28th, Still in this dreary cave. Who would have believed that we could have borne such a life for five weeks? The siege has lasted 42 days and yet no relief—every day this week we have waited for the sound of Gen. Johnston's guns, but in vain. (Lord, 6)
> Some families had light bread made in large quantities, and subsisted on it with milk (provided their cows were not killed from one milking time to another), without any more cooking, until called on to replenish. Though most of us lived on

corn bread and bacon, served three times a day, the only luxury of the meal consisting in its warmth. . . . (Loughborough 1864, 60)

Nevertheless, both women, despite their repetitious menu, fared far better than many of their fellow citizens who ate garbage, or mule meat, or rats to keep from starving.

During the weeks preceding the siege of Petersburg, Mrs. Roger Pryor, refugeeing in an abandoned overseer's "hovel" with her two young sons, later recalled the desperate plight of the city.

> Never had Petersburg been so healthy. No garbage was decaying in the streets. Every particle of animal or vegetable food was consumed, and the streets were clean. Flocks of pigeons would follow the children who were eating bread or crackers. Finally the pigeons vanished having been themselves eaten. Rats and mice disappeared. The poor cats staggered about the streets, and began to die of hunger. At times meal was the only article attainable except by the rich. An ounce of meat daily was considered an abundant ration for each member of the family. To keep food of any kind was impossible—cows, pigs, bacon, flour, everything, was stolen, and even sitting hens were taken from the nest. (Pryor 1904, 267)

By April 2, 1863, shortages had reached the critical stage in Richmond, and a crowd assembled in the city square to protest the scarcity of food. As the numbers of women and boys grew, emotions escalated to proportions of near mass hysteria and the women vented their anger by smashing windows and looting stores. (There were food riots in other cities as well as in Richmond.) Mrs. Roger Pryor's friend "Agnes" wrote that she singled out a pale, emaciated young girl in the crowd that was gathering in the streets and asked:

> "What is it? Is there some celebration?"
> "There *is*," said the girl solemnly; "we celebrate our right to live. We are starving. As soon as enough of us get together we are going to the bakeries and each of us will take a loaf of bread. That is little enough for the government to give us after it has taken all our men." (Pryor 1904, 238)

"Agnes" concluded her letter:

> Your General [Mrs. Pryor's husband] has been magnificent. He has fed Lee's army all winter—I wish he could feed our starving women and children. (Pryor 1904, 239)

Judith McGuire also registered her distress over the food riots and the hunger that sparked them.

> We were shocked when the gentlemen returned, to hear of the riot which occurred in Richmond today. A mob, principally of women, appeared in the streets, attacking the stores. Their object seemed to be to get any thing they could; dry-goods, shoes, brooms, meat, glassware, jewelry, were caught up by them. The military was called out—the Governor dispersed them from one part of the town, telling them that unless they disappeared in five minutes, the soldiers should fire among them. This he said, holding his watch in his hand. Mr. Munford, the President of the Young Men's Christian Association, quieted them on another street by inviting them to come to the rooms of the Association, and their wants should be supplied; many followed him—I suppose those who were really in want. Others there were, of the very worst class of women, and a great many who were not in want at all, which they proved by only supplying themselves with jewelry and other finery. The President was out speaking to them, and trying to secure order. The Mayor made them a speech, and seemed to influence them, but I dare say that the bayonets of the soldiers produced the most decided effect. It is the first time that such a thing has ever darkened the annals of Richmond. God grant it may be the last. I fear that the poor suffer very much: meal was selling to-day at $16 per bushel. It has been bought up by speculators. Oh that these hard-hearted creatures could be made to suffer! Strange that men with human hearts can, in these dreadful times, thus grind the poor. (202–3)

Hunger frequently bordered on starvation. Her situation had become so intolerable that Cornelia McDonald wished for death rather than a continuation of her suffering.

> One day, I can never forget it. I had been sitting at the table eating nothing. How could I eat bean soup and bread? I loathed

it and could not taste it. The children did, however, though it was easy to see they disliked it. But I was starving; I felt so weak and helpless and every thing seemed so dark, that for a time I was seized with utter despair. I felt that God had forsaken us, and I wished, oh! I wished that He would at one blow sweep me and mine from the earth. There seemed no place on it for us, no room for us to live.

I laid on a sofa through all those dreadful hours of unbelief and hopelessness; I had lost the feeling that God cared for us, that He even knew of our want. The whole dreadful situation was shown to my doubting heart; the empty pantry, for even the beans and bread were exhausted, and I should have to send the servant away. The house rent to be paid, and no money for it, although it had been due and demanded some time before. The coming cold weather and the want of everything that could make life bearable, made me wish it would end. I did not think; nor did I dare to pray the impious prayer that God would destroy us, but I wished it; I desired at that moment to be done with life, for no one seemed to care for us, whether we lived or died. How long I lay there I do not know, but after a while came the remembrance of the goodness my God had shown me . . . with that remembrance came the resolve, "Though He slay me, yet will I trust in Him." (267–68)

The South experienced acute shortages of clothing as well as food. Perhaps the most desperate need for clothing was revealed in Helen Maria Sharp's plaintive declaration to her soldier husband:

as for money i do wish it would come for i am near necked. (499)

Now and then imported goods brought in by blockade runners appeared in Southern stores or in makeshift shops. The wares provided a temporary solution for some women; others frowned on such self-indulgence. Louisa McCord Smythe recalled:

My mother set her face entirely against the importation of articles of clothing for women as she thought blockade running should be carried on entirely for the benefit of the Government and army. So for a long time she never let us buy anything that had run the blockade and I don't think she ever got anything for herself. So you can imagine we were put to it to contrive anything like respectability or comfort. Our best winter dresses through the latter part of the war were made of old riding habits ripped up and cleaned, and our best summer dresses were old pink evening barege dresses died black. These were so hot that we could hardly wear anything under them for fear of being overcome by the heat. Nobody minded looks for nearly everyone was in the same fix and to be too well dressed was a disgrace. (50)

In the North, although shortages were not nearly so pronounced as in the South, patriotic women organized groups to deter women from

buying any imported goods whilst this war lasts. They should especially give up buying expensive silks, laces, shawls, wines, etc., to stop the wild extravagance which seems the fashion by making it vulgar. (Hammond 1962, 290)

Maria Lydig Daly, of New York City, as president of the Women's Patriotic Association for Diminishing the Use of Imported Luxuries, devoted considerable time to the organization's work. Her observations in the spring of 1864 must have had a familiar ring to late twentieth-century American economists.

On Tuesday last there was a women's meeting at Cooper's Institute to take some measures to put down this extravagance in dress and entertainment which has been the rule for the last two years. The first year of the war our imports were less than our exports by fifteen million dollars from our great harvests, the scarcity of grain in Europe, and the general economy of our people. Last year, our imports exceeded our exports 50 million dollars, and this year the amount will be greater still. (Hammond 1962, 297)

With little or no merchandise to sell, many store owners in the South simply closed up their shops. Even making change had become almost impossible. Betty Herndon Maury, writing from Fredericksburg in the spring of 1862, explained in her diary:

> Goods of every kind are, of course, very scarce, and most of
> the stores are closed. . . . We never see a piece of silver however
> small, and are reduced to all sorts of devices to make change.
> I bought a spool of cotton the other day. It cost *37½ cts.* I gave
> the shop man half a dollar, and he handed me in change *two
> five cent stamps and a row of pins.* (64)

Despite the meticulous care given clothing, shoes wore out, material
gave out, dresses took on a tired, shabby appearance. In describing
the worrisome clothing problems facing most Southern women, Mary
Chesnut pointed out:

> We were all in a sadly molting condition. We had come to the
> end of our good clothes in three years, and now our only
> resource was to turn them upside down or inside out—mending,
> darning, patching. (Chesnut 1981, 459)

Several Southerners claimed they even "patched the patches."
Although sewing apparently was not her favorite activity, Catherine
Edmondston congratulated herself on her work in turning one of
her husband's overcoats.

> A miserable day, mist and rain until the earth is like a soaked
> sponge and smokes like a seething cauldron. I hard at work
> alone all day turning one of his thick overcoats! Think of it!
> Did I ever in former days think that I would come to sewing
> or he to wearing a turned coat. However it looks nice and I
> am thankful that it is worth the labour. (98)

Material for making dresses and undergarments soon became exceedingly difficult to obtain. Maria Beard Stewart remembered that
her mother was reduced to cutting up an old flag to make clothes
for the family during their refugee life in Biloxi. The linen "awn-
ings" that kept the porch cool in the summer were soon turned into
clothes that kept the children warm in the winter. (Scarlett O'Hara
was certainly not at all innovative when she pulled down the draperies
for material for a sorely needed new dress.)

Susan Bradford Eppes noted that as the lists of casualties grew, even
black material for mourning dresses and veils grew impossible to find.

. . . the demand for black dresses, for crape, for mourning veils,
stripped the Confederacy of these emblems of mourning and,
after that, you could not tell, when you saw a bright dress, how
much of bitter sorrow was hidden beneath it. (187)

The scarcity and price of cloth sent the more enterprising women
of both sections back to the spinning wheel and loom. Often the
women picked the cotton or sheared the wool themselves. Then came
the tedious work of carding, spinning, winding, dyeing, and weaving—the latter a slow process that took ten or twelve hours to produce
one or two yards of cloth. Virginia Norfleet, who had grown up during the war near Franklin, Virginia, recalled:

> For the four years of the war every piece of cloth that we
> used was made in this way.

Weavers who did not spin their own yarn, however, were frequently
hard put to secure "factory" thread. Not infrequently customers were
required to draw lots in order to be able to purchase even one bunch.
Sallie Jewell, of Oglethorpe County, Georgia, writing to her brother,
a private in the Confederate army, complained about the difficulty
of obtaining the much sought after thread.

> I have no news to write only we have a great deal of work to
> do. Ma is busy making soap. . . . May is weaving and I have
> been spinning . . . factory thread is selling $4½ a bunch but
> you can never get any of it for when you go after it they will
> not let you have it for anything but provisions. Carry that and
> they want money. Take [that] back and then they will say they
> cannot let you have any for they have got to pay their debts
> and so it is you have to go back home and take to the cards
> and wheel. But what is the worst of all you have to give $10
> for a wheel and $16 or $20 for a loom and $16 for a pair of
> cards without any backs and by that time you can spend a
> pocket full of money. (18 March 1863)

In time the demand for thread became so great that, as Mrs.
Sylvester Bleckley explained, it often could be obtained only through
bartering.

225

> Confederate money got so cheap it was hard to buy thread with money. We had to barter tallow, beeswax, leather, and sheep's wool for thread. I have often thought what a blessing we had a cotton factory then to supply our country and town in thread for our use. A neighbor woman would get ready to make a trip to the factory in a buggy, sending word around to her neighbors that she would carry anything she could for them. So she started off in her buggy or one-horse wagon, loaded up with articles for barter from many families, and great would be the excitement when she returned, bringing the needed requirements for our clothing. One bunch of thread would warp about thirty yards. Ladies in the country who took in weaving would have to be paid in something more valuable than Confederate money. I heard of one woman who had thirty yards of cloth woven for a half-pint of castor oil. (T. Taylor 1903, 362)

Thread was not only hard to come by, it was usually very expensive. Mrs. Warren Akin wrote of her delight in being able to purchase two bunches of factory thread for $56 a bunch.

> It is selling here at $100.00 per bunch or 25 lbs of bacon if its paid in that. Spools of thread sell here for $10.00 per spool, needles from 10 to 20 dollars a paper. I tell you when I have a needle taken from my cushion now I am angry and scold shamefully. (127–28)

As Mrs. Akin pointed out, needles were at a premium. One lady kept her only needle secreted away in the clock in order to keep it out of the hands of "meddlesome busybodies." Catherine Edmondston noted in her diary that her husband

> bought me a paper of 000 needles for which he paid ten dollars. He brought me a piece of long cloth from Halifax to look at and buy if I wished, at forty-five dollars a yard for the piece— fifty dollars for part of it. I decided we could not afford it. I was unwilling to wear the price of three barrels of corn in one chemise. Think of $1800.00 for a piece of long cloth! (98–99)

Pins also became scarce and therefore were carefully guarded. According to Mrs. Roger Pryor:

People walked about with downcast eyes; they were looking for pins! Thorns were gathered and dried to use as pins. (Pryor 1904, 266)

Surprisingly, very few women registered serious complaints about their made-over, pieced, and patched clothing. In fact, Virginia Norfleet took great pride in her fashionable, homemade outfit of 1863.

> I must tell you of the first time I was ever well dressed. I have never felt that I was as fine or elegantly gowned as I was the first time I put on that new spring suit for church. I have had silks and beautiful, nice clothes and lovely hats and bonnets and pretty nice shoes since, but none could ever be compared with that lovely, beautiful costume. . . . The shoes were made of dog skin that my brothers had gotten from some place, I do not know whether it was a hound or some nice bird dog or a yellow cur. One thing I do know is that they were the easiest and nicest shoes to the foot and so soft and comfortable, and when you walked one could not hear you, the step was so light and easy, and that was the one joy of my heart to have one pair of shoes that made no noise, because it was considered very rude to walk heavy. I shall never forget those shoes, they were to me beautiful.
>
> I wish you could have one dress that would come as near to your idea of perfection, just the dress you had been dreaming of and wishing for, but never expected that it could be possible for you to really possess it; that would be too good to be true. Well, this was my dress. I watched and helped in the process of making from the picking of the cotton all the way through, for there was just one dress planned in the weaving of the cloth, it was a blue and small black check, fast good colors, the cloth was very smooth and pretty, mother had taken so much time and thought to make it the very best and prittiest of all the cloth she ever made. I am sure that that was one of the reasons I appreciated it so much. . . .

The family had splurged on a fashionable straw hat for Virginia which was home-trimmed with a small piece of black silk and festooned with Virginia's pride and joy—a plume made of corn shucks!

As more and more items became unobtainable the need to discover substitutes taxed women's imagination to the utmost. Scarcities of coffee, tea, salt, sugar, raisins, paper, candles, buttons, dyes, and other basics became favorite topics of conversation and their substitutes the subjects of thousands of newspaper columns. Problems in obtaining coffee and tea caused almost universal consternation. As Kate Cumming noted:

> The scarcity of coffee seems to affect the spirits of the people more than any thing else. I have noticed that some who did not touch it before the war, talk as gravely about its loss as if their very existence depended upon it, and indeed they are quite melancholy about it. It is amusing to see how seriously it is discussed. I have said jestingly that I do believe it will yet be the means of subjugating us. When invited any place, if we are certain of getting a cup of pure coffee, or even a cup of that which "cheers," there is no sending "regrets" to that invitation. (248)

Southern women who gasped at paying fifty cents a pound for coffee in the early days soon wished they had squirreled away mass quantities of the precious bean when prices quickly rose to fifty dollars a pound. Coffee, indeed, became a luxury. Its scarcity set housewives to work frantically attempting to "manufacture" substitutes out of ochre, chestnuts, rye, sweet potatoes, beans, wheat, and chicory.

Tea, though less popular than coffee, also became scarce and women experimented with drying raspberry, huckleberry, blackberry, currant, holly-tree, and various vegetable leaves as replacements for expensive tea leaves. The gift of a small amount of "real tea" was a godsend to Malvina Gist; however, Malvina encountered a small problem when she added the sugar.

> It is next door to starvation with us, and no mistake. Each day we send to headquarters for a little bacon and some meal, and that is what we live on, if it may be called living. It is true, we have a little sugar, and a small quantity of real tea a dear old lady gave me in Newberry, but the sugar was buried while the Federal army was here, and in consequence is infested with those pestiferous little creatures who never fail to make the best of their opportunities. Now, some who may chance to read these lines might say that they couldn't go ant-tea. But I go it! It is

much better than no tea at all. Moreover, I manage it after a way of my own which vastly increases its palatability. I found out how to do it. I skim all I can conveniently off the top, then I shut my eyes tight and fast, then I open my mouth (which is a good-sized mouth) and it all runs down (ants too), and then I open my eyes and put the cup down and say to myself, "Good! Very good! I like tea." (T. Taylor 1903, 288)

Salt, of course, was important not only to cooking but also to the preserving of meat. Scores of diaries described the process of digging up the floors of smokehouses and "boiling the earth until the dirt and salt were separated. This required many boilings and skimmings before the salt was left clean" (T. Taylor 1903, 142). Honey and sorghum were substitutes for sugar.

Catherine Edmondston marveled over a "raisin" cake made of dried cherries and whortle-berries which was served at a wedding.

"Confederate raisins" are dried peaches clipped to bits with the scissors, and quite nice puddings they make. "Puddings!" what a reminiscence! Seems ages since I dabbled in sugar—currants—macaroni—and sago. "What shall I have for dessert?" seems a question of medieval times—so long it is since the question perplexed me! (61)

The scarcity of leather and therefore the inability to replace outgrown or worn-out shoes became an immense problem for the South. (The need for shoes, of course, accidentally helped set the stage for the Battle of Gettysburg when on July 1, 1863, General Harry Heth sent troops out on a search for a rumored supply of shoes at that "quiet little crossroads town.") The fashionable Mary Chesnut exulted in the gift of a pair of shoes from her uncle, even though they were not her size.

He gave me an excellent pair of shoes. What a gift! For more than a year I have had none but some dreadful things Armsted makes for me—and they hurt my feet so. These do not fit, but that is nothing. They are large enough and do not pinch anywhere. Absolutely a respectable pair of shoes!! (Chesnut 1981, 464)

Imaginative women employed wood, carpets, cloth, and pigskin in their attempts to create shoes that would serve, if not for the duration, at least for a month—or a few days. Mrs. Roger Pryor told of making shoes "of carpet lined with flannel" for her baby.

> I could in one day make a pair which she wore out in three! (Pryor 1904, 316).

Parthenia Hague described the family's futile attempts to make long wearing shoes from pigskin tanned at home.

> . . . and I smile even now when I remember how we used to hold our self-made shoes at arm's length and say, as they were inspected: "What is the blockade to us, so far as shoes are concerned, when we cannot only knit the uppers, but cut the soles and stitch them on? Each woman and girl her own shoemaker; away with bought shoes; we want none of them!" But alas, we really knew not how fickle a few months would prove that we were. (54)

Kid gloves were much in demand by members of the social set. Susan Dabney Smedes recalled:

> The only bridal present bought for one of our brides during the war was a pair of green kid gloves—white could not be bought—they cost fifty dollars, and were both for the left hand! (213)

As might be expected, the scarcity and prices of women's hats created great havoc. Untold hours went into the fashioning and refashioning of hats and bonnets. A new flower, a pretty ribbon, a piece of veiling added to a prewar hat often gave the homespun-clad wearer a brief moment of at least quasi-stylishness. Virginia Tarrh remembered:

> One bonnet did me during the whole war. It underwent many changes and divers colors of trimmings. Sometimes it would have a piece of pasteboard put on in front to give the additional

height known in those days as sky-scrapers; then when fashion changed, the pasteboard could be taken off to diminish the shape. (T. Taylor 1903, 191)

Plaiting hats from palmetto leaves frequently produced extremely satisfactory results which now and then could turn a profit for an imaginative stylist. Sallie Jewell, of Oglethorpe County, Georgia, wrote to her brother about her resourceful "millinery business."

> I sold the two [hats] I made at $2 apiece. It was not the highest prices . . . they are selling at $5 . . . but I have not got that high yet but may ask some that are able to pay it before I get through. (3 July 1863)

From Richmond Judith McGuire wrote admiringly of the plaited straw hats that had become so popular everywhere in the South.

> Almost every girl plaits her own hat, and that of her father, brother, and lover, if she has the bad taste to have a lover out of the army, which no girl of spirit would do unless he is incapacitated by sickness or wounds. But these hats are beautifully plaited of rye straw, and the ladies' hats are shaped so becomingly, that though a Parisian milliner might pronounce them old-fashioned, and laugh them to scorn, yet our Confederate girls look fresh and lovely in them, with their gentle countenances and bright, enthusiastic eyes; and what do we care for Parisian style, particularly as it would have to come to us through Yankee-land? The blockade has taught our people their own resources. (196–97)

Before the war's end almost everything was in short supply in the South: hairpins, toothbrushes, buttons, soap, cologne, pencils, pens, ink, candles, stationery. The paper shortage was reflected in newspapers that were sometimes printed on wallpaper; that almost daily varied in size—sometimes a single column, sometimes a half sheet, sometimes a normal-sized sheet; that many times were not printed at all. The scarcities of stationery and ink would have discouraged most correspondents. Undaunted, Civil War women economized by writing "crosswise." They first wrote left to right on

231

the paper and then turned their letters and wrote bottom to top over their earlier writing. Making the ink involved experimentation with oak balls, green persimmons, various tree barks, elderberries, and rusty nails—the latter to add more color. Envelopes were turned and used again. New envelopes were fashioned out of wallpaper or wrapping paper. Letters were often sealed with peach tree gum.

The era's diarists wrote on a variety of papers. Frances Peter used military hospital supply sheets; Catherine Virginia Baxley recorded her journal in a copy of Tennyson's *Enoch Arden*; Eliza Frances Andrews wrote with homemade ink in an old daybook.

Buttons were at a premium and pasteboard, persimmon seeds, pine bark, gourd shells, and thorns with waxed ends served in their stead. Candles became extremely scarce. The fortunate few who still had molds melted tallow and made candles as in former years. As the supply of tallow disappeared, women made "Confederate candles" by dipping cloth into melted wax (beeswax, myrtle wax, turpentine, or rosin) and then wrapping it around an old candlestick, a corn cob, or a hickory stick. "Confederate lamps" were tumblers of lard with wicks. Pine knots from the forest were probably the most universally used illuminants.

Of course no book about women, at least about women living in the nineteenth century, would be complete without some mention being made of weddings. And unfortunately, wartime weddings were no exception to shortages—often of groomsmen, and from time to time of grooms themselves.

Betty Maury's brother, Dick, tried numerous times to obtain leave to marry his fiancée, Sue Crutchfield. On October 18, 1861, Betty Maury wrote:

> Mrs. Hart, Sue Crutchfield's cousin, was here yesterday to invite us to her house Tuesday evening. She says that her oysters and ice cream will not keep, and that if Dick comes it will be his wedding, and if not, it will be her party. I do not see how she or aunt Lucy can have the heart to prepare a party or wedding entertainment in these times, when we cannot look one day into the future, and everything before us is so dark and

gloomy. The very night of the party Dick and many other dear
ones may be engaged in a *terrible* battle. (43–44)

When a telegram from Dick announced that he would be unable
to get home for his wedding, his sister lamented:

> Dick's wedding day, and he is not here! How entirely the con-
> dition of the country changes everything! Six months ago a
> gentleman who failed to keep such an engagement would have
> been forever disgraced. Now it is scarcely a matter of comment.
> (44)

A second wedding date set for the following Christmas Day seemed
promising, yet once again the bridegroom wired his inability to get
a leave. In fact, that frantic attempt to get home resulted in his arrest and a threatened court martial. Finally, six months later on July
17, 1862, Dick and Sue were married.

The safe return of Louisa McCord's fiancé was made even more
joyous by the young couple's decision to marry at once. However,
their frustrations in procuring wedding attire, food for the reception, and even the ring itself were undoubtedly typical of hundreds
of Southern wartime weddings. Louisa's trousseau, scraped together
from the generous contributions of a few yards of cambric and
makeovers from family and friends, was apparently a monument to
needlework ingenuity. Old gloves were re-dyed with ink as were two
pairs of ragged slippers.

A suitable wedding dress, however, presented the greatest problem
of all. Inquiries throughout the town (Columbia, South Carolina)
failed to turn up a *white* wedding gown. Throughout the war, Louisa's
mother had adamantly refused to purchase goods that had been pro-
cured through the blockade and at war's end she was equally resistant to trading with the hated Yankees. However, in desperation
Mrs. McCord, "anxious to do this one thing so desired," swallowed
her pride, compromised her convictions, and sought to purchase a
few rare yards of white muslin from a Yankee entrepreneur who had
set up shop among the ashen remains of Columbia. Mrs. McCord's

humiliation quickly changed to anger when the shopkeeper resolutely refused to part with the material for anything other than ten dollars in greenbacks, which in those times in Columbia were extremely rare.

Still undaunted, determined to see her daughter married in style, Mrs. McCord sent a piece of carpet, which had been "too stiff" to cut into soldier's blankets, along with the chairs from her room to an auction, but alas, they did not bring the hoped for ten dollars. Louisa recalled:

> And then, what did my mother do, *my* mother! with all her pride! She went and begged that Yankee to keep the muslin a few days, which he hemmed and hawed about doing . . . and she drove round town selling lard and butter until she made up the deficiency in the $10.00, bought the dress [material] and brought it home to me! Do you think I can ever forget that? (Smythe, 75)

Unfortunately, by the end of the war the fine jewelry of most Southern women had been appropriated by the Yankees or had been bartered for food or clothing and therefore even the securing of a wedding ring became a challenge. It looked as though the ceremony would have to be postponed a few weeks when, shortly before the wedding, Louisa's young bridegroom-to-be hurried over from his home in Clarendon district to announce sadly that "none of his people in Clarendon" had a ring. He would be forced to make a trip to another part of the state to try to borrow a ring from his aunts or cousins. Fortunately, once again Louisa's family came to the rescue. Her sister offered a ring given to her on her sixteenth birthday, her mother provided the guard ring, and the wedding took place as scheduled.

Although Louisa had hoped to be married in the church, the McCords had no appropriate transportation, their buggy having been confiscated, and therefore the bride, reluctant to walk a long distance in her wedding dress and veil, agreed to being married at home. There were few wedding guests and even two would-be-guests, who had come to Columbia for another wedding, were unable to stay for Louisa's ceremony "because their supply of horse feed gave out!" A friend contributed some raisins to help fill out the meager refreshments and six candles, which the family cut in half to furnish the traditional candlelight. (If it is true that every bride should wear "something old, something new, something borrowed, and something blue," Louisa's wedding certainly qualified on at least three counts!)

As conditions worsened, women soon realized their pet household economies and imaginative substitutions provided merely superficial answers to the deepening crisis. Once again, women showed their mettle—they rolled up their sleeves and went to WORK.

Selling or trading off expensive jewelry and clothing constituted the first divestiture, soon to be followed by the sale of the family's silver, oil paintings, and fine furniture. Sallie Brock Putnam remembered the parade of blacks who called at her door with baskets of goods to sell for their owners.

> The situation of the refugees was often painful in the extreme. It was no unusual thing to have presented at our doors a basket in the hands of a negro servant who sold on commission articles disposed of by the necessitous to obtain food. Handsome dresses, patterns of unmade goods, purchased perhaps before the commencement or in the beginning of the war, a piece of silver, or sets of jewelry, accompanied by a note anonymously sent, attested the poverty and noble pride of some woman who doubtless wore a cheerful face, and when asked if she desired peace, would reply "Only with liberty." (253)

Jewelry stores in cities throughout the South resold valuable bracelets, necklaces, rings, and watches for citizens forced to sell their most treasured possessions in order to procure food. Bookshops served as middlemen for families compelled to relinquish a few books at a time or whole libraries of cherished volumes.

Susan Blackford was among the many reduced to selling their homes and furniture as a means of securing some small income.

I still think it wise we should break up housekeeping; indeed we are shut up to that course, as starvation is the only other alternative, and this necessity gives me nerve to bear it. (218)

Mrs. Roger Pryor's trunk full of ball gowns and evening cloaks (worn during her gay antebellum days in Washington while her husband served as Congressman from Virginia) proved a lifesaver during the latter months of the war. When her husband, a general with the Confederate forces, was captured and imprisoned, Mrs. Pryor grew desperate for a means of support for her family. As history has shown, "necessity is the mother of invention" and Mrs. Pryor cleverly hit on the idea of cutting up the lace from the dresses, refashioning it into collars and sleeves and sending them off to a Richmond store. The collars proved immensely popular with women who still had money to purchase goods and the proceeds from the sales put food on the Pryors' table.

> After I had converted all my laces into collars, cuffs, and sleeves, and had sold my silk gowns, opera cloak, and point lace handkerchiefs, I devoted myself to trimming the edges of the artificial flowers, and separating the long wreaths and garlands into clusters for hats and *bouquets de corsage*. (Pryor 1904, 315)

With inflation at outrageous heights, even Mrs. Pryor's temporary "affluence" was ephemeral. Her first purchase—a barrel of flour—cost $1300. Greater ingenuity was needed.

> The time came when the salable contents of the Washington trunk were all gone. I then cut up my husband's dress-coat, and designed well-fitting ladies' gloves, with gauntlets made of the watered silk lining. Of an interlining of gray flannel I made gray gloves, and this glove manufacture yielded me hundreds of dollars. (Pryor 1904, 317)

Although Mary Chesnut was able to help to some degree in relieving the family's financial burdens, she bemoaned the fact that the receipts for her dresses and her butter and eggs sales were in depreciated Confederate dollars.

My pink silk dress I have sold for six hundred dollars, to be paid in installments, two hundred a month for three months. And I sell my eggs and butter from home for two hundred dollars a month. Does it not sound well—four hundred dollars a month, regularly? In what? "In Confederate money." Hélas! (Chesnut 1981, 643)

As the war wore on and inflation continued its ruinous course, desperate Southern women saw no alternative but to seek some form of remunerative work—almost any kind—few jobs were too menial.

Heretofore, in the antebellum South, relatively few women had held jobs outside the home. Even teaching was looked upon as an expedient, an occupation relegated to spinsters or daughters of impoverished families. During the war years, however, numerous Southern conventions, including the reluctance to see women enter the teaching profession—or any other profession for that matter—were gradually, although not universally, modified. In the absence of their husbands, women of both sections took up public work in shops, in factories, and in government offices. In Richmond and Columbia, for example, positions signing bills in the Treasury Department were opened to women, with widows and refugees usually given priority.

Initially, Judith McGuire was incensed at the demeaning aspects of having to take an arithmetic test preliminary to obtaining a job as a clerk with the Commissary Department in Richmond; however, she was most eager to accept the position and thus supplement the family's income. (Mrs. McGuire received a salary of $125 per month, later raised to $150, for six hours of accountant work per day. Afternoons, Mrs. McGuire usually devoted to her hospital work.)

They [officials] require us to say that we are really in want of the office—rather a work of supererogation, I should say, as no lady would bind herself to keep accounts for six hours per day without a dire necessity. (244)

As for the arithmetic test:

> This requirement may be right, but it certainly seems to me
> both provoking and absurd that I must be examined in arith-
> metic by a commissary major young enough to be my son. If
> I could afford it, I would give up the appointment, but, as it
> is, must submit with the best grace possible, particularly as other
> ladies of my age have to submit to it. (244–45)

Faced with families destitute of food and clothing, a great many
energetic women devised their own sources of revenue by market-
ing their homemade wine and condiments, baking pies and cakes
for the soldiers, working as seamstresses for the government and/or
the townspeople, taking in boarders, or conducting schools. Judith
McGuire described some of the successful enterprises undertaken
by her friends in Richmond.

> Several of us are engaged in making soap, and selling it, to buy
> things which seem essential to our wardrobes. A lady who has
> been perfectly independent in her circumstances, finding it
> necessary to do something of the kind for her support, has been
> very successful in making pickles and catsups for the restaurants.
> Another, like Mrs. Primrose, rejoices in her success in making
> gooseberry wine which sparkles like champagne, and is the best
> domestic wine I ever drank; this is designed for the highest
> bidder. . . . A gentleman, lately from Columbia, tells me that
> the South Carolina girls pride themselves on their palmetto
> hats; and a belle of a large fortune, who used to think no bonnet
> presentable but one made by the finest New York or Parisian
> milliner, now glories in her palmetto. . . . (196–97)

Hundreds of women discovered a livelihood doing government
sewing. The Quartermaster's Department of the Confederate Army
came up with a plan which helped to relieve some of the financial
difficulties of the poor and at the same time helped to provide much
needed clothing for the troops: the government supplied the material
and then paid needy women to construct the jackets, pants, and
drawers at home. One such family was befriended by "Miss Abby,"
a keen observer of the disastrous inflation and unreasonable prices
existing in Atlanta long before the appearance of General Sherman
and his men.

238

A woman came to see me to day, and bursting into tears said—"My husband can't get detailed any longer. He has already been published as a deserter, and how *am* I to get bread for my children, when meal is twenty dollars a bushel, and I have such poor health"! Then she cried out again—"O, I wish these Yankees would ever get here, before we are all murdered and starve to death"! This woman has five children; the eldest, a daughter about sixteen, has a bad cough—but walks two miles to town to obtain Goverment sewing—pants, coats &c. She stops here frequently to rest, for the material is of the heaviest kind. She gets one dollar for pants, a dollar & a half for coats, and fifty cents for shirts. She has been sewing for months to get a pair of shoes, and came yesterday to show them to me—she was so delighted. She is now saving her tickets, and not drawing the money for her sewing, fearing she would have to spend it—until she has enough to buy her a calico dress. Calico is ten and twelve dollars a yard. Is it any marvel that crime and prostitution are so common? This girl is intelligent and refined in her feelings, and she often cries when she tells me of the insults she receives from the men who deal out the work.

Many a woman walks eight or ten miles to town to get sewing; they often have no shoes, or only those made of cloth "pitched within & without"—and rarely ever wear stockings—for the simple reason they have none. The dresses of the countrywomen are sometimes made of flour sacks dyed with bark; gingham "Sunbonnets" were long ago dispensed with,—and those made of straw or the long leaved pine take their place. (6)

In the North, Miss H. A. Severance, of Leydon, Massachusetts, kept a diary of her lonely experiences as a worker in a Northampton hoopskirt factory in the spring of 1863. "Tired almost to death" and with raw, sore hands, Miss Severance had difficulty making enough hoops each day to pay for her room and board. Her later work as housekeeper for her uncle proved much more to her liking.

With most of the male educators in the armies, countless women took up teaching as a practical solution to their financial problems. Although at first some husbands and fathers (particularly in the South for female teachers were more generally accepted in the North) voiced strong objections, in time, resistance to women in the teaching profession subsided and a bright new future for women in the field of education was opened.

Susan Blackford, of Lynchburg, Virginia, took in boarders to help defray expenses, and as the family's debts continued to mount she approached her husband about taking a teaching position.

> If you think best, I can try and get a small school with which to eke out our small means. I am sure I can make enough to meet my own wants. Let me hear from you at once. I know that at first you will be shocked at the idea of your wife going to work to support herself, but you are so situated you can do nothing more and I should bear my share of the burden. (217)

Anne Frobel's black servant was greatly embarrassed that Anne's sister Lizzie would stoop to teaching school.

> Old mammie was always very much scandalized that Lizzie should teach the children of the neighborhood. Seems to think it entirely beneath her dignity. . . . She feels this [the Frobels' scarcities of food and money] a great degradation, and thinks it is her province to keep up the honour of the family. She has a vast deal of family pride. (159)

Although the John B. Grimballs were opposed to having their daughter accept a teaching position at a nearby school, their financial situation offered no other alternative. After considerable discussion, a friend of Emma Holmes finally won over her family and took a job teaching at a village school.

> Her father and brothers were much opposed to it at first but she, like myself, was very desirous of doing something for herself, especially in these times, and they at last consented that she should do so for a few months. (Holmes 1979, 172)

When she first discussed setting up a business to help with the family's war losses, Harriet McLellan met with great opposition from her husband on the grounds of "public opinion." Convinced that she could throw "foolish prejudices aside," Harriet remained oblivious to what others might say or think. Through a series of trips to the North to purchase fancy goods to sell in Marietta, Georgia,

Harriet managed to conduct a successful business which saw the family through the difficult times resulting from the war and from her husband's apparent addiction to the "intoxicating cup."

In their battle with privation on the homefront, most women met their hardships head on, exhibiting the steely determination and ingrained resourcefulness that carried them through the war. After selling off or bartering everything of value that could be spared, women entrenched themselves for the duration. Women who had never worked outside the home gratefully accepted menial jobs with the government. Women with young children to care for set up soap making or fruit canning "businesses" in their homes. Others took in boarders and in a sense became "slaves" themselves to their demanding patrons. Still others were out of bed before dawn each morning to begin exhausting work in the fields.

For four arduous years war and deprivation presented women on the homefront with momentous trials of stamina and resiliency, with illimitable challenges to their capabilities and ingenuity. For four long years women proved that they too were fighters, that courage and bravery and boldness were to be found on homefronts as well as on battlefronts.

CHAPTER VII

"Much to Do"
Part I

> . . . while men are making a free-will offering of their life's
> blood on the altar of their country, women must not be idle.
> We must do what we can for the comfort of our brave men.
> We must sew for them, knit for them, nurse the sick, keep up
> the faint-hearted, give them a word of encouragement in season
> and out of season. There is much for us to do, and we must
> do it!
> —*Judith Brockenbrough McGuire* 1889, 12–13

Although an ardent Southerner, Judith Brockenbrough McGuire
in her May 1861 diary entry vividly set forth the wartime responsibilities facing the women of both sections. In time, as the war gained
momentum, virtually every woman in America became involved in
working for the war effort in one way or another—as a volunteer
in the ubiquitous soldiers' aid societies, as a vital force in the production of food supplies for the armies and the homefront, as a com-
forter and morale booster through letters and hospital work.

At first the prospects of two or three years without the protection
and support of their husbands tended to frighten and bewilder many
a young wife as she watched her husband march off to war. In a
letter to her sister, Janette Stoddard, of Fairgrove, Michigan, despaired

> . . . what will become of me with my poor health and with
> three helpless little ones dependent upon me, for everything.
> Or of him with poor health, exposed to hardships, danger and
> death? We all call this a cruel war, but when it takes our loved

ones from us, *then* it comes right home and we begin to feel
that it is cruel indeed.

Southern women, such as Matilda Champion, of Mississippi, expressed many of the same feelings of apprehension and loss when
their husbands left to serve with the Confederate forces.

> ... if only you can only be spared to me I shall be satisfied but
> Oh my God if I should lose you my precious where should I
> turn for some one to lean against. One of my first thoughts when
> you joined the army was that Pa was old and might die, you
> might get killed, and then I would be without a protector in
> the world with my four children to raise. (Champion 8 July 1864).

For most women, however, including Janette Stoddard and Matilda
Champion, their self-pity soon subsided. Most quickly recovered their
equanimity, realizing that the tremendous responsibilities for maintaining their homes and farms, caring for their families, and buoy-
ing the morale of their soldier husbands were now settled squarely
on their shoulders for the duration of the war.

When Emily Liles Harris's husband left their hundred-acre farm-
home near Spartanburg, South Carolina, to serve with the Confederate army, Emily was already burdened with caring for their seven
children ranging in age from one year and nine months to fourteen.
Suddenly she found herself faced with the additional responsibilities of managing their farm and their black labor force.

> The trial has come at last, my husband has gone to the war,
> he left me yesterday afternoon. I thought I would rather not
> go with him to the depot but after he had gone I felt an almost
> irresistible impulse to follow him and keep his beloved coun-
> tenance in my sight as long as possible. It was hard parting,
> a bitter farewell. Ninety days* how long to be without him,
> how long for him to bear the privations and hardships of the
> camp and ... how I shudder to think I may never see him
> again. A load of responsibilities are resting upon me in his

---

*Southerners as well as Northerners anticipated a very short war. David Harris's serv-
ice extended not for merely ninety days but from November of 1862 to the war's end.

absence but I shall be found trying to bear them as well as I can. (Racine 1980, 388–89)

In the early days following Fort Sumter chaos reigned. Neither side was prepared for war; neither side expected the conflict to be of lasting duration. Almost overnight both sides found themselves hopelessly ill-equipped to meet the basic needs for food, clothing, and shelter required by the tens of thousands of volunteers and hastily recruited soldiers. All too soon came a desperate need for hospitals, medical attention, and nursing care for untold numbers of wounded, sick, and dying soldiers.

The emergency at first seemed overwhelming. Within days, however, both sections experienced an incredible "uprising of women." Wives, mothers, sisters, and lovers everywhere rushed forth to volunteer their time and talents to the war effort. Soldiers' aid societies sprang up overnight in towns and cities all across the country. The enthusiasm was unbridled; the activity often chaotic. Everyone wanted to help.

Catherine Edmondston noted in her diary the sustained fervor of Southern women, many of whom were unaccustomed to such rigorous activity.

> One thing struck me throughout the whole progress of the summer; the universality—and the eagerness with which the women entered into the struggle! They work—as many of them had never worked before steadily and faithfully to supply the soldiers with clothing and the hospitals with comforts of various kinds—everything must be given to them and everything must be done for them. (Edmondston n.d., 34)

In the North, women by the tens of thousands devoted their days and even nights to the work of the myriad of newly founded soldiers' aid societies. In local, as well as in the big city organizations, every volunteer was welcomed and put to work. Those with exceptional speaking abilities trod the lecture circuit soliciting funds; those with organizational talents planned benefits, concerts and theatricals. Others devoted their days to cutting, sewing, and packing the tons of clothing, bandages, and hospital supplies that were sent to the various camps. Still others spent untold hours cooking, canning, and drying the foodstuff that helped supplement meager army rations. Sarah Jane Full Hill's observation that in St. Louis "Every loyal household became a soldier's aid society" held true not only for St. Louis but for communities everywhere.

Typical of this unflagging commitment by women to alleviating the suffering on the battlefields was the Ladies' Springfield (Illinois) Soldiers' Aid Society. (Payment of twenty-five cent dues constituted membership.) Their annual report of September 11, 1862, noted that during the year they had furnished

> 50 cotton shirts . . . 522 pairs of cotton drawers . . . 122 pairs of cotton socks, 259 pairs of woolen socks, 155 pairs of slippers . . . 213 handkerchiefs, 234 towels . . . 154 pillow ticks . . . 676 pillow cases . . . 2,492 bandages, and large quantities of cornstarch, barley, tea, crackers, soap, jars, jellies, pickles, fruits. . . .

Similar contributions from affluent as well as poor women prompted Mary Livermore to write:

> It was from these and similar sources, multiplied thousands of times, that the stream of supplies for the sick and weary of the army maintained its vast and constant proportions to the very close of the war. The supplies varied according to the needs of the men at the front. But whatever was the need as to quality, quantity, or cost, it was soon apparent that in the zeal and intense nationality of the women of the North there was a certainty of its being supplied systematically and bountifully. No rebuffs could chill their zeal; no reverses repress their ardor; no discouragements weaken their devotion. The women had enlisted for the war. (154)

Both Confederate and Union women devoted countless hours to knitting "the everlasting sock" or glove. (Quaker women, of course, knitted mittens to insure there would be no trigger finger.) As her contribution to the war effort, one woman knit a sock a day (a total of

750 pairs), even compromising her religious scruples to knit on Sunday.

Years later, Louisa McCord Smythe recalled the continual preoccupation with knitting.

> Through all this the knitting went on—all of us knitted—all the time. My mother knit day and night, walking, driving, under all circumstances. When troubles and sorrows came thick and fast and sleep came no longer to comfort her, I used to wake at night and listen to the click, click of her needles, and shudder at the groans and sobs that accompanied them when she supposed no one heard her. (50)

Ladies took their knitting with them everywhere, as Emma Holmes noted in her diary, "even when they go out to take tea." She continued, "This evening . . . out of eleven ladies gathered, eight were knitting stockings . . . " (93).

Making pillowcases, underclothing, handkerchiefs, hospital gowns, shirts, and tents (referred to as "cloth houses" by some of the slaves) kept great numbers of women busy. Catherine Edmondston wrote of sewing uniforms "which may ere long be drenched in blood—perhaps of my own husband" (29).

> Brought home yesterday another tent on which my forces are busily engaged. The cloth for these uniforms and tents is bought by private subscription, not waiting for the State to equip its men—and this is going on all over the South. Thousands of ladies who have never worked before are hard at work on coarse sewing. (Edmondston n.d., 29)

Sewing for the troops, for many Southern women, ranged from making a husband's or a son's uniform to outfitting whole companies. Mrs. John T. Johnstone and her daughter Helen fitted out three companies with Confederate uniforms and kept a bevy of seamstresses constantly at work on their Annandale plantation in Madison County, Mississippi, supplying clothing for the soldiers. The Johnstones, as did many of their compatriots, patriotically cut up their luxurious velvet carpets to make blankets for the troops. In fact, as Mrs. Roger Pryor noted:

There was absolutely nothing which a man might possibly use that we did not make for them. We embroidered cases for razors, for soap and sponge, and cute morocco affairs for needles, thread, and court-plaster, with a little pocket lined with a bank-note. "How perfectly ridiculous!" do you say? Nothing is ridiculous that helps anxious women to bear their lot—cheats them with the hope that they are doing good. (Pryor 1904, 133)

Supplementing the generous contributions of food, clothing, and hospital supplies that poured in from women were the benefits, concerts, tableaux, suppers, lotteries, theatricals, and raffles held to raise funds for soldiers' relief. Admission was often accepted "in kind," i.e., in provisions or clothing for soldiers. Describing one of the "benefits" conducted by women in thousands of towns throughout the country, Miranda Spalding's half-sister wrote:

We have a Ladies Loyal League here in town for the benefit of soldiers families, that is needy ones, that don't have enough to be comfortable. We made a supper the 22nd of February; tickets fifty cents a piece and took in two hundred and forty dollars, with the help of the fancy table and grab bag. There was fifteen dollars worth in that at five cents a grab. We expect to use some of this money for the aid of sick and wounded soldiers. . . . (Spalding n.d.)

In the South the soldiers' aid societies functioned throughout the war essentially as local or state organizations. Although their activities were often localized, the women's generosity was immense. In surveying the tons of food and clothing that arrived from women on the homefront for distribution in her Richmond hospital, Phoebe Pember noted that "it appeared as if the non-fighting people of the Confederacy had worked as hard and exercised as much self-denial as the soldiers in the field" (58).

In the North, however, women immediately sensed the need for some sort of direction and focus to the work of the hundreds of local societies, and on April 29, 1861, a large gathering of women met at Cooper Institute in New York City and there formed the Woman's Central Association for Relief. Two weeks later a delegation was dispatched to Washington to secure President Lincoln's approval for the creation of a United States Sanitary Commission—an organization which would supplement the work of the government in providing for the comfort and welfare of the men of the U.S. Armed Forces, in sickness or in health. Reluctantly, Lincoln signed the order, cynically remarking that the organization might well become "a fifth wheel to the coach." Despite petty jealousies and early skepticism, the United States Sanitary Commission came to play a crucial role in "battlefield relief" activities and in time gave birth to the Red Cross (Maxwell 1956).

The Sanitary Commission coordinated the work of the smaller societies, sent agents to report on the food and sanitary conditions in the army camps and hospitals, and provided aid for the sick and wounded in warfront emergencies. It helped secure conscientious, trained nurses for hospitals, helped set up soup kitchens for temporary encampments, helped soldiers obtain back pay or pensions. Much of the money used to purchase supplies was raised through donations and by the aforementioned benefits in some 10,000 aid societies throughout the North (Maxwell 1956).

Ten "headquarters," such as the branch depots in New York, Boston, and Chicago, were set up to channel the bounteous contributions of clothing, bandages, and "delicacies" that flowed in from the local societies. Part of the work of the sub-depots involved the repacking, storage, and eventual distribution of goods and supplies to frontline hospitals and army camps.

Over the years, as noted, vast amounts of food were sent by women anxious to provide "something special" to tempt the appetite of some poor hospitalized lad. Mary Livermore, a devoted worker for the Northwestern Sanitary Commission (the Chicago "sub-depot" for the U.S. Sanitary Commission) explained that often the repacking of the thousands of boxes that poured into the Chicago center proved a dire necessity. Upon occasion local groups in their eagerness to send off their contributions failed to take into consideration the problems created by long delays in transportation and brutal baggage handling.

Women rifled their store-rooms and preserve-closets of canned fruits and pots of jam and marmalade, which they packed with clothing and blankets, books and stationery, photographs and "comfort-bags." Baggage cars were soon flooded with fermenting sweetmeats, and broken pots of jelly, that ought never to have been sent. Decaying fruit and vegetables, pastry and cake in a demoralized condition, badly canned meats and soups, whose fragrance was not that of "Araby the blest," were necessarily thrown away *en route.* And with them went the clothing and stationery saturated with the effervescing and putrefying compounds which they enfolded. (Livermore 1889, 122)

Meticulously packed or carelessly bundled off, the boxes were physical manifestations of the devotion and appreciation of the senders. Caring notes and special messages tucked inside a sock or rolled up in a handkerchief expressed the heartfelt gratitude of a mother or a wife whose loved one was serving with the army she knew not where. Other tear-stained notes came from women whose loved ones would no longer need the mittens or the warm overcoat.

The accompanying articles were worn for the last time by one very dear to the writer, who lost his life at Shiloh. They are sent to our wounded soldiers as the most fitting disposition that can be made of them, by one who has laid the husband of her youth—her all—on the altar of her country. (Livermore 1889, 139)

There was always the concern that possibly the surgeons or members of the hospital staff might appropriate the foodstuff and that the "delicacies" might never reach their intended recipient. A huge box of cookies, for example, arrived at the Chicago depot with a warning attached.

These cookies are expressly for the sick soldiers, and if anybody else eats them, *I hope they will choke him!* (Livermore 1889, 139)

Single young ladies hoping to strike up a correspondence with lonely young soldiers frequently included slips of paper noting their age, build, and hair color along with their names and addresses. One frisky hopeful added a P.S.:

> If the recipient of these socks has a wife, will he please exchange socks with some poor fellow not so fortunate? (Livermore 1889, 138)

In Bowling Green, Kentucky, Josie Underwood's mother was in charge of helping to gather and distribute supplies for needy soldiers and hospitals.

> Ma has been appointed—receiver and distributor of sanitary stores, sent by various societies throughout the north. The first consignment came today and never in all my life did I see so many good and thoughtful things provided for poor sick and wounded soldiers. Boxes and boxes of everything on earth good to eat—breads—jellies—dried fruits—canned, preserved, wines, cordials, many of the wine demijohns were labelled *"for sick soldiers, not for* nurses and surgeons." Then there are all sorts of nice warm double comforters and shirts for wounded soldiers buttoned up in such ways that they could be put on comfortably no matter in what condition the man might be—bandages of all kinds—boxes of linen lint and even cases for wounded fingers.
>
> Ma had a room on the back porch cleared for them—but it would not hold half—so they are piled up on the porch and a soldier has been detailed to guard them. The Doctors of the different hospitals are fast making requisitions for what they need and many poor sick fellows call down God's blessing on the good women who have added so much to their comfort and indeed to their recovery. A right funny thing happened today. Two soldiers were opening the boxes for Ma and five or six others were waiting to take things to the hospitals. A box of quilts was opened—on one was pinned a paper—with these lines written on it.
>
>
>
> "Mary Jackson is my name
> Single is my station
> Happy will be the soldier boy—
> Who makes the alteration."
>
>
>
> All the soldiers there—clamored for it, declaring their desperate lack of covers. Ma told them to stand in a row and draw straws for it. When the man who got the shortest straw was

about to take possession of the quilt—the others protested saying he was a married man. So Ma put it by, saying she would give it to some "soldier boy" who proved himself worthy of the industrious and patriotic Mary Jackson. (Nazro, 144–45)

Josie also pointed to the physical strain on her mother brought about by overwork.

> Dear Ma is wearing herself out—in her constant work at the hospital and for sick soldiers, and the constant excitements, anxieties and unavoidable irregularities and confusions in this crowded household are trying, in the extreme to her in her overwrought nervous condition. (Nazro, 145)

Most families made generous, freewill offerings to the soldiers' relief funds; however, after the initial enthusiasm subsided, keeping the flow of supplies steady and appropriate to immediate needs often involved real work. As provisions in some areas declined, it became the thankless task of countless volunteers to make the rounds of neighboring areas to remind the townspeople of the continuing need for contributions. Dozens of both Union and Confederate diaries reported the "begging committee" activities of the writers.

While Marjorie Ann Rogers's husband was serving as a surgeon with the Thirteenth Iowa Infantry, Mrs. Rogers spent much of her time working with the Marshalltown (Iowa) Sanitary Commission. Part of her work consisted of canvassing the countryside for donations.

> I organized an auxiliary and gave instructions for packing and shipping. This was not hard to do, but where I had to drive over the prairie and call at every house, it required a good deal of tact and patience, and grace even, to meet a rebuke or refusal without being, or seeming to be, impatient or surprised that anyone could refuse to aid in such a cause at such a time as this, when in nearly every house a son or husband or brother was missing, was on the battlefield or perhaps in the hospital suffering for the very things we were asking for and so anxious to receive. (604)

Soliciting donations is rarely an easy task, and Mrs. Rogers's usual courteous reception was marred by exceptions that at times made the work difficult and unpleasant. There were occasions, she wrote,

> when I would feel ready to faint from being denied or ordered out of the house with a string of abuse after me. I did not count on this when I accepted the work. . . . (605)

According to Mrs. Rogers, the women were more often abusive than the men. Some women indicated that their husbands would not approve of their generosity, others simply announced: "No, indeed, you will get nothing here. You can just go on" (16).

It should be remembered that there were areas of Copperheads in Iowa, and now and then a woman would send Marjorie on her way, saying

> "My man is not at home. I am glad he is not as he might give you some hams, we have plenty, but I am glad he is not here, and as for me I have no sympathy in your work. I know you are all right and I do not wish to hurt your feelings, this is your work and you believe you are doing your duty, but I cannot see it mine." (16)

The soldiers' aid societies and the Sanitary Commission, as well as the Christian Commission, the various state agencies, churches, and other special local organizations provided a wide array of opportunities for women to help their country and at the same time discover outlets for their abilities and energies. Scores of women, for example, worked for these auxiliary groups as special agents to help relieve shortages of supplies at or near battlefield areas or to assist in the inspection and efficient operation of field hospitals.

As a volunteer worker for the Ladies' War Committee, Ann Hosmer, of Chicago, made numerous trips to army camps and hospitals with her companion, Mrs. Tinkham, to deliver supplies, to help care for the wounded, and to set up diet kitchens. Recalling one of her early assignments which included assisting with amputations, Mrs. Hosmer wrote:

> I need hardly say that we worked unceasingly, being literally
> our own servants. . . . Our labor in the kitchen was intense,
> working harder than any hired servant I ever had in my house
> at home. The amount of food we daily prepared seems to me
> now incredible, we thought nothing of twenty loaves of bread
> cut and made into toast—at one time, and we daily made up
> a barrel of dried apples into sauce. . . . We made egg nog and
> milk punch for the Erysipelas and gangrene hospitals, indeed,
> we prepared most of the nourishing food for these patients. . . .

The work was always demanding and at times dangerous. On one occasion Mrs. Hosmer was captured by the enemy and on another almost murdered in an overnight stay in what proved to be a Secessionist's house. Upon her return home, Mrs. Hosmer continued to work daily (and often three or four times a week throughout the night) at the Soldiers' Home and Soldiers' Rest, Chicago facilities that provided food and lodging for soldiers in need or in transit. The Chicago Soldiers' Home, of course, was just one of forty soldiers' homes that gratuitously provided a total of over four and one-half million meals and over one million nights' lodgings for soldiers during the war years.

Feeding the troop trains or preparing food for the makeshift hospitals that were necessitated by sudden, massive encounters with the enemy demanded both fortitude and resourcefulness on the part of the nurse-"dietitians." An anonymous handwritten letter from the Chicago Historical Society collection, simply signed "your own dear mother," described that woman's work at Stoneman's Station.

> . . . I am very tired, as until last night, I have not laid on
> a bed or undressed myself for six nights. Last Friday morning,
> we left in our team . . . for "United States Ford". . . . So we took
> possession of a little old house in the field with the ambulances.
> As the battle had commenced we wrote a note to the Medical
> Director of the 5th Corp, telling him we were there with sup-
> plies. Soon came an "orderly" bringing a note, requesting to
> have supper ready as soon as possible for an ambulance train
> containing about eighty wounded men. When it came we were
> ready with camp kettles of beef, chicken, and oyster soup, also
> hot coffee.

The next night, after having worked until midnight feeding the wounded men who crowded their "headquarters" and the grounds surrounding it, she attempted to salvage a few moments of sleep by lying "down on the bare floor, a quilt rolled round me and a bundle of rolls of bandages for my pillow." She was soon awakened by the Rebs who had

> commenced "shelling" us. . . . A general stampede for the woods took place, *whirrrr* went the shells, and though I was very calm, still prudence led us hastily to put on our bonnets and sacks and "skedaddle" with the rest. As we walked toward the woods we could see these ugly missiles flying over our heads and striking on either side of us. Two men were killed and several wounded but it did not last long and we soon returned to the house and went to work again.

Some hours later:

> the doctor gave me a blanket and showed me a little corner in an attic all full of wounded men, and piles of rubbish, where, in the dark, surrounded bv our poor, suffering boys, all strangers to me, I rolled myself, all soaking wet, in the blanket and curled up in the corner till five o'clock.

In the early morning hours she

> set the ambulance drivers to work hunting up camp kettles, building a fire and getting water, so that about seven o'clock I had a breakfast of beef soup, crackers and coffee ready for *150* wounded men. They had not expected to remain there and if I had not been detained with our team they would not have had a mouthful to eat.

Volunteer work also involved "social work": in the South finding homes and clothing for refugeeing white families or in the North helping settle the trainloads of Negroes pouring into the free states. During church services one Sunday morning, Marjorie Ann Rogers, of Iowa, recalled a request from the pulpit for women volunteers to leave the church in order to complete their Sunday dinners to send down to a railroad car full of "cold, hungry negroes" who would be arriving at one o'clock. The response was 100 percent. "Every woman in that congregation rose to her feet and all were in tears" (21).

Times were hard and whole towns often got together to help needy families. Mrs. Rogers and several of her neighbors pooled their expertise and their resources to procure a piano and recruit students to help a young refugee from East Tennessee to eke out a living. The initial venture proved so successful that the young teacher soon had a steady stream of youngsters to help her to support her family and to keep her from dwelling on the troubles that had befallen her (600–2).

"Fairs" soon captured the public interest in both Northern and Southern small towns and villages as excellent sources of revenue for the various soldiers' relief funds.* The first large-scale fair, however, was Chicago's great Northwestern Sanitary Commission Fair of 1863, an enterprise which was so successful that Boston, New York, Philadelphia, and other large cities set about planning similar events. Such projects were no small undertakings and energetic, patriotic women from all walks of life spent inestimable hours securing donations of money and goods; setting up booths, exhibits, and games; organizing the extensive publicity campaigns waged; and preparing the food for the thousands of meals served and "delicacies" sold. So exhausting was the work that during the New York Metropolitan Fair two members of the executive committee died from overwork and were in a sense deemed casualties of war. Maria Daly reported the deaths in her diary:

> I learned today of the death of Mrs. Dudley Field. This Fair has probably killed her, as it is said it did poor Mrs. Kirkland. . . . They were both members of the executive committee of the Fair and very active and enthusiastic about it. (Hammond 1962, 293)

By the fall of 1863 the Northwestern Sanitary Commission had already sent over 30,000 boxes of clothing and sanitary stores, the

---

*Because of the numbers of people involved, the hours of work contributed, and the handsome profits earned, the fair mania warrants special attention.

equivalent of about $1.5 million, to U.S. battlefronts, and the Commission's treasury was rapidly evaporating. As a means of augmenting the Commission's coffers and at the same time drawing attention to its work, thus eliciting greater numbers of contributions and volunteers, Mary Livermore and her faithful co-worker, Mrs. Hodge, proposed the holding of a huge Northwestern Sanitary Commission Fair. The Fair, which netted almost $100,000 for the Commission, marked an important milestone in women's history in that it represented a tremendously successful venture which was created and conducted primarily by women. As Mary Livermore pointed out:

> This first Sanitary fair, it must be remembered, was an experiment, and was pre-eminently an enterprise of women, receiving no assistance from men in its early beginnings. The city of Chicago regarded it with indifference, and the gentlemen members of the Commission barely tolerated it. The first did not understand it, and the latter were doubtful of its success. The great fairs that followed this were the work of men as well as of women, from their very incipiency—but this fair was the work of women. (412–13)

At first the men scoffed at the women's dreams of raising $25,000, and only after observing the widespread enthusiasm expressed at a pre-fair convention of women from throughout the Midwest held on September 1, 1863, in Chicago, did the men finally join in with contributions of money and merchandise. Plans quickly mushroomed: 20,000 circulars were sent out soliciting donations and at one time fourteen bushels of mail were received in connection with the Fair. Women canvassed businesses and neighborhoods, knocking on doors to secure contributions. Soon donations by the thousands came pouring in, including knitted scarves and mittens, appliances, jewelry, agricultural and dairy products, evergreens, flowers, food supplies, war relics and trophies, works of art, and manufactured goods such as pumps, reapers, and cultivators. There was "cologne by the barrel," wine, pianos, organs, washing machines, nails, and lumber. Unexpected donations of livestock were gratefully accepted and auctioned in front of the hall. A newspaper, *The*

Volunteer, was published daily. There were booths featuring knitted goods, jams and jellies, baked goods, and fancy work. A dining hall was set up with fourteen tables which were reset four or five times daily to accommodate some twelve to fifteen hundred patrons each day. Tickets for the Fair ranged from twenty-five cents for single admissions to one dollar for "season tickets." Admission was free for any soldier or sailor. Dinner tickets sold for fifty cents. Additional revenue came from the extra charges levied for special events and exhibits such as concerts, lectures, and "allegorical, statuary, and classical tableaux."

One of the most adroit solicitations was tendered President Lincoln. In a stroke of genius the committee asked Lincoln for some donation "not so much for the value of the gift, as for the eclat which this circumstance would give to the Fair." It was suggested that the original draft of the Emancipation Proclamation would serve just such a purpose. The request noted:

> There would seem great appropriateness in this gift to Chicago & Illinois, for the benefit of Western soldiers, coming as it would from a Western President. (Northwestern, CHS)

Lincoln's reply was succinct and in the affirmative:

> Ladies having charge of the North Western Fair For the Sanitary Commission, Chicago, Illinois:
> According to the request made in your behalf, the original draft of the Emancipation proclamation is herewith enclosed. The formal words at the top, and the conclusion, except the signature, you perceive are not in my handwriting. They were written at the State Department by whom I know not. The printed part was cut from a copy of the preliminary proclamation, and pasted on merely to save writing—
> I have some desire to retain the paper; but if it shall contribute to the relief or comfort of the soldiers that will be better.
>
> Your obt. Servt.
> A. Lincoln
> (Northwestern, CHS)

The Fair's opening was heralded by a huge parade. Schools, banks, stores, and businesses were closed as thousands of Chicagoans lined the sidewalks and rooftops to cheer the seemingly endless file of officials, bands, banners, singers, and carriages carrying captured rebel flags and jubilant convalescing soldiers. Garnering the greatest attention was the long procession of farmers from the Lake Country driving wagons piled high with vegetables for the Fair. The lead wagon carried a large sign "THE GIFT OF LAKE COUNTRY TO OUR BRAVE BOYS IN THE HOSPITALS, THROUGH THE GREAT NORTHWESTERN FAIR." Mary Livermore noted:

> There were no small loads here. Every wagon was filled to overflowing with great heaps of potatoes and silver-skinned onions, mammoth squashes, huge beets and turnips, monster cabbages, barrels of cider, and rosy apples—load after load, with many a gray-haired farmer driving. (423)

The beneficence tugged at the heartstrings of even the roughest characters.

> On the sidewalk, among the spectators, was a broad-shouldered Dutchman, with a stolid, inexpressive face. He gazed at this singular procession as it passed,—the sunburned farmers, the long narrow wagons, and the endless variety of vegetables and farm produce, the men with their sober faces and homely gifts,—until, when the last wagon had passed, he broke down in a flood of tears. He could do nothing and say nothing; but seized upon the little child whom he held by the hand, and hugged her to his heart, trying to hide his manly tears behind her flowing curls. (Livermore 1889, 423)

One driver seated with his wife and carrying two young girls and a baby in the back of his wagon had stayed up all night gathering produce to bring to the Fair. Asked if he had a son in the army the man replied,

> "Well, no," he answered slowly. . . . "No, we haven't *now*. We had one there once. He was buried down by Stone River. He

was shot there. That's his wife there with the baby," pointing
over his shoulder to the rear of the wagon without looking back;
"but I should not bring these things any quicker if he were alive
now and in the army. I don't know as I should think so much
as I do now about the boys way off there. He was a good boy."
(Livermore 1889, 425)

The negotiations for the Fair also provided a remarkable learning
experience; both Mrs. Livermore and Mrs. Hodge were given an important lesson in women's rights when they undertook to contract
the building of a temporary hall next to the main building. The
lumber was donated and the contract drawn up; however, at that
point, Mrs. Livermore and Mrs. Hodge ran head-on into a serious
complication.

"Who underwrites for you?" asked the builder.
"What?" we inquired in concert.
"Who endorses for you?" he explained.
"We wish no endorsers. We have the money in bank, and
will pay you in advance, if you will draw the contract accordingly. We have more faith in you than you manifest in us," we
replied.
"It isn't a matter of faith at all," was his answer, "but of law.
You are married women; and, by the laws of Illinois, your names
are good for nothing, unless your husbands write their names
after yours on the contract."
"Let us pay you then in advance," we said. "We have money
of our own earning, and are able to settle your bill on the spot.
Instead of a contract, give us a promissory note, like this: 'In
consideration of ____ dollars, I promise to build for Mrs. Hoge
and Mrs. Livermore a hall of wood,' etc. Can't you do that?"
"The money of your earning belongs to your husbands, by
the law. The wife's earnings are the property of the husband
in this state. Until your husbands give their written consent
to your spending your earnings, I cannot give you the promise
you ask. The law must be respected."
Here was a revelation. We two women were able to enlist the
whole Northwest in a great philanthropic, money-making enterprise in the teeth of great opposition, and had the executive
ability to carry it forward to a successful termination. We had
money of our own in bank, twice as much as was necessary
to pay the builder. But by the laws of the state in which we

lived, our individual names were not worth the paper on which they were written. Our earnings were not ours, but belonged to our husbands. . . .

We learned much of the laws made by men for women, in that conversation with an illiterate builder. It opened a new world to us. We thought rapidly, and felt intensely. I registered a vow that when the war was over I would take up a new work—the work of making law and justice synonymous for women. I have kept my vow religiously. (435–36)

The building was begun only after the contract was countersigned by their husbands.

At the conclusion of Chicago's Fair the lady managers met and unanimously passed the resolution

That this Fair has been an unparalleled success—not merely in a pecuniary point of view, but as a great uprising of women of the Northwest, in signification of their devotion to the cause of our beloved and imperiled country. (*History of NWSF,* 46)

The "fair mania" swept the South as well. Fairs, although not on so ambitious a scale as the Northwestern Sanitary Fair and other big city fairs of the North, were sponsored by organizations ranging from the various Ladies' Gunboat Societies (groups seeking to raise funds to help build gunboats for the Confederacy) to small, local soldiers' aid societies. There, too, the fair organizers were rewarded with the same generous outpouring of donations as in the more extravagant Northern productions.

Emma Holmes described her pleasure in attending the Ladies' Gunboat Fair in Charleston on May 10, 1862. Unfortunately, she failed to disguise a faint hint of class consciousness as she penned the second paragraph, the afternoon entry.

Almost everything at the fair is raffled and today there is to be a grand lottery of all the silver, jewellry, watches, china sets, etc. which have been given. 4000 chances at one dollar each and 200 prizes. Some of the articles are very elegant—an entire pearl set and a diamond ring among others. . . .

I attended the grand raffle which was admirably conducted. The pearl set was won by a Miss Broadie, a Baptist, a respectable woman in the lower walks of life [but] one certainly who will never make any use of it except to sell it. I don't know who got the other handsomest prizes. (160)

From her home in Atlanta, Lizzie Ozburn sent her husband a somewhat amusing account of her participation in a fair conducted by the Ladies of the Association.

Hall and I went & carried a pound of chiped beef & a beef tongue & 6 bottles of that wine I had that was so poor but I mixed some rye whiskey & sugar with it & it was nearly good & we sold not quite 3 bottles of it and it brought 5 or 6 dollars & I sold two slices of beef tongue for 15 cents so what I carried made them 8 or 9 dollars but it would not if it had not been for Mrs. Luther Glen. She is the great[est] dramseller I ever saw but it was against my feelings carrying it to sell but I never saw that it turned out any harm for she would not let them have enough to hurt them.

She sold about an inch deep in a tumbler for 25 cts called it Confederate wine & she came very near making a man break his pledge but when he said it I saw he told the truth that he was a son of temperance. I said well don't drink it. O she said it is nothing more than sweet cider. Well it is wine & that is forbidden in the pledge etc. Well sir I have poured it out & you must take it. I saw him about to yield & I said look here if you are a son of temperance dont drink it for I made it & know what is in it & then told him.

So he looked puzzled for she still declared she could not pour out for less than 25 cts so he said I'll pay for it but not drink it, that will do said she & so he did (& Pa if he had drank it I should have felt bad yet but as it was I feel so glad I strengthened his resolution but I thought it looked very inconsistent to carry wine & preach temperance & I should never make my living by selling ardent spirits for it is against my conscience), and by the way tell me if you have anything to drink in that line now, dont forget to tell me. Well the Ladies made about 100 dollars clear at their fair last night. I brought back three bottles and kept one dollar for myself so you see I did not expend much & still helped the Society a good deal. (24 August 1861)

Men could join in the projects of the Eutawville Aid Association of South Carolina. Rule Six required each member "to contribute the sum of 25 cents at every regular meeting." The women, apparently in a compromise over charges of discrimination, added a final note:

> Gentlemen may become members of the association by contributing the sum stated in Rule 6, but not entitled to a vote, as they can't participate in the pleasure of sewing, cutting, etc. (T. Taylor 1903, 59)

Columbia, South Carolina, was engaged in planning a large bazaar for the benefit of the hospitals just weeks prior to Sherman's rampage through the city. Grace Elmore, in a seemingly pensive mood, commented on the preparations in her diary.

> How strangely is the serious and the gay intermingled in our life, one moment gloomily considering the many chances of Yankee rule and the next looking with equally anxious earnestness after the pleasures and interest of the Bazaar. For with the Yankees almost at our doors, we still think of, work for and cheer our soldiers, sick and wounded in the hospitals. Money is scarce, so we will have a Fair to which the whole State is contributing. Each house has its corner to which tobacco bags, cloth babies, cushions, all odds and ends that can be raked or scraped from our needs, is consigned, there to rest until the great day when they shall appear in the State House to tempt the fancy of every true Confederate. Since early in November we've been ransacking the house for scraps, and bemoaning our extravagance in the first years of the war, in using up most of our material in foolishness for the soldiers. I remember cutting up two pretty dresses, and spending a lot of money on tassels, to make a lot of smoking caps for Capt. Hokes' company. I presented them myself and was immensely pleased when the men whirled them around their heads and gave three cheers for "the ladies." If I only had those dresses now, how many cute things I could make for the Bazaar and our sick soldiers would be much better served by the money than the well ones were by the caps. (32)

Less dramatic but certainly no less important were the activities of thousands of other women, particularly those in the agrarian sectors, who made significant contributions to the war effort from their own, often isolated, farm homes. In cities, machines could frequently take up the slack caused by the loss of some two million men who left the labor force of the North to serve their country. However, in the agricultural areas, which predominated in the North and to an even greater extent in the South, it was the women who took over the farm work, even going into the fields, if necessary, in order to keep up the agricultural production and supply the troops with needed food. Suddenly thrust into the positions as farm managers, bookkeepers, bankers, overseers—responsibilities which they of necessity combined with their normal duties as housekeepers, seamstresses, "handymen," bakers, teachers, and mothers—most women took to their new roles with alacrity and dedication.

Mary Livermore, in her travels in Wisconsin and eastern Iowa, recalled stopping by the roadside and visiting with some of the hundreds of women busily engrossed in harvesting grain. One of the women explained that with her three brothers, cousins, and most of the able-bodied men in the area serving in the army, there was no alternative other than for the women to literally "pitch in" with the heavy farm work.

> "I tell mother . . . that as long as the country can't get along without grain, nor the army fight without food, we're serving the country just as much here in the harvest-field as our boys are on the battle-field—and that sort o'takes the edge off from this business of doing men's work, you know." (148–49)

Directives (often antiquated by wartime scarcities and fluctuating markets) arrived almost daily from the battlefield with instructions about paying taxes, or handling mortgages, or borrowing money, or harvesting crops, or selling livestock.

Matilda Champion, who was caring for their plantation near Vicksburg, received the following instructions from her soldier husband:

Don't plant that bottom piece of corn before the 15th or 25th of April and not then unless in good condition. Save some of it for Rice. Plant your sugar cane and peas by 15 or 20th of April and rice about the 20th of May. I can't say all things I wish to. Talk to some gentleman about planting and you will get some idea of things. . . . I hope you will get along finely and make something to eat. . . . (Champion, 17)

All too often the advice was vague and general: "Do as you see fit" or "You must decide what to do about planting" or "You are the best judge of when to sell." Vital decisions were suddenly forced on many heretofore inexperienced women who soon found that not only could they handle the planting, cultivating, and harvesting of crops and the negotiating of business transactions, but they could do so shrewdly and skillfully.

Sarah Chapin, of Courtland, Michigan, accounted for her financial transactions in her husband's behalf in a letter to him dated February 6, 1863.

I have paid our taxes. They were 11 dollars this year. Yesterday I paid Mr. Emmonds $2. I should have paid him more but I am determined to keep some money to help you home if there is a chance for you to come. I have paid the smallest note of Pixley's and the interest on the large one.

A few weeks later she explained:

There is a great deal of wheat going into market at present. It has been bringing twelve shillings for some time. But many still held on to their wheat thinking it would yet bring $2 but for a few days it has been falling and now brings ten shillings a bushel. I sold our wheat the other day for $1.35. (24 February 1863)

Three months later she wrote:

Mr. Emmonds has sawed up that pile of logs into stove wood and is to take his pay in team work during the summer. I let him have hay enough to pay up that note he had against us today. (20 May 1863)

A great many women served as bankers—or collection agents—for their sons or husbands. Benton Lewis's mother loaned her son's money out at 10 percent interest. Dr. John James Love, of West Bloomfield, New Jersey, instructed his wife to collect outstanding bills carried over from his prewar days in private practice.

> Jacob Van Riper deceased owes me for 3 visits—one a night visit at 1½, 2 day visits each making the above amt. $3.50. don't take one cent less I don't ride 3 miles for 50 cents—never did. (10 November 1862)

In a letter to his mother, a "loving Soldier Boy" marveled over the independence of the women in the area around Knoxville, Tennessee.

> Most of the women around here who live on farms have to do all their work alone their husbands being in the army. I got some butter the other day of a woman who has six little children and a place of fifty acres which she has cultivated alone and supported herself and children besides. Don't you think this is doing pretty well for one woman? (Walsh)

It was with great admiration that Mrs. D. D. McColl looked back on her mother's accomplishments during the war years.

> I have often thought my own mother's (Mrs. Thomas) life was a daily struggle and a certain triumph. Left by my father with seven young children, she managed to make the farm produce enough for their support, gave a tithe for army support, and was shrewd enough and wise enough to pay almost all of a small debt, which seemed very large to us. . . . My father's salary as captain was about all we had, and "the wolf" seemed seldom very far from the door. (T. Taylor 1903, 35)

When her husband and his brother volunteered their services to the Confederacy, Grace Pierson James Beard, mother of three, was pleased with her success in taking on the overseer's work on the two adjoining plantations near Columbia, South Carolina.

After my husband, as well as every other man in our family, had gone to the war I decided to relieve the overseer and let him have a chance to go too. This I did and mounted my pony day after day to attend to both plantations and it seemed the blessings of heaven were upon all my efforts. (1)

Louisa Jane Phifer, of Vandalia, Illinois, had seven young children to care for in addition to operating the family's farm. In December 1864, she proudly reported to her husband:

Well father we are getting along first rate with our work. We have about all the Corn husked but what is in the dry. The Corn Crib is full even with the door of the best kind of Corn. Corn is from 75 to 80 cts per bushel. We have the Sheep stable finished. We have put a little manure around all the apple trees. We have paid Tom Pilcher his 5.00 Dollars and Hickerson his Corn. The Wheat looks Just as good as it Could Look the early and late sewing. This has been the best fall on Wheat that I ever saw being warm and Wet. The Old mare and Colt looks well and so do the Ewes. The hogs fatten fast and look nice. (389–90)

Farming was particularly demanding during the war years. Scarcities of some commodities, surpluses of others, special taxes, worn-out equipment, labor shortages, and crop restrictions in the South were but a few of the problems confronting farmers. Adaline Lyon, of Milford, Michigan, wrote to her sister in 1861:

It is hard with farmers in this place. Especially those that are in debt and we come under that head. Butter will sell for no price, there is no sale for wool. We have not sold ours and taxes will be very high. An extra tax to support the war. We shall have to pay but we need to be very thankful that we are not in the immediate vicinity of the war. (Phelps-Lyons 4 August 1861)

Benton Lewis's mother despaired of the farmers' plight in a letter to her son in 1864.

The prospect is dull about farming this season for labor is so high that it is not possible for people to hire, so they will have to do what they can alone and let the rest go. We have only eight acres of wheat on the ground to harvest and I am glad there is no more. (16 February 1864)

In Sparta, Michigan, Mary Noble was experiencing great difficulties scraping together the money to pay the taxes on their farm.

Our taxes is 8 dollars & 14 cents. I don't know how I shal get them paid but I shal trust in providence there will be some way provided. (3 February 1862)

In South Carolina, Emily Harris enumerated some of her problems.

Husband gone to the army again, every thing resting on me, children troublesome, company forever, weather very cold, negroes in the newground, cows, calves and sheep on the wheat. To day I have heard that the Yankees were sheelling Charleston. Oh! God preseve my husband! (Racine 1990, 273)

Managing a farm frequently involved back-breaking physical labor. Mary Austin Wallace, wife of Robert Bruce Wallace, assumed full responsibility for the family's 160-acre farm in Calhoun County, Michigan, when her husband joined the 19th Michigan Volunteer Infantry in August 1862. The Wallaces were engaged in building a new home at the time of Robert's enlistment and, therefore, much of Mary's time, not taken up with caring for her two-and-a-half year-old son and six-month old daughter, was devoted to overseeing and actually working on the project.

A random sampling of her daily activities as recorded in her diary in the fall of 1862 attests to her perseverance and courage during her husband's absence.

October 24: I come home loaded the remainder of the sugar cane took it to mill . . . got my molasses over 17 gallons. . . . I covered the corn crib.
October 25: Unloaded my molasses loaded up seven bags of chess [a brome grass] and two bushel of wheat for flour. . . .

October 28: I dug the early June potatoes buried them for winter. . . . I put a door in the corn crib I husked some corn.

October 29: I hitched up the horses on the waggon went in the north cornfield husked a load of corn drawed it to the crib unloaded it drawed a load of pumpkins.

Nov 3: . . . Ma and myself went and got six hundred and fifty of brick. . . .

Nov 10: I lathed some in the forenoon the afternoon pulled baggas trimed them I finished Jonnies apron. . . . (M. Wallace 1963, 142)

Replacements for farm implements or stolen horses became increasingly difficult to procure as the war progressed, and in some destitute cases, a woman herself or her young sons drew the plow to prepare the sod for the year's crop (Livermore 1889, 698).

A lone woman could sometimes look to family members and/or neighbors to band together to provide needed assistance. Catharine and Thomas Baker, of Barry County, Michigan, asked Catharine's youngest brother to help her run their farm while Thomas served with the Union Army, and in the interests of expediency, the Bakers deeded the farm over to him. When Catharine's husband died of typhoid fever as a prisoner of war and her brother enlisted in the army, the whole family came to her aid. Charles L. Stanton, Catharine's son-in-law, later wrote about how everyone pitched in and "got up sawings" and "corn huskings" to help distressed families during the war years.

> It was no uncommon occurrance, for the neighbors to make a bea and harvest the crop, cut the wood, or even provide provision for some deserving family. (Hardenberg)

While some women found neighbors eager to help those less fortunate, Helen Maria Sharp, living near Des Moines, Iowa, complained bitterly of the lack of concern of her neighbors.

> we most freeze chopping this morning. i guess i have frosted one of my feet some. you said that i would not have anything

to see to but i tell you if i should wait to have someone come and see if i wanted anything i would both freeze and starve for no one comes in the house unless i go beg for it and sometimes not then. you wrote that you would send some more money the first of january but now the 16th and you have not even wrote in this month. i cant write any more for i have no more stamps or paper but write oftener or i shall give up all hopes. (488)

In Oxford, Wisconsin, *most* of Mary Burwell's neighbors appeared indifferent to her situation. Mary wrote her husband:

[The townspeople] think that the women are alone, and what they can't do themselves, they have to pay dear for. Our nearest neighbor has not even asked us if he could do a chore or shovel snow, or do a single turn for us and . . . I don't want them too, we can do our own chores as long as we have our health. When I go out to clean out the stables, there is most always two or three men on the tavern steps gauping at me but I don't care it is a honest trade, one day I was out cleaning out the stable, and Seir Miller's young brother stood looking at me. I had a mind to throw him a fork full. . . . (6 January 1865)

Some women firmly disdained all offers of assistance. With help both difficult and expensive to procure, Marjorie Ann Rogers undertook numerous trips to their farm in the Iowa countryside to bring in corn, potatoes, and vegetables to sell in town. Several of the older men sought to dissuade her, fearing she would be unable to manage the horses and the wagon over the steep hills. Marjorie persisted, however, refusing even to be helped down from the wagon. "I declined their kindness and said I would get down the same as a man did if I could do a man's work" (599).

Now and then farm work proved more embarrassing than onerous. In a letter to her husband, David, a volunteer with the First Michigan Mechanics and Engineers, Mary Noble, of Sparta, Michigan, explained:

Bill Vond [?] says if we want to raise a colt this year to send Wilbur up there with the mare. It is mortifying to see to such work but it seems as though we ought to raise a colt. . . . (24 April 1862)

To be sure, not all women responded enthusiastically to the challenges incurred in meeting the incessant demands of a lively household of four or five young children coupled with the debilitating sun-up to sun-down responsibilities of operating the family farm or plantation. Helen Maria Sharp's letters to her soldier husband reflected the loneliness and frustrations of an Iowa woman left to manage the family and farm affairs on her own. At times, she almost succumbed to the pressures. Her husband's intermittent pay, their mounting debts, problems of feeding and clothing their children, and anxieties over her own, her family's, and her husband's health brought her to the brink of suicide.

> Dear John . . . we are all well in body but i cant say as much about my mind. i can hardly tell you how much trouble i see . . . now what my family will do for the winter is more than i can tell. . . . it makes me low spirited so that i cant help writeing to you to not for gods sake if you want to save me from getting rid of myself lend your money till you relieve your family. . . . now do not raise any more false hopes for dissapointments nearly kill me. i cant eat nor sleep. my back hurts me so that i cant stand it to chop hardly at all. i shall have to brake up housekeeping before long. if i was only out of the way folks would take care of my children but to scatter them while im alive is more trouble that i can bare to think about. . . . the children miss you very much but they will cry a while and then it is all bright again but with me i have only seen a few pleasant hours since you went away. (484–85)

Her husband's irregular correspondence further added to Maria's despondency. Maria's letter dated May 3, 1865, was signed "from your afflicted wife."

> if you would write once in a while it would seem better but all the boys but hugh writes twice to your once but i have all the brunt to bare any way so it might as well be one thing as another. (519)

The days were long and exhausting for Emily Liles Harris during the absence of her husband. In December 1862, Emily's journal entries, written from Spartanburg, South Carolina, reflected her despair.

> It has rained all day, the children have been cross and un-governable. Old Judah and Edom [slaves] were both sick. Ann is trying to weave, and a poor weave it is, the sewing must be done, everything must be attended to, Laura is cough-ing a rough ominous cough, has scarcely any shoes on her feet, and no hope of getting any this week, West has the croup. I am trying to wean the baby and the cows laid out last night, and last and worst of all I know my husband is somewhere miserably cold, wet, and comfortless. (Racine 1990, 270)

Perhaps it was Emily's basic make-up, or the constant demands of not two or three, but of seven children, or simply the economic problems of the times that contributed to her feelings of inadequacy. She was remarkably successful in raising bumper crops; however, the harvests brought about additional stress. The extra workers she needed to gather in her crops demanded food rather than money. Her oat crop, for example, was almost lost because the workers had to be paid in wheat and her supply ran low. Emily lamented to her confidante, her diary:

> I shall never get used to being left as the head of affairs at home. The burden is very heavy, and there is no one to smile on me as I trudge wearily along in the dark with it. I am constituted so as to crave a guide and protector, I am not an independent woman nor ever shall be. (Racine 1990, 309)

Despite a few exceptions here and there, women, for the most part, blossomed in their newly acquired independence. While Ellen Elmore's two brothers were serving with the Confederacy, she, her mother, and five sisters were left to care for their home in Columbia, South Carolina; their large cotton and grain plantation in York County; and "a mill place with a provision farm in Lexington County, about ten miles from Columbia." When one overseer after another was called up by the Southern army, most of the management of the plantation fell to Ellen herself. As overseer, Ellen supervised the care of the cattle, hogs, and sheep; made daily checks of the slave quarters and the carpenter's and blacksmith's shops; canvassed the countryside for thirty miles around for additional provisions; looked after the sick, and prescribed and doctored when circumstances required it. She recalled:

> For myself, I never questioned if I *could* do the work that came to my hands, but did it as well as I had ability for, and *never* looking backward with heartbreaking regrets, which I felt would take from me all strength. (T. Taylor 1903, 206)

In addition, Ellen took over the management of the mill.

> I recall my consternation when my Uncle Alex Taylor told my mother that I could manage a lumber mill and make all the lumber accounts . . . and thus I became my mother's business agent to the close of the war, and had the honor of supplying to the government most of the heavy timbers required here; and, moreover, had the satisfaction of hearing from all parties that the business had never been so satisfactorily conducted. . . .
>
> This was truly a feather to my woman's cap; but we feminines, before that war ended, were to pick up many a one dropped from the helmets of our brave fellows who had work to do beyond our powers, and in which we could aid them only by doing what it had been theirs to do hitherto. (T. Taylor 1903, 198)

For Ellen Elmore, and for thousands of women like her, their tremendous contribution to the war effort as volunteers, as business women, as farm managers, was indeed a "feather to their woman's cap."

CHAPTER VIII

"Much to Do"
Part II

We shall with pleasing remembrance everbear in mind that
woman . . . with her fountain of affection, and lofty patriotism,
though the weaker sex accomplishes as much in this momentous struggle for liberty as the marshalled hosts of our soldiery.

—*Frank N. Marks*
Commander Co B Quachita Blues
23 March 1862

In addition to their work as volunteers or as farm or small business managers, women also struggled valiantly to bolster the morale
of their loved ones fighting at the warfront. Camp visits, long letters,
and overstuffed boxes of food proved their most effective methods.

A visit to a husband, son, or brother at his encampment constituted one of the greatest morale boosters for both the visitor and
the visited. Mary Logan, wife of General John Logan, recalled the
vast influx of visitors in the area around Cairo, Illinois, where Federal
troops were encamped to protect key positions on the Mississippi
River. The soldiers, of course, could not be granted leaves to visit
their friends and relatives in the surrounding area.

No law, however, could prevent friends from coming to
them, and ere they had been encamped two months, a new
army made its appearance. Fathers, mothers, brothers, sisters,
wives, and sweethearts came sweeping down in caravans of carriages, wagons, and every conceivable vehicle, and in every

imaginable manner, pitching their tents and building their brush houses as near the regiment in which they were interested as the commanding officers would permit. Every moment off duty one could see company officers and men wending their way to the camps outside the lines, where devoted ones were waiting to greet them. (109)

Now and then officers' wives were fortunate enough to be able to join their husbands for brief, or sometimes even lengthy, periods of time by taking up residence near their husband's battlefield headquarters. For some wives this meant a transitory visit fraught with long, arduous delays en route and deplorable living conditions. Miranda Spalding set off by boat from her home in remote Sault Ste. Marie, Michigan, and then "took the cars" for a long awaited visit with her husband at Camp Nicholsville near Cincinnati. Their time together was a matter of hours before her husband was called out on a mission and she was left to wind her lonely way back home again. Later, she wrote her husband:

> Your image is before me constantly as I saw you on "Billy" riding farther and farther from me, and taking my heart with you. . . . After returning to the parlor and giving vent to my tears for a few moments, to prevent the heart from breaking, a thought of the loved ones at home who require my care and attention made me feel the necessity of rising above my own heart's sadness, of trying to be cheerful, and to begin to think of turning my face homeward. (12 September 1863)

Added to her despair was the loss en route of her luggage, packed with possessions not inexpensively nor easily replaced. Seeking a bit of sympathy from her husband, she wrote:

> It will really be quite a loss to me if I do not [recover the trunk]—four of my best dresses—that new black silk which cannot be replaced short of $30 or $35—my bonnet, shawl, parasol, nearly all my underclothes, two night gowns, all my night caps, 8 pocket handkerchiefs all my collars and undersleeves, and last and dearest of all, that *beautiful album* which I prised *so highly for your sake*. (12 September 1863)

Their brief visit had been a happy occasion for her husband as well as for Miranda, and in his next letter he lovingly reassured her that her dresses could be replaced, that they represented but a small mishap attending their blissful reunion.

Laetitia LaFon Ashmore Nutt agreed to her husband's enlistment in the Confederate army only on the condition that she be allowed to accompany him as closely as possible on his campaigns. Her travels, as recorded in her diary, chronicled a peripatetic journey to innumerable battle areas, where all too infrequently, while waiting for his division to pass or marking time between assignments, he was able to spend a few precious hours with Laetitia and their three young daughters. On rare occasions she could take dinner with him at his headquarters and observe the rigors of camp life firsthand. One evening following dinner, Mrs. Nutt was led to an awesome panoramic view of long lines of both Blue and Gray troops ominously maneuvering into battlefield position for the next day's bloody encounter.

> As I gained the summit of Missionary Ridge and took a last look at the two great armies filling the valley below, I thought how much nearer the millennium would be if the two nations instead of devoting all their energies to the destruction of human life and happiness, had been bent upon establishing "peace on earth and good will towards men." O terrible at the last day will be the reckoning of those upon whose conscience rests the guilt of this *human* warfare. (29)

Repeated diary entries such as "We packed our trunks as soon as possible," or "We spent Saturday night cooking our rations and packing up," denoted yet "another interrupted and hasty move." Mrs. Nutt's living conditions were often spartan ("beds on the floor . . . one penknife for all of us") and their situation at times became precarious. On at least three occasions, Laetitia and her daughters were overrun by Yankee troops, experiences which proved frightening as well as ruinous. In December 1863, her husband's visit at their temporary quarters near Chattanooga was cut short by the report of the advance of the enemy. Scarcely two hours after her husband and two fellow officers made their escape back to camp

> . . . the "detestable Blue Coats" came in. Our house was filled with them in a few moments, but they had not completed the search when we heard the most alarming notes of distress from the pig sty, hen house and goose pen. I had just said to Mary that I must get up before daylight and have all the fowls killed, to keep the Yanks from getting them, but with their natural canine instinct they had scented the fowls, made a night attack, outgeneralled me, and left not even a cock to crow in the morning. (37)

In time as their situation grew ever more perilous and their provisions ever more scarce, Laetitia finally lamented:

> If I had realized at the beginning what "grim-visaged war" meant, I think I would have left the children with my Mother and devoted all my time and energies to our sick and wounded, many that I have seen died for lack of careful nursing that I would have given if not tied down by the children. (82)

For three years Septima Collis was one of the lucky wives able to join her husband at his winter headquarters. Their homes, she explained, were often "canvas houses," and their table service tin instead of silver. Their social life consisted of intermittent officers' parties, frequent horseback riding outings, and regular regimental reviews. As an officer's wife living close to the battlefield, she was well-acquainted with the horrors of war, and on one occasion she herself was almost cut down by gunfire. Surprisingly, it was only when the officers' wives were ordered home that Mrs. Collis sensed the full implications of the war.

> Extraordinary as it may appear, I did not fully realize that we were in the midst of a great war until I returned to Philadelphia. In camp the constant round of pleasurable excitement and the general belief that hostilities would be of short duration presented a bright picture. . . . But at home all was bustle and excitement; a dozen large stores on Chestnut Street

had become recruiting stations; public meetings were being held every night to encourage enlistment; politicians were shouting: "On to Richmond!"; young girls were declaring they would never engage themselves to a man who refused to fight for his country, and the fife and drum were heard morning, noon, and night. . . . The Girard House had, for the time being, been converted from a fashionable hotel into a vast workshop, where the jingle of the sewing-machine and the chatter of the sewing girl, daytime, nighttime, and Sundays gave evidence that the government was in earnest. Every woman who could use her needle found employment, and those who did not need compensation worked almost as assiduously. (11–13)

Mrs. R. J. Bell was delighted to be able to share at least a few hours each week with her husband, a doctor serving with the Confederate forces; however, she was continually on the move in her efforts to escape the path of the enemy. In April 1864 she complained to her diary that in the three years they had been married, she and her husband had been unable to spend more than six months together.

Difficulties finding places to stay, exorbitant board bills ($250 for two-and-a-half weeks in Shreveport—"Just think of charging such a price for a refugee"), the uncertainties endured in their transient living quarters, and an ever-changing circle of friends rendered great numbers of these young wives increasingly more depressed and lonely. On March 10, 1864, Mrs. Bell wept

I can scarcely write at all to night for tears: and what are they for! Dr. Bell [her husband] said he would be sure and come to-night. I am so sad to-night. What have I to live for? No friends! O! it is so hard!

Mrs. Bell should have considered herself lucky indeed had she compared her lot with that of Hetty Cary, considered by many to be the most beautiful woman in the South, who, on January 19, 1865, married the handsome General John Pegram in a ceremony performed before a gathering of Richmond's social elite. Their time together totaled less than twenty-one days. The happy couple was barely settled in their Petersburg quarters when, during the fighting around Hatcher's Run, General Pegram was killed instantaneously by a sharpshooter's bullet through the heart. Exactly three weeks to the day the young widow and her friends were gathered for the funeral of her husband in the same church that had so recently been the scene of their nuptials (Harrison 1911, 201–5).

Countless women were understandably distressed that costly traveling expenses, the care of small children or aged parents, or the lack of accommodations prevented them from visiting their husbands' battlefield encampments. Still more wives were annoyed when their husbands, believing the conditions too primitive or too hazardous, strictly forbade any visitation. Betty Herndon Maury, writing from Fredericksburg, complained to her diary of her husband's unwillingness to allow her to join him.

> I cannot help feeling hurt at my husband's determination to leave me here to the Yankees when I am willing to follow him *everywhere*. I think he will repent it. (66)

Some wives became impatient waiting for an invitation. Sophia Buchanan, for example, gave up hinting and finally wrote: "When are you going to send for me to come & make you a visit?" (Blackburn 1965, 53–57).

Susan Blackford clearly understood the expense involved and frankly inquired of her husband as to the feasibility of joining him.

> Tell me candidly if you can stand the expense of our trip to Petersburg. I know your means are running short and I will not be hurt if you tell me not to come. I will be very economical. . . . I do not expect to stay over two weeks, indeed I cannot, as . . . I must be here to look after the garden, which will be our principal source of support this summer. (171)

The uncomfortable and often transitory accommodations at the battlefield often sent the faint-hearted scampering for home. Other wives gladly put up with the inconveniences of tents, army cots, camp tables, stools, improvised tables and couches in the hope of a few hours of togetherness with their otherwise preoccupied husbands. George Farmer observed the departure of the less resolute army wives from his encampment in the spring of 1862:

> All the Ladies of our Regiment have left us. They were all young married ones and had romantic ideas of following their husbands all through the war and they did as long as they Boarded at a Hotel in York but beat a precipitate retreat on arriving here when it was Barracks or nothing. (20 March 1862)

The importance of letters as morale boosters can scarcely be overestimated. General William Dorsey Pender summarized the crucial role of letters when he wrote his wife:

> Darling, keep up your spirits. Cheer the men portion of the population. The ladies of the South have, morally speaking, done much more in this war than the men, but for them many a faint hearted soldier would long ago have given up, but so long as we have such wives, mothers, and sisters to fight for so long will this struggle continue until finally our freedom will be acknowledged. (152)

Letters were the lifeblood flowing between home and camp. According to Mary Livermore, letters sent to the army on the Atlantic coast averaged about forty-five thousand daily and as many as one hundred and eighty thousand letters were estimated to have been sent each day through the mails.

> On one day of the week preceding the battle of Pittsburg Landing, or Shiloh, there were sold to the soldiers, from the Pittsburg post-office, seven hundred dollars worth of postage-stamps. (141)

Letters from the warfront begged their readers to "tell me all the news." Letters from the homefront sought information about "where you sleep," "what you eat," and "are you well?" *Never* were there enough letters to satisfy the correspondents.

The receipt of a long-awaited letter sent those at home into paroxysms of joy. Virginia Gray's delight over a letter, one of the first in several months from her husband, was apparently shared vicariously by everyone in the room.

> Oh, goody—I looked so happy that all the men were made happy, too. The bestest letter. That is all I can say. Even Gen. Fagan himself had to come and ask me what I had. (151)

While the women on the homefront pleaded for longer, more frequent letters from their absent ones, the soldiers in turn chided their correspondents for their neglect in writing.

From a hospital near Suffolk, Virginia, Granville Belcher reproached his wife for her apathy:

> Our post office is in fifty yards of the hospital and I go out every time the mail comes and there is letters for everybody but me. I have frequently—because I cold not here from home I would be glad to here from you every three or four days. I have never received the scratch of a pen from you since I saw you. You must wirte soon and often. . . . (26 February 1862)

In much the same vein and with similar hostilities and deficiencies in spelling, Day Elmore wrote his brother and sister:

> I think you would write oftener to have the male come time after time with nothing for me as usal. Why I can not march half as far nor eat my meals half as well as when I hear from you often. . . . Pleas write ofterner if you want me to do my *Soldiering all right.* (20 September 1863)

Letters were moments of togetherness: times of remembering, of talking over problems, of sharing baby's first steps and first words. John W. Potter wrote his wife that her letters would be "like angels visits to me" (4 January 1865). For Harriet Jane Thompson her letters to her husband were "little talks."

Although it is now after ten o'clock and the rest are all in bed I could not go to sleep until I had a short talk with you. (229)

Lizzie Ozburn, writing from near Atlanta, found considerable emotional relief in writing to her husband.

> I have not received a single line from you yet I heard though you was at Petersberge but I knew you was some where so that did not satisfy me much. . . . Now I do not know whither to direct this to P—[Petersburg] or R—[Richmond] but I want to write any how & I want to cry too. I don't cry often but there are times I cant help it. . . . I rather talk to you & when I have the blues I dont feel like work. I have been sad all the eve. (24 August 1861)

If there were children in the family the letters almost invariably mentioned their health and activities. Sarah Chapin wrote her husband about the help in letter writing provided by their young son Gene.

> . . . for Gene is right on hand and wants to write too. I presume he would have forgotten about his Papa if he did not hear you spoken of so often. But as it is he talks about you a great deal and sometimes I almost think he remembers something about you yet for if he sees either a soldier dressed in his uniform or a picture of one, he always calls him Papa. He is a great soldier himself. He usually has any quantity of guns around and will often shoulder one and say, "Mama, Gene is going to sojir'." He thinks a great deal of the baby, his Bruner baby as he calls him. (24 March 1863)

Although modern women may be critical of the disproportionate number of letters extant in archives and attics that were written by women to soldiers in comparison to the vast number of letters from soldiers to women, the disparity can be attributed not so much to the lack of sentimentality as to the limited amount of space in haversacks. As one soldier explained in somewhat blunt terms in a letter to his sister:

> Your letter came to hand in due time—was read with the
> interest that only an absent bro. can have in reading sentences
> penned by the hand of his dearest friends and with the satis-
> faction resulting from knowing that you are all still well—and
> was thrown into the fire! for you ought to know that we have
> no place for such useless things as a read letter and must not
> burden our carryalls with them. (W. Hale 22 February 1862)

The mails, of course, carried innumerable courtship letters and,
as would be expected, they have been some of the most numerous
and best-preserved Civil War letters. Various collections depict the
evolution of a romance. The first letters began with a formal "Dear
Miss—" or "Dear Friend—" and were signed "Respectfully yours."
As the relationship gained momentum the salutation warmed to
"My Dearest" and concluded with "Much love your devoted—."
At first there were somewhat formal letters signifying a relationship just beginning to blossom.

> You can hardly imagine how much good it does me to receive
> and peruse your kind letter. No lady who writes such an in-
> couraging [sic] and patriotic letter can be called anything but
> a true and noble hearted woman. One who values her coun-
> try and its institutions with the highest esteem. Such letters
> do more to encourage the soldier in the field to do their duties
> bravely than anything else I can think of. (Weller 1980, 86)

On another occasion Ed Weller wrote:

> To Nettie from Raleigh, N.C. I was thinking, but yesterday,
> what a lonely life mine would have been since I returned to
> the Army from home had it not been for the sweet misives
> I have received from you, always full of hope and encourage-
> ment. I am quite confident that you can not fully realize what
> a source of pleasure and hope they have been to me. . . . (183)

In other letters, however, Ed Weller, the author of the two preceding paragraphs, grew considerably less formal and considerably more
ardent as indicated by the following postscript:

P.S. I was wishing while writing this letter that I should love to be where Charley Duryea imagined me, when writing me while I was home, tonight on a sofa with my arms full of calico or any other kind of goods, only that it contained a nice young lady. Say one about your size and I think should surely have a go-away-trouble expression on my face, if such was the case. I do not know whether you would enjoy it or not—but think you would. I would risk it if I were that woman.

Ed. (69)

Although some wives evidenced a typical nineteenth century modesty in their letters to their husbands, others were far less inhibited and wrote with implied as well as outright explicit sensualness. Harriet Jane Thompson told her husband, "Billy," an officer serving with the Twentieth Iowa Volunteer Infantry:

I have very pleasant times with you in my dreams and that is every night. . . . Do you not think of our bed at home when you lay down on your cot? Every night that I lay down I wonder where you are and what kind of a place you have to sleep. But I hope we may both live to see the day when you can be at home with me. (221–22)

In another letter she fantasized:

Oh, how I wish I could sleep with you tonight. Would you like to sleep with me? But I can only dream of being with you and that is very pleasant for I see you every night in my dreams. (231)

Mrs. John B. Gordon, wife of Brigadier General Gordon, thanked her husband for his recent letter which had been handed to her in a train station.

Your note was short but o so sweet. . . . I pulled down my veil & under it hid from all eyes, I pressed to my lips *over & over* the spot that yours had touched, & tried to imagine I could feel your own *precious lips* & that dear moustache that I love so much. (15 May 1864)

285

From Sparta, Michigan, Mary Noble wrote to her husband:

> O how I wish you was here these cold nights for your sake &
> mine to for I dont believe it is very comfortable sleeping on the
> ground & I know it aint very sleeping alone. (27 January 1862)

Even more precious than letters were the exchanges between
servicemen and their loved ones of their "likenesses." Soldiers as
well as their families implored one another to "send me your likeness." Louisa Jane Phifer, of Vandalia, Illinois, reported her compliance with her husband's request and gave a cost accounting of
the process.

> Now George you wrote to have us send you our likenesses.
> We did so. They were Ambrotypes and cost $1.00 apiece. They
> were the cheapest we could get. They are pretty fair pictures.
> We got your likeness cased for 75 cts so that it would not in-
> jure. (395)

Lizzie Ozburn, of Atlanta, at first thought it too expensive to have
her "likeness" made. She quickly reconsidered and in a realistic reap-
praisal informed her husband

> . . . I will have mine & Bobbie's likeness taken tomorrow
> morning. I thought once twas to hard times but then again
> I thought it might be the last request you ever might make. . . .
> (6 September 1861)

Photographs were treasured as visages to be adored as well as talked
to. Miranda Spalding's young son Genie reported to his father:

> We like to talk about you and often wish you was here with
> us. Mother has your photograph in her trunk where she can
> see it every time she goes to it and she kisses it and talks to
> it just as if you could hear every word she says. (16 January 1864)

Vying in importance with letters and "likenesses" as morale
boosters were the thousands upon thousands of boxes of food

lovingly prepared for the voracious appetites sharpened by poor, insufficient army fare. The traffic in "boxes," especially in the North, was appreciable, great numbers of them sent in response to plaintive letters detailing the bleak, repetitious camp food. These boxes were carefully packed and sent not to the general Sanitary Commission offices or to hospitals, but to special soldiers, with specific names and addresses.

Webster Teachout, of the 11th Michigan Cavalry, begged for some good food from home. (Whatever Webster lacked in spelling he apparently made up for in appetite.)

> Mother, I wish you would bake up about a dozen mince pies and two or three loaves of bread and some frid cakes and a saucage or so and send down to me also a piece of cheas if you have got it and a few pounds of butter also a piece of dried beef would go very well and a few apples to fill up if it don't fill without. If some of the rest of the neighbors want to send put it togather but put a good supply fried cakes and cookeys and bread and pies in and a good role of butter. Send a good big boxful so it will last a good while for a kind of lunch when hungry. (19 January 1865)

Sometimes the boxes were the contributions of whole networks of family members: mince pies made by an aunt, bread and cookies and sweetmeats from cousins, a plum cake, a turkey, and a ham, pickles, nuts and dried fruits from still other relatives.

Often entire towns gathered up provisions and "delicacies" to be sent to soldiers in neighboring hospitals. Judith McGuire, a Southerner, noted in her August 1, 1861, journal entry the weekly gathering of a wagonload of food for hospital patients. "This whole neighborhood is busy today loading a wagon with comforts for the hospital at Fairfax Court-House." On another occasion, Mrs. McGuire helped with the packing of "a barrel of grapes, and another with tomatoes and others with fresh vegetables, and yet another Mrs. M. has packed with bread, biscuit, and a variety of things for the sick" (65).

Amanda Chittenden walked miles out into the country near her Franklin, Indiana, home to try to obtain fresh butter and "good homemade cheese" to send to her husband and to her brother. Although she resisted the urge to make a large cake to slip in, the "delicacies" included were myriad. Her letter of April 12, 1863, enumerated the contents of the boxes "in case you *don't* get them."

> One smoked ham (bacon) 1. ham dried beef, one peck dried apples, half peck dried peaches, a *little* bit o'cheese, 1. jar pickles, two cans peaches, two green apples, one apple butter, 1. jar blackberries, 1. fresh butter, half peck onions, potatoes, green apples, mustard, & pepper, 1. box cigars, 1. box smoking *tobacco*.
>
> Now I know how highly you prise the two last named articles. I know what a happy influence good cigars and "cut & dried" has upon you. You will be in such a glorious good humor that you will write me letters *about* every day as long at least as the cigars and tobacco last. Then when they are gone, I'll send you more and only ask in return plenty of *good long* letters. (12 April 1863)

Women also sent off countless boxes of clothing in answer to the repeated requests for mittens and underwear and trousers. For example, Miranda Spalding's husband wrote from Blains Cross Roads, Tennessee:

> My ink is frozen up this morning and I will scratch a few lines in pencil. . . . We cannot move for the reasons the men have no clothing or shoes and provisions are not to be had for a long march. We live in hopes of having clothing soon but have been disappointed so many times that we put little dependance upon anything. . . . I am completely reduced in clothing. The pair of pants I have on are my all and have had to roll up in my blanket once to have them mended. (11 January 1864)

Morale played a vitally important role on the homefront as well as at the battlefront. Sustenance for those left at home was provided in part by the aforementioned letters as well as by the indispensable support derived from neighbors and close family ties. The emotional support of large, closely-knit families and devoted friends was often crucial to the sanity of the women who waited anxiously at home for the safe return of their loved ones. As Clara Maclean pointed out, "It is easier to bear afflictions when surrounded by affection and soothed by sympathy" (503).

With the mounting lists of fatalities, more and more women found themselves cast in the perennial roles of those providing sustenance or of those desperately needing sustenance. Jane Howison Beale's isolated position in Fredericksburg, which was surrounded by Federal troops; the economic loss of her black servants; her lack of food; her acute need for wood for heat—all were minor afflictions compared to the news of the death of her son, Charles, on May 5, 1862. In the days that followed, Jane Beale gratefully acknowledged the kindnesses shown her by the townspeople.

> In the midst of so much that is painful added to the deep sadness which environs our household, we are not left to feel ourselves forsaken, the kindness and sympathy of the dear Fred'g people was never more manifest to me than now, scarcely an hour of the day passes in which I do not receive some token of remembrance from friends, either a kind message, a lovely bunch of flowers, a waiter of nice things to eat or, best of all a visit from some dear Christian friend who talks to me of my dear boy who has fought the battle of life and so early won the crown of victory to cast at the Redeemer's feet. Surely there has been great mercy mingled with this stroke, there should be no murmurings in my heart but an humble acquiescence in the Divine will and a heart-felt reliance upon Him who "doeth all things well." (43–44)

Often, however, it was only women's deeply rooted religious faith, the very core of their being, that ultimately provided solace and helped in their eventual acceptance of life's adversities. Illness, death, and even the war itself were viewed by many as manifestations of the will of God.

Following the death of her son Seth, of brain fever, in a regimental hospital, Mrs. Ingersoll wrote to a second son who was serving with the Union Army as an ambulance driver. In her letter she expressed the widely-held conviction that all death reflected Divine will.

> It is a year today since Seth left us for the last time. I can hardly make it seem, even now, as though we should never see him again. But we must submit to the ways of an Allwise and ever Merciful God and try to feel that he will order all for our good. If we can but feel an assurance that we shall all meet in a better world, when the journey of life is ended, it will serve to bear up our spirits under the trials, and separations we have to meet here. (Rundell 1964, 357)

This same generally accepted doctrine of submission was succinctly phrased by Sallie Van Rensselear in her diary entry of January 16, 1862.

> We must feel that our Heavenly Father does all that is right & for the best & *therefore* we must be resigned.

The physical death of a beloved son or grandson was horrendous in itself, but for many women their anguish was coupled with deep anxieties concerning his spiritual life. Samary Sherman from Brown's Island grieved over the death of her grandson, Lyman, serving with an Ohio regiment in a battle near Winchester, Virginia, and was gravely troubled lest he had been "sent into eternity unprepared." She wrote to her cousin Lucretia:

> Lyman embraced religion when about 14 and has been a consistent member of the Methodist Episcopal Church ever since but whether he was prepared when he fell God only knows, but we will hope he was, and is now with his dear Mother in Heaven. (Sibley 7 March 1865)

To many women, sickness and the suffering wrought by the war were unquestionably God's punishment imposed upon a wicked and ungrateful people. Sunday diary entries noted attendance at church services and frequently included an explication of the sermon. Laura Nisbet Boykin, a faithful churchgoer, almost invariably summarized the Sunday sermon and added her personal comments.

> Attended afternoon service, and heard a still more edifying discourse from the text, "Faint yet pursuing." Mr. Wills said, every wave of sorrow or affliction that swept over us, cast up pearls and gems to the shore. I believe it is true. Affliction sanctifies. (46)

Hannah Ropes, a Georgetown nurse, viewed the war as God's War.

> This is God's War, in spite of uncertain generals, in spite of ill success; in spite of our own unworthiness; the cause is that of the human race, and must prevail. Let us work then with a good heart, here and at home. We are all scholars in the same school. Having failed to learn in prosperity, we ought to be glad of the Divine Mercy which gives us another chance in the upheaving of all social comforts and necessities. (113)

Lucy Breckinridge devoted numerous passages in her diary to a discussion of sermons she had heard or had been reading. Her nagging doubts and guilt feelings, however, seem to depict a young woman seeking to find herself, the comfort of a religious faith, and an acceptance of the will of God. After a walk through the cemetery following a visit to the grave of her brother John, who died in the Battle of Seven Pines in 1862, she mused:

> The sun always casts its last, lingering rays on Johnny's grave. It is such a quiet, beautiful spot. How I long to rest there. It is not the fear of the troubles and sorrows of life that makes me wish to die now. I am willing to bear my cross, but I feel such a yearning to be with Jesus. I wonder if it is wrong for me to think as I do. I am so sinful, so weak to resist temptation. I am always doing wrong, and yet my heart thrills with love for Christ. When I am alone I think of Him all the time, and resolve to lead a new life, but I always fail. There is so much to discourage anyone who tries to do right. May God help me! (57)

Almost two years later, Lucy was still troubled over her "sinfulness."

> I have been so sinful. I read my Bible and prayed, but the light of God's countenance was withdrawn from me. I longed so for some kind friend or pastor to guide and comfort me. . . . Sorrows are too apt to harden my heart against God, yet, I must reconcile myself to a life of hardship and sorrow. We are born to suffer and to die. The gloomy state of the country depresses me so terribly I cannot see the dawn of peace that I hear some people talk about. . . . But I *will* try to believe that "He doeth all things well." (189)

The war news continued to depress Lucy. Despite certain reservations, she, as did many others, firmly believed in the ultimate connections between God and war.

> I am right despondent about the times. It is so hard to believe that war is a punishment to a nation, administered by a merciful and just God. If it was a fiery ordeal through which we would come out purified and humbled, I could see the mercy of it; but it seems to me that people are more reckless and sinful than ever. It ruins our young men and has an immoral effect upon everyone. But, of course, it is just and wise, as God orders it so. (62)

Innumerable diary entries included prayers, Bible verses, religious admonitions, and reminders of one's duty to be submissive to the will of God.

> Oh I will believe that God is Love & his promises are yea and amen. (Howes 14 February 1864)
> God help us, and guide us onward and upward, for the Saviour's sake! (McGuire 1889, 326)
> The Lord save us, or we perish! (McGuire 1889, 342)

Mary Elizabeth Humphrey Howes, of Macon, Georgia, epitomized some of the more devout defenders of the faith. While the rest of the country was engaged in a bloody battlefield struggle with enemy soldiers, Mrs. Howes was engaged in moral combat with an ever-present, soul-threatening Satan. Her religious convictions were more personally and family centered than war related.

> May God be merciful & not chastise me for my impious thoughts. I have been to the house of God with my children but my thoughts are continually of my troubles. I do pray to God. I do cry in anguish of Spirit for energy of mind to rise above the buffetings of Satan. (8 February 1863)

Mrs. Howes's emotional outpourings reflected an almost fanatical concern over her husband's apparent disinterest in religion. She repeatedly cautioned her daughters against marrying "an ungodly man" for it had cost her "a lifetime of tears of agony of wrestling prayers of wretchedness of soul" (9 August 1864).

Much of Mrs. Howes's time was devoted to church activities, and one of her special projects was the establishment of a Sunday school for poor children. As a Good Samaritan and probably with the hope of a possible conversion, Mrs. Howes opened her home to a desperately ill, indigent. (Apparently proselytizing failed, for the woman unfortunately turned out to be a morphine addict.)

Judith McGuire, a clergyman's wife, magnanimously offered prayers for all soldiers—friend or foe alike.

> About to go to church. I trust that this Sabbath may be instrumental of much spiritual good, and that the hearts of the people may be busy in prayer, both for friends and enemies. Oh, that the Spirit of God may be with the soldiers, to direct them in keeping this holy day! We are in the Lord's hands— He alone can help us. (37)

Despite Mrs. McGuire's concerns for the suffering of the enemy, she and several million like her fervently prayed for a Confederate victory.

> Arise, O God, in thy strength, and save us from our relentless foes, for thy great name's sake! (159)

Writing from the perspective of a loyal Southerner, Virginia Conner, upon reading the Federal casualty list in June 1861, confided to her diary: " . . . I think the result clearly shows that God is on our side" (12 June 1861).

Sarah Butler Wister tended to repress the Biblical injunctions to "love thine enemy." Caught up in her intense loathing for the Confederacy, she wrote:

> Went at 9 o'clock a.m. to a service which is to be performed twice a week during these present troubles, who can say how long? The De Profundis, the full litany & those touching prayers which have been written for this present strait. I wish any church going could take some of the hatred out of my heart, but I cannot wish the war to stop. I cannot but hope that some lives may be lost in battle & some on the gallows, & I cannot speak or even think of the English without almost going into spasms. . . . (304–5)

Some parishioners believed their ministers were becoming increasingly distracted by their war-related activities. Sarah Alexander Lawton considered the sermons in her Richmond church rather poor.

> Our ministers have no time for study—they are so engaged with visits to the afflicted, to hospitals, to the wounded & with funerals. (Gilmer 19 June 1864)

Oftentimes neither letters nor family nor religion could dispel the overwhelming loneliness and anxieties experienced by women left at home—to wait. In desperation, Amanda Chittenden threatened her husband: "I am pretty near making up my mind to have a *'spell of the typhoid'*—and make you come home" (23 August 1861). Amanda quickly recognized her selfishness and apologized to her husband. In their exchange of letters, however, her husband's efforts to placate her seemed to annoy rather than to soothe.

> You must not call me a brave and contented girl, because *I ain't one bit.* And onething more I want you to quit *flourishing about* over the hills and valleys when you are in the midst of so many secessionists. I know you are very brave an all that *But I want you to do just as I tell you.* (September 1861)

Interwoven with women's concerns for their own and their absent ones' morale were worries over their tremendous responsibilities on the homefront. Although Jane Howison Beale, of Fredericksburg, Virginia, was describing a typical day in her life in 1850, circumstances would not have changed greatly had she been describing a day in her life or that of many of her contemporaries in the early 1860s.

> Spent part of the day greening pickles, cutting our work, cleaning lamps, learning lessons to the children, superintending the cleaning of the yards and whitewashing part of the house, paring peaches, mending clothes, cleaning bedsteads of insects, seeing the cow milked & fed, nursing the baby, and after putting the children to bed sat down to knit and talk. . . . (6)

Keziah Brevard, even though in her late fifties, oversaw her plantation near Columbia, South Carolina, essentially by herself. She sounded exhausted in her journal of 1860–61 and understandably so, for it was she who rationed out the meal and the clothing for the slaves; attended to the planting of rye, corn, cabbages, peas, potatoes, cucumbers; and supervised the harvesting, the killing of the chickens and turkeys, and the care of the fruit trees. In addition, she made butter and sausage, canned, and raised flowers.

Sarah Bovard, of Alpha, Indiana, described days in which she had "so much work to do I am most troubled to death." She wrote of boiling soap, spinning sock yarn, doubling and twisting it, going to market where she and her husband sold some of their produce: "65¢ for wheat, 50¢ for peaches, 5¢ for eggs and 25¢ for feathers." From the proceeds she bought delaine dress material for 12½¢ a yard, indigo, cotton, coffee and calico. Other days, Mrs. Bovard spent dyeing cloth, sewing eight pairs of jeans and five jackets, weaving carpet, including hackling the flax, spinning the tow out, spooling her linen, warping her linen then beaming it, getting it through the gears, and then putting her linen through the reed, and commencing weaving. In other diary entries she recorded a different though similarly enervating routine. "I bake, patch, wash, starch, iron."

Household activities similar to those of Mrs. Bovard's were duplicated throughout the South in homes where there were few or no household servants to help carry out the work. Some days, of course, the work proved less strenuous; however, there were always the minutiae of life to attend to. Cornelia Chase, living near Owosso, Michigan, recorded her activities in a popular phrase of the day: "I chored around."

Women everywhere could (and can) relate to Harriet Smith's near dinner fiasco:

> The meat scorched—my Fritters hissed & boiled over—the corn bread cooled, & yet the dinner was at last done &, *wonder of wonders*—tasted good. (S. Smith, 21)

The monotonous routine for Northern women of preparing three meals a day, seven days a week, was somewhat lightened in the South where, because of growing food shortages as the war continued, families subsisted on only one or two meals per day. However, the proximity of many Southern families to the battle scene frequently required the feeding—voluntarily or upon request—of hundreds of their own Confederate soldiers as they passed through the area or encamped in their yards and fields. The most despised task, however, involved feeding upon demand (sometimes at gunpoint) the enemy troops of occupation—often when the cupboard was almost bare. Many diarists recorded feeding over fifty soldiers a day.

Amanda Virginia Edmonds, for example, described the frenzy of activity to provide food for their gallant Confederate troops as they marched through Paris, Virginia, in July of 1861:

> They poured through all night and everybody in town and country was cooking and could not begin to satisfy the craving hunger of a third, though we were cooking as hard and as fast as fire and hands could do it. (53)

In July 1863 as Major General Burnside's cavalrymen passed near West Union, Ohio, in hot pursuit of raider John Hunt Morgan,

Lena Sheldon wrote her mother of the town's concerted efforts to help feed the hungry soldiers:

> Evening: We are feeding 141 cavalrymen. I have gathered one basketful of bread and butter and meat—everybody is bringing something. I came toiling in from a cross street with my basket load in one hand and a dish of pickles in the other. Laura is waiting for me with a big pan of bread, butter and pie, and such a nice plate of fried steak. One soldier leans over with his plate, on horseback, asking for a dinner for "just four." I fill his plate with my fingers and away he goes. They feed their horses on the pavement. These men are from Georgetown and Ripley. At last they dash away—a whole streetful—to overtake our Army. Just to think! Both those tremendous armies have been within 7 miles of us, and so close together! (61)

As the North's anaconda grip tightened, countless Southern families were given the alternative of boarding officers of the occupation troops or of giving up their homes. Most Southerners opted for the former course of action, hoping their compliance would help protect their homes from looters and stragglers. Even those families who were not coerced into furnishing long-term board and lodging accommodations were often plagued by the occupation troops for handouts and meals. Again most Southerners were too wary of the consequences to refuse. Irate Southern women, however, considered providing meals quite sufficient; they were not about to suffer harassment in addition.

Two Union diners, clearly unwelcome "guests" at Amanda Edmonds's home in Paris, Virginia, must have spent some uncomfortable hours if Amanda's diary entry in any way reflected the tenor of the evening.

> We were *dishonored* with two at the supper table—Shumaker and Memenger, whom I hope will be registered with the fallen. They are very chatty and extremely inquisitive as to the country and farming. One remarked, "Virginia was a garden spot; indeed it was a beautiful and fine country." Yes, and I hope you may all get a home on her soil not larger than six by three. (78)

Always there was a need for food in army hospitals. Women who lived nearby often deprived themselves to take food and "delicacies" to the patients. Fannie Beers, a nurse during the war, poignantly described the oft repeated scenes of women shyly proffering their gifts for "the boys."

> How often I have marshalled into the hospital wards mothers and wives, who for the sake of some absent loved one had come from homes many miles away, to bring some offering to the sick. Timid, yet earnest women, poorly dressed, with sun-browned faces and rough hands, yet bearing in their hearts the very essence of loving kindness towards the poor fellows upon whose pale faces and ghastly wounds they looked with "round-eyed wonder" and pity. After a while they would gain courage to approach some soldier whom they found "sort o' favored" their own, to whom they ventured to offer some dainty, would stroke the wasted hand, smooth the hair, or hold to the fevered lips a drink of buttermilk or a piece of delicious fruit. Ah, *how many* times I have watched such scenes! To the warmly expressed thanks of the beneficiaries they would simply answer, "That is nothing; 'mebbe' somebody will do as much *for mine* when he needs it." (200–1)

Southern hospitality assumed heroic proportions during the war years. According to numerous diarists, almost every Southern home in the vicinity of a battlefield became a hospital. The welcoming into their homes of wounded or ill soldiers, the nursing and caring for even those suffering from deadly contagious diseases, and the sharing of their own often scanty provisions with perfect strangers was a lifesaving accommodation provided generously and gratuitously in thousands of homes throughout the South. Amanda Virginia Edmonds, for example, told of being interrupted at dinner by the arrival of a soldier wounded at Manassas and seeking a room, food, and nursing care.

> We welcome him to our home, poor fellow—away from home and kindred and disabled. Who could but show our Confederate soldiers kindness and attention? (55)

A similar welcome was usually tendered refugees with the exception of areas where their increasing numbers threatened to produce greater shortages and ever-higher prices. Louisa McCord Smythe, of Columbia, South Carolina, remembered:

> In those days hospitality was unlimited. The whole up country was crowded with people from the coast who had been obliged to leave their homes. Uncle Haskell's house . . . was full of his relatives and strangers too—all helpless women and little children. No one ever complained or fussed that their homes were made unendurable by this—it was simply borne like everything else as a matter of course. It was then that Lewis Haskell's mother used to let me sleep with her and her children, five in a bed! (52)

In the absence of their husbands, women were suddenly faced with the sole responsibility for raising their children. For widows whose husbands died as casualties of war and who were left with a large family of young children to support, their first priority centered on keeping the family together.

Upon the death of her husband, Cornelia McDonald was counseled by family and friends to parcel out her seven children to the older members of the family who would be in a better financial position to care for and educate her brood. Repeated urgings made her even more adamant about keeping her family together.

> I listened, but was resolved no matter what happened not to part with my children; but often when pressed, and reminded how hopeless my condition was, and indeed how unreasonable it was to persist in refusing to do what was the only thing that could be done, as far as any one could see, if my heart was inclined to yield for fear I would not be doing the best for the children, the thought of my poor little lonely ones, for they would have been lonely without me and each other, the thought of not being there to hear their prayers at night, to soothe them if they were worried, or comfort them if they were troubled, that thought would nerve me for resistance. (241–42)

Even a well-intentioned minister called to see Cornelia to press the family's advice

> that it was perfectly hopeless for me to attempt to keep them together with no means, not even my husband's pay; that it ought to be a source of satisfaction to me to have them so well provided for. (242)

Mrs. McDonald, however, remained unmoved.

Finally, from the proceeds acquired by taking in boarders and teaching, Mrs. McDonald was able to care for her family. Some Southern women in similar straits took over many of the farming and dairy duties of their plantations themselves, working halves with their former slaves in order to help support their children. Northern farm women, already acquainted with field work, survived by sowing less acreage and accepting help from neighbors and friends.

Since schools were suspended in most areas of the South, the problem of educating their children introduced innumerable frustrations for mothers with young children. It soon became expedient to teach the children at home. (Even in antebellum days planters often hired tutors for their own children and invited other parents in the neighborhood to send their youngsters and share in paying the teacher's salary.) As more and more tutors were called into the army, the teaching responsibilities devolved upon mothers, aunts, grandmothers, or older sisters.

One mother described the added burden in a letter to her sister:

> This being Saturday, and a holiday for the children, I have a leisure hour to devote to you. I have undertaken to teach my children this year, in consequence of the pressure of the time. The war tax, together with our other expenses, make it necessary. And I find it a difficult matter, to teach half the day, and attend to household matters besides with numerous other vexations thrown in. (L. Richardson 1 February 1862)

Older sisters who struggled to serve as schoolmistresses for their younger siblings often found it difficult to maintain discipline and to keep their young charges steadily at work "learning their lessons." Occasionally, loud complaints about the difficulty and distastefulness of the work were voiced by some women who had no interest in teaching and had accepted positions in schools or homes only as a temporary stopgap to their financial problems. Countless other women, however, rejoiced in the discovery of the pleasures of awakening young minds.

Anne Frobel, of Fairfax County, Virginia, noted in an April 1863 diary entry her sister Lizzie's work in opening a school for the neighborhood children—a project which proved most rewarding.

> There is not a school in town, or any where in the neighbourhood, and where there are children, the parents are so anxious to have them taught, that Lizzie determined to collect all together that live within a convenient distance and teach them every day. And to-day she opned [*sic*] her school for the first time. The people around have been so kind to us, and done so many things, kind and considerate, and it was the only way she had of showing her gratitude. (127)

Two months later, Anne boasted:

> L.'s little school is added to every few days. The people are perfectly delighted with the idea of having some one to teach their children, of course the war broke up all the schools in this vicinity, and for more than two years now the children all are entirely without instruction. Some good kind lady friends in town hearing of the work L. is engaged in, went from house to house among their friends and collected up all the old school books they could find, and sent them out to her, a whole carriage load—and O such a treasure as it was to her, she was delighted, and so were the children, if only to rummage them all over. (148–49)

Caring for small children and nursing them through colds and fevers is always difficult in the best of times. Frequently, however, the teenage years become even more worrisome. Civil War women were certainly no strangers to "generation gap" problems. Unable

to cope with her daughter's impudence and late hours, Ann Cotton
despaired to her husband:

> She is so fond of gentlemens society, & is certainly the *fastest*
> girl for her age that I ever saw, I am completely at a loss to
> know what to do with her. . . . (17 August 1864)

A week later after a "slumber party," Ann again reported her distress over "the younger generation."

> . . . girls are not of much account in these days. I do not ex-
> pect mine will ever do anything for me, but I do not care for
> that so much, only I want them to be good & happy. (25
> August 1864)

Maria Daly and her friends lamented

> how the young acted without regard to the experience or wishes
> of their parents or elders. Someone said that there was no
> family government in America. The answer was, in no coun-
> try was there so much, but it was the young who governed.
> (Hammond 1962, 192)

Nor were Civil War mothers immune from problems of alcoholism,
drug addiction, or suicide in their children and their friends. Many
a diary and letter detailed family troubles: sibling rivalries, in-law
vexations, the need to house and care for elderly parents, and the
need for a stern father's hand at home to help discipline young children and teenagers.

To be sure, life on the homefront was not always gloomy and
foreboding. Interspersed between the anxieties and grief there were,
of course, happy occasions: a birthday party, a picnic, a church
supper, a wedding. Soldiers' aid society "socials" or "donations" entailed days of cooking and baking and precious evenings spent sharing news, experiences, and above all, hopes. Now and then there
was jubilant news to report: Mrs. Theodore Chapin's birth of a son;
Mrs. Williams's announcement several months following her visit

to her husband's battlefield headquarters that "a little stranger" was on the way. Even so, there was trepidation:

> I trust you will not feel sad dearest, at the prospect of this increase to our already interesting family—when so many of our brave countrymen are going to an untimely grave, we must do our part to fill their places. . . . (Mary Williams 17 April 1862)

Some diarists reported in detail the gala social festivities held in the large cities, dances where a forced gaiety prevailed, parties where many of the gallant young soldiers were literally dancing their last dance. Most social activities, however, took on a more somber wartime mien.

In Lexington, Kentucky, Frances Peter detailed the formation of a Sociable Club.

> None but ladies can be members but each member has the privilege of inviting & bringing with her any gentlemen whom she may chose, always providing that it is not one whose society is disagreeable to any of the other members. The refreshments are limited to three kinds to be left to the choice of the member at whos[e] house the club happens to meet. Ladies are not allowed to come in evening or party dresses, but must wear promenade or 'at home' villetes. No music to be engaged, but dancing is allowed if there is a piano. The Club met at our house tonight. (It meets once a week at the house of each member in turn.) (51)

Similar gatherings called "Starvation Parties" were the rage in Richmond. Constance Cary Harrison recalled Richmond's "Starvation Club," of which she was a founder.

> It was agreed between a number of young women that a place for our soldier visitors to meet with us for dancing and chat, once a week, would be a desirable variation upon evening calls in private homes. The hostesses who successively offered their drawing-rooms were among the leaders in society. It was also decided that we should permit no one to infringe the rule of suppressing all refreshment, save the amber-hued water from

the classic James. We began by having piano music for the dances, but the male members of the club made up between them a subscription providing a small but good orchestra. Before our first meeting, a committee of girls waited on General Lee to ask his sanction, with this result to the spokeswoman, who had ended with: "If you say no, general, we won't dance a single step!" "Why, of course, my dear child. My boys need to be heartened up when they get their furloughs. Go on, look your prettiest, and be just as nice to them as ever you can be!" (150)

Several paragraphs later, she continued:

The oft-told stories of damask curtains taken down to fabricate into court trains over petticoats of window curtain lace, and of mosquito nettings made up over pink or blue cambric slips, now took shape. Certain it is that girls never looked prettier or danced with more perfect grace than those shut-in war maidens, trying to obey the great general's behest and look their prettiest for the gallant survivors of his legions. (152)

Fannie Beers, surrounded as she was by suffering and dying men at her various hospitals, found it difficult to "make merry."

I could not rid myself of this feeling, and can truly say that during those fateful years, from the time when in Richmond the "starvation parties" were organized, until the end, I never found a suitable time to dance or a time to laugh or a time to make merry. (115)

Somehow, creatively inclined women salvaged time to write—short stories, articles, books—and diaries. A small sampling of authors focusing on their own wartime experiences and interests included Elizabeth Meriwether, who responded to a short story contest sponsored by the *Mississippian* in 1863 and was awarded first prize of $500 for "The Refugee," the story of her personal experiences following her banishment from Memphis by Sherman. Mary Abigail Dodge, under the pen name "Gail Hamilton," wrote articles chastising women for being backsliders and failing to courageously maintain Union morale. Louisa May Alcott used her experiences as a nurse in a Washington hospital as the basis of her book *Hospital Sketches*.

Although Southern women were at first less public than Northern women in their outspokenness on military and political issues, Augusta Jane Evans (Wilson), as a result of her novels and newspaper and magazine articles in support of "The Cause," earned a handsome reputation and was considered by many to be "the foremost propagandist of the Confederacy" (A. J. Wilson, City of Mobile Museum; Sterkx 1970, 83). As a critic she was credited with exerting considerable influence on women and even on high-ranking military officers. In a letter to her friend General Beauregard, she wrote:

> It is not my privilege to enter the ranks, wielding a sword, in my country's cause, but all that my feeble, womanly pen could contribute to the consummation of our freedom, I have humbly, but at least, faithfully and untiringly *endeavored* to achieve. (A. J. Wilson, Historic Mobile Preservation Society 4 August 1862)

In the North, Anna Elizabeth Dickinson achieved fame as an orator speaking on abolition as well as on political and military subjects.

Women were also faithful recorders of the passing scene. For many women, diary keeping was their salvation during times of trouble. Some women kept diaries as a record of their lives and times. Others seemed to have kept diaries as a way of releasing their emotions, as a sounding board for their thoughts, as secret revelations to a trusted friend—a confidante, or as a "listening ear." One diarist, a pro-Union woman living in Confederate territory, explained that "Keeping journals is for those who cannot, or dare not, speak out" (Straubing 1985, 181). In much the same vein, Sarah Morgan explained how her diary served as an emotional outlet.

> "I can suffer and be still" as far as outward signs are concerned; but as no word of this has passed my lips, I give it vent in writing, which is more lasting than words, partly to relieve my heart, partly to prove to my own satisfaction that I am no coward; for one line of this, surrounded as we are by soldiers,

and liable to have our houses searched at any instant, would be sufficient indictment for high treason. (Dawson 1960, 94)

Catherine Edmondston also shared Sarah Morgan's fear of her journal falling into the hands of the enemy.

> And now old friend—you, my Journal—for a time Farewell. You are too bulky to be kept out exposed to prying eyes and thievish fingers. You go for a season to darkness and solitude— and my record must be kept on scraps of paper, backs of letters or old memorandum books which I can secrete. Think how Sheridan's burning officers would seize on the Journal of a Secesh Lady, a record of daily life spent in the Southern Confederacy from July 1860 to April '65. And how would I feel thus dragged from the recesses of private life! I trust you to Owen's fidelity—hoping the time may yet come when I can withdraw you from your retreat and finish you with a triumphant announcement of Peace. (Edmondston n.d., 101)

According to many women, diary keeping was a vital part of their lives, "one of the greatest sources of comfort" they possessed. Amanda Edmonds was apologetic that her diary

> like all other Confederate articles . . . must be homespun, but better that than none, for Oh! what had I not rather relinquish than writing privately as I have done for years. (14 September 1862)

Without her diary, Sarah Morgan was convinced she

> would have fallen victim to despair and "the Blues" long since; but they have kept my eyes fixed on "Better days a-coming" while slightly alluding to present woes; kept me from making a fool of myself many a day; acted as lightning rod to my mental thunder, and have made me happy generally. (Dawson 1960, 76–77)

Emily Liles Harris and Cornelia McDonald kept journals at the request of their husbands for a record of what was taking place at home. Mary Jane Chadick's diary was a consolation. On May 26,

1865, as the war concluded, she wrote: "Whenever my eyes rest upon you, it will be with feelings of gratitude and affection for the consolation you have afforded me in these days of trial. Farewell!" (88).

At the end of the war, or when the responsibilities of family and homelife grew too great, the diarists expressed deep regret at the thought of having to part with their "friends." Helen Hart wrote in her diary for relief from stress: "Many times I have used it as a sort of escape valve for feelings that pressed upon me." After her marriage she was saddened to give up her diary writing.

> Goodbye my ever silently sympathetic friend. . . . I wrote here first when a great war was just commencing. The end has come at last, but with fearful cost to many hearts and lives. A fearful cost, but not too much to pay for freedom.
> Goodbye little book, I can't think why my eyes are so full of tears. Goodbye dear little book, goodbye. (98–99)

Scores of Civil War diaries, including those of Judith McGuire, Mary Chesnut, Kate Cumming, Sarah Morgan, Emma Holmes, and Catherine Edmondston were published in later years.

Most women, however, devoted what little free time they could capture to visiting, gossiping, and reading. "Visiting" for minutes, hours, days, or weeks at a time was a high priority for Southern as well as Northern women. Most often, women visited, or were visited by, family members—cousins, uncles, aunts, grandparents, older married brothers and sisters, and numerous nieces and nephews. For those women living in town or in close proximity to their neighbors, visiting or receiving friends appeared to occupy a goodly part of each day. In some social circles, especially in large cities and with less intimate acquaintances, "formal calls" were conducted according to prescribed rules of etiquette. Callers, dressed in their good silks and armed with engraved calling cards, alighted from their carriages during "at home" hours. Such formalities, however, were not representative of the majority of women for whom drop-in company and "neighboring" served as their communications systems, their support groups, and welcome respites from the trials and/or boredom of the day.

The diary of Julia LeGrand, living with her sister in New Orleans, reveals a steady stream of visitors calling during morning, afternoon, and evening hours. At times, the numbers and lengths of their visits left Julia and her sister with precious little time to themselves.

> Kate W—, Mrs. Randolph and Betty Harrison have taken up my morning. I like them all, but love best to be alone of all things. I am so worn out sometimes by the constant stream of talk around me that I am nearly crazy. (153)

A few weeks later the volume of company again became oppressive:

> We have company all day long. I think I prefer the fashionable way of receiving—only on reception days. (175–76)

Upon at least one occasion the LeGrand girls gave instructions to their "maid" to inform the half-dozen callers that they were "not well." When the "maid" announced that they were "not at home" Julia suffered pangs of guilt.

> Indeed there should be some decent, yet truthful, way of denying one's self to people when one is weary and out of spirits. (187)

Much of the conversation, Julia reported, was "war talk." Rumor habitually intensified the search for news and companionship. The threat of an enemy attack, for example, touched off excited rounds of visiting among Elizabeth Lindsay Lomax's neighbors.

> We had company today from breakfast time until midnight. People are in such a state of excitement they cannot stay at home. (212)

Visiting usually involved a pleasant break in routine, and Mrs. Warren Akin appeared somewhat wistful as she commented to her husband:

> I went to see Cousin Sally but as usual she had gone visiting.
> She loves to visit, and I believe most of the ladies here visit
> a good deal. (126)

Even military orders, as Henrietta Barr pointed out in her diary,
failed to curtail "visiting."

> The all abounding topic [of conversation] was Dan Frost's
> [the town's Yankee commander] latest *proclamation* wherein
> he enjoins the "secesh" to quit visiting and stay quietly at home.
> I wonder if he thinks we are going to mind him. (11)

And, of course, along with visiting came "spinning street yarn,"
a then popular term for gossiping. Emma Holmes, for example, noted
there was considerable speculation about town concerning the pater-
nity of a baby born to a woman whose husband had been absent for
well over a year as a soldier serving with the army. Still other gossip surrounded a neighbor who Emma discovered was not a widow
after all, but rather a woman whose husband had deserted her and
left her with six little children. Frequent diary entries referred to gossip about women "being in a family way" before they were married.

Following her attendance at a festive New York ball, Maria Daly
recounted several choice observations about guests and their dress
in her diary entry of January 11, 1865, and smugly added:

> I had quite a pleasant time, having heard some ill-natured
> things and said some myself. (Hammond 1962, 331)

Gossip was frequently included to spice up letters to the warfront.
Ann Cotton shared with her husband the rumors about a certain
lady in town who was having her wedding clothes made—

> & as the *crape* on Mr. Newton's hat is getting narrowed very
> fast it is surmised that he is to be the happy man, no new thing
> for him as he has been married three times already. (22
> November 1863)

Mrs. Warren Akin wrote her husband:

I thought you knew long ago that Joe Hardin was separated
from her husband. I am told she "flies around" as gay as a
young widow, goes to Milledgeville and every where else she
can and has a string of beau following her everywhere. Joe
Shackleford told me that last piece of news about her. Joe had
not named her baby when she was here and he is as ugly as
babies can get to be. (134)

Reading was a particularly welcome diversion for the women of
both the North and the South. Most diaries included notations
about the books the writer was reading along with comments about
the subject matter. Virginia Davis Gray, of Princeton, Arkansas,
for example, was an avid reader. Although she appeared to prefer
history and fiction, she was often reduced to reading "in any book
I can find." She indicated that she was somewhat displeased with
Sybil Tennard and amused by the *Quiet Husband*. She appeared to
take minor interruptions as a matter of course.

> Am now up in the corner where I have been reading Bayne's
> Criticisms, having only *once* [been] disturbed to have the mouse
> trap taken from the closet. (67)

Apparently, most of the household was occupied with reading that
evening; however, once again they were interrupted and Virginia
commented wryly:

> Capers has brought out the trap again—this time with *three*
> mice, and we have four cats—all growing fat on *trap mice*. (68)

Mary Wilson Gilchrist's reading included Shakespeare, Charlotte
Bronte, *Confessions of an Opium Eater*, *Vanity Fair*, *Lucille*, *Tom Jones*,
The Wandering Jew, Wordsworth, Virgil, and Sophocles, as well as
history and biographies (Lady, 213–14). Julia LeGrand proved to
be a voracious reader and expressed a great desire to have personally
known Tennyson, Hawthorne, George Eliot, and Edmund Burke.
Vanity Fair gave Julia a shock, and Wilkie Collins she deemed too
long on plot.

Civil War women seized upon books as opportunities for education, escape, entertainment, or vicarious experience, and during the widespread paper shortages in the South there was the oft-repeated complaint of "having nothing to read." Now and then husbands and wives discussed books in their letters. Some passionate readers gathered up books instead of food as they fled their homes prior to an enemy attack, and many mourned the destruction of their libraries as one of the greatest losses accompanying the devastation of their homes.

Louisa McCord Smythe extolled the advantages of combining reading and knitting.

> . . . with all the knitting we managed to get a good deal of reading done, for with constant practice we were able to prop the books up and read away without interruption to the work. In this way we got through a good many of the standard books we already possessed, and we devoured eagerly the few new books that came to us printed on brown paper and bound in wall paper of such a gritty nature that it gave us the shivers to touch them with bare hands. (50)

The Bible, history, and Shakespeare constituted "approved" reading material; certain other books did not. Novel reading, for example, was frowned on by some members of the clergy. Virginia Gray reported in her diary a sermon in which the minister delivered

> a most disgusting tirade against novel reading—calling it the most "dark, filthy, fiendish, infernal, devilish babble ever lighted by the fire of hell," etc. and said if he was the circuit rider here, "by the help of God he would make us come to tow in double quick time" etc. (148)

Despite the minister's remonstrances, Virginia Gray continued to read novels. So did other women. In fact, Dickens, Thackeray, Hugo, and Dumas were some of the country's most popular authors. Although Letitia Dabney Miller's mother loved to read, she considered it "a sinful waste of time to read in the week." Reading, her mother believed, should be indulged in only on Sunday.

311

Families frequently read aloud to each other. Helen Hart, living near Cleveland, Ohio, described her family's habit of reading nightly from history, Shakespeare, *The Atlantic*, each member in turn.

Reading clubs enjoyed a great popularity during the war years as an opportunity to share one's ideas with friends. Emma Holmes, for example, founded a club in Camden, South Carolina, patterned after the group she had found so enjoyable in Charleston. While visiting her husband at his army headquarters, Sarah Jane Full Hill participated in a reading group formed by officers and their wives.

> We formed a whist club for amusement and a reading club. Our friends and relatives kept us well supplied with reading matter from home, and we would procure new books. Some one would read aloud, usually one of the young officers, and we women would busy ourselves with our fancy work and sewing. We read *Adam Bede* and *Mill on the Floss* which were new at that time. We liked Thackeray better than Dickens and we also had Charles Reade and Wilkie Collins, and I must not forget Miss Evans, with *Beulah* and *St. Elmo*. Then, too, we liked Shakespeare and read and discussed him. E. M. had been quite a student of Shakespeare, and could recite several of his plays from memory. He had a pleasing voice and good delivery, and we would prevail on him to recite *Othello* or *Macbeth* for us. (286)

What did women do during the Civil War years? Well, they knitted, they sewed, they cooked, they rolled bandages, they scraped lint, they held lotteries, they staged fairs, and they begged for money and food and clothing for their soldiers.

If they were "the weaker sex" no one told them about it. They plowed and planted and harvested. They dug potatoes, hoed corn, chopped cotton. They cleaned and patched and washed and ironed for those at home. They cooked for their families, for the hospitals, for their own armies and, on occasion, for the enemy.

They worked unceasingly to bolster morale with letters by the millions and with boxes of food by the trainload. They kept up their own morale through their abiding faith in God and their neighbors' morale through friendship and caring. As much needed diversions from their incessant wartime anxieties, most Civil War women sought escape in the simple pleasures derived from visiting, gossiping, and reading.

CHAPTER IX

The Florence Nightingales of the Civil War

> Had a talk with Dr. Boice in regard to the rude manner in
> which he treated me . . . because I took a cup of tea to a sick
> man. . . . I told him it was the first time I was ever treated in
> a rude manner by one who called himself a gentleman. . . .
>
> *—Julia Susan Wheelock (Freeman)*
> Michigan Relief Agent "Nurse"
> from her Journal, 6 December 1862

Julia Wheelock, Louisa May Alcott, Katherine Prescott Wormeley,
Cornelia Hancock, and Phoebe Yates Pember were five of the 3,000
women who served as nurses during the Civil War. Thanks to their
dedication and courage, the hospital experiences of thousands of
soldiers were made more bearable.* Thanks to these pioneers, nursing was opened as a career for women in America and the ground-
work was laid for the modern hospital.

Civil War nurses were trailblazers in a field heretofore strictly
reserved for men. Hospital nursing was definitely not considered
a "proper" occupation for "genteel" women at that time. Teaching
was almost the only work available for "proper" ladies outside the
home. Here and there, perhaps, a lady might undertake a small

---

*According to statisticians, the Civil War resulted in 620,000 deaths and 10,000,000
cases of sickness. "The overriding element was the microbe, not the minie. Approxi-
mately 225,000 Federals and 164,000 Confederates simply 'died of disease.' For the
first year over one-quarter of the Union army and close to one-half of the Confederate army were on sick call, and just about five times as many died of disease as of
wounds on both sides" (S. Brooks 1966, 106).

dressmaking business or open up a millinery shop or write senti-
mental novels to stretch a meager income, but otherwise and often
in addition, her domain was her home. It took the legendary Florence
Nightingale's work in the Crimean War to pave the way for public
acceptance of nursing as a career for "refined" women. Even so,
her success failed to translate into unqualified approval with many
dissident American men.

Although Samuel Gridley Howe had personally encouraged
Florence Nightingale in her pursuit of a nursing career when she
came to him for advice, he was adamantly opposed to any kind of
public career for his wife, Julia Ward Howe, author of the words
of "The Battle Hymn of the Republic." He strongly disapproved
of the publishing of her poems and greatly deplored her public speaking appearances. When Julia questioned his inconsistency, he replied that "if he had been engaged to Florence Nightingale, and had
loved her ever so dearly, he would have given her up as soon as
she commenced her career as a public woman." Woman's sphere,
according to Dr. Howe and thousands like him, involved only activities directly connected with home and church (Howe, 138;
Clifford, 82–83; Young, 61). Walt Whitman, a hospital volunteer
"nurse" himself, praised the work of middle-aged or elderly women,
but disapproved of *young* women in the role of nurses.

> Then it remains to be distinctly said that few or no young
> ladies, under the irresistible conventions of society, answer the
> practical requirement of nurses for soldiers. (Lowenfels, 116)

Julia Grant, wife of General Ulysses S. Grant, wrote in her introduction to Annie Wittenmyer's book that although she had earnestly wished to come to the assistance of Mrs. Wittenmyer as a
nurse, her husband forbade it. Mrs. Grant's heartrending stories
of the suffering she observed during her volunteer nursing work
caused him to protest:

> Julia, cease, cease; I cannot listen; I hear this all day, every
> day, and I must have some rest from all this sorrow and misery.

If you insist on going again to the hospitals, I will have to send
you home. (Wittenmyer Intro.)

The objections of her family, *"especially my brothers,"* forced
Augusta Jane Evans (Wilson), a well-known novelist of her day, to
give up plans to join Ella Newsom as a nurse with the Confederacy.
She wrote to Mrs. Newsom:

> when the boys learned of my application, they opposed it so
> strenuously, and urged me so earnestly to abandon the idea,
> that I feel unwilling to take a step which they *disapprove* so
> vehemently. . . . I have very *reluctantly*, and with *great disap-*
> *pointment* given up the hope of being with you.
>   The boys have heard so much said about ladies being in the
> hospitals, that they can not bear for me to go. (Richard 1914,
> 93)

Criticism of women nurses was frequently expressed in gossip and
innuendo. Maria Daly noted in her diary the rumors being circulated by disapproving males in New York City—and elsewhere, no
doubt.

> Some of the men say that they [the nurses] are closeted for
> hours with the surgeons in pantries and all kinds of disorders
> go on. The surgeons dislike, as a body, the Sisters of Charity
> because they are obliged to be respectful to them. (Hammond
> 1962, 173)

The services of the Sisters of Mercy and the Sisters of Charity,
titles used to refer to various Catholic women's religious communities, many of whose members were trained and experienced in caring for the sick, came to be highly valued by both surgeons and
patients during the war years (Maher 1989). At first, however, even
the Archbishop of New York had reservations about Catholic sisters serving in army hospitals.

> I am now informed indirectly that the Sisters of Charity in
> the diocese would be willing to volunteer a force of from fifty

317

to one hundred nurses. To this last proposition I have very strong objections. (G. Barton 1897, 7)

Soon thereafter the Bishop withdrew his objections and all Sisters of Charity and Sisters of Mercy in the diocese who wished to volunteer at the various hospitals did so with his stamp of approval.

According to Kate Cumming, a devoted Confederate nurse, Southern women were slow to volunteer as hospital nurses, many on the grounds of respectability and modesty. In a September 1863 diary entry she chided women for their apathy.

> Are the women of the South going into the hospitals? I am afraid candor will compel me to say they are not! It is not respectable, and requires too constant attention, and a hospital has none of the comforts of home! About the first excuse I have already said much; but will here add, from my experience since last writing on that subject, that a lady's respectability must be at a low ebb when it can be endangered by going into a hospital. (136)

Later, in exasperation, Kate wrote:

> There is scarcely a day passes that I do not hear some derogatory remarks about the ladies who are in the hospitals, until I think, if there is any credit due them at all, it is for the moral courage they have in braving public opinion. (178)

Capable women who hid behind "conventional modesty" rather than volunteering for nursing assignments were severely chastised by Phoebe Pember, matron of Chimborazo Hospital in Richmond from 1862 to 1865.

> There is one subject connected with hospitals on which a few words should be said—the distasteful one that a woman must lose a certain amount of delicacy and reticence in filling any office in them. How can this be? There is no unpleasant exposure under proper arrangements, and if even there be, the circumstances which surround a wounded man, far from friends and home, suffering in a holy cause and dependent

upon a woman for help, care and sympathy, hallow and clear the atmosphere in which she labors. That woman must indeed be hard and gross, who lets one material thought lessen her efficiency. In the midst of suffering and death, hoping with those almost beyond hope in this world; praying by the bedside of the lonely and heart-stricken; closing the eyes of boys hardly old enough to realize man's sorrows, much less suffer by man's fierce hate, a woman *must* soar beyond the conventional modesty considered correct under different circumstances.

If the ordeal does not chasten and purify her nature, if the contemplation of suffering and endurance does not make her wiser and better, and if the daily fire through which she passes does not draw from her nature the sweet fragrance of benevolence, charity, and love,—then, indeed a hospital has been no fit place for her! (146)

Even though her husband was a surgeon with the 92nd Infantry, Ohio Volunteers, Ann Cotton, of Marietta, Ohio, was aghast at the sending of a woman surgeon to the battlefront. She queried her husband:

What did the Secretary of War mean by sending a woman to act as surgeon. If Col. McCok was my husband I should be the least bit jealous. The army is no place for women, & one with any delicacy would not wish to be in it don't you think so? (10 May 1864)

While Ann appeared to have been distressed about women serving as surgeons with the armies, she seemed to have made a distinction between women surgeons and women nurses, for she earnestly counseled her husband to accept with gratitude the nurses who volunteered to serve in the army hospitals.

If you should have a battle & after it, any ladies should come as nurses you must not forget how much *good* they can do, & how glad the poor sufferers are to have them there. There is at present about fifty of the best & experienced nurses, from here, in Murfresborough & other places near there, taking care of the sick & wounded, & the most of them are mothers & have left children, husband & pleasant homes for the sake of doing good, such women should be treated with the greatest respect by the Surgeons. (1 February 1863)

Cornelia Hancock's Quaker friends at home were skeptical of her service as a nurse until an article praising her work was published in the New York *Daily Tribune* and excerpted in her hometown paper. Suddenly, everyone registered approval. In June 1864, Cornelia Hancock's mother wrote her:

> Dear Cornelia
> I am inclined to write frequently to thee fearing thee will not get near all my letters. The piece published in the Salem paper extracted from the New York "Daily Tribune" is creating a sensation in this neighborhood. It has reminded me of a scripture passage "When a man's ways please the Lord he maketh even his enemies to be at peace with him," as those who we used to consider thy enemies are foremost in extolling thee now. Aunt Ruth says Nelly always *was* a good nurse. William Bradway says not *one* in a *thousand* could perform so much. Mary has so many beautiful things to say I cannot remember them, but closed with saying she hoped thee would not break down under the work in which desire I most sincerely join. (111)

Actually, the very term "nurse" had vague, nebulous parameters in 1861. At that time there were no nursing schools, no diplomas, no credentials. The word "nurse" might refer to a variety of people: a woman appointed by Dorthea Dix, Superintendent of Women Nurses for the Union Army; or a "nurse" or "agent" with the U.S. Sanitary Commission, the Christian Commission, or a state Soldiers' Aid Commission; or a woman specifically requested by a surgeon at a particular hospital; or a nun from the Sisters of Mercy or the Sisters of Charity. In an even looser sense the appellation sometimes applied to officers' wives who accompanied their husbands to the battlefields or women who rushed to the bedside of wounded sons or husbands or brothers and then remained to care for the sick and dying once they sensed the great need for surrogate mothers to buoy up "the boys." Often laundresses or matrons attached to state regiments took over nursing duties in between housekeeping chores. Still other "nurses" were volunteer helpers from the area. N. R. Wallace's letter to her cousin, Captain Latta, early in the war, typified family volunteerism.

> Cousin Sam, if you should get sick or wounded and want a nurse you have but to let me know, and I will go to you at once. You have always seemed just as near and dear to me as a brother. (Latta 7 June 1861)

More often, however, the Civil War nurse was a male (the male to female ratio was five to one for both the North and the South) who was attached to a particular regiment by the terms of his enlistment or by assignment. In many hospitals the nursing staff consisted of or was supplemented by convalescents, recuperating soldiers, who themselves were barely able to maneuver around the cots, men who frequently abused or at best neglected their patients.

The problem of securing experienced, conscientious nurses was the subject of a handwritten report to the Committee on Nurses Corp for the Army of the Cumberland.

> That the supply of nurses—both male and female—is inadequate to the necessities of the service. . . . The "Regulations" allow one nurse for every ten patients on beds—but the present "orders" take away all able bodied men, and supply their places with invalids, disqualified by lack of training, and physical disability, the number *not increased*, but the efficiency diminished one half or two thirds. (Report to Committee)

Mary Ann Bickerdyke's introduction to her nursing duties clearly illustrated the problems resulting from using hospitalized soldiers as nurses.

> It was far worse than the doctor's faltering pen had been able to picture. Ten men were crowded into the first tent, one or two on cots, most of them on straw pallets spread with an army blanket or a winter overcoat. The beds were so close together that there was scarcely room to move between them. The mud

floor was foul with human excrement. A swarm of blue-bottle flies circled low over the sufferers, keeping up an angry humming almost as loud as the groans and moans and painful labored breathing. The patients lay in shirts and underdrawers, filthy with vomit, rank with perspiration. On a cot near the door a human scarecrow sat, dressed like the others, feebly stirring the fetid air with a palm-leaf fan. At his feet was a tin water pail with dipper. It was empty. It should have been full, for this man was the nurse, and one of his duties was to fetch drinking water from the nearest storage barrel. He tottered off the cot as the doctor entered and stood shakily at salute. . . . The others [tents] were no different, and no better. (Baker 1952, 40)

Even at best, according to Mary Newcomb, there was a decided difference in the attitudes of male versus female nurses.

The boys never liked a man for a nurse. A man goes into the ward in the morning and he says: "Well, boys, I see you haven't all kicked the bucket!" Then he goes on to the next ward and says: "Well, boys, you are all here yet, I thought some of you would have passed in your checks before this!" Then to another ward: "Why, I expected to see some of your toes turned up this morning!" That sort of talk was not particularly *cheering* to a sick man. Now, a woman goes into the ward with a pleasant face and takes each one by the hand and says: "Good morning! How do you feel this morning? You are looking better! Did you have something good for breakfast? Keep up good courage! You will soon be able to go home." It made a great difference with their feelings who was the first to greet them in the morning. (108)

Apparently because of the resentment many male physicians harbored for women entering the field of medicine, neither Elizabeth nor Emily Blackwell (both pioneer women physicians) was awarded a top position with the Medical Department. In a letter to Barbara Smith Bodichon dated June 1, 1861, Emily Blackwell pointed to Dorthea Dix's inexperience in hospital management and predicted confusion in the appointment of nurses.

The jealousy of the physicians of the City [New York], and the fear of many of our leading managers lest our name should

322

make the work unpopular if we took any prominent part became so marked that we have to a great degree withdrawn as
the affair went on.

Dorthea Dix (world famous for her work as a reformer of insane
asylums) was named Superintendent of Female Nurses instead of
either of the Blackwells. In the interests of keeping her appointees
above reproach Miss Dix issued the following stipulations:

> No woman under thirty years need apply to serve in govern-
> ment hospitals. All nurses are required to be very plain look-
> ing women. Their dresses must be brown or black, with no
> bows, no curls, no jewelry and no hoop skirts. (Young 1959, 98)

Furthermore, nurses

> . . . must be in their own rooms at taps, or nine o'clock unless
> obliged to be with the sick; must not go to any place of amuse-
> ment in the evening; must not walk out with any patient or
> officer in their own room except on business; must be willing
> to take the forty cents per day that is allowed by the govern-
> ment. . . . (Adams 1952, 177–78)

In fact, so rigid were Miss Dix's restrictions about appointing only
middle-aged, homely women as nurses, that she perfunctorily refused Esther Hill Hawks's application, despite Mrs. Hawks's credentials as a bona fide medical doctor, an 1857 graduate of New England
Female Medical College (E. H. Hawks 1984, 15).

Cornelia Hancock also failed to pass Dorthea Dix's inspection;
however, she succeeded in making important contributions to the
Union Army and to the field of nursing during the war. With the
departure of her only brother and "every male relative and friend
that we possessed," Cornelia Hancock, a twenty-three year old
Quaker from near Salem, New Jersey, was unwilling to stand idly
by and decided that she also "would go and serve my country." On
July 5, 1863, following the carnage at Gettysburg, Cornelia's brother-
in-law, a doctor, sent for her to come to the battlefield to help with
the ill and wounded. Despite Miss Dix's immediate rejection of her

as being too young, Cornelia sneaked past her and traveled on to Gettysburg where her age became an exceedingly unimportant consideration.

At first it was understood that the nurses would serve without pay, but they were soon allotted $12 a month, army rations, and a certain amount of free travel. Countless nurses, however, served on a strictly voluntary basis. Mary Newcomb steadfastly refused to accept money or a commission for her work in the hospitals as a volunteer nurse. Once, on being questioned as to her authority, she retorted:

> "I have a commission from a higher power than any on earth, and you need not interfere. I shall go where I please and stay as long as I please." (49)

Even when approached by Dorthea Dix, she replied that she had not come for pay.

> " . . . I will accept no commission from any one. . . . When the doctors don't want me they will say so, and I will go, but you can't give me a commission. I am doing the work my husband wished me to do when he died." (57–58)

Amy Bradley was highly incensed when one of the surgeons inquired whether she was a "contract nurse."

> If I had been a man I believe I should have knocked him down! To think that I *poor Amy Bradley* would come out here to work for *money* and that, the paltry sum of twelve dollars per month and Rations! (July 1862)

The appearance of women on the scene in this previously male-dominated field aroused considerable antipathy on the part of many skeptical surgeons. Georgeanna M. Woolsey wrote of her Civil War nursing experience:

> No one knows, who did not watch the thing from the beginning, how much opposition, how much ill-will, how much unfeeling want of thought, these women nurses endured.

Hardly a surgeon of whom I can think, received or treated them
with even common courtesy. Government had decided that
women should be employed, and the army surgeons—unable,
therefore, to close the hospitals against them—determined to
make their lives so unbearable that they should be forced in
self-defence to leave. It seemed a matter of cool calculation,
just how much ill-mannered opposition would be requisite to
break up the system.

Some of the bravest women I have ever known were among
this first company of army nurses. They saw at once the
position of affairs, the attitude assumed by the surgeons,
and the wall against which they were expected to break and
scatter; and they set themselves to undermine the whole thing.
(Dannett 1959, 88)

In the first days of Nurse von Olnhausen's service (and her experience was not unique), she wrote: "A nurse told me he [the sur-
geon] said he would make the house [the hospital] so hot for me
I would not stay long" (Munroe 1903, 33).

Sophronia Bucklin corroborated Nurse von Olnhausen's reports
concerning the great aversion of the surgeons for female nurses.

Many surgeons, at this date of the war, were determined, by
a systematic course of ill-treatment toward women nurses, to
drive them from the service. To this class the surgeons in Wolf-
street Hospital belonged, without any shadow of doubt. (124)

Even at the end of the war, the book *The Medical and Surgical
History of the War of the Rebellion* belittled the work of women nurses:

Female nurses were borne on the rolls of many of the hospitals. . . . According to the testimony of all medical officers who
have referred to this point their best service was rendered in
connection with extra diets, the linen room and laundry. Male
help was preferred in the wards, save in special cases of pros-
tration and suffering where particular care was needful in the
administration of dietetic or remedial agents. (958)

The Sanitary Commission also minimized women's contributions
in a bulletin issued March 15, 1864:

Skilled and judicious women, offering their services as nurses, and accepted through the free and hearty consent of the surgeons in charge, have rendered invaluable service to the sick ever since the hospitals were opened. But they have owed their usefulness to their strict obedience and conformity to army regulations, and only those docile enough and wise enough to respect the superior knowledge and authority of the Surgeons have been for any considerable time able to keep their places or to make themselves generally serviceable. Perhaps two hundred such women exist in the whole army; to whose noble devoted, and gentle hearts, skillful hands and administrative faculties are due a considerable part of the success which attended the operation of our military nursing. (*U.S. Sanitary Commission Bulletin*, 295–96)

In many cases the surgeons' reluctance to share their domain was not without reason. Imagine the chaos engendered by the arrival of one volunteer and her fiancé, who arrived in a wagon loaded with medical supplies and 400 loaves of "freshly baked bread" at the field hospital which had been hurriedly set up following the Battle of Chantilly. After distributing the bread to the hungry soldiers, according to Agatha Young in *The Women and the Crisis*, the young lady continued her mission of mercy by entering the hospital.

The floor was slippery with blood. She averted her eyes and bent over a soldier with a bandaged arm. The bandage was tight and he was in considerable pain and, never stopping to think that the tight bandage might have a purpose, Elida took it off. At first everything was all right. A shot had gone completely through the arm and a scab had formed, but Elida decided the scab should be washed off. She found some water and went to work. The scab loosened. Then she saw little spurts of bright red arterial blood coming out of the wound. In a second the whole artery opened and she was drenched by a pulsing jet of blood. (204)

The young woman in question thereafter found other avenues more suited to her talents for her volunteer work. (To her credit she was a most generous volunteer, organizing concerts for soldiers and founding a reading room in Washington.)

Writing from her hospital in Jeffersonville, Indiana, on October 18, 1864, Elvira Powers pointed out in her diary that clearly not all volunteers were cut out to be nurses.

> One lady came here a few days since, who staid only two days. She was "not used to any such fare, such cold rooms, and couldn't work for any such pay." There are others here who do not work for the "pay," but for something higher & better. (121)

Phoebe Pember told of a newly acquired "nurse matron" who arrived at her hospital with seven trunks. Dissatisfied with her living accommodations, the woman quickly appropriated space of her own. It soon became clear that she was also appropriating the whiskey toddies issued as stimulants for her patients, and she was finally carted off "very drunk."

It was uncommitted women, who had little to offer but good intentions, who created more problems than they solved. Nurses repeatedly disparaged well-intentioned volunteers who were enthusiastic though hopelessly inept. Harriet Douglas Whetten wrote of the crowds of Philadelphia women who were gathered to welcome the wounded soldiers

> and insist upon feeding our boys, pouring their stuff into the eyes and noses of such as were on stretchers, and insisting upon drenching a young hearty nurse. (The Diary, 218)

Katharine Wormeley's day was spoiled by "a visit from a Sunday picnic of Congressmen and ladies." After one of the gentlemen complained to their superior about conditions on their hospital ship, the nurses facilitated his hasty exit.

> This gentleman came into the ward with a rose held to his nose; and when told they were all typhoid-fever cases ("That one by you is the worst case I ever saw," Georgy said maliciously), he went abruptly away. (147)

There were also other troublesome though well-meaning groups. These were women looking for excitement and adventure who bounced into camp headquarters announcing that

"they did not wish much . . . simply a room, a bed, a looking glass, someone to get their meals and do little things for them," and they would nurse the "sick boys of our gallant Union Army." (Brinton 1914, 43)

Those who came for business, however, stayed to work through the sixteen hour days, catching what sleep they could perched atop baggage on the hospital boats or amongst boxes in the supply rooms. Still clad in their blood-stained skirts, they forgot to eat, anguishing over the insistent march of death. Most of the women were older, often widows with sons in the service. Many had been activists for blacks and women's rights. Although at times outspoken, most were indeed "proper." They indulged in neither alcohol nor dancing; their associations with the soldiers were motherly or sisterly. Their uniforms consisted of calico dresses, bonnets and shawls. Even in the privacy of their diaries, legs were "limbs," panties were "unmentionables," and close associates were "Dr." and "Miss."

Over the years Civil War nursing took on many aspects. There was full-time or part-time work, for salaried or volunteer nurses, at battlefields or local hospitals. Assignments ran the gamut from managing the diet kitchens to assisting the surgeons with amputations.

Some of the most courageous women found their true calling in attempting to help alleviate the suffering on the battlefields. No stretch of the imagination can possibly envision the horrors those nurses encountered. The nurses themselves were sickened at the sight of amputated arms and legs "thrown out of one of the windows [of an operating room] until they made a pile *five feet high just as they fell*" (Newcomb 1893, 43). At times they walked out on battlefields where "the dead and dying lay so thick that we might have walked a mile with every step on a dead body" (Newcomb 1893, 43). They crossed battlefields slippery with blood until "the edge of my dress was red, my feet were wet with it" (Beers 1888, 153). At Gettysburg "it took nearly five days for some three hundred surgeons to perform the amputations that occurred here" (Hancock 1956, 13). Sophronia Bucklin helped a wounded soldier who

> had been struck by a piece of shell, and the cavity was deep and wide enough to insert a pint bowl. This cavity was absolutely filled with worms; not the little slender maggots from which a woman's hand is wont to shrink in nervous terror, but great black-headed worms, which had grown on the living flesh, and surfeiting the banquet some of them crawled into his hair, and over his torn clothing. (270)

Cornelia Hancock's experiences at Gettysburg were to stand her in good stead when she accompanied Dr. Child, her brother-in-law, to help with the casualties from the Battle of the Wilderness. When she arrived in Fredericksburg, Virginia, in May 1864 in the company of Drs. Detmold and Vanderpool, she compared the scene to that of Gettysburg. Even the doctors were stunned by the slaughter.

> On arriving here the scenes beggared all description and these two men, eminent as they are in their profession, were paralyzed by what they saw. Rain had poured in through the bullet-riddled roofs of the churches until our wounded lay in pools of water made bloody by their seriously wounded condition. On these scenes Dr. Detmold and Dr. Vanderpool gazed in horror and seemed not to know where to take hold. My Gettysburg experience enabled me to take hold. The next morning these two surgeons came to me and said: "If we open another church under better conditions than these, will you accompany us?" and I said "Yes." After they got their nerve their splendid executive ability asserted itself and they had the pews knocked to pieces; under the backs and seats put a cleat and made little beds to raise the wounded from the floor. 'Tis true the beds have no springs, but it keeps them from lying in the water. Here day by day things are improving. An amputating table is improvised under a tree in the yard where these two good men work indefatiguably. (92)

The threat of her own death by enemy gunfire constantly hung over the battlefield nurse as she attended to the debilitating work of seeing her patients "on their way to heaven or *home*" (Hancock 1956, 24). Annie Wittenmyer, for example, narrowly escaped death from a bullet fired through a train window. On another occasion she was subjected to enemy fire while aboard a transport ship and once was almost killed when a shell crashed some forty feet behind the carriage in which she was riding. Stray bullets killed men in the seeming safety of the hospital tents while their "guardian angels" were tending them.

Some of the most demanding work—and some of the least publicized—was undertaken by the nurses on the hospital transport ships that in the East plied the Atlantic coastline and in the West sailed the Mississippi and other midwestern rivers. These government steamers that were converted into hospital ships to transport the sick and wounded soldiers from Southern battlefields to well-equipped hospitals in more healthy northern climes literally proved to be "life preservers" for thousands of men who would otherwise have perished from heat and disease. These "floating hospitals" were staffed with surgeons and nurses and equipped with "kitchens" for the preparation and distribution of food.

Annie Wittenmyer related the moving story of two thousand half-dead, despondent soldiers in Helena, Arkansas, in August 1863, who had given up the will to live, but who suddenly came alive with her news that hospital transports (secured through the efforts of Mrs. Wittenmyer) would soon be coming to take them to cool, clean, efficient Northern hospitals. The men went wild with anticipation.

> My anxiety was intense. What if the boats should not come? I stepped out of the tent and looked up the river, and there in full view the little fleet of four boats were coming around the bend of the river.
> We both cried out in our joy, "The boats! the boats are coming!" but tears of thankfulness almost choked our voices. The excitement was intense. No one stood on the order of his going. The surgeons were willing all should go, and desired to go with them, and they did. Every man who could, rushed for the

boats. Some who were not able to walk managed some way to get from their cots and crawl out toward the boats.

Oh! it was pitiful to see the helpless ones, the wounded ones, who could not move, waiting with anxiety for their turn to be carried to the boats, and pleading, "Please, ladies, don't let me be left behind."

"No, no! Don't be alarmed, you shall go," was repeated over and over. At last all were crowded into the four steamers, and the boats steamed away with their precious freight up the Mississippi River. We stood at the landing as the boats moved away. The poor fellows out on the guards tried to give three cheers, but the effort was a failure. We waved our handkerchiefs, and they waved their hats, or their hands, as long as the boats were in sight. (113)

During their first weeks of service, however, many of the transport ships were ill-prepared with either beds or food for the hundreds of wounded brought from the battlefield with little or no advance notice. All too frequently the horribly wounded soldiers had been jolted in rough army ambulances over fifteen or twenty miles of corduroy roads and had been given nothing to eat for hours or days. Oftentimes the nurses were completely overwhelmed by the sudden arrival of trainloads of wounded men who were carelessly unloaded by insensitive stretcher-bearers on the hard, wooden decks with only their knapsacks as pillows.

Katharine Prescott Wormeley, of Newport, Rhode Island, who served with the Hospital Transport Service, described in letters to her mother and friends the chaos created by the appearance of thousands of suffering soldiers who needed to be accommodated and cared for.

> Conceive of the Medical Director sending down over four thousand five hundred wounded men without—yes, almost literally without—anything for them: without surgeons; no one authorized to take charge of them; nothing but empty boats to receive them. . . . You *can't conceive* what it is to stem the torrent of this disorder and utter want of organization. . . . To think or speak of the things we see would be fatal. No one must come here who cannot put away all feeling. (101–2)

The endless trainloads of wounded who had been dispatched from the battlefields were sights to repel even the most robust workers. According to a U.S. Sanitary Commission officer working with the hospital ships:

> They were packed as closely as they could be stowed in the common freight-cars, without beds, without straw, at most with a wisp of hay under their heads. Many of the lighter cases came on the roof of the cars. They arrived, dead and living together, in the same close box, many with awful wounds festering and swarming with maggots. Recollect it was midsummer in Virginia, clear and calm. The stench was such as to produce vomiting with some of our strong men, habituated to the duty of attending the sick. (Olmsted 1863, 106)

On some boats there were no provisions for feeding the men; on one boat there were not even mattresses. Katherine Wormeley was aghast.

> We went on board; and such a scene as we entered and lived in for two days I trust never to see again. Men in every condition of horror, shattered and shrieking, were being brought in on stretchers borne by "contrabands," who dumped them anywhere, banged the stretchers against pillars and posts, and walked over the men without compassion. . . . The men had mostly been without food for three days, but there was *nothing* on board either boat for them. . . . (103–4)

Everyone—patients, nurses, surgeons, ships' officers—suffered from the massive overcrowding. Katharine Wormeley continued:

> Imagine a great river or Sound steamer filled on every deck,— every berth and every square inch of room covered with wounded men; even the stairs and gangways and guards filled with those who are less badly wounded; and then imagine fifty well men, on every kind of errand, rushing to and fro over them, every touch bringing agony to the poor fellows, while stretcher after stretcher came along, hoping to find an empty place. . . . (105)

332

In time, food was provided and order restored on the transports; however, the horror remained with the nurses.

> I do not suffer under the sights; but oh! the sounds, the screams of men. It is when I think of it afterwards that it is so dreadful. (Wormeley 1889, 108)

Despite the frantic pace, the lack of sleep, the miserable conditions, Katharine Wormeley assured her friend in a May 16, 1862, letter that

> We all know in our hearts that it is thorough enjoyment to be here,—*it is life*, in short; and we wouldn't be anywhere else for anything in the world. . . . Hundreds of lives are being saved by it. I have seen with my own eyes in one week fifty men who must have died without it, and many more who probably would have done so. I speak of lives saved only; the amount of suffering saved is incalculable. (44)

While dangerous service at the battle scene occupied hundreds of brave women in both the North and the South, even greater numbers of women (particularly Southern women) restricted by young children, elderly parents, or finances worked in nearby hospitals or opened their homes and their hearts to sick and wounded soldiers, generously sharing their miniscule resources with their patients. (Some writers noted that almost every other home in Richmond was a "hospital" by the end of the war.)

Many of those unable to attend to nursing duties themselves contributed thousands of dollars and countless hours to founding and maintaining "Wayside Homes" or "Soldiers' Homes" (houses, buildings, or mere rooms established in scores of towns where convalescent soldiers or soldiers in transit could find food and accommodations). One particularly successful venture was the Soldiers' Home founded during the early days of the war by the Ladies' Hospital Association of Montgomery, Alabama. As a result of increased demands, the society soon decided to enlarge the project and to create the Ladies' Hospital of Montgomery, which became famous as one of the best hospitals in the Confederacy.

Juliet Opie Hopkins and her husband, of Mobile, Alabama, founded and funded several hospitals (in Richmond, at Culpeper Court House, and at Yorktown). Mrs. Hopkins volunteered money and time and was herself twice injured in helping wounded soldiers from the battlefield. Although financial help soon came from the Alabama government and from generous citizens, Mrs. Hopkins apparently contributed most of her personal income to the hospitals. Immense praise for her work as a benefactor and as an administrator came from people throughout the South, including Robert E. Lee and General Joseph E. Johnston. The latter called her "The Angel of the South" and General Lee commended her as having "done more for the South than all the women of the Confederacy" (Sterkx 1970, 119–22). Mrs. Ella King Newsom, known as "The Florence Nightingale of the South," devoted most of her wealth to the Southern cause and seriously impaired her health during her wartime nursing career (Richard 1914).

During the early years of the war, nurses had their work cut out for them in attempting to dispel the soldiers' terrifying image of the hospital as a "death house," a place far more ominous than the battlefield itself. Most soldiers viewed hospitals as places where "butchers" presided over overcrowded wards and underfed patients. A brave soldier's death on the battlefield could be considered heroic. Dying a slow agonizing death in a hospital, however, was the embodiment of one's worst nightmares. From his encampment at Murfreesboro, William Hale wrote home on June 8, 1862:

> I have to leave you now for the very sad duty of going to see a very dear friend die. . . . I could see him die on a battlefield with a stout heart—but this Hospital death, O, its awful—The lack of nursing care & nourishment carries these poor boys off by scores.

In a postscript he added: "You can know little of the horror of a hospital death."

Civil War field hospitals were spartan in the extreme, often hastily established in converted schools, hotels, churches, barns, private homes, boats, even in the halls of Congress. Often the beds were boards set atop church pews or laid on the ground; mattresses were sacks of straw or corn shucks; many operating tables were benches set up under the trees. Frequently sheets and pillows were non-existent.

Furniture, sparse even in the general hospitals, usually included some sort of bedside table on which the soldier's few possessions were kept in a box. Civil War patients frequently hid their "naughty" pictures underneath the lids of these "personal boxes." One nurse was so infuriated by the "depravity" of some of the men's pictures that she quickly confiscated the boxes, removed the pictures, and sanctimoniously replaced them with tracts (Young 1959, 225). Handkerchiefs were luxuries and the gift of a box of handkerchiefs to be distributed on the wards was a treat—freshened with cologne, these handkerchiefs helped mask the vile hospital odors. This was such a common practice for nurses as well that Louisa May Alcott, a hospital volunteer and later the author of *Little Women*, became known as "the nurse with the bottle" (Alcott 1960).

Ambulances were frequently horsecars whose wheels often failed to keep to the two parallel ruts called roads. These punishing rides aggravated already serious trauma. Following some battles, the wounded lay unattended on the ground overnight; at other times the slaughter was so great and the surgeons so few that the wounded waited from three to five days before being seen by a doctor.

Nurse Hannah Ropes credited exhaustion, extreme exposure to the elements, and primitive ambulance services with the high death rate among her patients at Union Hospital, Georgetown, D.C.

> Our house is one of constant death now. Every day some one drops off the corruption of a torn and wounded body. It is more from the worn condition of the soldier before the wound, and the torture of exposure on the field, added to which a forced removal in heavy wagons to the hospitals, than to the dangerous nature of the wounds. (68)

Even when a Civil War soldier survived the elements and his jar-ring ambulance ride, his chances for survival were still slim. Mrs. P. G. Robert, a volunteer Confederate nurse in a Richmond hospi-tal, pointed to the overcrowding and lack of medicine that greeted a patient upon his arrival at a hospital.

> Great was the suffering in the field, in the hospital it was greater. Our magnanimous foe having declared medicine and Bibles contraband of war, our supply of both articles was most limited, and medicine had to be reserved for extreme cases. The exigencies of the times were such that in the arrangements of the hospitals the laws of hygenics had to be entirely dis-regarded, and men with open wounds were placed in the room with typhoid fever patients, cases of measles and cases of malarial fever. Patients were indiscriminately brought in until the room was filled, and then they proceeded to fill up another one. (Missouri Division 1920, 86)

During those years there was scant knowledge of first aid and few pain killers. Although ether was generally accepted as safer, chloro-form was often used because of its quick action, effectiveness in small quantities, and nonflammability in "operating rooms" lit by candles. If there was no chloroform or ether, whiskey served.

In the absence of any anesthetic, including whiskey, speed was of the utmost importance. An experienced Civil War surgeon took 40 seconds to amputate a leg at the thigh.

Now and then surgeons employed whiskey as a disinfectant or a combination of whiskey and chloroform, which proved particu-larly successful with maggot-infected wounds. Paradoxically, the beneficial effects of maggots as scavengers were recognized. Quinine, considered the wonder drug of the Civil War, was essential in treating malaria. Stethoscopes and thermometers were beginning to appear but were used only by the more experimental.

Drugs and medical supplies were always in short supply. In emer-gencies, corn husks served as bandages for many frontline injuries. During the early part of the war, hundreds of ladies aid societies devoted themselves to "scraping lint" for the hospitals, a process that involved unraveling soft pieces of material and scraping them with a sharp knife. Widely used for packing wounds, the lint was probably more effective in spreading infection. Repeated use of soiled bandages also transmitted infection.

Fresh wounds were kept moist by positioning water above the patient's bed to drip onto the bandages. Suppurating wounds were treated by applying an ointment consisting of two parts fresh lard and one part white wax.

Fire, unclean water, and lack of sanitation proved to be formidable enemies in Civil War hospitals. The hazard of fire precipitated by candles and wood stoves was a constant threat to the hospitals as well as to whole encampments. The hospital water supply, usually seriously limited, was communally used for bathing, laundering, dishwashing, and as a watering hole for the horses and other livestock. In the interests of conserving the precious commodity, nurses used the same sponge dipped into communal basins for as many patients as possible. Later hygienists have claimed that the sponge "killed more men than the bullets of the enemy" (Young 1959, 223). Antiseptics, if used at all, were too often used after the fact. A scarcity of tableware in some hospitals also contributed to unsanitary conditions. T. N. Chapin wrote from his erysipelas ward in a Nashville hospital that the entire ward was forced to share three spoons, a situation more conducive to relapse than to recovery.

> The doctor came in the morning and pronounced my wound covered with erysipelas and I had to be removed to another room in which were 7 other cases. We are allowed a pretty good bunk and that is about all we have. We have one cup and that has to suffice for all eating and drinking and everything else. They will not even allow us a spoon. There are three spoons in the room belonging to the boys. (16 January 1863)

Poor plumbing systems, contaminated water, and general hospital filth greatly contributed to the spread of disease. George Worthington Adams noted that "the soldier was five times as likely to die of disease as was the civilian" (224). It was as if the warfare between North and South provided a backdrop for the natural biological warfare being waged: people against invading bacteria and viruses.

Complaints from both patients and nurses about hospital food, especially in the field hospitals, were caustically detailed in Civil War diaries and letters. Most nurses were well aware of the critical relationship between nourishing food and good health; however, indifferent kitchen help, inadequate facilities, and lack of money were responsible for monotonous, often inedible hospital food. Nurse Mary von Olnhausen described in her letters some of the problems in supplying wholesome, appetizing meals for her patients.

> I know what all the Sanitary committees in the North have done and how much they think the poor soldiers are comforted; but I can assure you that in the way of delicacies they get mighty little,—none in fact,—and, so far, not even good, nourishing food. As I told the Inspector General a few days since, both in quality and quantity it is intolerable. . . . The day before he came bean soup was sent up so salt[y] that no one could swallow a second spoonful; the beef tea was in the same state; and the beans were so hard that all would have had cholera morbus if they could have eaten them.
>
> Moreover, the cooks are so overbearing that it is like begging for life to get a thing for the really sick ones who cannot eat common diet. Yet the nurses are obliged to do all extra cooking and are not allowed the use of anything but tin cups or plates; and if we ask for spoon or knife or milk or eggs, you better hear the fuss! The kitchen is a perfect Babel at mealtimes, and, rather than encounter the noise, every day I buy eggs and milk, in fact almost every nice thing for the sick ones. I know I have a right to them here; but I've learned enough to know that all who make complaints to headquarters are not only unpopular there but are pitched into by all the house; so I just speak to nobody, get what I can, and buy the rest. Sometimes I can *make eyes* at the ice-box man and he'll give me a bit of chicken and mutton; but he isn't always to be melted any more than his ice, though he is the only one who really seems to work for the soldiers. (Munroe 1903, 38–39)

Sophronia Bucklin's experiences nursing and feeding the wounded near Petersburg in 1864 were even more distressing.

We had a full diet kitchen, but it was insufficient to furnish all the hospital, and at times some of the soldiers were in a *starving* condition, or reduced to wormy, mouldy "hard tack." It was resolved to remedy this defect by starting an extra diet kitchen, and in this corn-starch was boiled, often burned, then thrown into an old tub, and allowed to stand until it had a green mould over the surface. Tea was cooked in an iron kettle and poured into another tub where hot or cold water, whichever seemed most convenient, was turned in to reduce it. These, with an occasional soup of the poorest quality, and deficient in quantity, and with bits of dry bread, were often and again served to the sick and dying men, whose appetites had been sharpened by the drain upon their systems of wound discharges. It was dreadful to have to take such food to men whose anxious eyes were evidently watching for something which looked inviting. . . .

I grew sick of the mould, which rose like dust when boxes were opened, and of seeing fat worms drop out of broken biscuits which, even poor as they were, could not be obtained for some days. These things were calculated to make any one grow wretchedly nervous. (290–91)

These and similar experiences led to an important contribution of Civil War nurses—the setting up of diet kitchens in army hospitals. Annie Wittenmyer, the State Sanitary Agent "nurse" from Iowa, has been credited with designing a master plan to provide more wholesome, nutritious, palatable food for hospital patients. Dismayed over much of the food served in army hospitals, Mrs. Wittenmyer was convinced that there was little food for "a well man to eat, much less a sick or wounded man" (210). With the support of the Sanitary and Christian Commissions she set about remedying deficiencies. As a result, the cooking departments of vast numbers of U.S. government hospitals were revolutionized by her organization of special-diet kitchens. A system, a forerunner of the one used in hospitals today, was inaugurated whereby a "bill of fare" was provided each special-diet patient. By making selections within the limits provided by the surgeon, the patient was thus able to choose foods which appealed to his particular tastes.

Instead of the slops dished out of vessels that looked like swill-buckets, there came to the beds of the very sick and severely wounded, baked potatoes, baked apples, beef-tea, broiled beefsteak (when allowed), and especially to the wounded, toasts, jellies, good soup, and everything in the best home-like preparation. (Wittenmyer 1895, 212).

Mrs. Wittenmyer's plan, with its detailed instructions for cooks and nurses, was soon endorsed by both government and army officials and was instituted in hospitals throughout the North.

It soon became an admitted fact that thousands of lives were being saved by this supply of better food, which many of them needed more than they did medicine. (263)

All too often, however, the problem was not the quality of food but rather the quantity of food—in many hospital kitchens there was scant food for the patients. Writing to her sister in May 1864 from Fredericksburg, Virginia, eleven miles away from the fighting at Spotsylvania Court House, Cornelia Hancock despaired of the suffering and lack of food. Trains were busy carrying ammunition to the front and, therefore, food of any kind was at a premium.

We have an awful time here. Have to submit to seeing the men fed with hard tack and coffee. Supplies are very limited, scarcely any soft bread reached us. There is no end to the wounded, they arrive any time, night or day. Guerilas infest the country and endeavor to cut off our supplies going to the front. (95)

In their efforts to relieve shortages, hospital workers planted gardens, kept cows, and frequently foraged for food. "Mother" Bickerdyke was challenged by the shortage of eggs and milk in her unit. At that time in Memphis, milk was in short supply and what there was cost 50 cents a quart for inferior quality. Ever a problem-solver, she wrangled a thirty-days' leave to Chicago during which time she managed to drum up contributions of over one hundred cows and a thousand hens, and with that mooing and clucking procession returned to Memphis (Livermore 1889, 512).

Julia Wheelock (Freeman) spent part of her off-duty time baking pies for the patients. When she and her friends sought to distribute them, they were surrounded

> literally taken prisoners; some begging for themselves, others for a sick comrade who was unable to leave the quarters. At such time how earnestly I have wished that the miracle of "the loaves and fishes" might be repeated. (Freeman 1870, 44–45)

At times when the food situation became desperate, nurses such as Mrs. von Olnhausen, used their own money to purchase food for "their boys." Oftentimes, the nurses deprived themselves of food in order to supplement their patients' inadequate or misappropriated hospital sustenance. Nurse Bucklin explained:

> I could do nothing but take the food frequently, which I needed myself to keep up strength and courage, and give it to them [the patients], which was also a forbidden thing, but we did it often and again, and for a whole day I have gone with wretched hunger gnawing at my healthy stomach—glad to do so, if not detected—that some poor fellow's hunger might be satisfied. (93)

Since there were no real nursing schools, there were, of course, few textbooks written on the subject of nursing. Some nurses, however, must have been familiar with a small book, a *Manual of Directions for Nurses in the Army Hospitals*,* apparently written by a committee of Hospital Physicians of the City of New York. In it are directions for making the famous beef tea, mentioned repeatedly in almost every nurse's diary. In addition, there are instructions for giving baths, making poultices, and applying leeches. The recipe for beef tea:

---

*This booklet was found among the papers of the former Georgeanna Woolsey (Mrs. Francis Bacon) and may have served as the textbook used in a short course offered some women in preparation for their nursing assignments.

> To a pound of lean, fresh meat, chopped fine, add a pint of cold water; put it on a slow fire, heating it gradually to the boiling point; boil for ten minutes, then strain with firm pressure.

The tiny booklet indicated that

> Poultices may be made of bread and water, bread and milk, flaxseed meal, ground slippery elm, half flaxseed and half bread or slippery elm, etc. . . .

To apply leeches:

> The part to which leeches are to be applied should be carefully cleansed with soap and water, and dried. The leeches will be made more active by putting them in fresh water just before applying them. They may be applied by means of a wine-glass or pill-box, or by placing them in a clean napkin to be laid over the part. Should they refuse to bite, the skin may be moistened with a little milk, or pricked so as to draw blood.

The spartan living conditions of Civil War nurses themselves left much to be desired. Although some civilians fantasized that the nurses were living in luxurious quarters and dining on delicacies contributed by women on the homefront for the soldiers, Elvira Powers, who served in Indiana and Tennessee hospitals, dispelled the rumors with the following description of their hospital fare.

> Wonder how many people at the North think we are living on champagne and canned fruits at Uncle Sam's expense. Wish such could see our table. Please imagine, dear friends, your humble servant as sitting down to a long table with some eighteen others—not tables but ladies—and viewing three plates of bread, three bowls of gravy, ditto of apple-sauce arranged at equal distances, and that each has the exquisite pleasure of chewing for a reasonable length of time a piece of tough meat which is strongly suspected of having once been the person of a mule, and of drinking a mug of coffee minus the milk— and oh! worse than all the rest, the table is minus the butter. These two last are regretted the most. I wish somebody would

make a raid and capture a dairy—milk-maid and all! Won't some good Northern body be so magnanimous as to send me a little pat of butter and a cup of milk? (157)

Nurses' quarters during the Civil War were often tents which became ovens in the summer and rain spouts themselves when wet if bumped accidentally by a sleeper's extended arm or a repositioned table or chair. Katharine Wormeley pictured her dining accommodations:

> our dinner-table being the top of an old stove, with slices of bread for plates, fingers for knives and forks, and carpet-bags for chairs,—all this because everything available is being used for our poor fellows. (27)

As a nurse at Gettysburg, Sophronia Bucklin related that their clothes were often so damp it was almost impossible to pull them on.

> As time passed, and the heavy rains fell, sending muddy rivulets through our tents, we were often obliged in the morning to use our parasol handles to fish up our shoes from the water before we could dress ourselves. (144–45)

Candlelight, with its silhouette potential, provided tremendous opportunities for peeping Toms, and a tent's lack of security provided optimum conditions for thievery. Fortunately, most nurses were so exhausted when they finally struggled into bed that the inability of the thin canvas walls to dim the camp noises and the painful outcries of the wounded was rarely a serious problem. Creepy, crawly creatures were thwarted by placing the legs of the nurses' beds in cans of water.

Despite all their efforts to keep their quarters, their patients, and themselves clean, Hannah Ropes, a nurse at Union Hospital in Georgetown, D.C., wrote urging her daughter not to join her at the hospital, explaining that it was no place for young girls.

> You have no idea of a hospital, nor has anyone who simply calls in to see me. We get *lousy*! and dirty. We run the gauntlet of disease from the disgusting *itch* to smallpox! My needle

343

woman found nine body lice inside her flannel waistcoat after
mending the clothes that had been washed! And I caught two
inside the binding of my drawers!

I don't know any price that would induce me to have you
here! (115–16)

Eventually resigning herself to the presence of cockroaches, bed-
bugs, and untold inconveniences, Mary von Olnhausen concluded
that "When one goes nursing all things must be expected" (Munroe
1903, 115).

Hannah Ropes, in spite of the deplorable conditions, was deeply
committed to nursing as were thousands of other women during
that fratricidal war. It was at Union Hospital in the winter months
of 1862–63 that both Hannah Ropes and Louisa May Alcott contracted typhoid pneumonia, an illness that terminated Miss Alcott's
nursing career and proved fatal for Mrs. Ropes.

From her hospital at Morehead City, North Carolina, Mary von
Olnhausen wrote to her family:

This is the first time I have sat down to-day, and with no sleep
last night I feel drowsy . . . but am really glad to be where I
can make comfort to so many. . . . I am a little weaker than
usual from being over-tired. (Munroe 1903, 154–55)

This little "tiredness" soon degenerated into a severe case of yellow
fever, the same disease that had claimed the life of her much-admired
doctor several weeks earlier.

These nurses were just three of dozens of other nurses so weakened
by the debilitating routine of hospital life that they succumbed to
the illnesses of their patients and sickened and oftentimes died. Yet,
thanks to the dedication of these stalwart women, some of the grime
and filth that naturally accompanied the hospitalization of thousands of sick and wounded men crammed into emergency quarters
was lessened.

Added to the frustrations of nurses in the army hospitals were
problems stemming from the appointment of large numbers of obviously unqualified physicians and from the hastily performed

physical examinations often administered to new recruits. Although the primary focus of this chapter centers on women as nurses, the reader should remember that there were also some extremely vague regulations pertaining to the commissioning of physicians in those days. Some men were appointed as "surgeons" who had never seen an amputating knife, who did not hold medical degrees, or who qualified by having served as a hospital steward and by having completed one year of study in a doctor's office. These unqualified physicians, according to George Worthington Adams, were in part responsible for the farcical or nonexistent physical exams often given soldiers prior to their induction into the army. Hundreds of men were so casually examined that the oversights (cases of epilepsy, hernia, and syphilis, for example) were a future source of trouble for physicians, nurses, and the men themselves. Soldiers who never should have been inducted were later occupying hospital beds badly needed for severely wounded soldiers. Sometimes whole regiments were paraded by the examining surgeon en masse; sometimes whole regiments were never even examined (Adams 1952, 9–13). One new recruit wrote home:

> There was considerable fun to-day when old Jimmy Burwell was examined. Though the old cuss hasn't a tooth in his head he passed muster by simply keeping his mouth shut, and felt so good over it that he put on one of his funny streaks, and has kept the boys laughing ever since.

He later continued:

> One fellow passed yesterday with only one eye by drawing his hat down so the Surgeon could not see the *minus* eye. (Kellogg)

The early opposition of surgeons to having women intrude on their formerly male profession often made them overbearing and ill-disposed toward their assistants. Most nurses reported at least one confrontation with an ill-tempered, arrogant physician who resented sharing his territory. Some nurses were admonished for keeping the wards too clean; others for working too hard. Surgeons often expected the nurses to meekly obey orders and keep their ideas and suggestions about more humane, more effective treatment to themselves; however, many of these women had minds of their own and were unwilling to tolerate incompetence or carelessness. Elvira Powers clashed with surgeons over her suggestions for patients' comforts and with the chaplain whom she chided for not ministering to a dying soldier. Having prided herself on the enormous amount of work she had devoted to cleaning the wards from the grime and disarray in which she found them, Mary von Olnhausen was unprepared for the dressing-down she received from Dr. S., who thundered at her:

> "Madam, I intend to remove you; I intend Mrs. R. to have this ward; this is the most important one in the house and I consider her the most splendid nurse in the country; and, by _____, those are the kind of women I intend to fill this house with."

Mrs. von Olnhausen must have chuckled to herself, for as she was leaving for her reassigned duties on another ward

> we heard a fearful noise in the entry, and along was dragged my lady [her replacement], by two officers, dead drunk and swearing like a trooper. So that's the way she took possession of her new ward! I think my exit was better than her entrance. (Munroe 1903, 44–45).

Soon thereafter, Dr. S. apologized and was most enthusiastic in his praise of Mrs. von Olnhausen:

> " . . . you have done and are doing more to elevate the tone of this hospital than any one in it . . . and more than that, every doctor and every man in the house likes you." (Munroe 1903, 62)

A good many nurses were chastised for their refusal to give up on a seriously ill patient. Fannie Beers was attempting to improve the circulation of a patient on the point of expiring when a doctor interrupted her.

> "What the devil is all this fuss about? What are you going to do with that mustard-plaster? Better apply it to that pine table; it would do as much good. . . . Don't bother that fellow any more; let him die in peace."

At that, Mrs. Beers exploded.

> "Sir," said I, "if you have given the patient up, I *have not* and *will not*. No true physician would show such brutality."

The enraged physician left, threatening to report Mrs. Beers; however, her ministrations proved successful and the patient soon recovered. The day after the confrontation it was the surgeon who was reprimanded, not Mrs. Beers (97).

While attempting to nurse an apparently dying patient, Mary Newcomb was admonished by a wardmaster for continuing to burn a light after the nine o'clock curfew. Knowing the importance of her work in keeping the poor soldier alive, Mrs. Newcomb retorted that she was "no hired nurse" and that she would break the rules "when humanity demands it." She concluded the conversation with "you mind your business, and I will attend to mine" (34).

Over-imbibing "contract" doctors (physicians who held no commission but worked under three- or six-month contracts, often for from $30 to $100 a month) and drunken stewards presented innumerable obstacles to nurses. Perhaps the most frequent area of contention, however, revolved around the pilfering of army rations on the part of the unscrupulous stewards, and their wholesale appropriation of boxes of "delicacies" sent by concerned families or generous citizens solely for the patients' enjoyment. Nurse Newcomb helped entrap two doctors who were secretly selling hospital supplies to civilians. Her investigation led to the dismissal of the doctors and the reduction in rank of two other conspirators (61–62).

Hannah Ropes, matron-nurse at Union Hospital in 1862, refused to condone the chief surgeon's arrogant manner with and general disregard for his patients. She was appalled by the steward's efforts to feather his own nest by starving the patients, stealing their clothes, and selling their rations. Although her first efforts to secure the removal of these officials went unheeded by Surgeon General William A. Hammond, Mrs. Ropes, undaunted, proceeded directly to Secretary of War Stanton when the steward punished one of the patients by locking him in a "dark hole" partitioned off in the cellar. Her persistence was rewarded by Stanton's immediate investigation of the situation and his trouncing both the steward and chief surgeon off to prison.

Mary Ann Bickerdyke, nicknamed a "cyclone in calico," frequently took matters of cleanliness and organization into her own hands, overstepping her boundaries, and causing friction with the surgeons and male nurses. However, even Generals Grant and Sherman recognized her uncommon ability to cut through red tape. One day, after listening to a complaint from one of the men about her bossiness, General Sherman replied that there really was nothing he could do. "She ranks me. You must apply to President Lincoln" (Young 1959, 266).

In time, run-ins with their superiors became the exception rather than the rule. Good nurses could always arrange a transfer out of the jurisdiction of doctors for whom they had lost respect.

Despite slights and shabby treatment, some nurses revealed in their diaries and letters a certain reluctance to complain, make suggestions, or call attention to the neglect of patients. There was always the fear of reprisals from the stewards or staff and the potential for falling out of favor and being sent home in disgrace.

> We were not cowered from any fear of corporeal punishment being inflicted; no thought of bearing a load of wood on our backs, and being marched around by a guard for hours, deterred us from speaking of the wrongs we endured; but rather thoughts of usefulness cut off, of the disgrace of dismissal, of being shut out where our hands could not minister unto the

brave wounded—those considerations argued against all complaints, and kept sentinel over our tongues to their every ut-
terance. (Bucklin 1869, 125)

Both Northern and Southern women discovered that nursing
during the Civil War involved literally "binding up the nation's
wounds." Caring for "Johnny Reb," for example, became a necessary though not necessarily an eagerly anticipated task, particularly
in the more southerly Federal hospitals. At Gettysburg, one half
of the hospital's wounded were Confederate soldiers. Nurse von
Olnhausen, writing from Morehead City, North Carolina, in January
1865, frankly admitted her prejudices.

> At first I had some Rebels in my ward; but I made the doctor
> take them out and fill the ward up with Union. The Rebels
> made me so mad, and are so presuming, too. It was always
> "Madam, will you look at my wound?" Now I didn't want to
> see their wounds, unless they were going to die from them. . . .
> I can't be good, and it makes me furious to see them treated
> just as well as our men. The only way I could spite them was
> to give them one less blanket than ours had. (Munroe 1903,
> 167)

Amy Bradley, concerned about the hospital staff's neglect of a
Rebel prisoner, devoted special attention to the poor man only to
be taken aside by the head surgeon and informed that she was
drawing heavy criticism for her efforts in his behalf. Amy retorted
caustically:

> "Doctor . . . I profess to be a Christian, and my bible teaches
> me if my enemy hungers to feed him—if he is thirsty to give
> him drink. . . . " (June 1862)

As a hospital volunteer, Kate Robson, loyal Southerner that she
was, found it difficult to nurse wounded Yankees. On one occasion she told a patient whose eye had been shot that she "hoped
he would get well and go back home, but if he ever fought against
the South any more, I hope he would get his other eye shot out."

Grace Elmore, of Columbia, South Carolina, also a volunteer, was angered to find that she had mistakenly passed out homemade delicacies to one of the horrid Yankees.

> I have an overpowering feeling of disgust when I pass the beds occupied in the hospital by one of their number and see them lying side by side with our own sick men. My satisfaction in visiting at the hospital has more than once been destroyed by my going by mistake to a Yankee and giving him a delicacy prepared by my own hands, which was so needed and would have been enjoyed by the poor true Confederate who cast long eyes from the next bed. (26)

Occasionally, a volunteer absolutely refused to aid the "murderers" and was dismissed.

Caring for sick and wounded soldiers from the enemy ranks was often galling. Caring for very young patients, many of whom were underage and had somehow enlisted on the pretense of being older, was heartbreaking. Judith McGuire wrote of the death of a fifteen year old.

> Spent yesterday in the hospital by the bedside of Nathan Newton, our little Alabamian. I closed his eyes last night at ten o'clock, after an illness of six weeks. His body, at his own request, will be sent to his mother. Poor little boy. He was but fifteen, and should never have left his home. It was sad to pack his knapsack, with his little gray suit, and colored shirts, so neatly stitched by his poor mother, of whom he so often spoke, calling to us in delirium, "Mother, mother," or "Mother, come here."
>
> He so often called me mother that I said to him one day, when his mind was clear, "Nathan, do I look like your mother?"
>
> "No, ma'am, not a bit; *nobody is like my mother.*" (104–5)

If over the years the outside world had any doubts about the contributions of female nurses in the army hospitals, at least one group was thoroughly convinced of their importance—their patients. Testimonials to the work of the "angels" came in whispered gratitude from feverish, horribly wounded patients and in touching letters from appreciative parents and army veterans. Thousands of former patients well knew they owed their survival to their devoted, caring nurses. Cornelia Hancock's letter from a soldier stationed at Camp Bradford, Baltimore, Maryland, was just one of the constant stream of letters that flooded in to nurses and hospitals from grateful soldiers.

> TO OUR SOLDIERS' FRIEND, MISS HANCOCK
> You will please excuse a Soldier for writing a few lines to you to express our thankfulness for your kindness to our poor wounded comrades after the late battle. You little know the pleasure a Soldier feels in seeing a woman at camp. I only wish that we were able to express our gratitude in a different manner, but "Uncle Sam" happens to be in debt to us and until he "comes down" with his greenbacks we are not able to do any more. You will never be forgotten by us for we often think of your kind acts and remember them with pleasure. Please excuse a Soldier for taking the liberty to write to you, for although we are Soldiers we know how to appreciate a kind act.
>
> Your sincere friend,
> "A SOLDIER" (17)

One soldier wrote his family of the esteem held for Mrs. Brainard and the company's attempts to show their appreciation:

> Mrs. Brainard's services are very highly thought of among the boys and she has the full charge of the hospital affairs, the boys of our company made up a purse of forty dollars for her in the appreciation of her services a short time since and she has paid out 20 dollars of her own money for the sick before that and the boys look up to her as a child does to its mother and she is a mother to us all. (R. Noble December 1861)

Anna Etheridge, who ministered to the troops on the move (two revolvers tucked beneath her belt and her saddle bags filled with bandages and medical supplies), earned a special place in the hearts of the soldiers. D. G. Crotty of the Third Michigan Volunteer Infantry believed praise not enough for "Gentle Annie."

351

I must mention in these pages Anna Etheridge, the heroine and daughter of our regiment. The world never produced but very few such women, for she is along with us through storm and sunshine, in the heat of the battle caring for the wounded, and in the camp looking after the poor sick soldier, and to have a smile and a cheering word for every one who comes in her way. Every soldier is alike to her. She is with us to administer to all our little wants, which are not few. To praise her would not be enough, but suffice to say, that as long as one of the old Third shall live, she will always be held in the greatest esteem, and remembered with kindly feelings for her goodness and virtues. (58)

Women who nursed the sick and wounded in their homes were showered with accolades as well. Absalom Roby Dyson, from Franklin County, Missouri, wrote to his wife twenty-three days after suffering a chest wound at the battlefront.

I am at a private house in this place and could not be better treated were I at home. It appears that among all my misfortunes I have the best of luck in meeting with kind friends who are careful to see that I have every attention necessary to my comfort. May God bless the ladies of Raymond [Mississippi] and surrounding country. I could write a volume about the kind treatment which the wounded soldiers receive from the hands of ladies but suffice it to say that every place where our boys get wounded the ladies appear to feel that they are in duty bound to see to their wants and many a poor fellow that is now living would have been dead, had it not been for the kindness of those fair creatures. (Dyson-Bell 8 June 1863)

Most nurses, however, needed neither adulation nor testimonials. Their rewards, they told their diaries and their families, came from cheating death and sending fully recovered patients back to their regiments or home to their appreciative families. That they could help relieve the suffering of even a few soldiers seemed recompense enough. Mrs. von Olnhausen believed she had a special calling as a nurse.

I'm in for the war until discharged; I can't for a moment regret it; I could never be contented now at home remembering what I can do here and how many need me. I know that all are not fitted for this life, but I feel as if it were my special calling and I shall not leave it, if God gives me strength, while I know there is a Union soldier to nurse. You can have no idea how one's patriotism grows while one sees those poor fellows lying so piteously. (Munroe 1903, 79)

According to Kate Cumming, there was no greater happiness in life than the pleasures derived from nursing.

I can truly say, that there is no position in the world that a woman can occupy, no matter how high or exalted it may be, for which I would exchange the one I have. And no happiness which any thing earthly could give, could compare with the pleasure I have experienced in receiving the blessings of the suffering and dying. (178–79)

Despite the early skepticism of the surgeons and the general public about the propriety as well as the ability of women to serve as nurses during the Civil War, some three thousand women showed the world they had the stamina, the commitment, the organizational abilities, and the talent to become a vital force in the Nation. Civil War nurses demonstrated their talents as dietitians and cooks; as laundresses boiling soldiers' clothing "until there was nothing left 'alive' in them" (Newcomb 1893, 55); as personal secretaries (writing letters home for their patients); as talking books (reading stories and articles for those unable to do so for themselves); as psychiatrists (helping "their boys" cope with the loss of a leg or an arm—or both); as chaplains listening to confessions and dying words; as mental health counselors rallying their patients to full productive lives; as entertainers, providing musical therapy for their patients; as innkeepers (sharing their rooms and food with mothers who came to spend the final days with their dying sons). Despite Dorthea Dix, these nurses also brought a soothing feminine presence. As one dying patient murmured: "Thank God—I can die easier now since I have seen a woman's face once more" (Powers 1866, 20).

Not only did Civil War women help establish nursing as "proper" work for "refined" young ladies, but also they provided impetus for the development of modern health care. In addition, they made significant contributions to the field of dietetics, ramifications of which were felt in hospitals throughout the country.

CHAPTER X

Peace At Last

We are scattered, demoralized, stunned—ruined. . . .

　　　　　　　　　—*Mary Chesnut 15 May 1865*

Mary Chesnut, a talented writer, famous as perhaps the most astute, prolific woman diarist of the war, in her May 15, 1865, diary entry, gloomily depicted the South's utter despair following Lee's surrender. In the same entry she wrote:

> I said I wished now, as Mother prayed two years ago, that we might all be twenty feet under ground before we were subjugated. (Chesnut 1984, 243)

In retrospect, the real surprise is not that Lee surrendered the Army of Northern Virginia to Grant on April 9, 1865; the wonder is that the South held out for as long as it did. In the weeks preceding the collapse of Richmond and Lee's surrender at Appomattox, thousands of Southern soldiers read the handwriting on the wall. Learning of the destitute conditions of their families at home and seeing their cause as "gone up," they deserted in record numbers. Army desertions in the South reached "epidemic" proportions in the last months of the war, an estimated 8 percent of the forces having left within a month. Cornelia McDonald admitted she despised the stragglers "for giving up while Lee was still there" and yet at the same time she pitied many of them.

355

March came in gloomy and melancholy, and brought with it a dreadful certainty of disaster and defeat. One thing that almost quenched the last hope in me, was seeing the men coming home; every day they passed, in squads, in couples, or singly, all leaving the army. What must have been the anguish of Lee's great heart when he saw himself being deserted by his men when pressed so sorely by the enemy. Many stopped at my house asking for food. I gave them a share of such as I had, though I felt a scorn for giving up when defeat was near, instead of remaining to the end. It is hard to call them deserters, but such they were, and they knew it, for each one would tell of how hard Lee was beset, and how impossible it was for him to hold out any longer, as if to excuse his own delinquency.

After all though, when I thought of it afterwards, I could not wonder that they did desert. The conscription had forced many unwilling ones to go to the army, leaving unprotected wives and children in lonely mountain huts to abide their fate whatever it might be, freezing or starvation. Though the conscription was made necessary by the exigency of the times, it was nevertheless a dreadful tyranny; and though I have never said so, I have often thought that no greater despotism could be than that government was in the last months of its existence. To those whose education and habits of life made them enthusiastic, or whose pride acted as an incentive for them to endure and suffer, as was the case with the higher classes, it wore no such aspect, but to those who had but their poor homes and little pieces of ground by which they managed to provide very little more than bread for their families, who knew that they would be as well off under one government as another, it was oppression to be forced into the army, and not ever to be free from the apprehension that their families were suffering.

One man told me that he had remained in the trenches till a conscript who had lately arrived from his neighborhood told him that his family was starving. . . . (248–49)

By the spring of 1865 immense losses of men and territory, a crumbling economy, and scarcities of most of the basic necessities of life had brought the Confederacy to the breaking point. The final blow came with the Union occupation of Richmond, the capital of the Confederacy. Sunday, April 2, 1865, dawned bright and beautiful in Richmond. It was a day, according to Mary Burrows Fontaine, when " . . . delicate silks that look too fine at other times, seem just to suit; when invalids and convalescents venture out in the sunshine . . . " (30 April 1865).

Before evening, however, tranquility had given way to chaos. News of the impending takeover, which had been quietly whispered to President Davis as he sat in his regular pew in St. Paul's Episcopal Church, sent shock waves through the city. Within a matter of hours the scene was absolute turmoil as clerks frantically sought to burn incriminating government documents; agitated cabinet members hurriedly grabbed up vital papers and a change of clothing for a speedy exodus; bankers and treasury employees desperately struggled to move their bullion out of the city. The commissary stores were opened and ravaged by hungry women and children; streets were choked with horses, wagons, and carts carrying terrified citizens to safer territories.

For hundreds there was no choice but to remain and resignedly await their fate. Anxiety intensified during the night as explosions, "the shouts of the soldiers and mob as they ransacked stores," the noise of the wagons and the ominous crackling of fires rendered sleep unthinkable. According to Mary Burrows Fontaine:

> Just before dawn explosions of gun boats and magazines shook the city, and glass was shattered, and new houses crumbled beneath the shocks. Involuntarily I closed the shutters, and then everything had become still as death, while immense fires stretched their arms on high all around me. I shuddered at the dreadful silence. Richmond burning and no alarm. It was terrible! I cannot describe my feelings as I stood at a window overlooking the city in that dim dawn. I watched those silent, awful fires, I felt that there was no effort to stop them, but all like myself were watching them, paralyzed and breathless. After a while the sun rose as you may have seen it, a great red ball veiled in a mist. Again the streets were alive with hurrying men and women, and the cry of "Yankees" reached me. I did not move, I could not, but watched the blue horseman ride to the City Hall, enter with his sword knocking the ground at every step, and threw the great doors open, and take possession of our beautiful city; watched two blue figures on the

Capitol, white men, I saw them unfurl a tiny flag, and then I sank on my knees, and the bitter, bitter tears came in a torrent. (30 April 1865)

Thirteen year old Emmie Sublett, in a letter to a friend, also described the raising of the flag and the bitterness it engendered among the citizenry.

> The Yanks came in at fifteen minutes before eight A.M. and first of all placed the *horrible stars and stripes* (which seemed to me to be so many bloody gashes) over our beloved capitol. O, the *horrible wretches!* I can't think of a name dreadful enough to call them. It makes us fifty times more southern in our feelings to have them here; though they have behaved very well indeed, no private property has been touched, and no insults have been offered to any of the citizens. They say they can't get anything to report the Richmond girls for, to save their lives. They all behave with such perfect dignity and coolness, always go out thickly veiled and never notice the Yanks in the least. I've nearly broken my neck holding such a high head, never condescending to look at one when I meet him. (29 April 1865)

Everywhere pandemonium reigned. Mary Fontaine continued her description of the tumult.

> Then our Richmond servants were completely crazed, they danced and shouted, men hugged each other, and women kissed, and such a scene of confusion you have never seen. Imagine the streets crowded with these wild people, and troops by the thousands, some loaded with plunder from the burning stores, whole rolls of cloth, bags of corn, etc., chairs, one old woman was rolling a great sofa; dozens of bands trying to drown each other it seemed; gorgeously dressed officers galloping furiously about; men shouting and swearing as I never heard men do before; the fire creeping steadily nearer to us, until houses next to us caught, and we prepared to leave; and above all, inconceivably terrible, the 700,000 shells exploding at the laboratory. I say imagine, but you cannot; no one who was not here will ever fully appreciate the horrors of that day. I have heard persons say it was like their idea of judgment day; perhaps it may be. So many shells exploding for five hours

would be fearful at any time; the heavens were black as with a thunder cloud, great pieces of shells flying about, oh! it was too awful to remember, if it were possible to be erased, but that can not be. (7 May 1865)

In the weeks that followed, the presence of the Federal soldiers, despite the victors' courteous treatment of their conquered foe, was painful in the extreme. Phoebe Pember observed:

> There were few men in the city at this time; but the women of the South still fought their battle for them: fought it resentfully, calmly, but silently! Clad in their mourning garments, overcome but hardly subdued, they sat within their desolate homes, or if compelled to leave that shelter went on their errands to church or hospital with veiled faces and swift steps. By no sign or act did the possessors of their fair city know that they were even conscious of their presence. If they looked in their faces they saw them not: they might have supposed themselves a phantom army. There was no stepping aside with affectation to avoid the contact of dress, no feigned humility in giving the inside of the walk: they simply totally ignored their presence. (136)

Hope for a victorious conclusion to the war had died slowly for most Southerners. Even news of the collapse of Petersburg and Richmond failed to dampen the spirits of the South's most ardent patriots. Following the fall of Richmond, General Lee's wife had rallied the townspeople by cheerfully announcing, "The end is not yet . . . Richmond is not the Confederacy" (McGuire 1889, 356).

At first the heartbreaking news of Lee's surrender met with disbelief. Mary Jane Chadick, living in Federally-held Huntsville, Alabama, completely discredited the rumors being circulated.

> If there was any truth in the late news, Huntsville would be vocal with the shouts of joy! Who knows but after all the star of the Southern Confederacy is in the ascendency. We will say to you in confidence, dear journal, right here that we in the Yankee lines have become so thoroughly accustomed to these lying rumors that, when they actually tell the truth, we don't believe them. Keep this between the leaves and never divulge! (81)

Elizabeth Avery Meriwether observed a similar disbelief of the reports from Appomattox.

> . . . could the report be true? . . . Was not Lee still there? Were his soldiers not as brave, as heroic as ever? No, the report of a surrender at Appomattox was merely another vile Yankee invention!
>
> But in their hearts our people knew the report was true and tears filled the eyes of men even as they stood in groups on the streets and declared they knew Lee had not surrendered, that the great Virginian would never surrender. I suppose these scenes which I witnessed in Tuscaloosa were only such scenes as occurred all over the South in the latter half of April 1865. (247)

In remote areas it was several weeks before people learned of the surrender and even then the problems of communication were so great that wild rumors surrounded the news. Some Southerners were convinced that the Federals had surrendered to Lee. Other zealots shouted, "We are not whipped yet! We will fight in the Trans-Mississippi. . . . " Still other rumors circulated that France "had sent a fleet which had whipped the Yankees in the Mississippi." Some slave holders clung hopefully to recurrent reports of liberal peace terms which stipulated that slavery would not be abolished for fifty years. Two-and-one-half weeks after Appomattox, Lizzie Hardin, a Southern stalwart, continued to remain optimistic about the possibility of a favorable outcome to the war. Although still sanguine of victory, Lizzie had at least resigned herself to an end of slavery.

> I believe myself it will end in our gaining our independence, and giving up slavery. Nothing will ever convince me that slavery, as it exists in this country, is wrong, but if it is necessary for our independence, let the Negroes go. (28 April 1865)

Eventually reports of the surrender were confirmed and at first a feeling of numbness seemed to engulf the Southland. Mrs. Roger Pryor recalled:

Everyone who has suffered an overwhelming misfortune must be conscious of a strange deadening of feeling—more intolerable even than pain. It may be a merciful provision of nature. Insensibility at a crucial moment may be nature's anaesthesia. . . . I was so completely stunned by the thought that all the suffering, all the spilt blood, all the poverty, all the desolation of the South was *for naught*; that her very fidelity, heroism, and fortitude, qualities so noble in themselves, had wrought her undoing, that I seemed to become dead to everything around me. (Pryor 1904, 372–73)

Some Southerners, however, still resolutely refused to admit defeat. Even General Lee's surrender and return to Richmond failed to daunt Mrs. Lee, who was reported to have proclaimed: "General Lee is not the Confederacy . . . [there is] life in the old land yet" (McGuire 1889, 356). Sarah Wadley, a rabid Southerner, must have been cheered by a letter dated April 28, 1865, from her brother serving with the Third Louisiana Cavalry. (Actually, "Willie's" regiment did not formally surrender until May 26, 1865.)

It is rumored that Johnston has had an engagement with Sherman in which Sherman was whiped. . . . President Davis says that we only have to be true to our caus and we are sure to win. (W. Wadley)

Kate Stone, dazed yet still defiant, advocated continued Southern resistance. Hope for a regrouping of troops in the West remained strong.

We know not what to believe. All are fearfully depressed. Lee's defeat is a crushing blow hard to recover from. Maybe after a few days we can rally for another stand. Now, most seem to think it useless to struggle longer, now that we are subjugated. I say, "Never, never, though we perish in the track of their endeavor!" Words, idle words. What can poor weak women do?

I cannot bear to hear them talk of defeat. It seems a reproach to our gallant dead. If nothing else can force us to battle on for freedom, the thousands of grass-grown mounds heaped on mountainside and in every valley of our country should teach

361

us to emulate the heroes who lie beneath and make us clasp
closer to our hearts the determination to be free or die. (333–34)

Even as late as May 20, in Tyler, Texas, for example, the news
from the East was still spotty. Kate Stone theorized:

> We do not know whether armed resistance is over or whether
> we are to fight on to the bitter end. If the news of the way
> in which the people of the Trans-Mississippi Department are
> ground to the earth is true, it would be better for us to resist
> as long as there is a man left to load a gun. Gloom and despon-
> dency cloud every face. Mrs. Savage's are the only people that
> rejoice and are glad that "this cruel war is over." Better years
> of battle than a peace like this is the cry of all we see. (342)

Countless other Southern diarists, particularly the young zealots,
persistently championed their cause, determined that the struggle
should continue down to the last man. Their hatred of the North
had become an obsession and any thought of reconciliation was
anathema. Although fearful of heavenly retribution for her unwavering, un-Christian abhorrence of the Yankees, Kate Foster found
herself unable to smother her rebellious spirit.

> *Now* I can no more record hopes of our successful Indepen-
> dence, only hopes of personal happiness but ever present will be
> the losses we have felt during this cruel war. Both of my noble
> brothers sacrificed upon our country's altar as far as I can see for
> nothing. God grant that I may some day feel they were taken
> for *some* good. How can I ever love the Yankees as brothers
> when *they* made these deep and everlasting wounds in my heart.
> No, as each day rolls around it is my constant thought how
> much more do I hate our oppressors to-day. (18 July 1865)

Elizabeth Avery Meriwether summarized the bitterness of
Southern women following the war and reiterated her particular
loathing of General Sherman.

> The feeling of that [hate] is an ugly feeling, it mars and scars
> the human soul; but I fear in those dark days just after the
> close of the war hate was a feeling that came into many a

362

Southern woman's breast. The Southern men were too busy trying to retrieve their fallen fortunes, but the women—they had more time to brood over the wrongs that had been done them, they had not had the excitement of battle to sustain them, they suffered even more than their husbands and sons and brothers. For these reasons, or perhaps just because women are less forgiving than men, it took the women of the South a long time before they were able to feel kindly toward their conquerors. To this day I cannot truthfully say I love a Yankee, but my dear husband who fought four years in the Confederate army, seemed to feel no bitterness in his heart, not even in the years immediately following Lee's surrender. Were he living now, more than fifty years after Appomattox, he would probably be as kindly and as just in his estimate of a northern, as of a southern, soldier. I cannot feel that way—at any rate, I cannot feel kindly toward Gen. Sherman. He was a monster and I want the whole world to know it. (252)

Five months after the armistice, Sarah Wadley still questioned the possibility of the South's ever cementing relationships with the Federal government.

Is it indeed possible for us who have for four years battled against the United States and hated the very sound of the name, is it indeed possible I say for us to acknowledge it as our country, to wish for its prosperity, to join hands with its citizens? It is not for me; as long as I must own this land as my dwelling place I have no country, as long as this army is the country's army I have no patriotism. (26 September 1865)

While the Yankees were cheering the war's end and reunification, Sarah Morgan was fuming:

Never! Let a great earthquake swallow us up first! Let us leave our land and emigrate to any desert spot of the earth, rather than return to the Union, even as it Was! (Dawson 1960, 436)

So totally abhorrent was the idea of reconciliation that many of the staunchest Southern patriots, as Sarah Morgan noted, seriously considered leaving the South to make new homes in California or South America. Those with the wherewithal and ambition to begin

a new life did emigrate. Louisa McCord's mother, for example, en-
tertained dreams of moving to Hawaii.

> She wanted to go to the Hawaiwan Islands and so did we all,
> but [un?]fortunately there wasn't money enough. She wanted
> to get rid of everything, sell everything and just go *anywhere*,
> anywhere to get away from our surroundings. Indeed it was
> a hard time to know what to do. (Smythe, 77)

Like the McCords, Lizzie Hardin desperately wished to leave the
country but was also prevented from doing so by lack of funds.

> I wish I had the power to describe the state of this country.
> The Constitution so much waste paper, the civil law a dead
> letter, slavery in such a condition that neither masters nor
> Negroes know whether it exists or not, lawlessness of every
> shade, from the lawlessness of the government at Washington
> to that of the Negro who steals his master's chickens, and in
> the midst of it all, between the Southerners and Union people
> a hatred, bitter, unrelenting, and that promises to be eternal.
> I would love to go to a foreign land. . . . As I can't go, I suppose
> I might as well do like others and try to make the best of life
> here. But it does seem too hard. (279–80)

With the passage of time Southerners came to accept their defeat
on the battlefields; however, there was still a spirited reaction against
what many regarded as a meek, passive submission to the postwar
dictates of their conquerors. Catherine Devereux Edmondston, for
one, readily denounced those of her countrymen who deferred to
their Union oppressors without a struggle.

> What is the use of my writing this record? None! None! Yet
> tho it is a pain to me I continue it from force of habit. We
> are *crushed!* Subjugated! and I fear, oh, how I fear Conquered!
> And what is the saddest part our people do not feel it as they
> ought. They accept the situation tacitly—fold their hands and
> say, "Resistance is vain." Their once high spirits—their stern
> resolve seems dead. Can the very spirit of freedom die out?
> The oath of allegiance is shortly to be enforced upon us—men,

women and children. Everyone is discussing it, but I have not
heard one resistant voice. (Edmondston n.d., 105)

The passivity of some of her fellow Southerners also infuriated
Sarah Wadley.

> It is worse than all to see the change that is taking place,
> it may be right but it is hard to see men quietly, cheerfully
> falling into the new state of things, taking the oath, going into
> office, talking of the President and of the Government as if
> there had never been Our President Davis and our govern-
> ment. (26 September 1865)

Although stunned and intensely bitter over the defeat of the
Confederacy, Southern women in their diaries and letters had
repeatedly expressed their hopes for an end (with a Confederate
victory, of course) to "this cruel war." Following the Grant-Johnston
armistice of April 26, 1865, Laura McRaven DeFrance wrote to her
brother from her home in Ravenswood, Hinds County, Mississippi.
During the war the enemy had robbed the family of everything outside the house "except *one old Hen & three little chicks*" and had
burned her mother's "Gin Press, Cotton, Stables & cabins." Mrs.
DeFrance was happy to see the end of the war.

> After being robed of every thing Ma had to *walk* in to Clinton
> to draw *rashions* from the Yankees & by so doing we have never
> suffered for anything to eat. We have once more gathered a little
> stock around us & have some servants with us. They become
> dissatisfied sometimes & leave but then there are plenty of others
> ready to take their place. This has been a cruel and relentless
> War but it is over with now & I for one rejoice to think that
> it is so although we have been defeated. (20 August 1865)

Gertrude Thomas's touching diary entry of May 1, 1865, speaks
for itself. Her brother had come home from the war and she realized

> *the war was over* and my husband and brother saved; that they
> had not fallen a sacrifice to the Molock of war. I burst into

tears and wept for joy. Mr. Thomas [her husband] said "Why what are you crying for" and could not understand it, but any woman will.

Northerners, of course, greeted the news of the fall of Richmond jubilantly and boisterously. Maria Lydig Daly of New York City noted in her diary on April 5, 1865:

> On Saturday when the news came [the fall of Richmond] there was an impromptu meeting in Wall Street. All business-es adjourned, a few speeches, and then the multitude sang the Doxology and the 100th Psalm in Wall Street, the seat of the money-changers; it was a good augury.

She continued:

> When I got the extra containing the great news, the tears rushed to my eyes, my heart to my throat. I could not speak. A few days more, and God be praised, it would seem as though this great trouble will be past. . . . May God's blessing come with it and make us less a money-loving, selfish, and self-sufficient people, purified by this great trial. (Hammond 1962, 349)

On April 10, 1865, Mrs. Daly wrote:

> Last night at midnight we heard an extra called. The Judge rushed to the door. "Surrender of Lee's army, ten cents and no mistake," said the boy all in one breath. . . . It was Palm Sunday, and hosanna may we well cry! Glory be to God on high; the rebellion is ended! Phil, my brother, is uninjured, and peace soon to descend to bless the land again. (Hammond 1962, 351–52)

In Chicago, the reports of Lee's surrender also met with exultation. Mary Livermore recalled:

> The day for which all loyal souls had prayed and waited for four long years had come at last. The nation was delirious with

the intoxication of good news telegraphed from Washington,—
"Lee has surrendered to Grant!" Just as the Sunday evening
church services were ended, the bells of Chicago clanged out
the glad tidings, and the event they rejoiced in was instinc-
tively understood by heart. All were waiting for it; all knew
it could not be long delayed. The iron-throated cannon took
up the jubilant tidings, and thundered it from a hundred guns.
Bonfires blazed it joyfully in all the streets, rockets flashed it
everywhere on the night air, the huzzas and songs of the people
rolled out from the heart of the city to the suburbs, and the
ordinary quiet of the Sunday night was broken by universal
rejoicing.

The next day, the rejoicing was renewed with more *abandon*
than ever. . . . Courts adjourned, banks closed, the post-office
was summarily shut up, schools were dismissed, business was
suspended. The people poured into the streets, frenzied with
gladness, until there seemed to be no men and women in
Chicago,—only crazy, grown-up boys and girls. (468–69)

Cornelia Hancock, a nurse from New Jersey stationed at City
Point, Virginia, visited Richmond a few days after its collapse and
upon returning to her headquarters learned of the surrender. In calm,
Quaker fashion she wrote home:

Lee has now surrendered. We were wholly unconscious of
it until we returned to City Point, when the great rejoicing
at General Grants headquarters proclaimed the fact. The
salutes were fired here yesterday at noon. A bloodless surrender
keeps our hospital still empty and we have time to give special
attention to a few who are dying just when they want most
to live. After nightfall, I walk up and down my long, deserted
stockade, I see the great change from war to no war, and brace
myself for a new order of things.

President Lincoln visited our hospital a few days since. When
the medical directors wanted to call his attention to the
appointments of the hospital, he said: "Gentlemen, you know
better than I *how to conduct* these hospitals, but I came here
to take by the hand the men who have achieved our glorious
victories." After that the men who were able stood in line and
he shook hands with them—and the others, he went to their
bedsides and spoke to *them*. He assured us the war would be
over in six weeks. (179)

The elation in Washington over Lee's surrender, witnessed by the Frobel sisters from their nearby Virginia home, was in sharp contrast to their own utter dejection. Anne exclaimed in her diary:

> O mercy! That was another day not to be forgotten. I neither ate nor drank. I threw myself down on my face and cried—O it was an exceeding bitter cry—But it is useless. I cannot depict the agony of that day. The next day soldiers were sent round to every house in the towns, and all about the towns, and ordered the people to throw open their houses at night and illuminate, on penalty if they failed to do it of being arrested. Many did it through fear, not by any means as a token of rejoicing, others refused, and their houses were stoned, and their windows broken by the soldiery. After that day after day reports would come in of first this army and that surrendering— until I thought my heart would brake. (162)

The war's end failed to bring a much hoped for cessation to the constant stream of soldiers passing by or through the Frobels' property. Arrangements for the big Victory Parade in Washington in May saw whole regiments once again setting up camp in their fields and continuing to make life miserable for Anne and her sister. Anne complained:

> They tell us that Sherman, Sheriden, and the army of the Potomac, are to lie around *Wa* [Washington] from now until August before they can possibly be mustered out, and we are to have them all on us again. O mercy, mercy! I think of it with feelings of intense horror. (168)

Although they were urged by the Federal officers to go to see the Grand Review and were even offered a carriage and guards, Anne and her sister were adamant in their refusal. Asking a neighbor if he planned to attend the parade

> he answered very brusquely indeed. "No. What do you think I want to see all them devilish yankees for. I can see more than I want to see at home!" (173)

In less than a week after Lee's surrender, the North's jubilation suddenly gave way to deep sorrow with the assassination of President Lincoln by John Wilkes Booth at Ford's Theater. Although there have been hundreds of reports of the murder, there have been only a few eyewitness accounts found in women's diaries. One such report was the brief, poignant diary entry of Gertrude Dunn.

> I went to the theatre and there I seen the President shot. . . .
> I sat opposite the private Box which the President and his wife occupied. There was the greatest time cheering and shouting when he came in but there was no such a time when he went out. Everybody was excited when they heard the President was murdered. (14 April 1865)

Word of the President's death met with mixed reactions in the South. A good many Southerners danced in the streets and celebrated with parties and toasts. Lincoln's assassination was his just reward, claimed Emma LeConte, still infuriated over the reports from Appomattox.

> Hurrah! Old Abe Lincoln has been assassinated! It may be abstractly wrong to be so jubilant, but I just can't help it. After all the heaviness and gloom of yesterday this blow to our enemies comes like a gleam of light. We have suffered till we feel savage. There seems no reason to exult, for this will make no change in our position—will only infuriate them against us. Never mind, our hated enemy has met the just reward of his life. . . . Could there have been a fitter death for such a man? At the same hour nearby Seward's house was entered—he was badly wounded as also his son. Why could not the assassin have done his work more thoroughly? That *vile* Seward—he it is to whom we owe this war—it is a shame he should escape. (91–92)

Family and friends rejoiced together over the "splendid" news, and Emma continued:

> The man we hated has met his proper fate. I thought with exultation of the howl it had by that time sent through the

369

North, and how it would cast a damper on their rejoicings over the fall of our noble Lee. The next thought was how it would infuriate them against us—and that was pleasant too. . . . Andy Johnson will succeed him—the rail-splitter will be succeeded by the drunken ass. Such are the successors of Washington and Jefferson, such are to rule the South. . . . What exciting, what eventful times we are living in! (93)

When news of Lincoln's assassination finally arrived in Tyler, Texas, where Kate Stone and her family were refugeeing, Kate exulted over the deed in an April 28 diary entry.

> We hear that Lincoln is dead. . . . All honor to J. Wilkes Booth, who has rid the world of a tyrant and made himself famous for generations. Surratt [Lewis Powell] has also won the love and applause of all Southerners by his daring attack on Seward, whose life is trembling in the balance. How earnestly we hope our two avengers may escape to the South where they will meet with a warm welcome. It is a terrible tragedy, but what is war but one long tragedy? What torrents of blood Lincoln has caused to flow, and how Seward has aided him in his bloody work. I cannot be sorry for their fate. They deserve it. They have reaped their just reward. (333)

Anne Frobel certainly held no love for Lincoln and upon hearing of his interment in Springfield, confided to her diary on May 4, 1865:

> I do hope it is the last we are to hear of President Lincoln. The yanks have been dragging him about for exhibition for the last three or four weeks, in every state, town and village east, north and west. . . . They seem to know no bounds in the lavish expenditures of public money on that miserable old carcass thousands upon thousands have been spent on catifalque and in shewing him up in every way to the gaze of the adoring multitudes. . . . But I really am glad he has reached Springfield at last and hope I shall never hear of him again. (168)

Lincoln's death saw houses throughout the nation draped with black crape signifying mourning. Reluctant Southerners, especially in occupied territories, were usually ordered by the government to display the funereal black crape. On the night following Lincoln's assassination, Annie Harper's family in Natchez, Mississippi, was fired at and threatened with arrest for burning too many lights, the illumination being considered disrespectful to a nation in mourning.

> They advised us to close the doors and windows and would ask for no music lest it should be misunderstood. Crape was ordered tied to every door knob, and a general grimness pervaded the air for days. . . . (23–24)

Sarah Morgan, an ardent Southern patriot refugeeing with her brother in New Orleans, reported what she believed to be insincerity among many of the Southern mourners.

> To see a whole city [New Orleans] draped in mourning is certainly an imposing spectacle, and becomes almost grand when it is considered as an expression of universal affliction. So it is, in one sense. For the more violently "Secesh" the inmates, the more thankful they are for Lincoln's death, the more profusely the houses are decked with the emblems of woe. They all look to me like "not sorry for him, but dreadfully grieved to be forced to this demonstration." So all things have indeed assumed a funereal aspect. Men who have hated Lincoln with all their souls, under terror of confiscation and imprisonment which they *understand* is the alternative, tie black crape from every practicable knob and point to save their homes. (Dawson 1960, 437–38)

There were, of course, those Southerners who exhibited a somewhat more benign attitude toward Lincoln, fearing perhaps they would suffer a much worse fate under Andrew Johnson. Annie Harper, at least in retrospect, deplored the South's denigration of Lincoln.

> None but cowardly, treacherous nations ever resort to such means to rid themselves of an enemy. . . . Lincoln was a good man and the best friend of the Southern people, and they lost one who would have helped them out of trouble if they had let him do so. (24)

From Richmond, Emmie Sublett remarked about the leniency of the Federal occupation troops and in the same letter to her friend Emily Anderson registered her dismay over the assassination.

> The Yanks are very lenient to us at present, but they are drawing the ropes tighter every day. I believe there is some villainy at the bottom of it all. I am so sorry Lincoln was killed I don't know what in the world to do, because I believe the whole South will be punished for it. Johnson will be such an awful president; he is a perfect old tyrant. (29 April 1865)

The tragedy left many Northerners and blacks shocked and grief-stricken. The great President who had led them to a glorious victory, who had abolished the despicable slave system, and who had envisioned such a bright future devoted to "binding up the nation's wounds," now lay dead. In Iowa an elderly friend stopped at Marjorie Rogers's home near Des Moines to convey the terrible news that Lincoln had been shot and was dying. Neither Mrs. Rogers nor her friend could speak.

> I was dumb with fear and astonishment, we could not talk about it. This was all we knew—no particulars—nothing official but reliable from a friend in Washington. This was trouble indeed, no wonder everything looked like an eclipse of the sun, our light and hope was gone. Who but Lincoln could lead and direct the great war, the great armies concentrating for victory or defeat? Our old friend weeping like a child rose and left me alone. I wandered listlessly about, could not realize the awfulness of the situation. What would be the result if he should die? Who could kill that good man and at such a time as this? It almost seemed as if God had forsaken us and that our cause was lost. The sorrow and sadness that the death of our beloved Lincoln caused cannot be written; no pen can tell it, only those who lived in those dreadful days can appreciate the pain we suffered. The whole land was in mourning, emblems of which were seen everywhere loyal men were found. The copperheads were ashamed even to show themselves in public when the loyal North was all mourning for their beloved president. (41)

In New York City, Maria Daly noted in her diary that her husband, in Washington the night of the assassination, had been scheduled to confer with the President the following day. Not until Judge Daly appeared for the meeting the next morning did he learn the dreadful news. "The shock was very great," her husband wrote her, "all were paralyzed" (Hammond 1962, 354).

Being a Northerner or even a Unionist, it should be remembered, did not necessarily mean being a supporter of Lincoln, as excerpts from Mrs. Daly's April 19 diary entry clearly indicate. (Historians remind us that there were thousands of Lincoln-haters in the North; it was long after Lincoln's death that his reputation as one of America's greatest presidents was attained.)

> Booth is not yet caught, but it is said it will be impossible for him to escape. Several arrests of men in female attire have been made. It would seem that it is a plot in which many are inculpated. It will make a martyr of Abraham Lincoln, whose death will make all the shortcomings of his life and Presidential career forgotten in, as Shakespeare says, "the deep damnation of his taking off." People had been arrested in the streets only for saying, "Pity it had not been done before," and the Loyal Leaguers are in a furious state of patriotism. The houses are all draped in mourning, each house striving to outdo the other.
> Easter morning, instead of the Resurrection and Christ has Arisen, the clergymen began with Abraham Lincoln, mentioning that he was sacrificed on Good Friday, and it seemed to me that they gave Our Lord only the second place in his own house. (Hammond 1962, 354)

In May the Union army amassed its troops outside of Washington for a triumphant two-day parade down Pennsylvania Avenue. Wave after wave of blue-coated men, sabers polished, bayonets shining, marched in precise cadence, eyes front, down the avenue where thousands upon thousands of jubilant spectators jammed the streets. Women and children thrust floral wreaths over the heads of the horses, tossed bouquets of flowers at the masses of blue, waved flags, and held up banners. Rousing band music was dimmed amid the swells of frenzied cheering that burst forth as each new unit appeared. Proud Americans felt the tears well up and spill over, tensed throats at times too full for speech.

373

There was also a not-so-grand parade of soldiers—men too weak, too ill to join their comrades in the celebration. Tired, emaciated, and feverish they poured into Jane Stuart Woolsey's Fairfax Seminary Hospital in Alexandria, Virginia.

> . . . all day long we heard the shouts and the brass-music. Squads of sick men came in, hourly, from all the outlying regiments, some in ambulance trains, some wearily creeping up on foot;—measles, chronic diarrhoea, typho-malarial fever;—men dragged about with their regiments, some in the third week of fever, came in speechless or wandering and died just after getting on a clean bed. This was the "grand march home." (174)

And then, too, there was yet another "parade"—all across the South—one that continued not just for two days but for weeks and months as the dispirited, ragged, hungry men in gray slowly made their way back home—or to "Sherman's sentinels" and the black ashes of what had once been home—to their waiting families.

> Most of them came on foot, tired & worn out—heavy of heart & longing to see their homes & loved ones again. Ragged & foot-sore they came, begging a piece of bread or something to eat as they came, from those who were fortunate enough to have it. Some led a mule or horse, too poor to ride, but hoping when he got home he could feed him & use him to help make a crop & so they came, day after day, straggling home, many to find their homes destroyed & families gone— desolation & fire had done its work & all were sad. (Prescott, 48)

Cornelia Spencer described similar scenes and the fervent attempts made to cheer up the flagging spirits of "their boys."

> So we endeavored to play out the play with dignity and self-possession, watching the long train of foragers coming in every day by every high-road and byway leading from the country, laden with the substance of our friends and neighbors for many miles . . . wondering where it would all end, and that we should have lived to see such a day; reviewing the height from which we had fallen, and struggling, I say, to wear a look of proud

composure, when all our assumed stoicism and resignation was put to flight by the appearance, on a certain day, of a squad of unarmed men in gray, dusty and haggard, walking slowly along the road. A moment's look, a hasty inquiry, and *"Lee's men!"* burst from our lips, and tears from our eyes. There they were, the heroes of the army of Virginia, walking home, each with *his pass* in his pocket, and nothing else. To run after them, to call them in, to feel honored at shaking those rough hands, to spread the table for them, to cry over them, and say again and again, "God Bless you all; we are just as proud of you, and thank you just as much as if it had turned out differently"; this was a work which stirred our inmost souls, and has left a tender memory which will outlast life. Day after day we saw them, sometimes in twos and threes, sometimes in little companies, making the best of their way toward their distant homes, penniless and dependent on wayside charity for their food, plodding along, while the blue jackets pranced gayly past on the best blood of Southern stables. (188–89)

In thousands of homes overpowering grief for the loss of a brother—or brothers—a son—or sons—who would not be returning tended to shroud a soldier's homecoming. Particularly tragic were the deaths of soldiers who fell during the final days of the war. For Frances Jane Robertson, of Clarke County, Mississippi, the end of the war was tinged with heartache. On May 14, 1865, she welcomed one brother home; a second brother, Frank, was killed by sharpshooters two months earlier near Cross Keys on April 16, one week after Lee's surrender.

> . . . I cannot describe the feelings I had on meeting the *only* brother I have now. With what feelings & delight would we have met him & Frank. All our country is ruined, we are in poverty but if Frank had only been spared us, how differently we would feel.

Everyone placed the blame for the fall of the Confederacy on a different person or set of circumstances. Some attributed its collapse to Jefferson Davis, to the "croakers," to the depreciation of the currency, to the disruption of the railroads and the impossibility of transporting provisions to the troops, to the loss of the South's slave labor and the consequent problems of food production, to excessive taxation, to the draft of young boys and old men, to all of the above and to a myriad of other "hindsight" insights. Mary Chesnut told her diary:

> Such a hue and cry—whose fault? Everybody blamed by somebody else. Only the dead heroes left stiff and stark on the battlefield escape. (Chesnut 1981, 814)

Whatever the cause or causes of the war, the enormity of Southern sacrifices in lives, and homes, and money was staggering. Fields lay in ruins, schools, churches, courts were disbanded, Confederate currency had sickened and expired.

The long awaited return to normalcy proved elusive for untold numbers of women whose husbands struggled home broken and disheartened by their appalling war experiences. Thousands of soldiers returned home alive but physically and mentally ruined by the war. Life was, in many respects, over for them. Although some Southern men made a feeble attempt to salvage their property and pay their back taxes, others simply gave up. The loss of an arm or a leg, which had seemed heroic at the time, brought on serious psychological problems after the war. Men who had taken orders from superiors for four years sometimes found it difficult to give orders and make decisions on their own in the postwar world. Even had some women hoped to once again take up their comfortable dependent roles, many had no choice but to continue as managers and directors of family farms and businesses. It remained for the women in many cases to pick up the pieces and to serve as the family mainstay—and in many cases as the family breadwinner.

The war, of course, spelled financial ruin for vast numbers of once affluent families. While some Southerners watched their property disappear overnight, others suffered a slow, painful erosion of their savings, their land, and finally their livelihood. Grace Elmore called attention to the plight of an elderly neighbor during the occupation of Columbia, South Carolina, by the Union forces.

The poor old lady literally descended in one night from great wealth to abject poverty, she whose recreation it had been to clothe the naked and feed the hungry, is now absolutely without clothing and bread except what others give her, and she is sheltered by a shanty knocked up in a few hours from planks picked out of the ruins. (10 March 1865)

The collapse of the Confederacy, the freeing of the slaves, and the demise of Confederate bonds and currency brought on economic chaos in the South. Throughout the war, Southern patriots, confident that victory and independence lay just around the corner, continued pouring their money into Confederate bonds and buying Confederate currency. Whatever remained of their disposable wealth not eaten away by inflation and taxes vanished with the South's surrender at the end of the war. Catherine Edmondston registered her despair in her June 26, 1865, diary entry.

At one blow we have lost a large portion of our property. Father's is diminished by 350,000 and 400,000 dollars and what is sadder still, his liabilities remain the same. The future stands before us forbidding and stern. The happy past smiles back with the luster of a vanished summer sunset! At present all is gloomy, as well it can be. . . . Their [Yankee] hated troops are now stationed at all points amongst us—they command all the railroads and other modes of travel—and they have the ability to force their detested oath down the throat of every man amongst us. (Edmondston n.d., 107–8)

Although experiencing momentous economic troubles herself, Cornelia McDonald still had great compassion for a friend who found himself with "not a dollar" by the end of the war. His entire fortune had been lost in depreciated bank stock, a tragedy which was compounded a few months earlier by his having invested an inheritance of $7,000 in Confederate bonds "to show his confidence in the cause, and inspire others with the same" (259).

When Louise Wigfall's grandmother somehow succeeded in getting $1,000 in gold through the lines from Rhode Island, the money was immediately converted into Confederate bills which quickly became worthless. Although the exchange was financially unwise, it was a matter of both confidence and principle. As Louise explained:

> I am sure my father would have felt he was recreant to his country if he had admitted to himself that Confederate money was not as good as gold. (Wright 1905, 221)

With the Federal occupation of their city, Richmond residents witnessed the death throes of their currency. According to Phoebe Pember, many people relied on bartering for needed food and supplies.

> It had been a matter of pride among the Southerners to boast that they had never seen a greenback, so the entrance of the Federal army had thus found them entirely unprepared with gold and silver currency. People who had boxes of Confederate money and were wealthy the day previously, looked around in vain for wherewithal to buy a loaf of bread. Strange exchanges were made on the street of tea and coffee, flour and bacon. (134–35)

Thousands of Southerners were suddenly penniless and as Mary Fontaine pointed out:

> . . . my coffers are dry; I have not one cent, and no prospect of any unless I go to work. You all don't understand how poor we are here, not even a friend to borrow from, for all are alike. (7 May 1865)

Upon the completion of her duties at Chimborazo hospital in Richmond at the end of the war, Phoebe Pember found herself "houseless, homeless and moneyless," except for a single ten-cent silver coin which she "squandered" on "a box of matches and five cocoa-nut cakes."

> The wisdom of the purchase there is no need of defending. Should any one ever be in a strange country where the currency of which he is possessed is valueless, and ten cents be

his only available funds, perhaps he may be able to judge of the difficulty of expending it with judgment. (144)

By April 1865 countless Southerners discovered themselves not only destitute but also debt-ridden. Mary Chesnut described the two classes of Southerners: those to whom money was owed and those who owed money and noted that the Chesnuts (like most people) fell into both categories.

> There are two classes of vociferous sufferers in this commu-
> nity: (1) those who say, "If people would only pay me what
> they owe me!" (2) "If people would only let me alone. I cannot
> pay them. I could stand it if I had anything to pay debts."
> Now we belong to both classes. Heavens! What people owe
> us and will not or cannot pay would settle all our debts ten
> times over and leave us in easy circumstances for life. But they
> will not pay. How can they? (Chesnut 1981, 830)

Gertrude Thomas's problems were no doubt typical of those of many Southern women. Like other patriotic Southerners, Mrs. Thomas's husband had invested large sums of money in Confederate bonds. Her July 31, 1863, diary entry, for example, noted Mr. Thomas's sale of their cotton and his purchase of $15,000 worth of 8 percent Confederate bonds. Following the war, their financial problems became overwhelming and her husband's business and their two plantations were lost to satisfy creditors. Although Mrs. Thomas tried desperately to help pay off their obligations by making many of her own clothes, teaching school, and exercising great frugality in her personal and household expenditures, the property, much of it hers, went for back debts. In his role as the dominant, self-sufficient husband, Mr. Thomas rebuffed her attempts to offer advice and in a fit of pique begged her not to interfere. Mrs. Thomas was deeply hurt but realized that

> Most men dislike to admit that their wifes own anything. It
> is all the masculine "my" and "my own" which they use and
> in polite circles it would be considered in bad taste for a woman

to say "my plantation," "my horse," "my cows" altho they are
really as much her own as the dress she wears. (19 June 1869)

Mrs. Thomas's postwar days were made miserable and depressing
by the changes in her husband. Given to profanity and alcoholism
over the loss of property, he grew ever more surly in his refusal to
discuss their financial problems with her. She confided to her diary
that she would not wish her worst enemy greater problems than
her husband had experienced with his war debts.

The John Berkeley Grimballs, of South Carolina, were yet another
of the thousands of families financially ruined by the war. In 1858
the family owned two plantations and 145 slaves. The 945-acre Grove
plantation was probably worth about $35,000; the Pinebury plan-
tation about $22,000. Slaves at that time were valued at about $550
each. By the end of the war the Grimballs had suffered severe financial reverses and apparently were reduced to living for some time
on the monies from Meta Grimball's inheritance of her father's estate
in New York (which *would have been* $150,000 were it not for the
war). The Grimballs also underwent considerable embarrassment
when their daughter, in attempting to help relieve the family's financial pinch, took a job teaching school. Following Lee's surrender,
Mrs. Grimball wrote:

> The boys [her sons] found us most happy to see them, but
> with an empty corn box, & no money, that could be so called;
> we sent about, & did as others, sold dresses and ornaments,
> and bought bacon, & corn. . . . (113)

Patty, one of their faithful "servants" who had been with the
Grimballs for thirty-six years, helped by selling articles for them
"going at all times, & would take nothing for her trouble." By working out as a seamstress, laundress, or ironer, Patty supplied Meta
with "grist, molasses, and flour, which she said was my share of what
she made" (113). The Grimballs should have found some comfort
in the great numbers of their friends who were also experiencing
serious financial difficulties. Mrs. Grimball noted:

The end of the war found the old aristocracy reduced to many straights to get on and applying for, & gladly taking, very inferior places. (117)

The war's conclusion also marked the end of a way of life for many Southerners. Mary Boykin Chesnut left the excitement and gaiety of Washington behind her when, following Lincoln's election in the fall of 1860, her husband resigned his U.S. Senate seat and they returned to South Carolina. In Richmond, while her husband served as an aide to President Davis, Mary Chesnut, as in Washington, maintained a prominent position among the wealthy, socially elite. During the war years Richmond became the center of the political and social activity of the Confederacy, and Mrs. Chesnut's "salons" attracted governors, generals, politicians, as well as the socially eminent. Mary's long, personal friendship with Varina Davis continued during their years in the Confederate capital, and the Chesnuts were frequent guests at the home of the President.

Even during her husband's reassignment to Columbia, South Carolina, and her refugee days in Lincolnton, North Carolina, and Chester, South Carolina, Mrs. Chesnut graciously extended her hospitality to the parade of friends and dignitaries who stopped to visit with them. Their reduced circumstance became even more acute, however, when, after the war, the Chesnuts returned to their home near Camden, South Carolina. There they found the cotton fields burned and the house ransacked. As they attempted to cross the river "the ferryman at Chesnut's Ferry asked for his fee. Among us all, we could not muster the small silver coin he demanded. There was poverty for you" (Chesnut 1981, 805).

The Chesnuts lived out the latter years of their lives burdened with debt. Cotton was selling at one dollar a pound following the war and had their fields not been leveled, Mary concluded that they would have been "comparatively in easy circumstances." In an effort to avert abject poverty, Mrs. Chesnut managed a thriving butter-and-egg business which she operated on shares with her maid. Early in May 1865 she told her diary: "The first solid half dollar [we earned was] for butter. . . . John C and my husband laughed at my peddling—and borrowed the money" (Chesnut 1984, 237).

Over the years the war had been particularly unkind to Margaret Crozier Ramsey and her family. Mrs. Ramsey had lost a son to the war and two daughters to illness. As the war concluded, Mrs. Ramsey, at sixty-two years of age, living as a refugee near Charlotte, North Carolina, took up teaching in order to earn money for food and other necessities. In a series of reflective diary entries written in May of 1865, Mrs. Ramsey looked back to happier days before the war.

> A sad and lonely feeling came over me today—took a walk to a place which reminds me of home. Sat down on a stump and gave vent to my feelings.
> Our beautiful home all came up before me—the large and stately trees—the grand rivers the deep and quiet French Broad—the more rapid Holston—the roaring of the shoals—and the grand old bluff so lofty—the green fields with growing grain etc—
> All these I was once mistress of—
> Now all occupied by the vandals who desolated our beautiful country. Now the old mansion where we dispensed hospitality with a liberal hand is in ashes—
> The shade trees where our children played so happily, now stand all black and charred, not by thunder-bolts, but by the ruthless hand of men—
> Is it any wonder that we sit solitary, like the children of Israel when in captivity. . . . Often . . . at our old home Dr. Ramsey in playfulness called me the duchess of Mecklenburg. . . .
> Now I am the poor governess.

To be sure, not all Southern women were destitute at the end of the war. Some women, either through blind luck or intelligence or pure chicanery, amassed huge fortunes. Adelicia Acklen, of Nashville, Tennessee, succeeded in playing a clever game of apparent double-dealing during the war. When it appeared imminent that the Federal troops were about to occupy Nashville following the fall of Fort Donelson on February 16, 1862, Mrs. Acklen encouraged her husband to flee to their plantation in Louisiana. Although her

husband had taken the Oath of Allegiance to the Confederacy and
had supposedly contributed $30,000 to the Southern cause, he sought
to convince the Union officers in Louisiana that he had not actively
supported the South and regretted having taken the Oath of
Allegiance. He further befriended the Federals by providing information about Confederate naval operations near his property. This
duplicity, of course, kept both sides guessing as to the Acklens' true
allegiance.

Following the sudden death of her husband in 1863, Mrs. Acklen
and a cousin set off for Louisiana in a daring attempt to save Mrs.
Acklen's bountiful cotton crop. The cotton represented a considerable sum of money and both the Confederates and the Federals were
determined to either capture or burn the cotton rather than allow
it to be confiscated by the other side. However, through some of
the cleverest scheming of the war, Mrs. Acklen succeeded in
deceiving both sides into helping her transport her cotton to a ship.
She worked a shrewd deal by securing Confederates to guard the
bales and then enlisting Yankee help in having them transported
to New Orleans and then to Liverpool. For her efforts she managed
to have 2,000 bales sent to Liverpool for which she received about
$960,000, probably in gold, or about $2,000,000 in greenbacks, thus
making her one of the wealthiest women in America (Acklen Papers;
Graham).

Elizabeth Meriwether, of Memphis, was one of the few refugees
who returned to find her home in relatively good condition. Even
her furniture and personal possessions, stored by friends in her absence, were returned to her. Luck plus Mrs. Meriwether's skillful
outwitting of a slick Memphis lawyer to obtain some of her funds
in gold during a secret trip through the lines into Memphis during
the war, rendered the Meriwethers considerably better off financially following Appomattox than many of their contemporaries.
The Meriwethers survived the war with $4,000 in the bank and much
as Elizabeth longed for a gorgeous new dress, Minor, her husband,
insisted that the money go toward paying off their home and helping less fortunate Confederate veterans.

> During the first year or two after Lee's surrender hardly a day passed but some poor Confederate soldier came to our door for help; they were ragged, shoeless, moneyless. Some wanted help to get on [to] their former homes in distant states, Texas, Louisiana and Alabama. Some wanted to get work in Memphis. Others were wounded and could not work. Every soldier who had come out of that dreadful war unhurt felt it his sacred duty to help those who were less fortunate, and so it was that a considerable part of that four thousand dollars which Minor brought back from Kentucky went for charity. (307)

Although Harriet McLellan and her family found themselves "better situated than many of our Southern friends" upon her return home from her refugee life in the North, Mrs. McLellan suffered painful alienation for supposedly having abandoned the South in its time of need. Many of those women who were neither banished nor evacuated to the North during the war, but who left voluntarily, seeking to distance themselves from the conflict, returned home to find themselves ostracized and denounced as "Yankees." At the urging of her husband, Harriet McLellan had left him to care for their Marietta, Georgia, property, had gathered up their young children, and taken refuge first in Baltimore and then in Brooklyn to wait out the war. Upon her return she was given a cool reception by many of her former friends and neighbors.

> Many looked upon me as an enemy to them because I went North. They seemed disposed to visit the sins of the whole Nation upon one individual. I wonder why it is thus? Why, I love my friends that I know to be the warmest secessionists as well as those at the North, but I hear I am called a "Yankee," & one friend has said she will never come to see me. (34–35)

Harriet had been home but a few days when in a chance meeting she encountered her former minister and his wife on the street. Although the cleric's welcome was enthusiastic, his wife icily rebuffed Harriet "because you left us & went North" (35).

For years after the war it was considered disloyal in many Southern communities to have any personal associations whatsoever with

Yankees. Madame Octavia LeVert, one of Mobile's wealthiest and most illustrious citizens, was ostracized for receiving Federal officers in her home following the war. Madame LeVert was "openly insulted in the streets" and her house and carriage were stoned. When vicious rumors were circulated that she had been a Yankee spy, Madame LeVert was forced to close her Mobile home and move to Augusta (Delaney).

Long before the war's end the South's slave population had begun eroding. With news of their freedom, or even with the circulation of rumors of their liberty, blacks had been disappearing from the plantations singly or en masse—some to wind their way north to what they hoped would be "The Promised Land," some to join the Union forces as soldiers or laborers, some to embark on an often peripatetic existence working here and there as field hands, as laborers, cooks, or laundresses. Thousands simply trailed along after the Federal armies, dependent on army handouts or scavenging for food on their own. The end of the war served to intensify an already smoldering racial problem.

Despite innumerable volumes of analyses, essayists and historians still fail to do justice to the grave economic, political, and social problems which engulfed both races at the end of the war. Former owners confronted with devastated homes, farmyards and fields, and Confederate dollars that would purchase nothing, willingly released their slaves knowing they could no longer support them.* A few owners offered their former servants land to farm independently. A few built homes for them. A great many contracted to work "halves" with their Negroes. Some still solvent owners paid wages.

---

*Even at the end of the war when it surely must have been clear to slaves as well as their owners that the Negro was at last free, some Southerners still persisted in the buying and selling of blacks. Mrs. James Crew, of Lawrenceville, Georgia, noted in a diary entry of May 4, 1865, almost a month after Appomattox, a most unusual purchase: "I did a queer thing to-day: bought a negro girl for $50 in gold. I think the institution about gone, but she had not a relative in the world. Seems affectionate and well disposed, and if she remains with me I will do my duty towards her, and it will be no great loss if I lose the $50."

With the collapse of the Confederacy, tens of thousands of newly freed blacks greeted the news of their long-awaited freedom with wild abandon. However, freedom necessitated important decisions: whether to remain with their former masters, secure in the knowledge that they at least would be provided with food, clothing, and shelter, or whether to strike out on their own in what might well be a cruel, indifferent world (see pages 75–88). Some blacks jubilantly set off for a new life convinced that they would never have to work again. Some remained loyal to their former masters—often reversing their former roles and sustaining their masters by sharing their government rations. Some continued on at their plantation homes for several months, contemptuous of their masters and work of any kind. Courted by politicians and carpetbaggers, promised forty acres and a mule, maltreated by Northerners who staunchly advocated their freedom but refused to recognize them as equals, many blacks quickly discovered that they were the helpless victims of an economically devastated Southland and a pervasive racism endemic to both sections that would take generations to eradicate.

> The most pitiable of all was the condition in which the negroes from the country were plunged, in their haste to "go to freedom." On every road they came in crowds, mothers carrying their babes, with every size and age streaming along behind. The day of jubilee had come—nearly all left food, clothing, & fires behind in their forsaken homes. They were gathered near the cities by the *thousands* in what were called "Kraals" (Corrales) without food or shelter. The Gov't issued rations to this great army of the unemployed, and for a short time they realized the bliss of freedom. . . . (A. Harper 1983, 31)

Unfortunately, there is a dearth of eyewitness accounts of the end of the war (or of the war itself) written by blacks. However, the WPA Writers' Project during the 1930s attempted to fill that gap by conducting scores of interviews with former slaves about their life in bondage. Among those interviewed was J. M. Johnson, who recalled the good fortune of three slaves who, after being freed, were given forty acre homesteads by their former owner. Amanda McCray told of an owner whose liberated slaves, in gratitude for her kindness during their enslavement, remained with her. Sometime after the war, their former owner rewarded all of her "servants" with land grants. According to Rebecca Hooks, the slaves on her old plantation were kept in virtual slavery for many years after they had been legally freed. They were intimidated by their former master who "predicted that they would fare much worse as freemen and so many of them were afraid to venture into the world for themselves."

Alex Thompson, in yet another interview, reported that after the war his master called them all to the kitchen door, explained that they were now free, but if they wanted to stay, he would pay them for their work. However, Thompson explained, "most of the colored people had been in one place so long that they wanted to move on and work different places."

Another owner, enraged over the emancipation of his slaves and their refusal to remain with him, took a gun and fired into the assemblage, killing some and maiming others for life. As a final act of desperation, he turned the gun on himself in an attempt at suicide (WPA).

Many Southerners were wary of the harsh, miserable existence they feared awaited the newly liberated blacks. Others were embittered by what they considered a breach of loyalty on the part of their former servants. Catherine Edmondston evidenced her Southern bias—and her exasperation—when she wrote:

> The negro emancipation has been accomplished—the unfortunates have been thrust blindfold upon the ills of a state of which they know nothing. They enter with confidence and pleasure—expecting that freedom from care which they have hitherto enjoyed together with an entire immunity from all work or all necessity for self-provision. But on the threshold of their new life disappointment awaits them. The Yankees tell them that Freedom does not mean "freedom from work," but freedom from the lash and from the degradation of being sold. Now, as but few of them have ever felt the first to any appreciable degree, and as the second always secured them a comfortable home and an assured subsistence, they prefer a degradation which they cannot understand to being turned adrift and told to shift for themselves. They have taxed their

masters' patience beyond human endurance. They occupy themselves ceaselessly trying on their new chains—seeing how little work they can accomplish and yet be fed, and endeavoring to be slave and free at the same moment—a slave on the food, shelter and clothing question, but free when labour is concerned. Accordingly they are in continual difficulty, and make our lives anything but beds of roses. (Edmondston n.d., 107)

In the absence of her brother, Emma Mordecai served as caretaker of his ailing wife and overseer of their plantation located about four miles outside of Richmond. With the death of the Confederacy, Emma's frustrations with their labor force intensified. Upon discovering one of their former slaves idly reposing near a hedge, Emma confronted him:

> I asked Cy, if he was not going to work any more?—He answered, "Not until I know who I gwine to wuck for". I said, "Why hadn't you as lief work for your mistress as for any one else if she compensates you for it?" He said I onderstand she an't got nothin' to compensate me wid.—"But" I rejoined "if you work the place, she *will* have something". "No," he couldn't work on dem terms. He informed me there was to be no more Master & Mistress now, all was equal, he "done hear dat read from the Court House Steps". I asked if he expected "to continue to live on '*Mrs. Mordecai*' without working for her?" "Yes" he said, "until I see how things is gwine to wuck. All the land belongs to the Yankees now & they gwine divide it out 'mong de coloured people". I listened with perfect self command: there was no redress, no refutation.

As she continued her journey into town, Emma was somewhat surprised by the response when she broached the subject of emancipation to Mary, another of the family's newly liberated blacks. Asking Mary "if she was mighty glad to hear she was free?—She replied 'No M'm' I just as leave be slave as not" (131).

By the end of the war, growing numbers of Southerners were becoming convinced that slavery had perhaps outlived its time (see chapter 2) and they not only accepted, but perhaps even welcomed, emancipation. Yankee promises of land and luxury, for example,

assured the above-mentioned Cy that part of the Mordecai plantation was certainly his "for all the work he had done on it." The
kitchen, in particular, he insisted, should be his in return for his having helped cut the wood to build it. Emma complained to her diary:

> Georgiana, for the last two days has been as sullen as a cow,
> and as perverse as a mule, & as slow as a snail. . . . To have
> to submit to the Yankees is bad enough, but to submit to negro
> children is a little worse. They will, I hope, get ready to go soon.
> We have now had nearly three weeks of this state of things. (141)

Although many Northerners considered the freeing of the slaves
one of the great redeeming features of the war, most vigorously
resisted accepting the blacks as equals, or allowing them to vote,
or to hold office, or to serve as jurors, or to live next door as neighbors, or to compete for jobs. In contrast, however, were the scores
of Northern women who, sensing the desperate plight of the blacks
and their immediate need for education and skills necessary to obtain
employment, volunteered for work in the South helping to teach
black men, women, and children to read and write (see chapter 2).

By June of 1865 fighting on the battlefield had ended, however
internal strife continued to rage. In both sections rival political fac-
tions struggled for control; seething sectional loyalties continued
to flare; widely divergent attitudes toward blacks resulted in discord and violence; the nation's leaders quarreled over reconciliation versus radical reconstruction; hopes for reunification ran the
spectrum from Lincoln's proposed "charity for all" to undying feelings of bitterness and revenge. Thus ran a few of the divisions which
continued to wrack the nation. The painful story of the aftermath
of the war and women's role in coping with postwar problems,
however, remain subjects for another volume.

As the war wound down and the nation struggled to pull itself
back together again, the women of both sections discovered they had
undergone a decided change in status. During the war years men,
either by choice or by default, turned over many of the homefront
decisions to the women. As a result, women in a heretofore male-

dominated society were suddenly being accorded unprecedented responsibility and authority. Grace Elmore sensed the change effected by Southern men's preoccupation with the war effort (she could have spoken for Northern men as well) and commented in her diary:

> How queer the times, the women can't count on the men at all to help them; they either laugh at us or when they speak seriously, 'tis to say they know not what to advise, we must do to the best of our ability. . . . Our men do depend on us a great deal, in fact their time and thought are so fully occupied with what concerns the public welfare that they have none to spare to private matters. They belong to the Confederacy, that is all who are worth anything, and their private concerns have in a great measure ceased to engage their attention. (41)

While the men were away at war, women not only assumed the full responsibility for their families, they ran the farms, planted, cultivated, harvested, butchered; they sent trainloads of boxes filled to overflowing with badly needed clothing and hospital supplies to battlefield hospitals; they planned and conducted fairs that earned hundreds of thousands of dollars for soldiers' relief; they taught schools in their own areas or traveled south to teach newly freed blacks to read and write. They operated businesses, and kept books, and cared for the sick and wounded.

Courageous Civil War women helped pave the way for women as nurses and as dietitians. Although the vote and true equality were a long way in the future, women associated with the U.S. Sanitary Commission had found themselves in the unique position of working with men as equals (Maxwell 1956, 303).

During the four years of conflict, the conduct of the war and its relationship to the safety and prompt return of their husbands, fathers, sons, and brothers had become of paramount importance to women. Few could resist speaking out on military and political matters. In time it was discovered that many women were well-read, that they evidenced a surprising amount of wisdom, and that they could be considerably more than decorative accessories to a discussion. Women had slowly begun to gain acceptance as writers and public speakers.

390

With the return of peace, some women welcomed their husbands home and promptly settled back into their former "cult of domesticity." Other women, however, had been awakened by their war experiences to a host of their own unexplored talents and to a much wider world beyond their immediate family and neighbors.

By the end of the war, gone or at least fast disappearing was the typical stereotype of women as delicate, submissive China dolls. The change was a welcome one for many women who savored their newly acquired independence and emerging feelings of self-worth. Fathers, husbands, and brothers in both the North and the South were often astonished at the resourcefulness and capabilities of their women. Several years after the war Thomas Smith Dabney wrote to his daughter Emmy:

> That you and Ida are quite able to take care of yourselves I entertain no doubt, but still it does me good to find you asserting the fact with so much boldness. Of all the principles developed by the late war, I think the capability of our Southern women to take care of themselves by no means the least important. (Smedes 1965, 264)

The ramifications of women's war work were widespread. Their achievements, for example, were no doubt considerations in their admission as equals with men in the formation of the Grange (the giant organization founded in 1867 and dedicated to the education and advancement of farmers).

As a result of their wartime accomplishments, the taboos against women working outside the home were gradually relaxed. Either from necessity or from choice, women began emerging from their kitchens to undertake both paying and volunteer jobs. Many war widows and wives of disabled veterans, of course, had little choice but to enter the workforce in order to support themselves and their families. True, some women could submit to a life of dependency, living off the charity of their families and friends, or they could work for the government or teach school or clerk in a store. A great many women chose the latter options.

Women's track record during the war years also helped make post-war volunteer work for hospitals, veterans' rehabilitation centers, temperance societies, or orphanages acceptable—in fact, even admirable—in the eyes of society at large. With or without the approval of their husbands, many women expended their time and energies on working for women's rights and women's suffrage. Others devoted themselves to working for the downtrodden in the slums, to contributing to the work of missionary societies, or to conducting fairs for the aid of handicapped veterans and their families.

Several wartime nurses went on to medical school and obtained medical degrees. Other women assumed active roles in disaster relief activities and in various philanthropic organizations. Some founded or edited magazines, or worked to secure pensions for veterans and nurses, or helped to alleviate the problems of immigrants and the aged. Hundreds of activists labored for prison, divorce, or dress reform. For many women the war years provided the conditioning necessary for the long arduous trek westward and the rigors of homesteading.

Their wartime experiences imbued women with a desire for more knowledge and for greater opportunities for cultural enrichment, goals which provided the impetus for the women's club movement. More women sought higher education, more colleges opened their doors to women, and more women attended college.

Years later Mary Elizabeth Massey summarized the advancement of women well when she concluded:

> A comparison of women's advancement during the seventy-eight years between the end of the American Revolution and 1861 with the forty-nine years between 1865 and the outbreak of the First World War shows that in the latter period they outran and outdistanced their predecessors. The Civil War provided a springboard from which they leaped beyond the circumscribed "women's sphere" into that heretofore reserved for men. (367)

The complete story of women's terrible suffering, as well as their important achievements for the war effort—and for women—can never be told. Through the years, however, these women clearly demonstrated they could with dignity and honor meet "the hour of need." They left no doubt about their stamina, courage, self-reliance, resourcefulness, and abilities. They proved to themselves, to their families, and to the world that they could indeed be counted on for considerably more than "just choring around."

High praise poured in for women and their war work from throughout the country. Among the tributes, some hoarsely whispered by dying lips, others proudly proclaimed from public address platforms, two commendations in particular warrant inclusion here. On August 19, 1864, Harry Hammond, serving with the Confederate forces at Chaffin's Bluff near Richmond, wrote his wife:

> I cannot feel tho' any pleasure in hearing you say that you wish you were not a woman. The only solution of this country is in the hands of women not only now in all that they inspire men to do and bear and to believe in, or in the present help and aid they render to the country—but if ever this war does end it will be their part to restore order and to reform society. It would not be easy to estimate the influence that the first generation of women after this struggle will exert upon the whole future history of this country. (Bleser 1981, 124)

Yet another accolade for women and their immense contributions to the war effort came from a most appreciative gentleman—this one a Northern man, a Union man.

> I AM NOT ACCUSTOMED TO USE THE LANGUAGE OF EULOGY. I HAVE NEVER STUDIED THE ART OF PAYING COMPLIMENTS TO WOMEN. BUT I MUST SAY THAT, IF ALL THAT HAS BEEN SAID BY ORATORS AND POETS SINCE THE CREATION OF THE WORLD IN PRAISE OF WOMEN WAS APPLIED TO THE WOMEN OF AMERICA, IT WOULD NOT DO THEM JUSTICE FOR THEIR CONDUCT DURING THIS WAR. I WILL CLOSE BY SAYING, GOD BLESS THE WOMEN OF AMERICA!
>
> —ABRAHAM LINCOLN

Bibliography

"Abby, Miss." Diary. Hargrett Rare Book and Manuscript Library. University of Georgia, Athens.

Acklen, Adelicia. Papers. Tennessee State Library and Archives, Nashville.

Adams, George Worthington. *Doctors in Blue.* New York: Henry Schuman, 1952.

Ainsworth, Garrett Smith. Journal, 1860–1865. McCain Library and Archives, University of Southern Mississippi, Hattiesburg.

Akin, Warren. *Letters of Warren Akin, Confederate Congressman.* Edited by Bell Irvin Wiley. Athens: University of Georgia Press, 1959.

Alcott, Louisa May. *Hospital Sketches.* Cambridge: Belknap Press of Harvard University Press, 1960.

Alexander, Manning P., and Pillone P. Alexander. Collection. Hargrett Rare Book and Manuscript Library. University of Georgia, Athens.

Alexander, Rebecca Ella Solomons. Journal. Archives, Atlanta Historical Society.

Allen, Gideon Winan-Annie Cox. Cox-Allen Correspondence. The Department of Special Collections, The Newberry Library, Chicago.

Anderson Family Papers. New Jersey Historical Society, Newark.

Andrews, Eliza Frances. *The War-time Journal of a Georgia Girl, 1864–1865.* New York: D. Appleton and Company, 1908.

Andrews, Marietta Minnigerode. *Scraps of Paper.* New York: E. P. Dutton & Co., Inc., 1929.

Andrews, Matthew Page, ed. *The Women of the South in War Times.* Baltimore: The Norman, Remington Co., 1923.

Andruss, Virgil Bell. Letters. Archives and Manuscripts Department, Chicago Historical Society.

Anonymous Civil War Letter. Schlesinger Library, Radcliffe College, Cambridge.

Anonymous Letter [Tone?]. Civil War Letters, Archives and Manuscripts Department, Chicago Historical Society.

Anonymous Letter Signed "Mother." Civil War Letters. Archives and Manuscripts Department, Chicago Historical Society.

Atkinson, Thomas. Letters. Jefferson Davis Museum, Biloxi, Miss.

Avary, Marta Lockett, ed. *A Virginia Girl in the Civil War, 1861–1865.* New York: D. Appleton and Company, 1903.

Avery, George Smith, and Lizzie Little. Letters. In the George Avery and Lizzie Little Collection. Archives and Manuscripts Department, Chicago Historical Society.

Bacon, Mrs. Francis. Memorabilia. Manuscripts Department, New York Historical Society, New York.

Baker, Nina Brown. *Cyclone in Calico: The Story of Mary Ann Bickerdyke.* Boston: Little Brown, 1952.

Baldridge-Thompson Collection of Civil War Papers. Historical Collections and Labor Archives, Pattee Library, Pennsylvania State University, University Park.

Baldwin, Helene L., Michael Allen Mudge, and Keith W. Schlegel, eds. *The McKaig Journal.* Baltimore: Gateway Press Inc., 1984. Microfilm.

Baldwin-McColl Family Papers. Burton Historical Collection, Detroit Public Library.

Balfour, Emma. *Vicksburg, A City Under Siege: Diary of Emma Balfour, May 16, 1863–June 2, 1863.* Vicksburg, Miss.: Phillip C. Weinberger, 1983.

Barber, Lucius W. *Army Memoirs of Lucius W. Barber Company "D," 15th Illinois Volunteer Infantry.* Chicago: The J. M. W. Jones Stationery and Printing Co., 1894.

Barnett, Family Correspondence. Indiana Division, Indiana State Library, Indianapolis.

Barr [Barre], Mrs. Henrietta Fitzhugh. *The Civil War Diary of Mrs. Henrietta Fitzhugh Barr (Barre) 1862–1863, Ravenswood, Virginia (West Virginia).* Edited by Sallie Kiger Winn. Marietta, Ohio: Marietta College, 1963.

Barton, Clara. Diary, 1863. In Clara Barton Papers. American Antiquarian Society, Worcester, Mass.

Barton, George. *Angels of the Battlefield.* Philadelphia: The Catholic Art Publishing Company, 1897.

Bascot, Ada. Diaries. South Caroliniana Library, University of South Carolina, Columbia.

Battle of the Handkerchiefs. Manuscripts Division, The Historic New Orleans Collection.

Battle of St. Paul's. Manuscripts Division, The Historic New Orleans Collection.

Baxley, Catherine Virginia. Diary. Manuscripts and Archives Section, New York Public Library.

Beale, Jane Howison. *The Journal of Jane Howison Beale of Fredericksburg, Virginia, 1850–1862.* Fredericksburg: Historic Fredericksburg, Inc., 1979.

Beard, Grace Pierson James. Beard Papers. Southern Historical Collection, Wilson Library, University of North Carolina at Chapel Hill.

Beers, Mrs. Fannie A. *Memories: A Record of Personal Experience and Adventure During the Four Years of War.* Philadelphia: J. B. Lippincott Company, 1888.

Belcher, Granville W., and Mary Caroline Belcher. Letters. McCain Library and Archives, University of Southern Mississippi, Hattiesburg.

Bell, Mrs. R. J. Diary. In M. M. Parsons Papers. Archives, Missouri Historical Society, St. Louis.

Benbury-Haywood Papers. Southern Historical Collection, Wilson Library, University of North Carolina at Chapel Hill.

Berry, Carrie. Diary. Archives, Atlanta Historical Society.

Billings, John D. *Hardtack and Coffee or The Unwritten Story of Army Life.* Boston: George M. Smith & Co., 1888.

Bingham, Mary (Warden). Diary. Michigan Historical Collections, Bentley Historical Library, University of Michigan, Ann Arbor.

Black, Nellie Peters. Reminiscences. Archives, Atlanta Historical Society.

Blackburn, George M., ed. "The Negro as Viewed by a Michigan Civil War Soldier: Letters of John C. Buchanan." *Michigan History* 47 (March 1963): 75–84.

———. "Letters to the Front: A Distaff View of the Civil War." *Michigan History* 49 (March 1965): 53–57.

Blackford, Susan Leigh. *Letters From Lee's Army or Memoirs of Life In and Out of The Army in Virginia During the War Between the States.* Edited by Charles Minor Blackford III. New York: Charles Scribner's Sons, 1947.

Blackwell, Emily. Letter to Barbara Smith Bodichon, June 1, 1861. Rare Book and Manuscript Library, Columbia University, New York.

Bleser, Carol K., ed. *The Hammonds of Redcliffe.* New York: Oxford University Press, 1981.

Blunt, Sarah R. Letters. Manuscripts Department, New York Historical Society, New York.

Boatner, Mark Mayo III. *The Civil War Dictionary.* New York: David McKay Company, Inc., 1959.

Boney, F. N., ed. *A Union Soldier in the Land of the Vanquished: The Diary of Sergeant Mathew Woodruff, June–December 1865.* Tuscaloosa: University of Alabama Press, 1969.

Bonner, James C., ed. *The Journal of a Milledgeville Girl, 1861–1867.* Athens: University of Georgia Press, 1964.

Boozer, Alice (Mrs. Simon P.). Collection. South Caroliniana Library, University of South Carolina, Columbia.

Bourne, Amelia. Diary. In Mrs. Henry L. Stone Papers. Filson Club, Louisville, Ky.

Boutwell, Mrs. Wineford. "A Poor Widow Asks for Food: 1865." Edited by Spencer B. King, Jr. *Georgia Historical Quarterly* 52 (December 1968): 449–50.

Bovard, Sarah. Papers. Indiana Division, Indiana State Library, Indianapolis.

Bowen, Clarissa Adger. *The Diary of Clarissa Adger Bowen Ashtabula Plantation, 1865.* Edited by Mary Stevenson. Pendleton, S.C.: The Research and Publication Committee Foundation for the Historical Restoration in Pendleton Area, 1973.

Boyd, Belle. *Belle Boyd in Camp and Prison.* Edited by Curtis Carroll Davis. New York: Thomas Yoseloff, 1968.

Boykin Papers. Southern Historical Collection, Wilson Library, University of North Carolina at Chapel Hill.

Boykin, Laura Nisbet. *Shinplasters and Homespun: The Diary of Laura Nisbet Boykin.* Edited by Mary Wright Stock. Rockville, Md.: Printex, 1975.

Bradley, Amy Morris. Papers. Special Collections Department, William R. Perkins Library, Duke University, Durham, N.C. Microfilm.

Brainerd, Morris. Letters. Connecticut Historical Society, Hartford.

Brandon, Zillah (Haynie). Diary. Alabama Department of Archives and History, Montgomery. Microfilm.

Brandt, Marie Ester. Diaries. Indiana Historical Society, Indianapolis.

Breckinridge, Lucy. *Lucy Breckinridge of Grove Hill: Journal of a Virginia Girl, 1862–1864.* Edited by Mary D. Robertson. Kent, Ohio: The Kent State University Press, 1979.

Brett, David. *"My Dear Wife. . . . "* The Civil War Letters of David Brett, *9th Massachusetts Battery Union Cannoneers.* Little Rock: Pioneer Press, 1964.

Brevard, Keziah Goodwyn Hopkins. Diary. South Caroliniana Library, University of South Carolina, Columbia. Typescript.

Brinton, John H. *Personal Memoirs of John Brinton.* New York: The Neale Publishing Co., 1914.

Brobst, John F. *Well, Mary: Civil War Letters of a Wisconsin Volunteer.* Edited by Margaret Brobst Roth. Madison: The University of Wisconsin Press, 1960.

Brockett, Linus Pierpont, and Mrs. Mary C. Vaughan. *Woman's Work in the Civil War: A Record of Heroism, Patriotism and Patience.* Philadelphia: Zeigler, McCurdy & Co., 1867.

Broidrick, Annie Laurie. "A Recollection of Thirty Years Ago." Southern Historical Collection, Wilson Library, University of North Carolina at Chapel Hill.

Brooks, Abbie M. Diary and Civil War Reminiscences, January 17, 1865–July 1, 1865. Archives, Atlanta Historical Society.

Brooks, Stewart. *Civil War Medicine.* Springfield, Ill.: Charles C. Thomas, 1966.

Brown, B. B. "Civil War Letters." *North Dakota Historical Quarterly* 1 (April 1927): 66–68.

Brown, Bergun H. Diary. Special Collections. Washington University Library, St. Louis, Mo.

Brown Family Correspondence. Manuscripts and Archives Section, New York Public Library.

Brown, Jasper. Papers. Burton Historical Collection, Detroit Public Library.

Brown, Mary Davis. Diary. South Caroliniana Library, University of South Carolina, Columbia. Microfilm.

Bryan, Mary Norcott. *A Grandmother's Recollection of Dixie.* N.p., n.d.

Buck, Lucy Rebecca. *Sad Earth, Sweet Heavens: The Diary of Lucy Rebecca Buck During the War Between the States, Front Royal, Virginia, December 25, 1861–April 15, 1865.* Edited by Dr. William P. Buck. Birmingham, Ala.: The Cornerstone Publisher, 1973.

Bucklin, Sophronia E. *In Hospital and Camp: A Woman's Record of Thrilling Incidents Among the Wounded in the Late War.* Philadelphia: John E. Potter and Company, 1869.

Burge, Dolly Sumner Lunt. *A Woman's Wartime Journal.* New York: The Century Company, 1918.

Burge, Louisiana D. Diary. Robert W. Woodruff Library, Emory University, Atlanta. Microfilm.

Burr, Barbara. "Letters from Two Wars." *Illinois State Historical Society Journal* 30 (April 1937–January 1938): 135–58.

Burwell, Andrew, and Mary E. Burwell. Letters. McCain Library and Archives, University of Southern Mississippi, Hattiesburg.

Butler, C. Ann. Paper. Georgia Historical Society, Savannah.

Butler, Lucy (Wood). Letters and Diary of a Civil War Bride. In the Lomax Family Papers. Virginia Historical Society, Richmond.

Byron, Anna. Diary. Rare Book and Manuscript Library, Columbia University, New York.

Campbell, Randolph B., and Donald K. Pickens, eds. " 'My Dear Husband': A Texas Slave's Love Letter, 1862." *Journal of Negro History* 65 (Fall 1980): 361–64.

Carney, Kate. Diary. Southern Historical Collection, Wilson Library, University of North Carolina at Chapel Hill. Microfilm.

Carr, Mary M. Diary. Special Collections Department, William R. Perkins Library, Duke University, Durham, N.C. Microfilm.

Carson, William G. B. " 'Secesh.' " *Bulletin of the Missouri Historical Society* 23 (January 1967): 119–45.

Carter, Robert Goldthwaite. *Four Brothers in Blue or Sunshine and Shadows of the War of the Rebellion: A Story of the Great Civil War from Bull Run to Appomattox.* Austin: University of Texas Press, 1978.

Chadick, Mary Jane Cook. Papers. Special Collections Department, William R. Perkins Library, Duke University, Durham, N.C.

Chamberlain Family Papers. Burton Historical Collection, Detroit Public Library.

Chambers, William Pitt. "My Journal—Chambers." *Publications of The Mississippi Historical Society* 5: 225–386.

Champion, Matilda M., and Sid Champion. Letters. Archives, Old Court House Museum, Vicksburg, Miss.

Chancellor, Sue M. "Personal Recollections of the Battle of Chancellorsville." *Register of the Kentucky Historical Society* 66 (April 1968): 137–46.

Chapin, T. N. and Sarah A. Underhill Chapin. The Civil War Letters of T. N. Chapin and Sarah A. Underhill Chapin. Compiled by Marie E. Charnley. Privately held.

Chapman, Mary Sumner. Diary and Correspondence. Rare Book and Manuscript Library, Columbia University, New York.

Chappelear, Amanda Virginia (Edmonds). Diary. Virginia Historical Society, Richmond.

Charles, Thomas C., and Ellen McRaven Charles. Letters. McCain Library and Archives, University of Southern Mississippi, Hattiesburg.

Chase, Cornelia. Diary. Michigan Historical Collections, Bentley Historical Library, University of Michigan, Ann Arbor.

Chesnut, Mary. *Mary Chesnut's Civil War.* Edited by C. Vann Woodward. New Haven: Yale University Press, 1981.

———. *The Private Mary Chesnut: The Unpublished Civil War Diaries.* Edited by C. Vann Woodward and Elisabeth Muhlenfeld. New York: Oxford University Press, 1984.

Child, Lydia Marie (Frances). Letters. Schlesinger Library, Radcliffe College, Cambridge.

Chittenden, George, and Amanda Chittenden. Letters. Indiana Division, Indiana State Library, Indianapolis.

Chunn, William A. Family Papers. Robert W. Woodruff Library, Emory University, Atlanta.

Cist, Elisa. Letters, August 9, 1863–November 14, 1865. In Cist Family Papers. Cincinnati Historical Society.

Clark, Edgar W. Civil War Recollections. Privately held.

Clay Papers. Georgia Historical Society, Savannah.

Clay-Clopton, Mrs. Virginia. *A Belle of the Fifties: Memoirs of Mrs. Clay of Alabama.* New York: De Capo Press, 1969.

Clemson, Floride. *A Rebel Come Home: The Diary and Letters of Floride Clemson, 1863–1866.* Edited by Charles M. McGee, Jr. and Ernest M. Lander, Jr. Columbia: University of South Carolina Press, 1961.

Clifford, Deborah Pickman. *Mine Eyes Have Seen the Glory: A Biography of Julia Ward Howe.* Boston: Little, Brown and Company, 1978.

Clinton, Catherine. *The Plantation Mistress: Woman's World in the Old South.* New York: Pantheon Books, 1982.

———. *The Other Civil War: American Women in the Nineteenth Century.* New York: Hill and Wang, 1984.

Collis, Septima M. *A Woman's War Record, 1861–1865.* New York: G. P. Putnam's Sons, 1889.

Conner, Virginia. Diary. In Conner Family Collection. Middle Georgia Archives, Washington Memorial Library, Macon.

Connor, Orange Cicero, and Mary America (Aikin) Connor. *Dear America, Some Letters of Orange Cicero and Mary America (Aikin) Connor.* Edited by Seymour V. Connor. Austin and New York: Jenkins Publishing Company, 1971.

Converse, James L. Letters. Archives and Manuscripts Department, Chicago Historical Society.

Cooper, Catherine. Letter. Tennessee State Library and Archives, Nashville.

Cory, Joseph. Letter. Alexander Library, Rutgers University, New Brunswick, N.J.

Cotton, Ann. Letters. In J. Dexter Cotton Papers. Library of Congress.

Cotton, Gordon A. *Yankee Bullets, Rebel Rations: Caught Between Two Armies, Vicksburg Citizens Recall the Horrors of the 1863 Siege.* Vicksburg, Miss.: The Office Supply Company, 1989.

Cotton, Gordon A. Civil War Women Collection. Archives, Old Court House Museum, Vicksburg, Miss.

Cowan, Eliza L. Diary. In George B. Atwood Papers. Archives, Missouri Historical Society, St. Louis.

Cormany. *See* Mohr.

Craighead, Rachel Carter. Diaries. Tennessee State Library and Archives, Nashville. Microfilm.

Crary, Catherine S., ed. *Dear Belle: Letters from a Cadet & Officer to his Sweetheart, 1858–1865.* Middletown, Conn.: Wesleyan University Press, 1965.

Crawshaw, Titus. Letters, 1853–1866. The British Library of Political and Economic Science, London.

Crew, Mrs. James R. Diary. Archives, Atlanta Historical Society.

Crossley, Martha Jane. "A Patriotic Confederate Woman's Diary, 1862–1863." Edited by H. E. Sterkx. *Alabama Historical Quarterly* 20 (Winter 1958): 611–17.

Crotty, D. G. *Four Years Campaigning in the Army of the Potomac.* Grand Rapids, Mich.: Dygert Bros. & Co., 1874.

Crozier, Elizabeth Baker. Journal. Special Collections, University of Tennessee at Knoxville.

Culpepper, John Wesley. Journal. McCain Library and Archives, University of Southern Mississippi, Hattiesburg.

Cumming, Kate. *Kate: The Journal of a Confederate Nurse.* Edited by Richard Barksdale Harwell. Baton Rouge: Louisiana State University Press, 1959.

Cumming, Katharine H. *A Northern Daughter and A Southern Wife: The Civil War Reminiscences and Letters of Katharine H. Cumming, 1860–1865.* Edited by W. Kirk Wood. Augusta, Ga.: Richmond County Historical Society, 1976.

Cunningham, Sarah Alexander. Collection. Georgia Historical Society, Savannah.

Currey, Mary Eliza. " 'What An Awful and Grand Spectacle It Is': Fear in the Heart of North Carolina." Edited by Ted Yeatman. *Civil War Times Illustrated* 22 (January 1984): 41–43.

Daly Papers. Maria Daly Correspondence, January 1861–December 1865. Manuscripts and Archives Section, New York Public Library.

Dannett, Sylvia G. L., ed. *Noble Women of the North.* New York: Thomas Yoseloff, 1959.

Darden, Susan Sillers. Diary. Mississippi Department of Archives and History, Jackson.

Davidson, John, and Julia Davidson. Letters. In Davidson Family Collection. Archives, Atlanta Historical Society.

Davis, Burke. *Sherman's March.* New York: Random House, 1980.

Davis, Caroline Kean (Hill). Diary. Virginia Historical Society, Richmond.

Davis, Lois Wright Richardson. Papers. Special Collections Department, William R. Perkins Library, Duke University, Durham, N.C.

Davis, William Van. Diary. McCain Library and Archives, University of Southern Mississippi, Hattiesburg.

Dawson, Sarah Morgan. *A Confederate Girl's Diary.* Edited by James I. Robertson, Jr. Bloomington: Indiana University Press, 1960.

De France, Laura McRaven. Letters. In Thomas C. Charles and Ellen McRaven Charles Letters. McCain Library and Archives, University of Southern Mississippi, Hattiesburg.

De Saussure, Mrs. N. B. *Old Plantation Days—Being Recollections of Southern Life Before the Civil War.* New York: Duffield & Company, 1909.

Delaney, Caldwell. "Madame Octavia Walton LeVert 1810–1877." Master's thesis, University of Alabama, 1952.

———. "Madame Octavia Walton LeVert: The South's Most Famous Belle." *A Mobile Sextet: Papers Read Before the Alabama Historical Association, 1952–1971.* Mobile: The Haunted Book Shop, 1981.

———. *The Story of Mobile.* Mobile: The Haunted Book Shop, 1981.

DeLeon, Thomas Cooper. *Belles, Beaux, and Brains of the 60's.* New York: G. W. Dillingham Company, 1907.

DeLonne, Mrs. A. B. Papers. Mississippi Department of Archives and History, Jackson.

Doak, Henry Melvil. Papers. Tennessee State Library and Archives, Nashville. Microfilm.

Dodge, Mary Abigail [Gail Hamilton]. "A Call to My Country-Women." *Atlantic Monthly* 11 (1863): 345–49.

Duer, Hannah Maria Denning. Diaries. Rare Book and Manuscript Library, Columbia University, New York.

Dunn, Gertrude. Diary. Manuscripts and Archives Section, New York Public Library.

Dyson-Bell-Sans Souci Papers. Joint Collection, University of Missouri Western Historical Manuscript Collection, St. Louis and State Historical Society of Missouri Manuscripts.

Eaton, Harriet. Diary. Southern Historical Collection, Wilson Library, University of North Carolina at Chapel Hill. Microfilm.

Edmonds, Amanda Virginia. *Journals of Amanda Virginia Edmonds: Lass of the Mosby Confederacy, 1859–1867.* Edited by Nancy Chappelear Blair. Delaplane, Va.: N. C. Baird, 1984.

Edmondson, Belle. Diary. Southern Historical Collection, Wilson Library, University of North Carolina at Chapel Hill.

Edmondston, Catherine Ann Devereux. *"Journal of a Secesh Lady": The Diary of Catherine Ann Devereux Edmondston, 1860–1866.* Edited by Beth G. Crabtree and James W. Patton. Raleigh: North Carolina Division of Archives and History, 1979.

———. *The Journal of Catherine Devereux Edmondston, 1860–1866.* Edited by Margaret Mackey Jones. Privately published, n.d.

Elliott, Jane Evans. Diaries. Library, Historical Foundation of the Presbyterian and Reformed Churches, Montreat, N.C.

Elmore, Day. Letters. Archives and Manuscripts Department, Chicago Historical Society.

Elmore, Franklin Harper. Papers. South Caroliniana Library, University of South Carolina, Columbia.

Elmore, Grace Brown. Diaries and Books. Southern Historical Collection, Wilson Library, University of North Carolina at Chapel Hill.

Embree, Lucius. Family Papers. Indiana Division, Indiana State Library, Indianapolis.

England, John. Letters. Manuscripts and Archives Section, New York Public Library.

Eppes, Susan Bradford. *Through Some Eventful Years.* Gainesville: University of Florida Press, Floridiana Facsimile Reprint Series, 1968.

Erwin, Margaret Johnson. *Like Some Green Laurel: Letters of Margaret Johnson Erwin, 1821–1863.* Edited by John Seymour Erwin. Baton Rouge: Louisiana State University Press, 1981.

Eschbach Letters. Privately held.

Faller, Leo W., and John I. Faller. *Dear Folks at Home: The Civil War Letters of Leo W. and John I. Faller With An Account of Andersonville.* Edited by Milton E. Fowler. Carlisle, Penn.: Cumberland County Historical Society, 1963.

Famous Adventures and Prison Escapes of the Civil War. New York: The Century Company, 1915.

Farmer, George E. Papers. Special Collections. Washington University Library, St. Louis.

Faw Family Letters and Diary. Kennesaw Mountain National Battlefield Park, Marietta, Ga.

Fisher, Julia Bryant. Letter. In Winston and Octavia Stephens Papers. The P. K. Yonge Library of Florida History, University of Florida, Gainesville.

Fletcher, Emily. Letter. Indiana Division, Indiana State Library, Indianapolis.

Fletcher, Louisa Warren Patch. Journal. Georgia Department of Archives and History, Atlanta.

Fletcher, Lucy Muse Walton. Papers. Special Collections Department, William R. Perkins Library, Duke University, Durham, N.C.

Fontaine, Mrs. Mary Burrows. Letters. Eleanor S. Brockenbrough Library, The Museum of the Confederacy, Richmond, Va.

Forbes, Charles. Diaries. In Prudence McCabe Collection. Special Collections, Western Michigan University, Kalamazoo.

404

Forbes, Henry Clinton. Letters. Archives and Manuscripts Department, Chicago Historical Society.

Forbes, Susan E. Parsons Brown. Diary. American Antiquarian Society, Worcester, Mass. Microfilm.

Forten, Charlotte L. *The Journal of Charlotte L. Forten.* Edited by Ray Allen Billington. New York: The Dryden Press, Publishers, 1953.

Foster, Kate D. Diary. In Kate D. Foster Papers. Special Collections Department, William R. Perkins Library, Duke University, Durham, N.C.

Fox, Virginia L. Woodbury. Correspondence in G. V. Fox Papers. Manuscripts Department, New York Historical Society, New York.

Fox-Genovese, Elizabeth. *Within the Plantation Household.* Chapel Hill: The University of North Carolina Press, 1988.

Francis, Anna Mercer LaRoche. Diary. Rare Book and Manuscript Library, Columbia University, New York.

Fraser, A. Letter. Kennesaw Mountain National Battlefield Park, Marietta, Ga.

Fraser, Walter J., Jr., R. Frank Saunders, Jr., and Jon L. Wakelyn, eds. *The Web of Southern Social Relations: Women, Family, & Education.* Athens: The University of Georgia Press, 1985.

Freeman, Mrs. Julia Susan (Wheelock). *The Boys in White; The Experiences of a Hospital Agent in and Around Washington.* New York: Lange & Hillman, 1870.

———. Journals. Burton Historical Collection, Detroit Public Library.

Frobel, Anne S. *The Civil War Diary of Anne S. Frobel of Wilton Hill in Virginia.* Edited by Mary H. Lancaster and Dallas M. Lancaster. Birmingham: Birmingham Printing & Publishing Co., 1986.

Fuson, Joseph B. Civil War Diary. Privately held.

Garrick [Garrioch], William. Letter from Grand Rapids, Michigan, to Brother in Perth, Scotland, February 29, 1862. The British Library of Political and Economic Science, London.

Garrison, W. C. J. (Mrs.). "A Bit of My Experiences During the Civil War." Archives, Atlanta Historical Society.

Gay, Mary A.H. *Life in Dixie During the War.* Atlanta: Foote & Davies Company, 1901.

Geary, John W. Collection. Archives, Atlanta Historical Society.

Gibson Family Papers. Virginia State Library, Richmond.

Gilmer, Louisa Frederika Alexander. Papers. Georgia Historical Society, Savannah.

Goodnight, Mrs. T. H. "War Recollections." *Virginia Historical Magazine* 43 (1935): 355–59.

Goolrick, Mrs. Frances Bernard. "The Shelling of Fredericksburg." *Confederate Veteran* 12 (December 1917): 573–74.

Gordon, Mrs. John B. Papers. Georgia Department of Archives and History, Atlanta.

Gorgas, Amelia. "As I Saw It." Edited by Sarah Woolfolk Wiggins. *Civil War Times Illustrated* 25 (May 1986): 40–43.

Goyne, Minetta Altgelt. *Lone Star and Double Eagle: Civil War Letters of a German-Texas Family*. Fort Worth: Texas Christian University Press, 1982.

Graham, Eleanor. "Belmont I. Nashville Home of Adelicia Acklen." *Tennessee Historical Quarterly* 30 (1971): 345–68.

Gratz, Miriam. Diary. Special Collections and Archives, King Library, University of Kentucky, Lexington.

Gray, Virginia Davis. "Life in Confederate Arkansas: The Diary of Virginia Davis Gray, 1863–1865." Parts 1, 2. Edited by Carl H. Moneyhon. *Arkansas Historical Quarterly* 42 (Spring, Summer 1983): 47–85, 134–69.

Green, Fannie. Journal. In Green Family Civil War Papers. Robert W. Woodruff Library, Emory University, Atlanta.

Greenbie, Marjorie Barstow. *Lincoln's Daughters of Mercy*. New York: G. P. Putnam's Sons, 1944.

Greenhow, Rose O'Neal. Papers. Special Collections Department, William R. Perkins Library, Duke University, Durham, N.C.

Greer, Alexander, and Joseph Thomas Greer. Papers, 1862–1865. McCain Library and Archives, University of Southern Mississippi, Hattiesburg.

Grimball, Meta Morris. Journal. South Caroliniana Library, University of South Carolina, Columbia. Also in Southern Historical Collection, Wilson Library, University of North Carolina at Chapel Hill.

Grinnell, Helen (Lansing). Diary. Manuscripts and Archives Section, New York Public Library.

Gwinn, Laban. "The Civil War Letters of Laban Gwinn: A Union Refugee." *West Virginia History* 43 (Spring 1982): 227–45.

Gwyn, Margaret. Diary. Special Collections Department, William R. Perkins Library, Duke University, Durham, N.C.

Habersham, Josephine Clay. *Ebb Tide As Seen Through the Diary of Josephine Clay Habersham, 1863*. Edited by Spencer Bidwell King, Jr. Athens: University of Georgia Press, 1958.

Haggard, Mrs. P. H. "A Sketch of My Early Life." Edited by James R. Jones. *Civil War Times Illustrated* 20 (August 1981): 34–43.

Hagle Diary. Special Collections, Western Michigan University, Kalamazoo.

Hague, Parthenia Antoinette. *A Blockaded Family: Life in Southern Alabama During the Civil War*. Boston: Houghton, Mifflin and Company, 1888.

Hale, Mary Taylor. Papers. Michigan State University Archives and Historical Collections, East Lansing.

Hale, William Dinsmore and Family Papers. Minnesota Historical Society, St. Paul. Microfilm.

Hall, Maria. Letters. Privately held.

Halsted, N. Norris, and Nancy Marsh Halsted. Papers. New Jersey Historical Society, Newark.

Hammond, Harold Earl, ed. *Diary of a Union Lady, 1861–1865.* New York: Funk & Wagnalls Company, Inc., 1962.

Hancock, Cornelia. *South After Gettysburg: Letters of Cornelia Hancock, 1863–1868.* Edited by Henrietta Stratton Jaquette. New York: Thomas Y. Crowell Company, 1956.

Hardenberg Family Papers. Michigan State University Archives and Historical Collections, East Lansing.

Hardin, Lizzie. *The Private War of Lizzie Hardin: A Kentucky Confederate Girl's Diary of the Civil War in Kentucky, Virginia, Tennessee, Alabama, and Georgia.* Edited by G. Glenn Clift. Frankfort: The Kentucky Historical Society, 1963.

Harding, Elizabeth McGavock. "Letters From Nashville, 1862, I: A Portrait of Belle Meade." Edited by Ridley Wills, II. *Tennessee Historical Quarterly* 33 (Spring 1974): 70–84.

Harper, Annie. *Annie Harper's Journal: A Southern Mother's Legacy.* Edited by Jeannie Marie Deen. Denton, Miss.: Flower Mound Writing Company, 1983.

Harper, Myra S. Letter. Archives, Atlanta Historical Society.

Harreld, Claudia White. Reminiscences. Schlesinger Library, Radcliffe College, Cambridge.

Harrison, Mrs. Burton. *Recollections Grave and Gay.* New York: Charles Scribner's Sons, 1911.

Hart, Helen Marcia. Diary. Schlesinger Library, Radcliffe College, Cambridge.

Harwell, J. D. Letters. McCain Library and Archives, University of Southern Mississippi, Hattiesburg.

Haskell, Sophia Lovell. Diary, 1862–1866. South Carolina Historical Society, Charleston.

Havens, Harry C. Letter. Alexander Library, Rutgers University, New Brunswick, N.J.

Hawks, J. M., and Esther Hawks. Papers. Library of Congress.

Hawks, Esther Hill. *A Woman Doctor's Civil War: Esther Hill Hawks' Diary.* Edited by Gerald Schwartz. Columbia: University of South Carolina Press, 1984.

Hawley, Mary. Diary, 1864. Manuscripts Department, New York Historical Society, New York.

Heath, Susan. Diary, 1861–1865. Heath Family Papers. Massachusetts Historical Society, Boston.

Hertzog, William F. Letters. Archives and Manuscripts, Chicago Historical Society.

Hesseltine, William B., ed. *Dr. J. G. M. Ramsey Autobiography and Letters.* Nashville: Tennessee Historical Commission, 1954.

Hill, Sarah Jane Full. "Reminiscences of the Civil War." Library of Congress.

———. *Mrs. Hill's Journal—Civil War Remniscences.* Edited by Mark M. Krug. Chicago: The Lakeside Press, 1980.

History of the North-Western Soldiers' Fair Held in Chicago. Chicago: Dunlop, Sewell & Spalding, Printers, 1864.

Hoehling, A. A., and Mary Hoehling. *The Last Days of the Confederacy.* New York: The Fairfax Press, 1981.

Holland, Mary A. Gardner, ed. *Our Army Nurses.* Boston: B. Wilkins & Co., Publishers, 1895.

Hollis, J. Rufus. Papers. Tennessee State Library and Archives, Nashville. Microfilm.

Holmes, Emma. *The Diary of Miss Emma Holmes, 1861–1866.* Edited by John F. Marszalek. Baton Rouge: Louisiana State University Press, 1979.

Homans, Ned. Letters. In Homans Collection. Manuscripts and Archives, New York Public Library.

Hooper, Ernest Walter. "Memphis, Tennessee: Federal Occupation and Reconstruction, 1862–1870." Ph.D. diss., University of North Carolina, 1957.

Horsman, Reginald. *Josiah Nott of Mobile.* Baton Rouge: Louisiana State University Press, 1987.

Hort, Mary. Journal. South Caroliniana Library, University of South Carolina, Columbia.

Hosmer, Ann P. (Mrs. O. E.). Reminiscences. Archives and Manuscripts Department, Chicago Historical Society.

Howe, Julia Ward. Reminiscences. Boston: Houghton, Mifflin & Co., 1899.

Howes, Mary Elizabeth Humphrey. Diary. Howes Davis Collection. Middle Georgia Archives, Washington Memorial Library, Macon.

Hume, Fannie Page. Diary. Library of Congress.

Humphrey, William T. Collection. Special Collections Division, Chicago Public Library.

Hunley, Mary. Diary. In Hunley Papers. Southern Historical Collection, Library of the University of North Carolina at Chapel Hill.

Hunt, Sarah. Letter. Hargrett Rare Book and Manuscript Library, University of Georgia, Athens.

Huntington, Mrs. Henry. "Escape from Atlanta: The Huntington Memoir." Edited by Ben Kremenak. *Civil War History* 11 (June 1965): 160–77.

Hurlbut, George. Letters. Kennesaw Mountain National Battlefield Park, Marietta, Ga.

Hurn, Ethel Alice. *Wisconsin Women in the War*. Wisconsin History Commission Original Papers No. 6, May 1911.

Ingraham, Elizabeth Mary Meade. "The Vicksbury Diary of Mrs. Alfred Ingraham (May 2–June 13, 1863)." Edited by W. Maury Darst. *Journal of Mississippi History* 44 (May 1982): 148–79.

Jackson, Eveline Harden. Diary. Special Collections, Hargrett Rare Book and Manuscript Library, University of Georgia, Athens. Microfilm.

James, John. Letter. Alexander Library, Rutgers University, New Brunswick, N.J.

Jenkins, Gertrude. Narrative. Special Collections Department, William R. Perkins Library, Duke University, Durham, N.C.

Jewell Family Civil War Letters. Joint Collection, University of Missouri Western Historical Manuscript Collection, St. Louis and State Historical Society of Missouri Manuscripts.

Johnston, Gertrude K. *Dear Pa—And So It Goes*. Harrisburg, Penn.: Business Service Company, 1971.

Johnston, Joseph Sturge. Letters. Archives and Manuscripts, Chicago Historical Society.

Johnstone, Helen. "What She Did for the Confederacy." Mississippi Department of Archives and History, Jackson.

Jones, John Beauchamp. *A Rebel War Clerk's Diary at the Confederate States Capital*. Vols 1, 2. Edited by Howard Swiggett. New York: Old Hickory Bookshop, 1935.

Jones, Katharine M., ed. *Heroines of Dixie: Confederate Women Tell Their Story of the War*. Indianapolis: The Bobbs-Merrill Company, Inc., 1955.

Jones, Martha B. Diaries. Filson Club, Louisville, Ky.

Jones, Mary Sharpe, and Mary Jones Mallard. *Yankees A'Coming: One Month's Experience During the Invasion of Liberty County, Georgia, 1864–1865*. Edited by Haskell Monroe. Tuscaloosa, Ala.: Confederate Publishing Company, 1959.

Jones, Sarah L. *Life in the South; From the Commencement of the War*. Vols. 1, 2. London: Chapman and Hall, 1863.

Jones, William Augustus. Letters. Memphis Room Collections, Memphis/Shelby County Public Library and Information Center, Memphis, Tenn.

Judd, Harriet Stewart (Mrs. Orange). Autobiography. Manuscripts Department, New York Historical Society, New York.

Keatinge, Harriette C. "Narrative of the Burning of Columbia, S.C., Feb. 17, 1865 and Journey to Fayetteville, N.C. with Sherman's Army, 1865." Library of Congress.

Keitt, Sue Sparks. "Sue Sparks Keitt to a Northern Friend, March 4, 1861." Edited by Elmer Don Herd, Jr. *South Carolina Historical Magazine* 62 (April 1961): 82–87.

Kellogg, F. N. Letters. In James B. Plessinger Papers. Indiana Division, Indiana State Library, Indianapolis.

Kemper, Mary Robinson. "Civil War Reminiscences at Danville Female Academy." Edited by Mary Lee Kemper. *Missouri Historical Review* 62 (April 1968): 314–20.

Kent, William T. Letter, April 15, 1865. Kennesaw Mountain National Battlefield Park, Marietta, Ga.

Kerr, William. Letters. Alexander Library, Rutgers University, New Brunswick, N.J.

Ketcham, Jane Merrill. Reminiscences. Indiana Division, Indiana State Library, Indianapolis.

Killin, Elizabeth Maddox. Papers. Indiana Historical Society, Indianapolis.

Kinchen, Oscar A. *Women Who Spied for the Blue and the Gray.* Philadelphia: Dorrance & Company, 1972.

King, Grace. *Memories of a Southern Woman of Letters.* New York: The Macmillan Company, 1932.

King, Spencer B., Jr., ed. "Fanny Cohen's Journal of Sherman's Occupation of Savannah." *Collections of the Georgia Historical Society* 41: 407–16.

King, William. Diary. Kennesaw Mountain National Battlefield Park, Marietta, Ga.

Kinsel Papers. Archives and Manuscripts Department, Chicago Historical Society.

Kinsland, Mary. Letter. Hargrett Rare Book and Manuscript Library. University of Georgia, Athens.

Kiser, John W. "Scion of Belmont. Part I." *Tennessee Historical Quarterly* 38 (1979): 34–61.

Knobeloch, Margaret Anna Parker. "The Rebels' Friend." Edited by M. Foster Farley. *Civil War Times Illustrated* 24 (October 1985): 26–31.

Koehler, Septima. Writings. In Hutchings-Koehler Collection. Indiana Historical Society, Indianapolis.

Ladies' Springfield [Illinois] Soldiers Aid Society Report, September 11, 1862. Archives and Manuscripts Department, Chicago Historical Society.

Lady, Claudia Lynn. "Five Tri-State Women During the Civil War: Day-to-Day-Life." Parts 1, 2. *West Virginia History* 43 (Spring, Summer 1982): 189–226, 303–21.

Langdon Papers. Hargrett Rare Book and Manuscript Library. University of Georgia, Athens.

Lamison, Martha. Letter. In the Gideon Winan Allen–Annie Cox Correspondence. The Department of Special Collections, The Newberry Library, Chicago.

Lanning, R. A. Correspondence. Manuscripts and Archives Section, New York Public Library.

Larcom, Lucy. Diary, August 20, 1862–February 10, 1865. In D. D. Addison Collection. Masachussets Historical Society, Boston.

Latta, Samuel. Letters. In Kay Averitt Collection. Special Collections, Western Michigan University, Kalamazoo.

Lauderdale, Maggie. Papers. Mississippi Department of Archives and History, Jackson.

Lauman, Jacob Gartner. Letters. Archives and Manuscripts Department, Chicago Historical Society.

LeConte, Emma. *When the World Ended: The Diary of Emma LeConte*. Edited by Earl Schenck Miers. New York: Oxford University Press, 1957.

Lee, Elizabeth Blair. " 'On the Qui Vive for the Long Letter': Washington Letters from a Navy Wife, 1861." Edited by Virginia Jeans Laas. *Civil War History* 29 (March 1983): 28–52.

LeGrand, Julia. *The Journal of Julia LeGrand*. Edited by Kate Mason Rowland and Mrs. Morris L. Croxall. Richmond: Everett Waddey Company, 1911.

Letters of Confederate Soldiers. Special Collections, Florida State University, Tallahassee.

LeVert, Octavia Walton. Collection. City of Mobile Museum, Mobile Ala.

LeVert, Octavia Walton. Collection. Archives, Historic Mobile Preservation Society, Mobile, Ala.

Lewis, Benton. Letters. In Lydia Watkins Collection. Michigan Historical Collections, Bentley Historical Library, University of Michigan, Ann Arbor.

Lewis, Charlotte. "Twelve Letters from Altoona, June–July, 1863." Edited by Michael R. Gannett. *Pennsylvania History* 47 (January 1980): 38–56.

Lewis, Levi. Letters. McCain Library and Archives, University of Southern Mississippi, Hattiesburg.

Lincoln, Abraham. Letter to Officials of the North-Western Sanitary Fair of 1863. Civil War Collection. Archives and Manuscripts Department, Chicago Historical Society.

————. *The Collected Works of Abraham Lincoln VII.* Edited by Roy P. Basler. New Brunswick, N.J.: Rutgers University Press, 1953.

Linderman, Gerald F. *Embattled Courage: The Experience of Combat in the American Civil War.* New York: The Free Press, Macmillan, Inc., 1987.

Lines, Jane Amelia (Akehurst). Diary. Special Collections, Hargrett Rare Book and Manuscript Library, University of Georgia, Athens. Microfilm.

Livermore, Mary Ashton. *My Story of the War: A Woman's Narrative of Four Years Personal Experience.* Hartford, Conn.: A. D. Worthington and Company, 1889.

Logan, Mrs. John A. *Reminiscences of a Soldier's Wife: An Autobiography.* New York: Charles Scribner's Sons, 1913.

Lomax, Elizabeth Lindsay. *Leaves from an Old Washington Diary, 1854–1863.* Edited by Lindsay Lomax Wood. Mount Vernon, N.Y.: S. A. Jacobs, The Golden Eagle Press, 1943.

Lord, Mrs. W. W. Journal. Library of Congress.

Loughborough, Mary Webster. *My Cave Life in Vicksburg.* New York: D. Appleton and Company, 1864.

Love, John James Hervey. Papers. New Jersey Historical Society, Newark.

Love-Scarborough Papers. Special Collections, Florida State University, Tallahassee.

Lowell, Anna Cabot. Papers II, 1808–1894. Massachusetts Historical Society, Boston.

Lowenfels, Walter. *Walt Whitman's Civil War.* New York: Alfred A. Knopf, 1960.

M[arsh], Mary B. Letter. Schlesinger Library, Radcliffe College, Cambridge.

Mackin, Sister Aloysius. "Wartime Scenes from Convent Windows: St. Cecilia, 1860 through 1865." *Tennessee Historical Quarterly* 39 (1980): 401–22.

Maclean, Mrs. Clara Dargan. "Return of a Refugee." *Southern Historical Society Papers* 13 (1885): 502–15.

Maher, Sister Mary Denis. *To Bind Up the Wounds: Catholic Sister Nurses in the U.S. Civil War.* New York: Greenwood Press, 1989.

Mallard, Robert Q. Papers. Library, Historical Foundation of the Presbyterian and Reformed Churches, Montreat, N.C.

Mallory, Stephen Russell. Letters. In Mallory Family Letters. Pensacola Historical Museum, Pensacola, Fla.

Marks, Frank N. Letter of March 23, 1862. In Wadley Papers. Middle Georgia Archives, Washington Memorial Library, Macon.

Massey, Mary Elizabeth. *Ersatz in the Confederacy.* Columbia: University of South Carolina Press, 1952.

———. *Refugee Life in the Confederacy.* Baton Rouge: Louisiana State University Press, 1964.

———. *Bonnet Brigades.* New York: Alfred A. Knopf, 1966.

Maury, Betty Herndon. *The Confederate Diary of Betty Herndon Maury 1861–63.* Edited by Alice Maury Parmelee. Washington: Privately Printed, 1938.

Maxwell, William Quentin. *Lincoln's Fifth Wheel: The Political History of the United States Sanitary Commission.* New York: Longmans, Green & Co., 1956.

May, Lisa. "Justice to the Women's Work." Master's Seminar Paper, University of Massachusetts, May 1990.

Mayo, Perry. *The Civil War Letters of Perry Mayo.* Cultural Series, Vol. 1, no. 3. Edited by Robert W. Hodge. East Lansing: Publications of the Museum, Michigan State University, 1967.

McBryde, Lucy Newton. Collection. South Caroliniana Library, University of South Carolina, Columbia.

McClatchey Family Papers. Georgia Department of Archives and History, Atlanta.

McClatchey, Minerva Leah Rowles. "A Georgia Woman's Civil War Diary: The Journal of Minerva Leah Rowles McClatchey, 1864–1865." Edited by T. Conn Bryan. *Georgia Historical Quarterly* 51 (June 1967): 197–216.

McCollum, Duncan. Diary. McCain Library and Archives, University of Southern Mississippi, Hattiesburg.

McCook, J. O. Civil War Letter. Georgia Department of Archives and History, Atlanta.

McCoy, Mary. Letters. Connecticut Historical Society, Hartford.

McDonald, Cornelia Peake. *A Diary with Reminiscences of the War and Refugee Life in the Shenandoah Valley, 1860–1865.* Nashville: Cullom & Ghertner Co., 1934.

McEwen, Sallie Florence. Diary. Tennessee State Library and Archives, Nashville.

McGregor, Frank. *Dearest Susie: A Civil War Infantryman's Letters to His Sweetheart.* Edited by Carl E. Hatch. New York: Exposition Press, 1971.

McGruer, J. Letter. Memphis Room Collections, Memphis/Shelby County Public Library and Information Center, Memphis, Tenn.

McGuire, Judith White (Brockenbrough). *Diary of a Southern Refugee, During the War.* 3d ed. Richmond, Va.: J. W. Randolph and English Publishers, 1889.

McIvison, John. Letters. Historical Collections and Labor Archives, Pattee Library, Pennsylvania State University, University Park.

McKay, Mrs. C. E. *Stories of Hospital and Camp.* Philadelphia: Claxton, Remsen & Haffelfinger, 1876.

McKee, Mary T. Diary. Library of Congress.

McKinley, Emilie R. Diary. Archives, Missouri Historical Society, St. Louis.

McKown, Bethiah Pyatt. "The Civil War Letters of Bethiah Pyatt McKown." Parts 1, 2. Edited by James W. Goodrich. *Missouri Historical Review* 67 (January, April 1973): 227-52, 351-70.

McLellan, Harriet (Tatem), Diary. Special Collections Department, William R. Perkins Library, Duke University, Durham, N.C. Microfilm.

McMullen, William E. Letters. Archives and Manuscripts, Chicago Historical Society.

The Medical and Surgical History of the War of the Rebellion. Part 3, vol. 1. Washington, D.C.: Government Printing Office, 1888.

Mellette, Margaret Wylie. *Maggie: The Civil War Diary of Margaret Wylie Mellette.* Edited by Joanita Kant. Watertown, S.D.: Codington County Historical Society, Inc., 1983.

Meriwether, Elizabeth Avery. Recollections. Southern Historical Collection, Wilson Library, University of North Carolina at Chapel Hill.

Merryweather, George. Letters. Archives and Manuscripts Department, Chicago Historical Society.

Metropolitan Fair Collection. Manuscripts Department, New York Historical Society, New York.

Michigan Soldiers' Relief Association. Papers. Burton Historical Collection, Detroit Public Library.

Michigan Women in the Civil War. Lansing: Michigan Civil War Centennial Observance Commission, 1963.

Millbrook, Minnie Dubbs, ed. *Twice Told Tales of Michigan and Her Soldiers in the Civil War.* Lansing: Michigan Civil War Centennial Observance Commission, 1966.

Miller, Elizabeth Perry. Reminiscences. Tennessee State Library and Archives, Nashville. Microfilm.

Miller, Letitia Dabney. Recollections. In Thomas Gregory Dabney Collection. McCain Library and Archives, University of Southern Mississippi, Hattiesburg.

Miller, Martha Davis. Papers. Mississippi Department of Archives and History, Jackson.

Mills, Ellen L. Journal. Library of Congress.

Minutes of the Louisiana Relief Committee. Archives and Manuscripts Department, Chicago Historical Society.

"Miss Abby." Diary. Hargrett Rare Book and Manuscript Library. University of Georgia, Athens.

Missouri Division, United Daughters of the Confederacy. *Reminiscences of the Women of Missouri During the Sixties.* Jefferson City: The Hugh Stephens Printing Co., 1920.

Mitchell, Martha Luttrell. Papers. Tennessee State Library and Archives, Nashville. Microfilm.

Mitchell, Robert. Letters. Archives and Manuscripts Department, Chicago Historical Society.

Mohr, James C., ed. *The Cormany Diaries: A Northern Family in the Civil War.* Pittsburgh: University of Pittsburgh Press, 1982.

Moore, Frank. *Women of the War; Their Heroism and Self-sacrifice.* Hartford, Conn.: S. S. Scranton & Co., 1866.

Moore, William H. "Writing Home to Talladega." *Civil War Times Illustrated* (November/December 1990): 56.

Mordecai, Emma. Diary. Southern Historical Collection, Wilson Library, University of North Carolina at Chapel Hill. Microfilm.

Morris, Mrs. L. C. Personal Recollections of the War—Girl Confederate Soldiers. In Crumley Family Collection. Archives, Atlanta Historical Society.

Morrow, Estelle. Diary. Indiana Historical Society, Indianapolis.

Morrow, Maud E. *Recollections of the Civil War.* Lockland, Ohio: John C. Morrow, 1901.

Morse, Charlotte Ingersoll, ed. *The Unknown Friends: A Civil War Romance: Letters of My Father and My Mother.* Chicago: A. Kroch & Son, Publishers, 1948.

Mortimer, Mrs. C. L. Diary. Archives and Manuscripts Department, Chicago Historical Society.

Morton, Richard L. "Contrabands and Quakers in the Virginia Peninsula, 1862–1869." *Virginia Historical Magazine* 61 (October 1953): 419–29.

Mott, Louisa D. Memoir. McCain Library and Archives, University of Southern Mississippi, Hattiesburg.

Mott, Ruth A. Diary. In Mott Family Papers. Manuscripts Department, New York Historical Society, New York.

Munroe, James Phinney. *Adventures of an Army Nurse in Two Wars.* Boston: Little, Brown, and Company, 1903.

Murray, Donald M., and Robert M. Rodney. "The Letters of Peter Bryant, Jackson County Pioneer." *Kansas Historical Quarterly* 27 (Winter 1961): 469–94.

Murray, Elizabeth Dunbar. *My Mother Used to Say*. Boston: The Christopher Publishing House, 1959.

Myers, Robert Manson, ed. *The Children of Pride: A True Story of Georgia and the Civil War*. New Haven: Yale University Press, 1972.

Nazro, Johanna Louise (Underwood). Diary. Department of Library Special Collections, Western Kentucky University, Bowling Green. Typescript.

Newcomb, M. A. *Four Years of Personal Reminiscences of the War*. Chicago: H. S. Mills & Co., Publishers, 1893.

Nickinson, Merritt L., ed. *Kiss the Children for Father*. Pensacola, Fla.: Pensacola Historical Society, 1985.

Nightingale Papers. Second Series. British Museum, London.

Noble, David, and Mary A. Knapp Noble. Letters. In Dorothy Keister Collection. Michigan and Family History Department, Grand Rapids Public Library.

Noble, Roger. Collection. Michigan State University Archives and Historical Collections, East Lansing.

Noddins and Baker Families. Papers. Michigan State University Archives and Historical Collections, East Lansing.

Norfleet, Virginia. Reminiscences. Privately held.

Northwestern Sanitary Fair. Archives and Manuscripts Department, Chicago Historical Society.

Northwestern Sanitary Fair. Special Collections Division, Chicago Public Library.

Northwestern Sanitary Fair. *Voice of the Fair*. Vol. 1, nos. 1–22 (April 27–June 24, 1865). Chicago: Rounds & James Printers.

Nutt, Laetitia LaFon Ashmore. *Courageous Journey: The Civil War Journal of Laetitia LaFon Ashmore Nutt*. Edited by Florence Ashmore Cowles Hamlett Martin. Miami, Fla.: E. A. Seemann Publishing, Inc., 1975.

Obrien, Michael. Letters. Burton Historical Collection, Detroit Public Library.

Ogg, Lizzie. Collection. Indiana Division, Indiana State Library, Indianapolis.

Olmstead, Frederick Law. *Hospital Transports: A Memoir of the Embarkation of the Sick and Wounded from the Peninsula of Virginia in the Summer of 1862*. Boston: Ticknor and Fields, 1863.

Otis, Esther S. Diary. Privately held.

Outwater, Harrison. Letters. Michigan State University Archives and Historical Collections, East Lansing.

Owen, William Miller. *In Camp and Battle with the Washington Artillery of New Orleans*. Boston: Ticknor and Company, 1885.

Owens, Cora. Journal. In William Garrison Hume Collection. Filson Club, Louisville, Ky.

Ozburn, Lizzie. Family Papers. Georgia Department of Archives and History, Atlanta.

Palmer Family Papers. South Caroliniana Library, University of South Carolina, Columbia.

Parkhurst, John G. Papers. Michigan State University Archives and Historical Collections, East Lansing.

Parsons Family Papers. Michigan State University Archives and Historical Collections, East Lansing.

Partin, Robert. "The Wartime Experiences of Margaret McCalla: Confederate Refugee from East Tennessee." *Tennessee Historical Quarterly* 24 (Spring 1965): 39–53.

Pearl, Louisa Brown. "The Civil War Diary of Louisa Brown Pearl." Edited by James A. Hoobler. *Tennessee Historical Quarterly* 38 (Fall 1979): 308–21.

Pearson, Elizabeth Ware, ed. *Letters from Port Royal, 1862–1868.* New York: Arno Press, 1969.

Pease, William H. "Three Years Among the Freedmen: William C. Gannett and the Port Royal Experiment." *Journal of Negro History* 42 (April 1957): 98–117.

Peck, Abel G. Papers. Michigan State University Archives and Historical Collections, East Lansing.

Pedrick, Joseph. Letter. Alexander Library, Rutgers University, New Brunswick, N.J.

Pember, Phoebe Yates. *A Southern Woman's Story: Life in Confederate Richmond. Including Unpublished Letters Written from the Chimborazo Hospital.* Edited by Bell Irvin Wiley. Jackson, Tenn.: McCowat-Mercer Press, Inc., 1959.

Pender, William Dorsey. *The General To His Lady: The Civil War Letters of William Dorsey Pender to Fanny Pender.* Edited by William W. Hassler. Chapel Hill: The University of North Carolina Press, 1965.

Pendleton Family Papers. Michigan State University Archives and Historical Collections, East Lansing.

Perry, Martha Derby. *Letters From a Surgeon of the Civil War.* Boston: Little, Brown, and Company, 1906.

Peter, Frances Dallam. *Window on the War: Frances Dallam Peter's Lexington Civil War Diary.* Edited by John David Smith and William Cooper, Jr. Lexington, Ky.: Lexington-Fayette County Historic Commission, 1976.

Phelps-Lyons Papers. Clements Library, University of Michigan, Ann Arbor.

Phifer, Louisa Jane. "Letters from an Illinois Farm, 1864–1865." Edited by Carol Benson Pye. *Journal of the Illinois State Historical Society* 66 (Winter 1973): 387–403.

417

Phillips-Myers. Papers. Southern Historical Collection, Wilson Library, University of North Carolina at Chapel Hill.

Pickett, George E. *Soldier of the South: General Pickett's War Letters to His Wife.* Edited by Arthur Crew Inman. New York: Houghton Mifflin Company, 1928.

Pigman, Mary Theresa. Diary. Georgia Historical Society, Savannah.

Poe, Clarence, ed. *True Tales of the South at War: How Soldiers Fought and Families Lived, 1861–1865.* Chapel Hill: The University of North Carolina Press, 1961.

Polley, J. B. *A Soldier's Letters to Charming Nellie.* New York: The Neale Publishing Company, 1908.

Poppenheim, Christopher Pritchard. Correspondence. South Carolina Historical Society, Charleston.

Porter-Griffin Collection. Indiana Division, Indiana State Library, Indianapolis. Microfilm.

Post, Eliza G. Memorandum Books. Archives, Missouri Historical Society, St. Louis.

Postel, Marie Monroe. "Sherman's Occupation of Savannah: Two Letters." *Georgia Historical Quarterly* 50 (March 1966): 109–15.

Potter Letters. Special Collections Division, Chicago Public Library.

Powell, Mildred Elizabeth. "Journal of Mildred Elizabeth Powell." Edited by Mary Stella Hereford Powell Ball. *Reminiscences of the Women of Missouri During the Sixties.* Jefferson City, Mo.: The Hugh Stephens Printing Company, 1920.

Powers, Elvira J. *Hospital Pencillings, Being a Diary While in Jefferson General Hospital, Jefferson, Ind. and Others at Nashville, Tennessee, As Matron and Visitor.* Boston: Edward L. Mitchell, 1866.

Pratt, D. D. Letters. Indiana Division, Indiana State Library, Indianapolis.

Prescott, Emma (Slade). Reminiscences of the War. Archives, Atlanta Historical Society.

Preston, Margaret. Reminiscences. Indiana Division, Indiana State Library, Indianapolis.

Pringle, Elizabeth Waties (Allston). Diary. South Carolina Historical Society, Charleston. Microfilm.

Pryor, Mrs. Roger A. *Reminiscences of Peace and War.* New York: The Macmillan Company, 1904.

———. *My Day: Reminiscences of a Long Life.* New York: The Macmillan Company, 1909.

Putnam, Sallie Brock. *Richmond During the War; Four Years of Personal Observation.* New York: G. W. Carleton & Co., Publishers, 1867.

Quaife, Milo M., ed. *From the Cannon's Mouth: The Civil War Letters of General Alpheus S. Williams.* Detroit: Wayne State University Press and the Detroit Historical Society, 1959.

Racine, Philip N. "Emily Lyles Harris: A Piedmont Farmer During the Civil War." *South Atlantic Quarterly* 79 (Autumn 1980): 386–97.

———., ed. *Piedmont Farmer: The Journals of David Golightly Harris, 1855–1870.* Knoxville: University of Tennessee Press, 1990.

Rainwater, Mrs. Charles C. Reminiscences. Special Collections Department, William R. Perkins Library, Duke University, Durham, N.C.

Ramsey, Margaret B. Crozier. Journal. Special Collections, University of Tennessee at Knoxville.

Ransom, John L. *John Ransom's Diary.* New York: Paul S. Eriksson, Inc., 1963.

Rawson, Mary. Diary. Archives, Atlanta Historical Society.

Ready, Alice. Diary. Southern Historical Collection, Wilson Library, University of North Carolina at Chapel Hill. Microfilm.

Realf, Richard. Letter, January 11, 1864. Special Collections, Chicago Public Library.

Reddick, H. W. *Seventy-seven Years in Dixie: The Boys in Gray of 61–65.* Santa Rosa, Washington County, Fla.: H. W. Reddick Publisher, 1910.

Reid, Mrs. Mary Martha. Papers. Samuel A. Swann Memorial Collection, Florida Historical Society, University of South Florida, Tampa.

Rennolds, Elizabeth Gordon. Papers. Virginia Historical Society, Richmond.

Report of the Western Sanitary Commission for the Year Ending June 1, 1863. St. Louis, Mo.: Western Sanitary Commission, 1863.

Report to the Committee on Nurses Corp for the Army of the Cumberland. Cincinnati Historical Society.

Reynolds, Mary Jane. Letters. Special Collections, University of Tennessee at Knoxville.

Rice, Marie Gordon (Pryor). Reminiscences. Virginia Historical Society, Richmond.

Richard, J. Fraise. *The Florence Nightingale of the Southern Army.* New York: Broadway Publishing Company, 1914.

Richardson, Louise. Collection. Special Collections, Florida State University, Tallahassee.

Richardson, Sue. Diary. Robert W. Woodruff Library, Emory University, Atlanta.

Roberts, Barbara. "Sisters of Mercy: From Vicksburg to Shelby Springs." *Alabama Heritage*, no. 11 (Winter 1989): 3–17.

Roberts, Helen. Diary. Indiana Historical Society, Indianapolis.

Robertson, Frances Jane (Bestor). Diary. Alabama Department of Archives and History, Montgomery. Microfilm.

Robertson, Wyndam. Papers. Special Collections, The University of Chicago Library.

Robinson, John Leroy. Papers. McCain Library and Archives, University of Southern Mississippi, Hattiesburg.

Robson, Kate Hester. Memoirs. Archives, Atlanta Historical Society.

Rogers, Marjorie Ann. "An Iowa Woman in Wartime." Parts 1–3. *Annals of Iowa* 35, 36 (Winter, Spring, Summer 1961): 523–48, 594–615, 16–44.

Root, Sarah. Diary. Rare Books, Boston Public Library.

Ropes, Hannah. *Civil War Nurse: The Diary and Letters of Hannah Ropes.* Edited by John R. Brumgardt. Knoxville: The University of Tennessee Press, 1980.

Rowland, Kate Whitehead. Journals, 1863–1878. Robert W. Woodruff Library, Emory University, Atlanta.

Ruck, Valliant. Letters. Mississippi Department of Archives and History, Jackson.

Rundell, Walter, Jr., ed. " 'Despotism of Traitors': The Rebellious South Through New York Eyes." *New York History* 45 (October 1964): 331–67.

Russell, Mrs. E. Letter, May 14, 1862. Manuscripts Department, New York Historical Society, New York.

Russell, Mrs. J. W. "Mrs. Russell and the Battle of Raymond, Mississippi." Edited by Allan C. Ashcraft. *Journal of Mississippi History* 25 (January 1963): 38–40.

Russell, Rebecca. Indiana Historical Society, Indianapolis.

Ryne, Charles. Letter. Alexander Library, Rutgers University, New Brunswick, N.J.

Sams, Sarah Jane. Letter-Diary. South Caroliniana Library, University of South Carolina, Columbia.

Satterlee Family Correspondence. Manuscripts Department, New York Historical Society, New York.

Schuyler, Louisa Lee. Collection. Manuscripts Department, New York Historical Society, New York.

Scott, Margaret. Letters. Manuscripts Department, New York Historical Society, New York.

Screven, Ellen Buchanan. Autobiography. Hargrett Rare Book and Manuscript Library. University of Georgia, Athens.

Seeyle, Sarah E. Papers. Burton Historical Collection, Detroit Public Library.

Selby Family Papers. Manuscripts Department, New York Historical Society, New York.

Severance, H. A. Diary. Schlesinger Library, Radcliffe College, Cambridge.

420

Sharp, John, and Helen Maria Sharp. "The Sharp Family Civil War Letters." Edited by George Mills. *Annals of Iowa* 34 (January 1959): 481–532.

Sheldon, Lena. "Peril in West Union: A Personal Account." *Civil War Times Illustrated* 23 (November 1984): 38–39.

Sherman, William Tecumseh. *Home Letters of General Sherman.* Edited by M. A. DeWolfe Howe. New York: Charles Scribner's Sons, 1909.

———. *Memoirs of General William T. Sherman.* Bloomington: Indiana University Press, 1957.

Sibley, Lucretia Cargill. Papers. American Antiquarian Society, Worcester, Mass.

Simkins, Francis Butler, and James Welch Patton. "The Work of Southern Women Among the Sick and Wounded of the Confederate Armies." *Journal of Southern History* 1 (1935): 475–96.

———. *The Women of the Confederacy.* Richmond and New York: Garrett and Massie, Inc., 1936.

Simmons Papers. Florida Historical Society, University of South Florida, Tampa.

Simons, Mrs. Harriet H. Reminiscences. South Caroliniana Library, University of South Carolina, Columbia.

Sloan, Mrs. Anna Toone. "Reminiscences of the Battle of Franklin." Tennessee State Library and Archives, Nashville. Microfilm.

Sloat, Philemon. Letter to Miss Hannah Sloat, June 30, 1864. Special Collections Department, Chicago Public Library.

Smedes, Susan Dabney. *Memorials of a Southern Planter.* Edited by Fletcher M. Green. New York: Alfred A. Knopf, 1965.

Smith, A. Y. Personal Memories. Manuscripts and Archives Section, New York Public Library.

Smith, George Winston, and Charles Judah. *Life in the North During the Civil War: A Source History.* Albuquerque: The University of New Mexico Press, 1966.

Smith, Janie. Letter, April 12, 1865. Kennesaw Mountain National Battlefield Park, Marietta, Ga.

Smith, John R. Diary. Archives and Manuscripts Department, Chicago Historical Society.

Smith, Ophia D. "The Incorrigible 'Miss Ginger.'" *West Tennessee Historical Society Papers,* no. 9 (1955): 93–118.

Smith, Stanley Barney. Collection. Special Collections, Western Michigan University, Kalamazoo.

Smythe, Louisa McCord. Recollections. South Caroliniana Library, University of South Carolina, Columbia. Typescript.

421

Soldiers' Aid Society of Michigan. Burton Historical Collection, Detroit Public Library.

Sosnowski, Sophie. "Burning of Columbia: (A Thrilling), a Faithful, & Graphic Description of a National Crime." *The Georgia Historical Quarterly* 8 (1924): 195–214.

Spalding, Miranda. Spalding Collection. Michigan Historical Collections, Bentley Historical Library, University of Michigan, Ann Arbor.

Spencer, Cornelia Phillips. *The Last Ninety Days of the War in North Carolina*. New York: Watchman Publishing Co., 1866.

Spight, Thomas. Letters. McCain Library and Archives, University of Southern Mississippi, Hattiesburg.

Starks, Kate. Letters. Indiana Division, Indiana State Library, Indianapolis.

Stearns, Nellie F. Papers. Special Collections Department, William R. Perkins Library, Duke University, Durham, N.C.

Stebbins, Laura V. Papers. Special Collections Department, William R. Perkins Library, Duke University, Durham, N.C.

Steiner, Paul Eby. *Disease in the Civil War*. Springfield, Ill.: Charles C. Thomas, 1968.

Stephens, Winston, and Octavia. Papers. The P. K. Yonge Library of Florida History, University of Florida, Gainesville.

Sterkx, H. E. *Partners in Rebellion: Alabama Women in the Civil War*. Rutherford, N.J.: Fairleigh Dickinson University Press, 1970.

Stewart, Marie Beard. Reminiscences. Schlesinger Library, Radcliffe College, Cambridge.

Stoddard, Janette. Letters. In Stoddard Family Papers. Michigan State University Archives and Historical Collections, East Lansing.

Stone, Kate. *Brokenburn: The Journal of Kate Stone, 1861–1868*. Edited by John Q. Anderson. Baton Rouge: Louisiana State University Press, 1955.

Straubing, Harold Elk, ed. *Civil War Eyewitness Reports*. Hamden, Conn.: Archon Books, The Shoe String Press, Inc., 1985.

Stull, Lydia J. Collection. Library of Congress.

Sublett, Emmie. Letter. Eleanor S. Brockenbrough Library, The Museum of the Confederacy, Richmond, Va.

Susanna. "Letters From Nashville, 1862, II 'Dear Master.'" Edited by Randall Miller. *Tennessee Historical Quarterly* 33 (Spring 1974): 85–92.

Sutton, Francena Lavinia (Martin). "A Civil War Experience of Some Arkansas Women in Indian Territory." Edited by LeRoy H. Fischer. *Chronicles of Oklahoma* 57 (Summer 1979): 137–63.

Swanson, Mrs. M. A. Reminiscences of the War. Georgia Department of Archives and History, Atlanta.

Swint, Henry L., ed. *Dear Ones At Home: Letters from Contraband Camps.* Nashville: Vanderbilt University Press, 1966.

Tallman, John N. Letters. Archives and Manuscripts Department, Chicago Historical Society.

Taylor, Maria Baker. Diary. The P. K. Yonge Library of Florida History, University of Florida, Gainesville.

Taylor, Susie King. *Reminiscences of My Life in Camp.* New York: Arno Press and The New York Times, 1968.

Taylor, Mrs. Thomas, Mrs. Smythe, Mrs. August Kohn, Miss Poppenheim, Miss Martha B. Washington, eds. *South Carolina Women in the Confederacy.* Columbia, S.C.: The State Company, 1903.

Teachout, Webster. Letters. Michigan State University Archives and Historical Collections, East Lansing.

Thomas, Anna Hasell. "The Diary of Anna Hasell Thomas." Edited by Charles E. Thomas. *South Carolina Historical Magazine* 74 (July 1973): 128–43.

Thomas, Ella Gertrude Clanton. Journal. Manuscript Department, William R. Perkins Library, Duke University, Durham, N.C. The journal is now published in large part in Virginia Ingraham Burr's book, *The Secret Eye: The Journal of Ella Gertrude Clanton Thomas, 1848–1889.* Chapel Hill: The University of North Carolina Press, 1990.

Thompson, Harriet Jane. "Civil War Wife: The Letters of Harriet Jane Thompson." Parts 1, 2. Edited by Glenda Riley. *Annals of Iowa* 44 (Winter, Spring 1978): 214–31, 296–314.

Thompson, Helen. Papers. Mississippi Department of Archives and History, Jackson.

Thompson, Kate. Collection. Archives, Atlanta Historical Society.

Thornton, Caroline (Homassel). Virginia Historical Society, Richmond.

Tinsley, Mrs. S. G. War Experiences. Virginia Historical Society, Richmond.

Todd, Andrew. Civil War Letters. Archives, Calvin College & Seminary, Grand Rapids, Mich.

Toffey, John James. Letters. Alexander Library, Rutgers University, New Brunswick, N.J.

Towne, Laura M. *Letters and Diary of Laura M. Towne Written from the Sea Islands of South Carolina, 1862–1884.* Edited by Rupert Sargent Holland. Cambridge: The Riverside Press, 1912.

Troutman, Richard L., ed. *The Heavens are Weeping: The Diaries of George Richard Browder 1852–1886.* Grand Rapids, Mich.: Zondervan Publishing House, 1987.

U.S. Sanitary Commission Bulletin 1, no. 10 (March 15, 1864): 295–96.

Underwood, J. L., ed. *The Women of the Confederacy*. New York: The Neale Publishing Company, 1906.

Van Der Weyde, Peter Henri. Papers. Manuscripts and Archives Section, New York Public Library.

Van Hook Collection. Indiana Division, Indiana State Library, Indianapolis.

Van Lew, Elizabeth L. Papers. Manuscripts and Archives Section, New York Public Library.

Van Raalte, Ben. Correspondence. In Albertus C. Van Raalte Papers. Archives, Calvin College & Seminary, Grand Rapids, Mich.

Van Rensselaer, Sallie B. Pendleton. Diary. Manuscripts Department, New York Historical Society, New York.

Van Wart, Mrs. Lizzie D. *Personal Recollections of the Civil War*. New York: Printed for Private Circulation, 1900. (Fredericksburg, Va.: Central Rappahannock Regional Library).

Vanderhorst, Adele Allston. Collection. South Carolina Historical Society, Charleston.

Wadley Papers. Middle Georgia Archives, Washington Memorial Library, Macon.

Wadley, Sarah Lois. Diaries. Middle Georgia Archives, Washington Memorial Library, Macon. Also in Southern Historical Collection, Wilson Library, University of North Carolina at Chapel Hill.

Wadley, William O. Letter. In Wadley Papers. Middle Georgia Archives, Washington Memorial Library, Macon.

Waite, Eunice Hale. Rare Books, Boston Public Library.

Walker, Georgiana Gholson. *The Private Journal of Georgiana Gholson Walker, 1862–1865 With Selections from the Post-War Years, 1865–1876*. Edited by Dwight Franklin Henderson. Tuscaloosa, Ala.: Confederate Publishing Company, Inc., 1963.

Walker, Susan. Journal. In Susan Walker Papers. Cincinnati Historical Society.

Wallace, Elizabeth Curtis. *Glencoe Diary: The War-Time Journal of Elizabeth Curtis Wallace*. Edited by Eleanor P. Cross and Charles B. Cross, Jr. Chesapeake: Norfolk County Historical Society of Chesapeake, Virginia, 1968.

Wallace, Mary (Austin). "Mary Austin Wallace: Her Diary, 1862." Edited by Julia McCune. In *Michigan Women in the Civil War*. Lansing: Michigan Civil War Centennial Observance Commission, 1963.

Walsh, Mrs. Kay. Letter. Special Collections, University of Tennessee at Knoxville.

Walton, William V. Letter to his Brother in England. British Museum, London.

Ward, Evelyn D. *The Children of Bladensfield.* New York: Viking Press, 1978.

Wardin, Able W., Jr. *Belmont Mansion: The Home of Joseph and Adelicia Acklen.* Nashville, Tenn.: History of Belmont Association, 1981.

Waring, Malvina Sarah Black. Occasional Diary. South Caroliniana Library, University of South Carolina, Columbia.

Waring, Mary. *Miss Waring's Journal, 1863 and 1865, Being the Diary of Miss Mary Waring of Mobile, During the Final Days of the War Between the States.* Edited by Thad Holt, Jr. Chicago: The Wyvern Press of S.F.E. Inc., 1964.

Washburn, Hannah Blaney Thacher. Diaries. Manuscripts and Archives Section, New York Public Library.

Washburn, Mrs. Samuel B. Diary. Manuscripts and Archives Section, New York Public Library.

Washington, Ella More Bassett. Diary. Virginia Historical Society, Richmond.

Washington, Ella. " 'An Army of Devils': The Diary of Ella Washington." Edited by James O. Hall. *Civil War Times Illustrated* 16 (February 1978): 18–25.

Waters Family. Correspondence. Michigan State University Archives and Historical Collections, East Lansing.

Welborn, Mrs. J. S. "A Wayside Hospital." *Confederate Veteran* 38 (1930): 95–96.

Welch, Spencer Glasgow. *A Confederate Surgeon's Letters to His Wife.* New York: The Neale Publishing Company, 1911.

Weller, Edwin. *A Civil War Courtship: The Letters of Edwin Weller from Antietam to Atlanta.* Edited by William Walton. Garden City, N.Y.: Doubleday & Company, Inc., 1980.

Westcott, Martin A. Diary. Special Collections, Western Michigan University, Kalamazoo.

Weston Family Papers. Letter, November 30, 1861. Burton Historical Collection, Detroit Public Library.

Wetmore, George. Letters. Connecticut Historical Society, Hartford.

Wheeler, Richard. *Witness to Appomattox.* New York: Harper & Row, Publishers, 1989.

Whetten, Harriet Douglas. "A Volunteer Nurse in the Civil War: The Letters of Harriet Douglas Whetten." Edited by Paul H. Hass. *Wisconsin Magazine of History* 48 (Winter 1964/1965): 131–51.

———. "A Volunteer Nurse in the Civil War: The Diary of Harriet Douglas Whetten." Edited by Paul H. Hass. *Wisconsin Magazine of History* 48 (Spring 1965): 205–21.

White, Caroline Barrett. Diaries, 1862–1865. American Antiquarian Society, Worcester, Mass.

Whitehead, P. F. Letters. McCain Library and Archives, University of Southern Mississippi, Hattiesburg.

Whittemore, Margaret L. Collection. Archives, Atlanta Historical Society.

Whittle, Grace Latimer, and Cloe Tyler Greene (Whittle). Diaries. Rare Books and Manuscripts, Swem Library, College of William and Mary, Williamsburg, Va. Microfilm.

Wilcox, William E. Letters. McCain Library and Archives, University of Southern Mississippi, Hattiesburg.

Wiley, Bell Irvin. *The Life of Johnny Reb.* Indianapolis: Bobbs-Merrill Company, Inc., 1962.

———. *Confederate Women.* Westport, Conn.: Greenwood Press, 1975.

———. *The Life of Billy Yank.* Baton Rouge: Louisiana State University Press, 1978.

Wilkeson, Frank. *Recollections of a Private Soldier in the Army of the Potomac.* New York: G. P. Putnam's Sons, 1887.

Williams, Frederick D. *Michigan Soldiers in the Civil War.* Lansing: Michigan Historical Commission, 1960.

Williams, Mary. Letters. In Thomas W. Williams Collection. Burton Historical Collection, Detroit Public Library.

Williams, Matthew J. Diary. Kennesaw Mountain National Battlefield Park, Marietta, Ga.

Williams, Richard Mortimer. "The Civil War Courtship of Richard Mortimer Williams and Rose Anderson of Rockville." Edited by George M. Anderson. *Maryland Historical Magazine* 80 (Summer 1985): 119–38.

Williams, Sarah Cornelia. Diaries. Joint Collection, University of Missouri Western Historical Manuscript Collection, St. Louis and State Historical Society of Missouri Manuscripts.

Williamson, Alice. Diary. Special Collections Department, William R. Perkins Library, Duke University, Durham, N.C.

Wills, Ridley, II. "Letters from Nashville, 1862, I. A Portrait of Belle Meade." *Tennessee Historical Quarterly* 33 (1974): 70–92.

Wilson, Amanda (Landrum). Diary for 1861. Cincinnati Historical Society.

Wilson, Augusta Jane Evans. Collection. City of Mobile Museum, Mobile, Ala.

———. Collection. Archives, Historic Mobile Preservation Society, Mobile, Ala.

Wilson, J. A. Letters. Jefferson Davis Museum, Biloxi, Miss.

Wilson, Moultrie Reid. Letters. South Caroliniana Library, University of South Carolina, Columbia.

Wister, Sarah Butler. "Sarah Butler Wister's Civil War Diary." Edited by Fanny Kemble Wister. *Pennsylvania Magazine of History and Biography* 102 (July 1978): 271–327.

Wittenmyer, Mrs. Annie. *Under the Guns: A Woman's Reminiscences of the Civil War.* Boston: E. B. Stillings & Co., Publishers, 1895.

Woolsey, Jane Stuart. *Hospital Days.* New York: D. Van Nostrand, 1868.

Wormeley, Katharine Prescott. *The Other Side of War with the Army of the Potomac.* Boston: Ticknor and Company, 1889.

Worthington, C. J., ed. *The Woman in Battle: A Narrative of the Exploits, Adventures, and Travels of Madame Loreta Janeta Velazquez.* Hartford, Conn.: T. Belknap, 1876.

WPA Federal Writers Project. Slave Days in Florida. Florida Historical Society, University of South Florida, Tampa.

Wray, Henry and Drucilla Wray. Paper. Georgia Historical Society, Savannah.

Wright, Mrs. D. Giraud. *A Southern Girl in '61: The War-Time Memories of a Confederate Senator's Daughter.* New York: Doubleday, Page & Company, 1905.

Wyatt-Brown, Bertram. *Yankee Saints and Southern Sinners.* Baton Rouge: Louisiana State University Press, 1985.

———. *Honor and Violence in the Old South.* New York: Oxford University Press, 1986.

Young, Agatha. *The Women and the Crisis: Women of the North in the Civil War.* New York: McDowell, Obolensky, 1959.

Trials and Triumphs: Women of the American Civil War

Production Editor: Julie L. Loehr
Editor: Kristine M. Blakeslee
Cover Design: Sean T. Harrington

Text Composed by Lansing Graphics, Inc.
in 11/14 Goudy Old Style

Printed by Edwards Brothers
on Glattfelter Offset B-16 55#

Bound in Holliston Crown Linen Burgundy #13708
Stamped with General Roll Leaf Lustrofoil